THE POLITICAL SOCIOLOGY OF FREEDOM

NEW THINKING IN POLITICAL ECONOMY

Series Editor: Peter J. Boettke
George Mason University, USA

New Thinking in Political Economy aims to encourage scholarship in the intersection of the disciplines of politics, philosophy and economics. It has the ambitious purpose of reinvigorating political economy as a progressive force for understanding social and economic change.

The series is an important forum for the publication of new work analysing the social world from a multidisciplinary perspective. With increased specialization (and professionalization) within universities, interdisciplinary work has become increasingly uncommon. Indeed, during the 20th century, the process of disciplinary specialization reduced the intersection between economics, philosophy and politics and impoverished our understanding of society. Modern economics in particular has become increasingly mathematical and largely ignores the role of institutions and the contribution of moral philosophy and politics.

New Thinking in Political Economy will stimulate new work that combines technical knowledge provided by the 'dismal science' and the wisdom gleaned from the serious study of the 'worldly philosophy'. The series will reinvigorate our understanding of the social world by encouraging a multidisciplinary approach to the challenges confronting society in the new century.

Recent titles in the series include:

Explaining Constitutional Change
A Positive Economics Approach
Stefan Voigt

Ethics as Social Science
The Moral Philosophy of Social Cooperation
Leland B. Yeager

Markets, Planning and Democracy
Essays after the Collapse of Communism
David L. Prychitko

Governance and Economic Development
A Comparative Institutional Approach
Joachim Ahrens

Constitutions, Markets and Law
Recent Experiences in Transition Economies
Edited by Stefan Voigt and Hans-Jürgen Wagener

Austrian Economics and the Political Economy of Freedom
Richard M. Ebeling

Anarchy, State and Public Choice
Edited by Edward Stringham

The Political Sociology of Freedom

Adam Ferguson and F.A. Hayek

Ronald Hamowy

Professor Emeritus of History, University of Alberta, Canada, and Affiliate Professor of Economics, George Mason University, USA

NEW THINKING IN POLITICAL ECONOMY

Edward Elgar
Cheltenham, UK • Northampton, MA, USA

Published by
Edward Elgar Publishing Limited
Glensanda House
Montpellier Parade
Cheltenham
Glos GL50 1UA
UK

Edward Elgar Publishing, Inc.
136 West Street
Suite 202
Northampton
Massachusetts 01060
USA

A catalogue record for this book
is available from the British Library

Library of Congress Cataloguing in Publication Data

Hamowy, Ronald, 1937–
   The political sociology of freedom : Adam Ferguson and F.A. Hayek / Ronald Hamowy.
      p. cm.
   Includes index.
    1. Political sociology. 2. Economics. 3. Ferguson, Adam, 1723–1816. 4. Hayek,
Friedrich A. von (Friedrich August), 1899– I. Title.

JA76.H379   2005
323.44'01—dc22

                                        2005044196

ISBN 1 84542 108 6

Printed and bound in Great Britain by MPG Books Ltd, Bodmin, Cornwall.

To Clement

Est enim amicitia nihil aliud nisi omnium divinarum humanarumque rerum cum benevolentia et caritate consensio, qua quidem haud scio an excepta sapientia nil quicquam melius homini sit a dis immortalibus datum.

Friendship is nothing else than an accord in all things, human and divine, conjoined with mutual goodwill and affection, and I am inclined to think that, with all the exception of wisdom, no better thing has been given to man by the immortal gods.

Cicero

Contents

Acknowledgements

I should like to thank Mario Rizzo for having originally suggested that I collect my essays on Hayek and Ferguson in a published volume and to Peter Boettke for having included this anthology in his edited series. I am also indebted to the Earhart Foundation, whose generous support allowed me the time to prepare these essays for republication.

The author and publisher wish to thank the following who have kindly given their permission for the use of copyright material:

Interpretation, Inc. for 'Progress and commerce in Anglo-American thought: the social philosophy of Adam Ferguson', 1986, *Interpretation: A Journal of Political Philosophy*, **14**(1), pp. 61–87 and 'Two Whig views of the American Revolution: Adam Ferguson's response to Richard Price', 2003, *Interpretation: A Journal of Political Philosophy*, **31**(1), Fall, pp. 3–35.

Blackwell Publishing for 'Adam Smith, Adam Ferguson, and the division of labour', 1968, *Economica*, **35**, August, pp. 249–59.

Southern Illinois University Press and the *Journal of the History of Philosophy* for *The Scottish Enlightenment and the Theory of Spontaneous Order*, 1987, Carbondale and Edwardsville: Southern Illinois University Press, published for the *Journal of the History of Philosophy*, pp. 3–36, 39–50 and Appendix.

The Cato Institute for 'F.A. Hayek on the occasion of the centenary of his birth', 1999, *Cato Journal*, **19**(2), Fall, pp. 279–87 and 'F.A. Hayek and the common law', 2003, *Cato Journal*, **23**(2), Fall, pp. 241–64.

Sage Publications for 'Book reviews: Hayek on Hayek: an autobiographical dialogue', 1996, *Philosophy of the Social Sciences*, **26**(3), September, pp. 417–21.

Duke University Press for 'A note on Hayek and anti-Semitism', 2002, *History of Political Economy*, **34**(1), pp. 255–60.

Univertità di Pavia for 'Freedom and the rule of law in F.A. Hayek', 1971, *Il Politico*, **XXXVI**(2), pp. 349–76.

Ludwig von Mises Institute for 'The Hayekian model of government in an open society', 1982, *Journal of Libertarian Studies*, **VI**(2), Spring, pp. 137–43.

Every effort has been made to trace all copyright holders but if any have been inadvertently overlooked the publisher will be pleased to make the necessary arrangements at the first opportunity.

Foreword

These are important essays, not only for the historian of ideas, but also, more generally, for economists and political theorists. They go to the core of what the Austrian economist Carl Menger said was 'perhaps the most noteworthy ... problem of the social sciences: How can it be that institutions which serve the common welfare and are extremely significant for its development come into being without a common will directed toward establishing them?'[1]

Adam Smith and Adam Ferguson, two of the important thinkers whose works are analyzed in this volume, wrote more than two centuries ago. Yet their ideas are fresh because they have not, by any means, been fully absorbed into mainstream economic, sociological or political thought. There are many unexploited opportunities for intellectual profit in these ideas. Even contemporary thinkers in the 'spontaneous order' tradition can learn from Professor Hamowy's analysis of Smith, Ferguson and Friedrich Hayek. Hayek, of course, was the twentieth century's foremost 'Scottish Enlightenment' thinker – he exposited and further developed the ideas of Scottish Enlightenment philosophers such as David Hume, Adam Smith and Adam Ferguson. But Hayek's work is not a closed book. It reminds us of the tremendous insights of this tradition and then challenges us to go on. The essays presented here are particularly useful in the latter regard because they never fail to stimulate the reader's own ideas. Ultimately, this is the greatest contribution Hamowy makes.

Hamowy's essays also shed light on both the analytical aspects of spontaneous order theory and upon its applications. Analytically, there are two issues: first, what generates the order? And second, what are the characteristics of the order generated? The Scottish philosophers never believed that the individual human behavior that generates an overall order was of the hyper-rational kind. Omniscient agents and lightning-fast calculators were the twentieth century's contribution to economics. Smith, Ferguson and Hume, on the other hand, each realized that men were sometimes guided by 'instinct', custom, habit and were prone to error.[2] They also recognized that chance played a role in the generation of spontaneous orders. Furthermore, the orders generated were not the static, finely-determined and, ultimately, brittle orders modeled by the older general equilibrium theorists. Instead, they were conceived as flexible orders that could and did accommodate change.

The issue of the proper application of spontaneous order theory is also evident in Hamowy's essays. Are the spontaneous-ordering forces limited to the generation of orders *within* a framework of private property and the rule of law? This is the approach taken since the formalization of economics by most economists. Or are these forces capable of generating the institutions or framework of liberty? Clearly, most of the Scottish Enlightenment took the latter, more expansive, view. But it is significant that the Welsh moral philosopher Richard Price believed that the framework can and should be the product of reason in the constructivist sense so denigrated by Hayek. It is further significant, as Hamowy shows, that many American revolutionaries found good in both approaches. After all, the American Revolution was both constructivist and evolutionary in different respects.

In recent years, however, the expansive view has found more and more support in the social sciences. There has been, as examples, both theoretical and empirical work on the evolution of cooperation and of moral norms, on contracts that are self-enforcing, on private arbitration and on the private provisions of public goods, including protection services. All of this work shows the contemporary and increasing relevance of the thinkers and debates of the Scottish Enlightenment.

Finally, these essays are a pleasure to read because they are well-organized, well-argued and well-written. You will learn a lot.

Mario J. Rizzo
Department of Economics
New York University
New York

March 2005

Notes

1. Carl Menger, *Investigations into the Method of the Social Sciences with Special Reference to Economics*, with a new introduction by Lawrence J. White, edited by Louis Schneider and translated by Francis J. Nock (New York: New York University Press, 1985), p. 146 (italics suppressed).
2. There is renewed emphasis on this theme among 'behavioral economists'. See, for example, Colin Camerer, George Loewenstein and Matthew Rabin (eds), *Advances in Behavioral Economics* (Princeton, NJ: Princeton University Press, 2004). The main difference is that these economists generally see these kinds of behavior as resulting in distortions of overall market activity. On the other hand, other scholars have emphasized the efficiency of the admittedly imperfect heuristics that people use to make decisions. See, for example, Gerd Gigerenzer, *Adaptive Thinking: Rationality in the Real World* (Oxford: Oxford University Press, 2000). The latter seems more consistent with the view of Scottish Enlightenment thinkers like Ferguson, Smith and Hume.

Introduction

Both Adam Ferguson and Friedrich Hayek, although separated by a period of almost two hundred years, have made original contributions of a similar nature to the field of theoretical sociology. Ferguson, one of the giants of the Scottish Enlightenment, can justifiably be credited with laying the foundations of what we now call theoretical history and with first proposing the idea that social institutions undergo evolutionary change such that, while they take their form at any point in time from the actions of human beings, they are not the product of human design. Somewhat less than two centuries later, Hayek extended this insight in dealing with the nature of economic and social interaction, arguing that the knowledge requisite for structuring the social institutions under which we live is far too complex to be comprehended by any one mind or group of minds and that these institutions had in fact evolved over long periods of time without deliberate design. In the same way, a command economy could not help but be inefficient since the knowledge requisite to creating viable markets, which were ultimately dependent on the subjective demands of all its participants, was far too diffuse to be possessed and processed by any directing body.

Adam Ferguson was one of a trio of thinkers that dominated the Scottish Enlightenment. A close friend of Adam Smith and David Hume, Ferguson was to have a profound effect on the future of the social sciences; indeed, he can be credited as one of the founders of sociology. Born in 1723 in Perthshire, Scotland, he became an ordained minister in the Scottish Kirk and was for a time chaplain to the Black Watch Regiment. In 1757 he left the ministry and, through the intercession of David Hume, became Librarian of the Advocates' Library in Edinburgh and, two years later, professor at the University of Edinburgh. Ferguson's interest in the nature of social interaction was rooted in his theory of ethics. Inasmuch as how men should behave, he maintained, was rooted in what men were in actuality like, it followed that any moral conclusions could only follow an empirical investigation of man's social history. Toward this end, in 1767 Ferguson published his *An Essay on the History of Civil Society*, in which he set out to chart the theoretical history of humanity by observing contemporary human society in its various stages of development.

In his natural history of mankind Ferguson offered a stadial theory of social evolution. He maintained that all societies pass through three distinct stages, savagery, barbarism and civilization, each marked by the extent to which private property prevailed. The movement from one stage to another, Ferguson claimed, was invariably associated with an expansion of the notion of private ownership and the subordination of rank that he associated with differences in wealth. While in savage communities, even those based on hunting and fishing, notions of private ownership were rudimentary and confined to a few household effects, property in most agrarian and pastoral societies had ceased to remain communal and distinctions in rank emerged as crucially important. Once these distinctions, both in rank and wealth, became even more extensive and formalized the clash of faction gave rise to civilized society, marked by a system of laws designed to restrain the more powerful from encroaching on the prerogatives of the weaker.

For Ferguson the social arrangements in which we live did not take their form from deliberate design nor from the conscious intentions of any person or group. They evolved without regard to their final form, the product of a massive number of individual interactions each having some immediate end in view but none seeking to shape the institution as a whole. In this sense, although Ferguson does not seem to have been aware of the similarity, all social institutions are like the market, where its form at any point in time (its 'price') is the result of countless inputs, each of which reflects certain ends (individual subjective demands) and where none of which aims at designing its final shape. It follows that all attempts to design complex social institutions *de novo* are doomed to the same fate as are efforts to simulate a price in the absence of a market.

It was this insight into the evolution of social arrangements that Friedrich Hayek found central to an understanding of how free societies develop. They are not, Hayek maintained, the product of conscious design and deliberate calculation but are, to use Hayek's terminology, generated spontaneously and evolve into their current form independent of the intentions of the participants whose actions contribute to their structure and character. Indeed, given the complexity of the social arrangements under which we live, viable institutions that conduce to man's well-being, Hayek insists, cannot form in any other manner.

When Friedrich Hayek was awarded the Nobel Prize in economics in 1974 he had achieved a substantial body of work in a variety of disciplines, including psychology, economic history, the history of ideas and, most importantly, social theory. His major writings in economic theory had been completed prior to his transfer from the London School of Economics to the University of Chicago in 1950 and he devoted most of his efforts from then on to the end of his life to political and social philosophy. It was while at Chicago that Hayek completed *The Constitution of Liberty*, his major essay on the institutional foundations of a free society, in which he discusses the nature of the rule of law and its relation to individual liberty and in which he elaborates his theory of spontaneous order.

During his tenure at the University of Chicago Hayek enlarged on the distinction between the English and French liberal traditions, which extended his insights on spontaneously generated orders to the history of political thought. Hayek maintained that nineteenth-century liberalism comprises two distinct approaches, one of which is more closely associated with English thinkers, the other with the French. English liberalism, like Ferguson's eighteenth-century Whiggism, reflects a theory of liberty that is based on a society whose political institutions evolved from numerous individual actions over a long course of time, none of which was deliberately designed with that end in view. These institutions molded themselves to the needs and desires of the people and thereby conduced to well-being and their notions of what constituted a relatively free society. French liberalism, on the other hand, Hayek asserted, was rationalist and was strongly indebted to the Cartesian tradition in French philosophy. It rested on the assumption that social institutions, regardless of their complexity, could, and indeed should, be deliberately designed in their totality, based on the ends contemplated by the designer. This approach to politics, Hayek concluded, was predicated on the erroneous assumption that all ordered arrangements require an orderer. This notion, that all social arrangements necessitate some central authority to coordinate their disparate elements or else chaos will follow, leads inexorably to totalitarianism inasmuch as it requires constant direction.

The relation between freedom, tradition and reason became one of Hayek's central concerns and informs all his last works, which deal with the structure of free societies and the dangers of social engineering. He is especially concerned with the nature of law and why it is not synonymous with legislation. Law, particularly the English common law, Hayek holds, is a particularly apposite example of a spontaneously generated institution, based on unarticulated custom and enforced by judges whose judgments are based on precedent. Legislation, or statutory laws, on the other hand, are clear examples of rules designed with deliberate intent and are enacted by individuals to achieve specific and usually immediate ends. Historically, Hayek argues, it was only in the fifteenth century that on the Continent legislation was understood in the same sense as was law, a process that did not occur in England until the seventeenth century.

It is worth observing that Ferguson was a product of mid-eighteenth-century Scotland, a period unmatched in creativity, originality and the sheer number of major intellectual figures produced by that small, isolated nation. Similarly, Hayek emerges from one of the most fruitful periods of Austrian culture and intellectual achievement, Vienna during the period between the world wars. Both thinkers clearly benefitted from the intellectual milieus in which they found themselves but even more significantly the contributions of both writers added lustre and distinction to the ages in which they lived.

The essays that comprise this volume deal with various aspects of the social and political thought of Ferguson and Hayek. Several have reference to both thinkers ('The Scottish Enlightenment and the Theory of Spontaneous Order' and 'Two Whig Views of the American Revolution: Adam Ferguson's Response to Richard Price') while most touch on one aspect or another of either Ferguson's or Hayek's life or their political philosophies. Taken as a whole, I hope that they provide some sense of the immensely important contributions these two thinkers have made to the sociology of freedom.

The first of these, 'Progress and Commerce in Anglo-American Thought: The Social Philosophy of Adam Ferguson' offers an outline of Ferguson's social philosophy centering on the crucial role the idea of spontaneous order plays in shaping his conclusions regarding advanced societies and commerce. 'Adam Smith, Adam Ferguson, and the Division of Labour' concerns itself with Ferguson's discussion of the division of labor that accompanies advanced commercial societies, his fears regarding what might follow from too great a specialization, his personal rift with Adam Smith over this issue, and his influence on Karl Marx. The third essay, 'The Scottish Enlightenment and the Theory of Spontaneous Order' concerns the development of the notion of spontaneously generated orders and its position in the social thought of the Scottish Enlightenment thinkers, especially Ferguson. This essay places Scottish thought within the larger context of British social thought on the topic from Mandeville to Edmund Burke. I should point out that the bibliographical Appendix to this essay differs substantially from that which accompanies the previously published version. It has been expanded to the size originally intended to incorporate all editions of all works (including translations) of the Scottish writers to which the monograph refers that were published up to approximately ten years after the death of the author.

The final article centering on Ferguson compares his views on the American Revolution with those of Richard Price, using as the framework Hayek's claim that there exist two distinct traditions of liberalism, British and French, and that only the former is consistent with free societies. Once again, the article differs from the version that appears in *Interpretation* by virtue of the fact that the original footnotes (which had to be removed) have been restored.

There are six essays whose central focus is the work of Hayek and particularly of his conclusions regarding social arrangements as the unintended consequence of human action. The first, 'F. A. Hayek on the Occasion of the Centenary of his Birth', is a brief biographical essay which discusses his earlier work as an economist and his increasing interest in questions arising in social theory, much of this a product of his conclusions regarding the dispersal of knowledge and its implications both for markets and for other complex social arrangements. The second, 'Book Reviews: *Hayek on Hayek*', and the third, 'A Note on Hayek and Anti-Semitism', further discuss certain biographical details as they emerged in Hayek's own autobiographical sketch and touch on his feelings towards his Jewish contemporaries. 'Freedom and the Rule of Law in F.A. Hayek' is a lengthy essay that examines a crucial aspect of Hayek's political theory, his notion of the rule of law, which Hayek equates with a society in which its citizens are personally free. Hayek lays down certain criteria for legislation, criteria that, by virtue of their evolving in an undirected and spontaneous manner, are formal and not substantive. This essay analyzes whether such criteria can in fact assure a free society and concludes that the rule of law alone can be consistent with a host of invasive legislation that Hayek himself would condemn. In 'The Hayekian Model of Government in an Open Society' I consider and offer a critical analysis of Hayek's specific proposals for what he believes will insure a free and open society, most importantly his suggestion that, while a lower chamber of the legislature could well be entrusted to tax and to manage the government, an upper chamber should be established with the power to pass 'enforceable rules of just conduct'. There are serious theoretical problems with this distinction and this article seeks to point them out. The final essay, 'F.A. Hayek and the Common Law', concerns itself with Hayek's strong defense of early British common law as a particularly apt example of a spontaneously generated social institution, evolving over time and based on precedent and not statute. I show this conclusion to be historically oversimplified and needing refinement.

Although a number of books and shorter essays on Ferguson and Hayek have appeared since the earliest of the articles in this collection were first published, I find little that needs revising. The interest in Hayek particularly has been intense, especially since the collapse of the communist regimes in Eastern Europe and the incontrovertible evidence that has emerged from that region that the absence of an effective price system made rational productive decisions impossible. Indeed, nothing better shows the bankruptcy of socialist planning than the experience of Eastern Europe, where whole continents were enslaved in the name of greater prosperity and where the result was the total immiseration of countless millions. Of the relevant articles and books that have been published in the past fifteen years, two essays deserve comment, primarily because they argue positions incompatible with the views expressed in this volume. The first concerns Ferguson's political philosophy and whether it can accommodate modern democratic theory, while the second is a book-length treatment of Hayek's debt to the Scottish Enlightenment conception of spontaneous order.

Andreas Kalyvas and Ira Katznelson, the authors of the article on Ferguson,[1] contend that Ferguson's notion of political obligation implies a constitutional structure akin to a modern democracy, in which almost every aspect of social life could legitimately be subject to political decision-making. In the nineteenth century Marx and other communist theorists had attempted to make of Ferguson a proto-socialist whose fears regarding the possible stultifying effects that accompanied the division of labor and the anomie associated with a market economy led him to oppose commercial society. This interpretation had been shown to be without merit and more recent scholarship has provided evidence that Ferguson, in the main, welcomed commerce and the extension of private property as civilizing forces that made for a fuller human being. However, Kalyvas and Katznelson, claiming to recapture 'the rich complexity of his political writings', argue that Ferguson's views were not nearly as Lockean and individualistic as had been suggested by some commentators. Stripped of its pretentious academic jargon, what the article maintains is that Ferguson was as keenly aware of the dangers associated with a regime based on Lockean liberalism as he was of a society that stifled individual integrity and that he was sympathetic to using the government as the instrument by which rampant individualism could be checked.

What Ferguson attempted in his work, Kalyvas and Katznelson write, was nothing short of reconciling 'the tension between republicanism and liberalism', that is, 'the conflict between political and individual autonomy and rights',[2] which was possible, the authors contend, through the mediation of modern democratic theory. In short, the authors interpret Ferguson's politics as having laid the groundwork for twentieth-century democracy inasmuch as a democratic regime alone provided 'the method to transform force into legitimate practice'. It should be noted that this interpretation lacks textual warrant. There is nothing in Ferguson that supports the view that he regarded democracy as the means by which the possible dangers of individualism and a society of commerce could be checked, nor that he even approved of democracy as a method of determining political policy. Indeed, his remarks on the French Revolution are a stinging indictment of this form of political organization. Nor did Ferguson maintain that commercial society would inevitably prove dangerous. He held that social progress, indeed, civilization itself, was intimately associated with the increasing extension of private property and that commerce and material progress tended to be accompanied by higher levels of morality. Kalyvas and Katznelson misconstrue Ferguson in two crucial ways. First, democracy can hardly be equated with 'political autonomy and rights', nor with a selfless concern for the public welfare. Equally important, Ferguson at no point maintained that the danger that existed that advanced societies might plunge into despotism could be best avoided by extensive political intervention into private life. Corruption and despotism threatened advanced commercial societies, Ferguson argued, by virtue of the fact that in such societies individuals were prone to limit their concerns to their own private interests, oblivious to any threats to the community. However, it hardly requires the intrusion of government to alert citizens to the need to be vigilant nor does Ferguson suggest as much.

Another recently published work warrants comment in part because its implications for Hayek's social theory are so far-reaching. The essay contends that Hayek has completely misconstrued the arguments put forward by the Scottish Enlightenment thinkers regarding the genesis of complex social rules and institutions and has imputed to these philosophers the theory that social conventions and arrangements took their form spontaneously and without conscious design and evolved independently of the actions of any particular actor, while in fact these thinkers made no such claims. Indeed, the book, entitled *Hayek's Liberalism and its Origins: His Idea of Spontaneous Order and the Scottish Enliahtenment*, maintains that 'the very thinkers Hayek cites as his intellectual ancestors can be used to provide a convincing critique of Hayek's own theory'.[3] Its author is Christina Petsoulas, who is identified as Associate Researcher at the Center for Socio-Legal Studies at Wolfson College, Oxford.

Despite its title, Petsoulas's monograph devotes no space whatever to the thought of Adam Ferguson, whose formulation of the theory of spontaneous order is probably the most elaborate and fully developed of all the Scottish thinkers. Instead, a substantial portion of her essay deals with the social philosophy of Bernard Mandeville, not a Scotsman but born and educated in the Dutch Republic before moving to London. Even more curious is the fact that the author at no point cites earlier scholarship on the same issue. Neither Norman Barry's essay nor my monograph on the subject[4] appear to have been consulted nor are they mentioned in Petsoulas's bibliography.

In writing of Mandeville, Hume and Smith, Petsoulas maintains that these thinkers espoused the theory that social rules were 'introduced intentionally and [came] to be observed because individuals recognise[d] their advantages, either to themselves or to the community as a whole'.[5] Now, while she might be correct with regard to a small portion of the rules under which society operates – and Hayek would not deny this – her conclusions are hardly applicable to the greater number of social conventions. Indeed, even Petsoulas's own discussions of Hume's treatment of justice and property and of Smith's analysis of the rules of morality suggest that, to a substantial degree, the conventions and institutions that govern society had their origin in the actions of men whose aim was substantially different from the general outcome that followed these actions. Yet, despite this the author concludes that 'contrary to Hayek's claims, both Hume and Smith attribute the selection of rules to individual intentionality and understanding of their benefits'.[6]

Nor does Petsoulas grasp the nature of ordered arrangements in the context of market forces. She seems oblivious to the notion that the complex network of prices that constitute an economy is not itself the conscious design of certain individuals but rather the unintended product of large numbers of individual actions, each aiming towards some private end. Petsoulas argues that intent and conscious choice are what give order to economic activity in the form of 'individuals reacting to price signals and adjusting their plans accordingly'. But she is oblivious to the origin of these 'price signals' to which individuals react, which themselves form the spontaneously generated order that is the market and which provide the mechanism within which individual actors may buy and sell without economic activity becoming chaotic.

It is difficult to know what to make of Petsoulas's book. It was written as a dissertation at Nuffield College, Oxford, and has appeared under the imprimatur of a reputable academic press, yet it falls so far short of what would ordinarily be expected of a serious exploration of the topic that the reader is at a loss to know why it ever saw print. Indeed, I have included these comments in part because Petsoulas's monograph, while the only work on Hayek and the notion of spontaneous order to appear since my own essay was published in 1987, seems to have escaped review in the academic literature and might therefore be thought the last word on the subject.

With the notable exceptions of the article by Kalyvas and Katznelson and of Petsoulas's book, almost all the literature on Ferguson and Hayek to have appeared since my own essays were first published have either reached conclusions not greatly dissimilar to mine or have extended the discussion of these two great social theoreticians into areas that I left untouched. This is not to suggest that all modern scholarship is in agreement with my conclusions, but to the extent we disagree it is over questions of emphasis – to what extent does Ferguson embrace a regime of commerce? does Hayek's theory of the rule of law provide sufficient safeguards for a free society? – rather than fundamental theoretical issues.

These essays, taken together, will, I trust, provide a fairly broad overview of the sociology of Ferguson and Hayek and will encourage the reader to further explore aspects of the writings of these two thinkers whose insights have greatly advanced our understanding of the political and social institutions in which mankind finds itself.

Ronald Hamowy
Rockville, Maryland

Notes

1. Andreas Kalyvas and Ira Katznelson, 'Adam Ferguson Returns: Liberalism through a Glass Darkly', *Political Theory*, **26** (April 1998): 173–97.
2. Kalyvas and Katznelson, 176.
3. (London and New York: Routledge, 2001): [i].
4. Norman Barry, 'The Tradition of Spontaneous Order', *Literature of Liberty*, **5**(2) (summer, 1982): 7–58; Ronald Hamowy, *The Scottish Enlightenment and the Theory of Spontaneous Order* (Carbondale, Ill.: Southern Illinois University Press, 1987).
5. Petsoulas, 187.
6. Petsoulas, 188.

[1]

Progress and Commerce in Anglo-American Thought: The Social Philosophy of Adam Ferguson

RONALD HAMOWY
University of Alberta

There can be little doubt that the influence of the Scottish Enlightenment on late eighteenth-century American thought was as thorough and as extensive as on British and Continental philosophy. It is true that some historians have recently exaggerated this influence to the point where it has been claimed that American revolutionary doctine was primarily a product of Scottish political philosophy.[1] Notwithstanding these distortions, however, there is strong evidence that, at least in the areas of ethics, economics, and social theory, the imprint of Scottish thinking was substantial. Not only did the Scottish universities serve as models for institutions of higher learning in the colonies,[2] but the works of the various writers who together comprised the Scottish Enlightenment were well-known and highly regarded on this side of the Atlantic.[3] Among this group were the greatest philosophers then writing in the English language, including Francis Hutcheson, David Hume, Adam Smith, Thomas Reid, Adam Ferguson, and Henry Home, Lord Kames.

Adam Ferguson is today perhaps the least known and appreciated of these

1. Perhaps the most extreme instance of this view is that contained in Garry Wills, *Inventing America: Jefferson's Declaration of Independence* (New York: Doubleday, 1979), wherein Wills attempts to interpret the philosophy embedded in the Declaration—at least as Jefferson originally intended it—as exclusively the product of Scottish Enlightenment thought, devoid of Lockean influences.

2. The Scottish impact on American higher education is fully examined in Douglas Sloan, *The Scottish Enlightenment and the American College Ideal* (New York: Teachers College Press, 1971). See also A. Bailey Cutts, "The Educational Influences of Aberdeen in Seventeenth-Century Virginia," *William and Mary Quarterly*, 2d Ser., xv(1935):229–49, and George S. Pryde, *The Scottish Universities and the Colleges of Colonial America* (Glasgow: Jackson, 1957).

3. Herbert W. Schneider has observed of the Scottish Enlightenment that it "was probably the most potent single tradition in the American Enlightenment. From Hutcheson to Ferguson, including Hume and Adam Smith, came a body of philosophical literature that aroused men from their dogmatic slumbers on both sides of the Atlantic" (*A History of American Philosophy* [New York: Columbia University Press, 1946], p. 246). See also the detailed discussion of the favorable reception given eighteenth-century Scottish moral philosophy and epistemology by American intellectuals in Elizabeth Flower and Murray G. Murphey, *A History of Philosophy in America* (2 vols.; New York: Capricorn Books, 1977), I, pp. 203–361. David Lundberg and Henry F. May's survey of early American library holdings and booksellers' lists bears out the conclusion that works by Scottish Enlightenment thinkers were extremely popular in America ("The Enlightened Reader in America," *American Quarterly*, XXVIII[1976]:262–93).

The relationship between Scotland and America in the eighteenth century has recently been the subject of a brief study by William R. Brock, *Scotus Americanus: A Survey of the Sources for Links Between Scotland and America in the Eighteenth Century* (Edinburgh: Edinburgh University Press, 1982).

thinkers, despite the distinctive contributions he made to eighteenth-century social theory. Although of lesser stature than were his contemporaries Hume and Smith, Ferguson was a man of letters of international repute during his lifetime, whose work was both as familiar to, and as esteemed by, most educated Americans as to Britons.[4] The recent resurgence of interest in the Scottish Enlightenment, therefore, makes it particularly appropriate that the character and quality of Ferguson's political and social philosophy be examined and assessed, especially as it touched on questions that interested both Britons and Americans at the close of the eighteenth and the beginning of the nineteenth centuries.

The youngest child of the parish minister, Adam Ferguson was born on June 20, 1723, at Logierait, Perthshire, on the border of the Scottish Highlands.[5] He received his early education both at the parish school and at the grammar school in Perth. In 1738, at the age of fifteen, he was sent to the University of St. Andrews, where he gained a reputation for classical scholarship. Ferguson took his M.A. degree in 1742 and, in the same year, entered the Divinity Hall at St. Andrews, but soon thereafter transferred to the University of Edinburgh to pursue his theological studies. Although having only completed two years of divinity school, Ferguson was offered the deputy chaplaincy of the Black Watch regiment in 1745. He joined the regiment in Flanders and accompanied it at the Battle of Fontenoy. Granted a dispensation from further study by the General Assembly, in part because of his knowledge of Gaelic, Ferguson was ordained in July, 1745, and given the rank of principal chaplain. He remained with his regiment, both at home and abroad, until 1754, at which time Ferguson resigned his commission and quit the clerical profession.

With the help of his friend David Hume, Ferguson was appointed to the post

4. With particular reference to Ferguson's reputation in America, see Gladys Bryson, *Man and Society: The Scottish Inquiry of the Eighteenth Century* (Princeton: Princeton University Press, 1945), p. 31, and Henry F. May, *The Enlightenment in America* (New York: Oxford University Press, 1976), p. 343.

Scottish moral philosophy was decisively established in America through the mediation of John Witherspoon, who arrived in the colonies from Scotland to take up the position of president of Princeton in 1768. Witherspoon, one of the more outspoken Evangelical ministers in the Church of Scotland, brought with him an intimate knowledge of the work of the leading Scottish writers, which he kept current and attempted to impart to his students. Thus, Ferguson's *Essay on the History of Civil Society* appears among the works comprising Witherspoon's recommended reading list for his course in political theory (Dennis F. Thompson, "The Education of a Founding Father: The Reading List for John Witherspoon's Course in Political Theory, as Taken by James Madison," *Political Theory*, IV[1976]:528). See also John Witherspoon, *Lectures on Moral Philosophy*, Varnum Lansing Collins, ed. (Princeton: Princeton University Press, 1912), p. 144.

A student of Witherspoon's, James Madison seems to have been especially receptive to Ferguson's writings. Madison's debt to Scottish Enlightenment thinking is discussed at some length in Roy Branson, "James Madison and the Scottish Enlightenment," *Journal of the History of Ideas*, XL(1979):235–50.

5. The standard biographical essay of Ferguson remains John Small, "Biographical Sketch of Adam Ferguson, LL.D., F.R.S.E., Professor of Moral Philosophy in the University of Edinburgh," *Transactions of the Royal Society of Edinburgh*, XXIII, Part III (1864): 599–655. See also the biographical chapter on Ferguson in David Kettler, *The Social and Political Thought of Adam Ferguson* (Columbus: Ohio State University Press, 1965), pp. 42–82.

of keeper of the Advocates' Library, Edinburgh, in 1757, having succeeded Hume to that office. Following the death of the professor of natural philosophy at the University of Edinburgh, Ferguson was named to that chair in 1759; five years later, in 1764, Ferguson transferred to the chair of pneumatics and moral philosophy, which he held until 1785. It was during his tenure as professor of moral philosophy that three of his four most important works were published: the *Essay on the History of Civil Society*, in 1767; the *Institutes of Moral Philosophy*, a synopsis of his lectures on moral philosophy, in 1769; and the *History of the Progress and Termination of the Roman Republic*, in 1783.

In 1778, having received permission from the University to temporarily absent himself, Ferguson served on the Conciliation Commission headed by the Earl of Carlisle, charged with negotiating a settlement with the American colonies. Upon arriving at Philadelphia, the Commission appointed Ferguson its secretary and immediately attempted to enter into negotiations with several members of Congress.[6] These proved a complete failure, nor was the Commission any more successful in prevailing upon Washington to grant Ferguson a passport through the American lines to treat directly with Congress.[7] Having been defeated at reaching agreement with the colonies short of recognizing their independence and withdrawing all British troops, the Commission returned home in late 1778, at which point Ferguson resumed his chair at the University.

Because of ill health, Ferguson resigned the professorship of moral philosophy in 1785, at the age of sixty-two, to be succeeded in the position by his one-time student, Dugald Stewart. The University arranged that Ferguson continue to draw a salary by awarding him the chair of mathematics as a sinecure; all lectures in the field were, in fact, to be delivered by a junior professor. During his retirement Ferguson completed his major work in moral philosophy, a revision and expansion of his *Institutes*, entitled *Principles of Moral and Political Science*, which appeared in two volumes in 1792. Ferguson died on February 22, 1816, in his ninety-third year, at St. Andrews, Scotland, and was buried in the grounds of the cathedral there.

Of Ferguson's principal writings, the *Essay on the History of Civil Society* is

6. Extensive discussions of the Carlisle Commission appear in Weldon A. Brown, *Empire or Independence: a Study in the Failure of Reconciliation, 1774–1783* (University, La.: Louisiana State University Press, 1941); pp. 244–92, and Carl Van Doren, *Secret History of the American Revolution* (Garden City, N.Y.: Garden City Publishing Co., 1941), pp. 63–116.

7. The Commission's official letter to Congress was accompanied by personal notes from both William Eden (later Lord Auckland) and George Johnstone—two of the Commissioners—to General Washington, warmly commending Ferguson. Eden referred to the favorable reception to which Ferguson was entitled by virtue of his eminence in the literary world (Eden to Washington, June 9, 1778, in Benjamin Franklin Stevens, ed., *Stevens's Facsimiles of Manuscripts in European Archives Relating to America, 1773–1783* [24 vols.; London: Issued only to subscribers and printed by Malby & Sons, 1889–1895], V, p. 401, facsimile 498), while Johnstone's letter was even more generous. "I beg to recommend to your private civilities my friend Dr. Ferguson," he wrote. "He has been engaged from his early life, in inculcating to mankind the virtuous principles you practise" (Johnstone to Washington, June 10, 1778, in Jared Sparks, ed., *Correspondence of the American Revolution . . .* [4 vols.; Boston: Little, Brown, 1853], II, p. 136).

64 · *Interpretation*

probably the most important; certainly it has generated the greatest interest among social scientists and intellectual historians in the last twenty years. The work went through seven editions during the author's lifetime,[8] in addition to appearing in French, German, and Italian translations.[9] So popular did the *Essay* prove that despite the ready availability of British editions of the work in America[10] at least two American editions appeared by 1819.[11]

The reception accorded Ferguson's essay was almost universally favorable. Not only did his Scottish contemporaries think highly of the work,[12] but it met with great success in London and on the Continent as well. The poet Thomas

8. The first edition was published simultaneously in Edinburgh, London, and Dublin. In addition to the seven authorized editions that appeared between 1767 and 1814, two pirated editions were apparently issued, the first carrying the imprint "Basil, J. J. Toureisen, 1789," and the second, "Basel, Thurneysen, 1791."

The edition used throughout this paper is a reprinting of the first edition, with a collation of the variants in the seventh edition which appeared in 1814, the last during Ferguson's lifetime, edited by Duncan Forbes (Edinburgh: Edinburgh University Press, 1966), hereafter cited as *Essay*.

9. Two French editions were published in Paris, in 1783 and 1796, under the title *Essai sur l'histoire de la société civile*, translated by Claude Bergier and Alexandre Meunier. A German translation by C. F. Jünger, entitled *Versuch über die Geschichte der bürgerlichen Gesellschaft*, appeared in Leipzig in 1768. In 1807 the work was published in an Italian translation done by P. Antonutti in Venice, under the title *Saggio circa la storia di civile società*.

10. Thus, the edition acquired by Jefferson that appears in his manuscript catalogue and that was included in the collection of books sold to the Library of Congress in 1815 is the second, corrected, edition, published in London in 1768 by A. Millar and T. Cadell (E. Millicent Sowerby, comp., *Catalogue of the Library of Thomas Jefferson* [5 vols.; Washington, D.C.: Library of Congress, 1952–1959], III, pp. 20–1, item 2348). Data presented by Lundberg and May indicate that between 1777 and 1813 the *Essay* appeared in twenty-two percent of the catalogues and booklists examined ("Enlightened Reader in America," 283).

11. There was a printing of the seventh edition, published in Boston by Hastings, Etheridge and Bliss in 1809, and an eighth edition, published in Philadelphia by A. Finley in 1819. Charles R. Hildeburn's bibliography of Pennsylvania imprints lists an edition of the *Essay* printed in Philadelphia by Robert Bell in 1773 (*A Century of Printing: The Issues of the Press in Pennsylvania, 1685 –1784* [2 vols.; New York: Burt Franklin, 1968], I, p. 164, [item 2878 originally published in 2 vols.; Philadelphia: Press of Matlack & Harvey, 1885–1886]). Hildeburn's evidence for the existence of such an edition is based on an advertising circular issued by Bell in that year, announcing that the *Essay*, "by a living Author of much Estimation whose elegant Performance will greatly delight," would be published by subscription in the fall of 1773 (*Ibid.*, p. 160, item 1857). There appear to be no copies of this edition extant. The editors of the Madison papers, however, state that the copy of the *Essay* obtained for James Madison by William Bradford in 1775 is that which Bell is reputed to have published in 1773 (William Bradford to Madison, January 4, 1775, in William T. Hutchinson and William M. E. Rachel, eds., *The Papers of James Madison*, I [Chicago: University of Chicago Press, 1962], p. 133 n.).

12. Both Hugh Blair and Principal William Robertson thought highly of the work (letter from David Hume to Blair, February 11, 1766, in *The Letters of David Hume*, J. Y. T. Grieg, ed. [2 vols.; Oxford: Clarendon Press, 1932], II, pp. 11–12). And Lord Kames wrote of the *Essay* that "the subject, not less beautiful than interesting, employs some vigour in writing, and much original thought" (letter from Lord Kames to Mrs. Edward Montagu, March 6, 1767, in Alexander Fraser Tytler, Lord Woodhouselee, *Memoirs of the Life and Writings of the Honourable Henry Home of Kames* [2 vols.; Edinburgh: William Creech, 1807], II, 48).

Gray found "uncommon strains of eloquence in it"[13] and Baron d'Holbach regarded it as "answering completely to the high opinion I had conceived of your great abilities and ingenuity."[14] So well received was the *Essay* that only two weeks after its appearance in London, David Hume was able to write Ferguson: "It is with sincere Pleasure I inform you of the general Success of your Book. I had almost said universal Success; and the Expression would have been proper, as far as a Book can be suppos'd to be diffus'd in a Fortnight, amidst this Hurry of Politics and Faction, I may safely say, that I have met with no body, that has read it, who does not praise it, and these are the People, who by their Reputation and Rank commonly give the Tone on these Occasions."[15]

Indeed, the only person who appears to have had reservations about the *Essay* was Hume himself. A large part of the work had been completed by Ferguson some years earlier, and, in manuscript form, had circulated among Ferguson's close friends under the title "A Treatise on Refinement." In 1759 Hume had examined it in this form and it had then met with his approval.[16] However, when the finished manuscript of the *Essay* was offered to Hume for his critical evaluation in 1766, Hume had different thoughts. In February, 1766, he wrote to Hugh Blair:

> I have perus'd Ferguson's Papers [the ms. of the *Essay*] more than once, which had been put into my hands, some time ago, at his desire. I sat down to read them with great Prepossession, founded on my good Opinion of him [and] on a Small Specimen I had seen of them some Years ago, . . . But I am sorry to say it, they have no-wise answer'd my Expectation. I do not think them fit to be given to the Public, neither on account of the Style nor the Reasoning; the Form nor the Matter.[17]

Hume's specific objections to the *Essay* have not been recorded, but the most plausible explanation is that offered by David Kettler, that where it was especially important that Ferguson be clear and precise, Hume found Ferguson's style both unsystematic and inexact.[18] Indeed, the *Essay* is filled with observations which, once made, are set aside without further discussion despite their be-

13. Letter from Gray to James Beattie, August 12, 1767, in Edmund Gosse, ed., *The Works of Thomas Gray* (4 vols.; New York: A. C. Armstrong, 1885), III, p. 279.

14. Baron d'Holbach to Ferguson, June 15, 1767, in John Small, *Biographical Sketch*, p. 611.

15. Hume to Ferguson, March 10, 1767, in Grieg, ed., *Letters of Hume*, II, p. 125.

16. Ernest Campbell Mossner, *The Life of David Hume* (Edinburgh: Nelson, 1954), p. 542. See also Hume's letter to Adam Smith, April 12, 1759, in Raymond Klibansky and Ernest Campbell Mossner, eds., *New Letters of David Hume* (Oxford: Clarendon Press, 1954), p. 52.

17. Hume to Blair, February 11, 1766, in Grieg, ed., *Letters of Hume*, II, pp. 11–12. Hume still held the same opinion of the *Essay* a year after its publication. Again writing to Blair, he commented: "The success of the Book, Dear Dr, which you mention, gives me great Satisfaction, on account of my sincere Friendship for the Author; and so much the rather, as this success was to me unexpected. I have since begun to hope, and even to believe, that I was mistaken; and in this Perswasion [*sic*] have several times taken it up and read Chapters of it: But to my great Mortification and Sorrow, I have not been able to change my Sentiments" (Hume to Blair, April 1, 1767, *ibid.*, II, p. 133).

18. Kettler, *Thought of Adam Ferguson*, pp. 58–60.

66 · *Interpretation*

ing pregnant with sociological and political implications. Hume's own disappointment clearly extended to these aspects of the *Essay*, its "reasoning, form, and matter," all of which were found wanting.[19] But despite these limitations, the *Essay* proved a remarkable success and gained for Ferguson an international reputation as a man of letters.[20]

Although the *Essay* is a study in the social history of man, Ferguson regarded the work as primarily an extension of his researches into moral philosophy. The starting point for any analysis of ethics, Ferguson believed, was the study of the way man functions, both as an individual and in conjunction with other people. If, furthermore, aprioristic notions of man's nature were to be rejected as unsatisfactory, then the only adequate method of gaining information about the rules of morality was by studying man within the context of his history.[21] It is because of the adoption of this empirical approach to the study of man's nature that Ferguson has been credited with being one of the founders of sociology.[22]

Ferguson's adherence to scientific description, to man as he is actually observed, led him to reject the notion of "man in the state of nature," in the sense of man before the advent of society. "Mankind are taken in groupes," he wrote, "as they have always subsisted."[23] That society is coeval with man is confirmed by

19. There is no evidence whatever to support the assertion recently made by Paul A. Rahe that Hume's reaction to the *Essay* stemmed primarily from his differences over Ferguson's claim that primitive societies displayed a vigor absent in more polished nations. Nor did Ferguson hold that "the emergence of commercial society would inevitably be accompanied by a decline in martial fervor that was the ultimate guarantor of political freedom" (Paul A. Rahe, "The Primacy of Politics in Classical Greece," *American Historical Review*, LXXXIX[1984]:280). Rahe is here confusing "martial fervor" with public-spiritedness and an active involvement in public affairs, characteristics Ferguson feared might diminish as societies became more commercial. In any case, Ferguson certainly did not regard the weakening of these social bonds as ineluctable. Indeed, the quotation from Ferguson that Rahe offers in support of his contention has no bearing on the value of martial fervor nor does it suggest that decline is inevitable. The quotation consists of two sentences joined by ellipses; in reality the two statements are taken out of context and are separated by no less than thirty-five pages of text in the Forbes edition of the *Essay*, with the second statement appearing first!

Rahe does no better with the quotation from the *Essay* that prefaces his article (*ibid.*, 265). Once again he has separated two sentences with ellipses. The first statement in fact appears as part of Ferguson's analysis of the dangers that might follow upon the increasing division of labor and is from part five of the *Essay*. The second sentence forms part of Ferguson's discussion of the naturalness of society and appears over 180 pages *earlier*, in part one. Such distorted quotations can only do a disservice to Ferguson's thought and, ultimately, to the cause of scholarship.

20. Among the many marks of favor the publication of the *Essay* conferred upon its author was the award of an honorary LL.D. by the University of Edinburgh.

21. "Before we can ascertain the rules of morality for mankind, the history of man's nature, his dispositions, his specific enjoyments and sufferings, his condition and future prospects, should be known" (Adam Ferguson, *Institutes of Moral Philosophy* [2d ed.; Edinburgh: A. Kincaid and W. Creech, 1772], p. 2, hereafter cited as *Institutes*).

22. See, for example, Harry E. Barnes, "Sociology before Comte," *American Journal of Sociology*, XXIII(1917):234; Theodor Buddeberg, "Ferguson als Soziologe," *Jahrbücher für Nationalökonomie und Statistik*, CXXIII(1925):609–12; and Werner Sombart, "Die Angänge der Soziologie," in Melchoir Palyi, ed., *Hauptprobleme der Soziologie: Erinnerungsgabe für Max Weber* (2 vols.; Munich and Leipzig: Duncker & Humblot, 1923), I, p. 9.

23. *Essay*, p. 4.

Progress and Commerce in Anglo-American Thought · 67

the fact that the individual is the bearer of social dispositions and that regardless of where we find man, we find him gathered together with others.[24]

Quoting Montesquieu's dictum that man is born in society and that there he remains,[25] Ferguson insisted that it was more than mere convenience that binds men together. Society is the product of an array of natural, one might almost say instinctive, drives impelling the individual toward social interaction. "We may reckon," he observed,

> the parental affection, which, instead of deserting the adult, as among the brutes, embraces more close, as it becomes mixed with esteem, and the memory of its early effects; together with a propensity common to man and other animals, to mix with the herd, and, without reflection, to follow the croud of his species. What this propensity was in the first moment of its operation we know not; but with men accustomed to company, its enjoyments and disappointments are reckoned among the principal pleasures or pains of human life. Sadness and melancholy are connected with solitude; gladness and pleasure with the concourse of men.[26]

Ferguson rejected the social contract theory as a valid account of the origins of government with the same force and with arguments not dissimilar to those earlier offered by Hume.[27] The establishment of formal rules enforceable by a permanent political institution emerged, not from the desire to create a stronger social union, but rather in response to the abuses that had arisen from an imperfect distribution of justice. Ferguson held that a system of formal political arrangements did not rest on consent but was gradually shaped to meet the interests of justice with respect to securing private property.[28] It is a useless analytical tool, he claimed, to posit the idea of universal consent to what was, in fact, the gradual emergence of formalized rules of action which took their origin in earlier modes of behavior. "What was in one generation of propensity to herd with the species," Ferguson observed, "becomes, in the ages which follow, a principle of

24. "If both the earliest and the latest accounts collected from every quarter of the earth, represent mankind as assembled in troops and companies; and the individual always joined by affection to one party, while he is possibly opposed to another; employed in the exercise of recollection and foresight; inclined to communicate his own sentiments, and to be made acquainted with those of others; these facts must be admitted as the foundation of all our reasoning relative to man" (*Essay*, p. 3).

25. The statement appears in letter XCIV of Montesquieu's *Lettres persanes*.

26. *Essay*, pp. 16–17.

27. David Hume, *A Treatise of Human Nature*, L. A. Selby-Bigge, ed. (2d ed.; Oxford: Clarendon Press, 1978), pp. 534–9. Useful analyses of Hume's views appear in Jonathan Harrison, *Hume's Theory of Justice* (Oxford: Clarendon Press, 1981), pp. 172–89, and Duncan Forbes, *Hume's Philosophical Politics* (Cambridge: Cambridge University Press, 1975), pp. 84–90.

28. *Essay*, 122–6. The notion that government itself, far from being the product of conscious design, took its form gradually and without deliberate intent has led one commentator to refer to Ferguson's rejection of the social contract as the boldest attack on the contractarian theory of political obligation that had been made up to that time (Herman Huth, "Soziale und Individualistische Auffassung im 18. Jahrhundert, vornehmlich bei Adam Smith und Adam Ferguson," *Staats- und Sozialwissenschaftliche Forschungen* [Leipzig: Duncker & Humblot, 1907], p. 46).

national union. What was originally an alliance for common defence, becomes a concerted plan of political force."[29]

The reader must turn to a consideration of Ferguson's ethics for a clear notion of what the term "state of nature" in fact refers to within the structure of Ferguson's own thought. Ferguson regarded a progression towards excellence or perfection as the governing principle of all moral life. The natural development of the individual and the species towards perfection *is*, for Ferguson, the "state of nature." Any point that lies along this continuum of development is as much man's "state of nature" as is any other point.[30] In his major work on moral philosophy, Ferguson noted:

> The state of nature or the distinctive character of any progressive being is to be taken, not from its description at the outset, or at any subsequent stage of its progress; but from an accumulative view of its movement throughout. The oak is distinguishable from the pine, not merely by its seed leaf; but by every successive aspect of its form; by its foliage in every successive season; by its acorn; by its spreading top; by its lofty growth; and the length of its period. And the state of nature, relative to every tree in the wood, includes all the varieties of form or dimension through which it is known to pass in the course of its nature.[31]

A sense of this unending improvement of the individual and the species is apparent from any study of the history of mankind. Thus, at one and the same time, Ferguson's law of perfection offers an explanation both for individual morality and for social progress. All acts generated by a desire for the preservation of what man most values and that are consonant with man's fellow-feeling, his sense of benevolence, work towards these ends.[32]

Ferguson's conclusions respecting the character of society and the nature of progress were totally antithetical to those of Hobbes, who understood progress solely in terms of man acting against his basic nature. The ends of society, for Hobbes, were easily determined by reference to the purposes which originally impelled man to enter into the social contract. The ends of society for Ferguson, on the other hand, followed directly from man's progressive nature. "In the human kind," he wrote, "the species has a progress as well as the individual; they build in every subsequent age on foundations formerly laid; and, in a succession

29. *Essay*, p. 121.

30. "If the palace be unnatural," wrote Ferguson in an often-quoted passage, "the cottage is no less; and the highest refinements of political and moral apprehension, are not more artificial in their kind, than the first operation of sentiment and reason" (*Essay*, p. 8).

31. Adam Ferguson, *Principles of Moral and Political Science* (2 vols.; Edinburgh: A. Strahan & T. Cadell, 1792), I, p. 192, hereafter cited as *Principles*.

32. "Man is by nature a member of society; . . . his perfection consists in the excellency or measure of his natural ability and dispositions or, in other words, it consists in his being an excellent part of the system to which he belongs. So that the effect of mankind should be the same, whether the individual means to preserve himself, or to preserve his community, with either intention he must cherish the love of mankind, as the most valuable part of his character" (*Institutes*, pp. 108-9).

of years, tend to a perfection in the application of their faculties, to which the aid of long experience is required, and to which many generations must have combined their endeavours."[33]

It is true that, unlike many of his French contemporaries,[34] Ferguson did not regard individual and social progress as inevitable,[35] although he held it as the natural end towards which all men strive. "Progression is the gift of God to all his intelligent creatures," he remarked, "and is within the competence of the lowest of mankind. . . . It is the nature of created mind in the course of experience and observation to improve its sagacity, and to make continual approach to the highest measure of intellectual ability of which it is susceptible."[36]

In his introductory comments to the 1966 edition of the *Essay*, Duncan Forbes has denied that the *Essay* can properly be said to belong to the history of the idea of progress, inasmuch as Ferguson devoted a lengthy section of the work to the dangers of luxury and to the irrecoverable loss of much primitive vigor brought about by civilization.[37] However, Ferguson's rejection of the idea of progress in its extreme form did not entail his having repudiated the notion of man's natural progress, however formulated. Forbes is no doubt justified in wishing to distinguish Ferguson (and the other Scottish Enlightenment writers) from those thinkers who embraced an uncritical faith in universal and inevitable progress directed by conscious design. But, though Ferguson would have rejected such a blindly optimistic view of social development, his belief in the progressive nature of man permeates the *Essay* and underpins all his moral philosophy. In the *Principles*, where Ferguson's moral theory is spelled out in great detail, Ferguson's optimism is far clearer and his predictions of unlimited progress unambiguous.[38] In light of his comments in the *Essay*, particularly as they are informed by the sentiments expressed in his *Principles*, the claim recently made that Ferguson "prophesied an inevitable decline" once societies had passed from barbarism to

---

33. *Essay*, p. 5.

34. Condorcet, in particular, comes to mind. Although portions of it are now somewhat dated, J. B. Bury's study of the idea of progress remains the best general work on the subject (J. B. Bury, *The Idea of Progress: An Inquiry into Its Origin and Growth* [London: Macmillan, 1920]).

35. Ferguson devoted an extensive portion of the *Essay* to the possibilities of retrogression (pp. 236–80). Consider also the following observation: "The public safety, and the relative interests of states; political establishments, the pretensions of party, commerce, and arts, are subjects which engage the attention of nations. The advantages gained in some of these particulars, determine the degree of national prosperity. The ardour and vigour with which they are at any one time pursued, is the measure of a national spirit. When those objects cease to animate, nations may be said to languish; when they are during any considerable time neglected, states must decline, and their people degenerate" (*ibid.*, p. 211).

36. *Principles*, II, pp. 403–4.

37. Duncan Forbes, "Introduction," *Essay*, p. xiv.

38. Lois Whitney has called attention to this fact some fifty years ago (Lois Whitney, *Primitivism and the Idea of Progress in English Popular Literature of the Eighteenth Century* [Baltimore: The Johns Hopkins Press, 1934], p. 153).

70 · *Interpretation*

commercialism[39] cannot stand up to examination.[40] Although it is clearly extravagant to assert that he posited "an inevitable, suprahuman logic of continual spiritual as well as material progress," as does one commentator,[41] it is equally questionable to claim that Ferguson held to a cyclical view of history,[42] or to deny, as does Forbes, that he should be considered a proponent of the idea of progress at all. Only a proponent of man's natural progressive development could have concluded that the progress of mankind "in its continual approach to the infinite perfection of what is eternal . . . may be compared to that curve, described by geometers, as in continual approach to a straight line, which it never can reach."[43]

All societies, Ferguson claimed, progressed from "rude" to "polished" nations, most evolving through three clearly distinct stages,[44] the first two of

39. Istvan Hont, "The 'Rich Country–Poor Country' Debate in Scottish Classical Political Economy," in Istvan Hont and Michael Ignatieff, eds., *Wealth and Virtue: The Shaping of Political Economy in the Scottish Enlightenment* (Cambridge: Cambridge University Press, 1983), p. 296. Nor, one might add, is there reason to accept Hont's conclusion that Hume's disappointment with the *Essay* was occasioned by Ferguson's play on "the Machiavellian chords" of "growth and decay, virtue and corruption" (*ibid.*, p. 295).

40. Indeed, Ferguson identified a higher degree of morality with the process by which the material progress that marks commercial societies emerges than with the more primitive cultures from which they progressed:

"The end of commercial art is, such a supply of accommodation and pleasure, as wealth may procure: But, suppose this end to be obtained at once, and without any effort; suppose the savage to become suddenly rich, to be lodged in a palace, and furnished with all the accommodations or means of enjoyment, which an ample estate or revenue can bestow; he would either have no permanent relish for such possessions, or, not knowing how to use and enjoy them, would exhibit effects of gross or ungovernable passion, and a brutality of nature, from which, amidst the wants and hardships of his own situation, he is in a great measure restrained.

"Such we may pronounce to be the effect of mere wealth, unattended with education, or apart from the virtues of industry, sobriety, and frugality, which nature has prescribed as the means of attainment: But, in the use of these means, the industrious are furnished with exercises improving to the genius of man; have occasion to experience, and to return the offices of beneficence and friendship; are led to the study of justice, sobriety, and good order, in the conduct of life. And, thus, in the very progress with which they arrive at the possession of wealth, form to themselves a taste of enjoyment, and decency of manners, equivalent to a conviction that happiness does not consist in the measure of fortune, but in its proper use; a condition, indeed, upon which happiness depends, no less in the highest, than in the lowest, or any intermediate state into which nations are led in the pursuit of these, or any other arts" (*Principles*, I, pp. 254–5).

41. Kettler, *Thought of Adam Ferguson*, pp. 219–20.

42. W. C. Lehmann, *Adam Ferguson and the Beginnings of Modern Sociology* (New York: Columbia University Press, 1930), p. 149.

43. *Principles*, I, pp. 184–5.

44. Ferguson's analysis of the stages of social development and their relation to changes in the notion of private property were adumbrated in slightly altered form by his fellow Scotsmen Sir John Dalrymple (*Essay Towards a General History of Feudal Property in Great Britain* [London: A. Millar, 1757]), Lord Kames (*Historical Law–Tracts* [2 vols.; Edinburgh: Printed for A. Millar, London; and A. Kincaid & J. Bell, Edinburgh, 1758] and the second edition of his *Essays on the Principles of Morality and Natural Religion* [2d ed.; Edinburgh: Printed for R. Fleming & A. Donaldson, 1758]) and, in particular, by Adam Smith, in his 1762–1763 lectures on jurisprudence (*Lectures on*

Progress and Commerce in Anglo-American Thought · 71

which are pre-political. Of the varieties of pre-commercial society, the most primitive are those based on hunting and fishing, and in these the notion of private property, except in its most rudimentary sense, is absent.[45] Lacking a concept of property, these communities possess no formal system of subordination and, consequently, no government.[46] Such societies Ferguson denominated *sav-*

Jurisprudence, R. L. Meek, D. D. Raphael, and P. G. Stein, eds. [Oxford: Clarendon Press, 1978], pp. 1-394). Dalrymple, Kames, and Smith had postulated the theory that societies progressed through four stages, defined by their primary mode of subsistence—hunting, pastoral, agricultural, and commercial—and that each of these stages reflected differing notions or property and distinct legal and political institutions. The origin and development of this theory has been examined by Ronald L. Meek, "The Scottish Contribution to Marxist Sociology," in Ronald L. Meek, ed., *Economics and Ideology and Other Essays: Studies in the Development of Economic Thought* (London: Chapman & Hall, 1967), pp. 34-50. (This essay originally appeared in slightly altered form under the same title in John Saville, ed., *Democracy and the Labour Movement: Essays in Honour of Dona Torr* [London: Lawrence & Wishart, 1954], pp. 84-102). Meek has since extended his researches to include a study of French, as well as Scottish, eighteenth-century advocates of the four-stages theory. See his "Smith, Turgot, and the 'Four-Stages' Theory," *History of Political Economy*, III(1971):9-27, and his book-length analysis, *Social Science and the Ignoble Savage* (Cambridge: Cambridge University Press, 1976). For a critical examination of the centrality of the four-stages theory to Adam Smith's thought, see Andrew Skinner, "A Scottish Contribution to Marxist Sociology?" in Ian Bradley and Michael Howard, eds., *Classical and Marxian Political Economy: Essays in Honor of Ronald L. Meek* (New York: St. Martin's Press, 1981), pp. 79-114.

45. The description of primitive communities as exhibiting a form of tribal communism was taken up by a number of nineteenth century social theorists, most notably by Friedrich Engels. Engels, who was familiar with Ferguson's writings, in commenting on the communal control over property that was reputed to exist among the early Germans, observed: "It has been established that among almost all peoples the cultivated land was tilled collectively by the gens, and later by communistic household communities such as were still found by Caesar among the Suevi" (*The Origin of the Family, Private Property and the State* [Zurich, 1884; first English edition, London, 1902] [London: Lawrence & Wishart, 1940], pp. 157-8). Engels, at other points in the study, discusses the same system of ownership as prevailing among the early Greeks (68-9), the Iroquois (99), and the Celts (149).

Tribal ownership of the land in primitive societies appears to have been so well accepted an hypothesis that even the great nineteenth-century legal scholar Henry Maine felt easy in noting: "The collective ownership of the soil by groups of men either in fact united by blood-relationship, or believing or assuming that they are so united, is now entitled to take rank as an ascertained primitive phenomenon, once universally characterising those communities of mankind between whose civilisation and our own there is any distinct connection or analogy" (Henry Sumner Maine, *Lectures on the Early History of Institutions* [New York: Henry Holt, 1875], pp. 1-2). See also chapter x, "Classifications of Property," in Maine's *Dissertations on Early Law and Custom* (New York: Henry Holt, 1886), pp. 335-61.

46. "Where no profit attends dominion, one party is as much averse to the trouble of perpetual command, as the other is to the mortification of perpetual submission" (*Essay*, p. 84).

That the institution of a formal political structure rests upon the prior establishment of a system of private property is a concept common to the Scottish historical school. Adam Smith's analysis is especially close to that offered by Ferguson. "Among hunters," Smith commented in his 1766 lectures on jurisprudence, "there is no regular government. . . . The appropriation of herds and flocks, which introduced an inequality of fortune, was that which first gave rise to regular government. Till there be property there can be no government, the very end of which is to secure wealth" (Adam Smith, *Lectures on Jurisprudence*, p. 404). Similar sentiments appear in the *Wealth of Nations* (Adam Smith,

72 · Interpretation

age. Even when savage societies base their mode of subsistence on some form of agriculture, their notion of property remains communal.[47]

Most agrarian and pastoral societies, however, are likely to be those in which property has ceased to remain communal and in which private wealth takes the form of agricultural products or of a herd of animals. Although private property will not have yet become institutionalized into a formal system of laws in these communities, it is a principal object of individual and social concern.[48] Societies thus marked by the emergence of personal property Ferguson called *barbarian*.

The causes for this transition from savagery to barbarism are unclear.[49] The motive for the emergence of private property appears to center upon the parent's desire for "better provision for his children than is found under the promiscuous management of many copartners."[50] At that point, when the labor and skill of some members of the community are applied apart, when they aim at *exclusive possession* and "the individual no longer finds among his associates the same inclination to commit every subject to public use, he [too] is seized with concern for his personal fortune; and is alarmed by the cares which every person entertains for himself." Such feelings, Ferguson added, begin to pervade all members of society as much from the desire to emulate and from jealousy as from economic necessity.[51]

With the advent of property, the members of the community can now be distinguished one from the other by unequal possessions, which in turn lays the foundation for a permanent subordination of rank. Just as savage societies appear to bear the crude outlines of democracies, so, Ferguson claimed, barbarous nations resemble monarchies.[52] However, the disparities of rank that mark barbarous states are not yet sufficiently formalized for a concerted plan of government

---

An Inquiry into the Nature and Causes of the Wealth of Nations, R. H. Campbell and A. S. Skinner, eds. [2 vols.; Oxford: Clarendon Press, 1976], II, pp. 709–10 [v.i.b.2]).

For a valuable discussion of the relationship between property and government among the members of the Scottish historical school, see Roy Pascal's seminal article, "Property and Society: The Scottish Historical School of the Eighteenth Century," *Modern Quarterly* (London), 1(1938): 167–79.

47. "After they have shared the toils of the seed-time, they enjoy the fruits of the harvest in common. The field in which they have planted . . . is claimed as a property by the nation, but is not parcelled in lots to its members. They go forth in parties to prepare the ground, to plant, and to reap. The harvest is gathered into the public granary, and from thence, at stated times, is divided into shares for the maintenance of separate families" (*Essay*, p. 82).

48. *Essay*, p. 82.

49. Indeed, in its naïveté and simplicity, the reader is reminded of Rousseau's analysis of the origin of private property that appears in his *Discourse on Inequality* (Jean-Jacques Rousseau, *Sur l'origine de l'inégalité parmi les hommes*, in *Œuvres complètes*, Barnard Gagnebin and Marcel Raymond, eds. [Bibliothèque de la Pléiade; Paris: Librairie Gallimard, 1964], III, pp. 164, 171.

50. *Essay*, p. 96.

51. *Essay*, pp. 96–7.

52. *Essay*, p. 100.

Progress and Commerce in Anglo-American Thought · 73

to have emerged.[53] The distinction between leader and follower continues blurred; their pursuits and occupations remain the same, their minds are equally cultivated. There is no civil control, only brute force; no formal set of rules, only habit and power. Yet, Ferguson noted, "property is secure, because each has a friend, as well as an enemy; and if the one is disposed to molest, the other is ready to protect."[54]

The chief threat to property in barbarous communities issues from outside the tribe, and war, whether offensive or defensive, is its main concern. While this state of affairs prevails, internal usurpation of power is impossible and no formal arrangement of laws nor any systematic and ongoing institutions to enforce them are found necessary.[55] However, once society has secured itself from its foreign enemies, "the individual at home bethinks him of what he may gain or lose for himself: the leader is disposed to enlarge the advantages which belong to his station; the follower becomes jealous of rights which are open to incroachment; and parties who united before, from affection and habit, or from regard to their common preservation, disagree in supporting their several claims to precedence or profit."[56]

This clash of faction, which emerges out of a desire "to withstand the encroachments of sovereignty" upon the rights and property of the subject,[57] gives rise to government restrained by law.[58] Government, for Ferguson, was in its origin a natural outgrowth of the conflict of party in domestic struggle. And from this struggle, he contended, issued the earliest political institutions, which were based on previously observed but not explicitly formulated rules.

Two themes emerge in Ferguson's discussion of the rise of government that are reiterated throughout his work and that are central to his social philosophy. The first concerns the ongoing value of social conflict and competition, while the

53. *Essay*, p. 103.

54. *Essay*, p. 106.

55. *Essay*, p. 125. But compare the description of the origin of political establishments that Ferguson at one point offered in his *Principles*. "Man," he wrote, "is born naked, defenceless, and exposed to greater hardships than any other species of animal; . . . His society, also, prior to any manner of political establishment, we may imagine exposed to extreme disorder; and there, also, we may fancy the spur of necessity no less applied than in the urgency of his mere animal wants. From these motives, accordingly, we admit the arts of human life, whether commercial or political, to have originated, and suppose that the consideration of necessity must have operated prior to that of convenience . . ." (I, p. 239).

56. *Essay*, p. 125.

57. The terminology that Ferguson here used is confusing. "Sovereignty" and "subject" are to be understood only in some metaphorical sense, since Ferguson's discussion at this point has exclusive reference to barbarous societies prior to the establishment of government.

58. I can find little evidence to support Kettler's contention that "Ferguson differs politically from Hume and Smith because he believes that political life is primarily about power and the assertion of will, and only secondarily about property and the satisfaction of interest" (David Kettler, "History and Theory in Ferguson's Essay on the *History of Civil Society*: A Reconsideration," *Political Theory*, v[1977]:453). Indeed, with respect to the ultimate purposes of government, Ferguson, Hume, and Smith appear to differ in only minor particulars.

74 · *Interpretation*

second has reference to the role of instinct and habit in shaping social institutions. Conflict, Ferguson contended, is a natural phenomenon; our very games and sports testify to our love of contention. This fundamental desire to compete, when manifested in the animosities of faction, assures a vigorous and flourishing society. Without the vigilance and spirit that accompany the divisions of party, free government becomes impossible and despotism quickly follows. Indeed, Ferguson went even further and claimed that war itself gives rise to many of the more noble sentiments of which mankind is capable.[59] In addition, war advances that shared feeling of community which cements social life. "The sense of a common danger, and the assaults of an enemy," he wrote, "have been frequently useful to nations, by uniting their members more firmly together, and by preventing the secessions and actual separations in which their civil discord might otherwise terminate."[60]

Conflict and rivalry are thus natural to men at all stages of social development and contribute substantially to a host of beneficial social ends.[61] Not only does war act to encourage social cohesion, but the struggle of faction contributes both to the original emergence of government constrained by law and to the public spiritedness and vigilance which forestalls the rise of despotism. Advanced societies, Ferguson maintained, were particularly prone to degenerate into despotism as each individual concentrated his activities on the private pursuit of fortune. A society secure from foreign attack and internal strife and comprised of citizens preoccupied with their private interests is easily corrupted[62] and may fall into a condition of political slavery. "Liberty," Ferguson contended, "is maintained by the continued differences and oppositions of numbers, not by their concurring zeal in behalf of equitable government."[63] Duncan Forbes has quite justifiably

---

59. "Without the rivalship of nations, and the practice of war, civil society itself could scarcely have found an object, or a form. Mankind might have traded without any formal convention, but they cannot be safe without a national concert. The necessity of a public defence, has given rise to many departments of state, and the intellectual talents of men have found their busiest scene in wielding their national forces. To overawe, or intimidate, or, when we cannot persuade with reason, or resist with fortitude, are the occupations which give its most animating exercise, and its greatest triumphs, to a vigorous mind; and he who has never struggled with his fellow-creatures, is a stranger to half the sentiments of mankind" (*Essay*, p. 24).

Adam Smith, in like vein, refers to the "ennobling hardships and hazards of war" (*Theory of Moral Sentiments*, D. D. Raphael and A. L. Macfie, eds. [Oxford: Clarendon Press, 1979], p. 134 [III.2.35]).

60. *Essay*, p. 22.

61. Several commentators have taken note of this apparent contradiction in Ferguson's thought: that he could view man's hostile and contentious instincts as of enormous social utility while at the same time advocating a system of ethics predicated on fellow-feelings of sympathy and benevolence. See, for example, Paul Janet, *Histoire de la science politique dans ses rapports avec la morale* (2 vols.; 3rd ed.; Paris: Ancienne Librairie Germer Baillière, 1887), II, pp. 565–6, and Duncan Forbes, "Introduction," *Essay*, pp. xviii–xix.

62. "The national vigour," Ferguson wrote, "declines from the abuse of that very security which is procured by the supposed perfection of public order" (*Essay*, p. 223).

63. *Essay*, p. 128.

Progress and Commerce in Anglo-American Thought · 75

noted that Ferguson's discussion of the dangers of political tranquility and the value of social faction are a critical running commentary on Hume's political philosophy.[64] Indeed, nowhere did Ferguson more clearly distance himself from Hume's politics than in his treatment of the relation between party faction and good government.[65] On this issue, Ferguson's views were at substantial variance from those of his fellow Scots while they tended to approach those of Edmund Burke, who wrote similarly that the existence of party divisions is inseparable from free government.[66]

What is somewhat more difficult to justify is Ferguson's conclusion that the ferocity of armed conflict plays a crucial role in the evolution and survival of civilized societies.[67] His emphasis on the value of dissension can probably be made more palatable if we include among the forces against which the will should be exerted, as I'm sure he meant to, the hostility of nature itself. There is, after all, great drama in the way in which the American West was tamed and settled by sheer strength of character, and its early settlers perhaps best reflect the active independent citizen whom Ferguson would have regarded with approval. There is, however, no denying that Ferguson saw in the rivalship of nations a device for cementing the social bonds and for providing an outlet for selfless action. In the process of pacifying man's anomosities, Ferguson wrote,

64. "Introduction," *Essay,* p. xxxvi.

65. Consider the following sentiments from Hume's essay on political parties: "As much as legislators and founders of states ought to be honoured and respected among men, as much ought the founders of sects and factions to be detested and hated; because the influence of faction is directly contrary to that of laws. Factions subvert government, render laws impotent, and beget the fiercest animosities among men of the same nation, who ought to give mutual assistance and protection to each other. And what should render the founders of parties more odious is, the difficulty of extirpating these weeds, when once they have taken root in any state. They naturally propagate themselves for many centuries, and seldom end but by the total dissolution of that government, in which they are sown" (David Hume, "Of Parties in General," *Essays Moral, Political, and Literary,* T. H. Green and T. H. Grose, eds. [2 vols.; new ed.; London: Longmans, Green, 1882], I, pp. 127–8 [reprint ed.: Vol. III, *The Philosophical Works* (Darmstadt: Scientia Verlag Aalan, 1964)]).

Smith too had grave reservations respecting the benefits of faction. See Donald Winch, *Adam Smith's Politics: An Essay in Historiographic Revision* (Cambridge: Cambridge University Press, 1978), pp. 158–60, and Smith's references to the dangers inherent in the clash of political and religious party that appear in the *Theory of Moral Sentiments,* p. 155 (III.3.43), p. 170 (III.5.13), p. 232 (VI.ii.2.15), pp. 241–2 (VI.iii.12).

66. Edmund Burke, "Observations on 'The Present State of the Nation'" (1769), in *Works* (12 vols.; rev. ed.; Boston: Little, Brown, 1865–1867), I, p. 271.

Herta H. Jogland, in commenting on Ferguson's discussion of the benefits arising out of political faction, implies an analogue between Ferguson's view of the role of healthy competition in political life, on the one hand, and commercial life, on the other (*Ursprünge und Grundlagen der Soziologie bei Adam Ferguson* [Berlin: Duncker & Humblot, 1959], p. 101).

67. Duncan Forbes has written of this aspect of Ferguson's thought: "None of the leading thinkers of the Scottish Enlightenment believed in perpetual peace, either as a practical possibility or as an ideal . . . ; and they were well aware of the creative as well as destructive role of war in the development of civilization. But Ferguson's is the most profound and disturbing of these glosses on the high hopes of the Enlightenment" ("Introduction," *Essay,* p. xviii).

76 · *Interpretation*

we may hope, in some instances, to disarm the angry passions of jealousy and envy; we may hope to instil into the breasts of private man sentiments of candour toward their fellow-creatures, and a disposition to humanity and justice. But it is vain to expect that we can give to the multitude of a people a sense of union among themselves, without admitting hostility to those who oppose them. Could we at once, in the case of any nation, extinguish the emulation which is excited from abroad, we should probably break or weaken the bands of society at home, and close the busiest scenes of national occupations and virtues.[68]

The positive but unintended effects that Ferguson claimed characterizes social conflict are illustrative of a more general social principle that emerges throughout his writings, namely, that social institutions take their form not from deliberate calculation but from instinct and habit. "The artifices of the beaver, the ant, and the bee," he observed,

are ascribed to the wisdom of nature. Those of polished nations are ascribed to themselves, and are supposed to indicate a capacity superior to that of rude minds. But the establishments of men, like those of every animal, are suggested by nature, and are the result of instinct, directed by the variety of situations in which mankind are placed. Those establishments arose from successive improvements that were made, without any sense of their general effect; and they bring human affairs to a state of complication, which the greatest reach of capacity with which human nature was ever adorned, could not have projected; nor even when the whole is carried into execution, can it be comprehended in its full extent.[69]

The conception here offered that social structures are formed spontaneously is possibly the single most spectacular contribution to social philosophy of the Scottish Enlightenment. Such a theory is able to provide an explanation for complex social phenomena without recourse to descriptions requiring the presence of a designer or coordinator. Regularities and orderly arrangements in the social sphere need not be the deliberate product of human design. Rather, the theory provides that the complex organization inherent in our social institutions can be, and indeed most often is, the result of countless individual actions, none of which is intentionally aimed at contributing to any preconceived plan. Society is not formed from any rational calculation, but spontaneously; its institutions are the outcome of men's actions that have as their objects more immediate private ends.[70]

68. *Essay*, p. 25.

69. *Essay*, p. 182.

70. It is important to underscore the fact that the theory here expounded does not make the claim that social structures take their shape independent of the action of individuals—but only independent of their intent. There is no attempt to reduce social institutions to products of arcane forces operating according to laws that do not provide for the intervention of any human agency. It follows that the theory of spontaneous order as propounded by Ferguson and the other Scottish writers cannot legitimately be regarded as a precursor to the anti-individualistic theories of social evolution that appeared in the nineteenth century, as has been claimed by some sociologists. See, for example, Buddeberg, "Ferguson als Soziologe," 625, and Roy Pascal, "Herder and the Scottish Historical School," *Publications of the English Goethe Society: Papers Read Before the Society, 1938–1939*, New Ser., XIV(1938–1939):28.

Progress and Commerce in Anglo-American Thought · 77

The revolutionary nature of this explanation of the essential characteristics of most complex social patterns should not be underestimated. Social institutions are exceedingly intricate and it is, at least at first blush, counter-intuitive to suppose that they take their shape from anything other than conscious intent. Indeed, the argument from design dictates that when objects reach a certain order of intricacy, such as the social arrangements under which men operate, we must suppose them to have had a designer.[71] The theory of spontaneously generated orders explicitly denies this conclusion; far from being the product of human contrivance, the theory provides that these arrangements emerged as the unintended and unanticipated result of human action through the process of adaptive evolution.

This account of the growth of institutions is, of course, not limited to Ferguson but appears in the writings of the other Scottish moral philosophers as well. David Hume, for example, examined the distinction between the motives behind individual actions and the emergence of general rules of justice in terms of this doctrine.[72] The principle perhaps presents itself most clearly in his account of the rights of property, right, and obligation. There Hume conceded that they served the public good but denied that the public good was the motive for their adoption. "If men had been endow'd with such a strong regard for public good," he wrote,

> they wou'd never have restrain'd themselves by these rules: so that the laws of justice arise from natural principles in a manner still more oblique and artificial. 'Tis self-love which is their real origin; and as the self-love of one person is naturally contrary to that of another, these several interested passions are oblig'd to adjust themselves after such a manner as to concur in some system of conduct and behaviour. This system, therefore, comprehending the interest of each individual, is of course advantageous to the public; tho' it be not intended for that purpose by the inventors.[73]

One of the most explicit presentations of the theory that complex social phenomena, especially economic phenomena, are self-coordinating and do not require conscious ordering, was offered by Adam Smith. Hence the centrality in Smith's thought of such notions as "natural justice" and the "invisible hand" in connection with the self-regulating mechanism of the market. Consider as an example Smith's account of the evolution of the division of labor as the unintended consequence of men's propensity to exchange goods. "The division of labour," Smith wrote, "from which so many advantages are derived, is not originally the effect of any human wisdom, which foresees and intends the general opulence

71. The relation between invisible-hand explanations and the argument from design is touched on in Edna Ullmann-Margalit, "Invisible-Hand Explanations," *Synthese*, XXXIX(1978):263–91.

72. Hume, "Of the Origin of Justice and Property," *Treatise of Human Nature*, pp. 484–501. For discussions of the role the theory of spontaneous order plays in Hume's social theory, see F. A. Hayek, "The Legal and Political Philosophy of David Hume," in V. C. Chappell, ed., *Hume* (Notre Dame, Ind.: University of Notre Dame Press, 1968), pp. 335–60. and Knud Haakonssen, *The Science of a Legislator: The Natural Jurisprudence of David Hume and Adam Smith* (Cambridge: Cambridge University Press, 1981), pp. 4–44.

73. Hume, *Treatise of Human Nature*, p. 529.

78 · *Interpretation*

to which it gives occasion. It is the necessary, though very slow and gradual consequence of a certain propensity in human nature which has in view no such extensive utility; the propensity to truck, barter, and exchange one thing for another."[74]

Smith first employed the concept of the invisible hand in his *Theory of Moral Sentiments*[75] in the context of his examination of the effects of the uneven distribution of wealth. With reference to the rich, he observed:

> They consume little more than the poor, and in spite of their natural selfishness and rapacity, though they mean only their own conveniency, though the sole end which they propose from the labours of all the thousands whom they employ, be the gratification of their own vain and insatiable desires, they divide with the poor the produce of all their improvements. They are led by an invisible hand to make nearly the same distribution of the necessaries of life, which would have been made, had the earth been divided into equal portions among all its inhabitants, and thus without intending it, without knowing it, advance the interest of the society, and afford means to the multiplication of the species.[76]

Smith again had recourse to the expression "invisible hand" in the *Wealth of Nations,* published some seventeen years later, when he once again used it to describe the beneficial but unintended social outcome of individual actions, each aiming at some distinct private end.[77]

Nor did Smith limit the scope to which the doctrine of spontaneously generated orders was applicable to economic phenomena. Duncan Forbes has employed the phrase "the law of the heterogeneity of ends" to describe this aspect of Scottish thought and has pointed out the pervasiveness of Smith's use of this principle in explicating social issues.[78] Indeed, Forbes provides an extensive list

74. Smith, *Wealth of Nations,* I, p. 25 [I.ii.1].

75. This is not, strictly speaking, correct. The term appears in Smith's "History of Astronomy" [III.2], which was probably penned before his *Theory of Moral Sentiments.* See Alec Macfie, "The Invisible Hand of Jupiter," *Journal of the History of Ideas,* XXXII(1971):595–9.

76. *Theory of Moral Sentiments,* pp. 184–5 [IV.1.10].

77. "As every individual, therefore, endeavours as much as he can both to employ his capital in the support of domestick industry, and so to direct that industry that its produce may be of the greatest value; every individual necessarily labours to render the annual revenue of the society as great as he can. He generally, indeed, neither intends to promote the publick interest, nor knows how much he is promoting it. By preferring the support of domestick to that of foreign industry, he intends only his own security; and by directing that industry in such a manner as its produce may be of the greatest value, he intends only his own gain, and he is in this, as in many other cases, led by an invisible hand to promote an end which was no part of his intention. By pursuing his own interest he frequently promotes that of the society more effectually than when he really intends to promote it. I have never known much good done by those who affected to trade for the publick good. It is an affectation, indeed, not very common among merchants, and very few words need be employed in dissuading them from it" (I, p. 456 [IV.ii.9]).

78. Duncan Forbes, "'Scientific' Whiggism: Adam Smith and John Millar," *Cambridge Journal,* VII(1954):643–70.

It should be pointed out that Forbes's law of the heterogeneity of ends is not quite synonymous with the principle of spontaneously generated orders as used in this essay. Forbes's law emcompasses

Progress and Commerce in Anglo-American Thought · 79

of examples where Smith employed the device to explain the unplanned consequences of human action. Instances include the "silent and insensible operation of foreign commerce" on the authority of the feudal barons[79] and the unintended effects on the political power of the nobility of their consuming the whole of the value of their rents.[80]

Although there are fewer instances of Ferguson's use of the theory of spontaneous order than appear in Smith's writings, mainly the result of Ferguson's lack of interest in purely economic questions, Ferguson's applications of the doctrine are, for the most part, much clearer and less ambiguous, especially when they have reference to non-economic phenomena. For example, Ferguson explicitly rejected the notion that the institutions we associate with government are the product of conscious design. "No constitution," he observed,

> is formed by concert, no government is copied from a plan. The members of a small state contend for equality; the members of a greater, find themselves classed in a certain manner that lays a foundation for monarchy. They proceed from one form of government to another, by easy transitions, and frequently under old names adopt a new constitution. The seeds of every form are lodged in human nature; they spring up and ripen with the season. The prevalence of a particular species is often derived from an imperceptible ingredient mingled in the soil.[81]

Ferguson concluded that we need put no credence in the theory that social arrangements are the creation of some original Lycurgus-like legislator, who deliberately structured the consistency and symmetry that marks our political and legal institutions.[82]

In contradistinction to Ferguson, one need only point to Rousseau, who, in his discussion of the legislator, noted that he must possess an almost superhuman intelligence that would allow him to stand above the ordinary human passions. He would thus be in a position not only to mold the new and perfect institutions by which men would be governed but to actually change the essential nature of

---

the whole spectrum of human actions that issue in significant but unintended social consequences. The doctrine of spontaneous order, on the other hand, has specific reference only to those human actions the unintended effects of which, in the aggregate, result in social institutions or complex social patterns. The principle of spontaneous order thus refers to a narrower range of unplanned effects than does Forbes's law.

79. *Wealth of Nations*, I, pp. 417–18 (III.iv.9–10).

80. *Wealth of Nations*, I, pp. 418–22 (III.iv.10–17). So embedded is this principle in Smith's thought that it has been seen as extending to his ethical theory as well. Thus, in discussing the role utility plays in shaping the rules of morality, Campbell and Ross refer to "Smith's repeated attempts to demonstrate the unintended utilitarian consequences of non-utilitarian motivations" (T. D. Campbell and I. S. Ross, "The Utilitarianism of Adam Smith's Policy Advice," *Journal of the History of Ideas*, XLII[1981]:76). And Haakonssen remarks of Smith's ethics that "the general rules of morality are thus the unintended outcome of a multitude of individual instances of natural moral evaluation" (*Science of a Legislator*, p. 61).

81. *Essay*, p. 123.

82. *Essay*, p. 123.

80 · *Interpretation*

man.[83] It is, therefore, not surprising that Rousseau felt such a profound admiration for Lycurgus.

The belief that it was within the power of the legislator to create social institutions of enormous complexity, which, in addition, would constrain men to live virtuous lives, was not an uncommon view among the more radical French revolutionaries, who all seem to have found their model of the ideal legislator in Lycurgus.[84] Nor did this belief stop at the Channel. It can, surprisingly, be found even in Burke, who wrote of "the wise legislators of all countries, who aimed at improving instincts into morals, and at grafting the virtues on the stock of the natural affections."[85] Ferguson, of course, was an adamant opponent of this view, which he, together with the other Scottish moral philosophers, successfully undermined by applying the theory of spontaneously generated orders to the origin and growth of political institutions.

Nor did Ferguson limit the application of this doctrine to explaining the development of systems of government. In a particularly insightful comment, Ferguson observed that language was an especially good example of an institution that takes its shape from the actions of countless individuals, who neither aim at nor are capable of comprehending the complexity that language displays. Language is one of the clearest examples of an intricately ordered social arrangement that, although the product of individual actions, is not consciously designed. "Parts of speech," Ferguson wrote,

> which, in speculation, cost the grammarian so much study, are in practice familiar to the vulgar: The rudest tribes, even the idiot, and the insane, are possessed of them: They are soonest learned in childhood; insomuch, that we must suppose human nature, in its lowest state, competent to the use of them; and, without the intervention of uncommon genius, mankind, in a succession of ages, qualified to accomplish in detail this amazing fabric of language, which, when raised to its height, appears so much

83. "Celui qui ose entreprendre d'instituer un peuple doit se sentir en état de changer, pour ainsi dire, la nature humaine; de transformer chaque individu, qui par lui-même est un tout parfait et solitaire, en partie d'un plus grand tout dont cet individu reçoive en quelque sorte sa vie et son être; d'alterer la constitution de l'homme pour la renforcer; de substituer une existence partielle et morale à l'existence physique et indépendante que nous avons tous reçue de la nature. Il faut, en un mot, qu'il ôte à l'homme ses forces propres pour lui en donner qui lui soient étrangères et dont il ne puisse faire usage sans le secours d'autrui. Plus ces forces naturelles sont mortes et anéanties, plus les acquises sont grandes et durables, plus aussi l'institution est solide et parfaite: En sorte que si chaque Citoyen n'est rien, ne peut rien, que par tous les autres, et que la force acquise par le tout soit égale ou supérieure à la somme des forces naturelles de tous les individus, on peut dire que la législation est au plus haut point la perfection qu'elle puisse atteindre" (*Du contrat social* [book II, chapter vii], in *Œuvres complètes*, III, pp. 381–2).

84. See Harold T. Parker, *The Cult of Antiquity and the French Revolutionaries: A Study in the Development of the Revolutionary Spirit* (Chicago: University of Chicago Press, 1937). *passim*, but esp. pp. 146–70. Duncan Forbes has remarked that the destruction of the Legislator myth, which found such favor among certain eighteenth-century intellectuals, "was perhaps the most original and daring *coup* of the social science of the Scottish Enlightenment" ("Introduction," *Essay*, p. xxiv).

85. "Letters on a Regicide Peace" (1796–1797), in *Works*, V, p. 311.

Progress and Commerce in Anglo-American Thought · 81

above what could be ascribed to any simultaneous effort of the most sublime and comprehensive abilities.[86]

Ferguson's application of the doctrine of spontaneous order as an explanation of the development of institutions is extensive. Most complex social arrangements, he contended, whether political, linguistic, economic, legal, or otherwise, are likely to have taken their form as the unintended consequence of the efforts of large numbers of actors, often acting over long periods of time. In a particularly elegant passage of his *Essay*, Ferguson noted:

> Like the winds, that come we know not whence, and blow whithersoever they list, the forms of society are derived from an obscure and distant origin; they arise, long before the date of philosophy, from the instincts, not from the speculations of men. The croud of mankind, are directed in their establishments and measures, by the circumstances in which they are placed; and seldom are turned from their way, to follow the plan of any single projector.
>
> Every step and every movement of the multitude, even in what are termed enlightened ages, are made with equal blindness to the future; and nations stumble upon establishments, which are indeed the result of human action, but not the execution of any human design.[87]

Ferguson's theory of spontaneous development, when wedded to his notions respecting man's natural progress towards excellence, led him to conclude that social arrangements took their ultimate form in the institutions that mark com-

---

86. *Principles*, I, p. 43. Dugald Stewart, in his own discussions of the origin and nature of language, twice quoted this passage with approval. See Stewart's *Dissertation: Exhibiting the Progress of Metaphysical, Ethical, and Political Philosophy, Since the Revival of Letters in Europe* (1815–1827), in Sir William Hamilton, ed., *The Collected Works* (11 vols.; Edinburgh: Thomas Constable, 1854), I, p. 365; and, *Elements of the Philosophy of the Human Mind* (1792–1827), Vol. III, *ibid.*, IV, p. 27.

87. *Essay*, p. 122. Despite the extensive literature dealing with Scottish Enlightenment social theory, the role played by the notion of spontaneous order in Scottish philosophy has been neglected by all but a handful of commentators. (Exception must be made for Friedrich Meinecke, whose *Die Entstehung des Historismus* [2 vols.; Munich: R. Oldenbourg, 1936] discusses this theory at some length.) Outside the field of economics proper, most scholars appear to have become aware of the doctrine and its widespread implications through the writings of F. A. Hayek, whose own work in political and social philosophy is explicitly indebted to the nonintentionalist aspects of Scottish thought. See especially Hayek's "Individualism: True and False" (1945), in F. A. Hayek, *Individualism and Economic Order* (London: Routledge & Kegan Paul, 1949), pp. 1–32; *The Constitution of Liberty* (Chicago: University of Chicago Press, 1960), pp. 54–70; and, "Kinds of Rationalism" (1965) and "The Results of Human Action but not of Human Design" (1967), in F. A. Hayek, *Studies in Philosophy, Politics and Economics* (Chicago: University of Chicago Press, 1967), pp. 82–95, 96–105. Of the intellectual historians who have recently discussed Ferguson's thought, the few who make reference to the relation between ordered arrangements and unintended outcomes appear to owe the structure of their analysis to Hayek. See, for example, Louis Schneider, ed., *The Scottish Moralists on Human Nature and Society* (Chicago: University of Chicago Press, 1967), pp. xxix–xlvii; Pasquale Salvucci, *Adam Ferguson: Sociologia e filosofia politica* (Urbino: Argalia, 1972), pp. 533–5; and, Alan Swingewood, "Origins of sociology: the case of the Scottish Enlightenment," *British Journal of Sociology*, XXI(1970):174. Both Schneider and Salvucci are expressly indebted to Hayek's interpretation of this aspect of Scottish social philosophy.

82 · *Interpretation*

mercial society. The establishment of private property—and, by implication, the formal governmental organization necessary to protect it—was, for Ferguson, so deeply rooted in man's nature that, despite Ferguson's references to its evolutionary character, he regarded the impetus towards private possession as universal and its institutionalization as essential to man's moral growth.[88]

Ferguson was prepared to concede that commercial societies, that is, those based on the principle of private property, would inevitably display an uneven distribution of wealth. But this, he contended, served the essential function of acting as a spur to the industry and an incentive to the labor of the great mass of the population.[89] The ultimate effect of the economic inequality that characterizes commercial societies is to encourage the production of ever-greater quantities of wealth, thus benefitting all members of the community. "The object of commerce is wealth," wrote Ferguson, and "in the progress, as well as in the result of commercial arts, mankind are enabled to subsist in growing numbers; learn to ply their resources, and to wield their strength, with superior ease and success."[90]

Ferguson did not back away from embracing a regime of commerce of the most extended sort, despite what he regarded as its potential dangers. Indeed, he argued in his *Principles* that active participation in commercial life encouraged men in the exercise of a host of virtues, including industry, sobriety, frugality, justice, even beneficence and friendship.[91] Although Ferguson contended that civilization was not invariably accompanied by a high degree of commercial activity,[92] he did insist that the prime motive force for individual and social progress was ambition, "the specific principle of advancement uniformly directed to this end, and not satiated with any given measure of gratification." And ambition, in turn, he noted, operated no less "in the concerns of mere animal life; in the provision of subsistence, of accommodation, and ornament," as "in the progress of society, and in the choice of its institutions."[93] Further, and more important, Ferguson saw no conflict between those social arrangements that acted as guarantees of individual liberty and those that encouraged an increase in wealth.[94] Indeed, he contended that the forces that lead to an expansion in population, which Ferguson equated with social wealth, required the successful pur-

---

88. "The dispositions which refer to the preservation of the individual, while they continue to operate in the manner of instinctive desires, are nearly the same in man that they are in the other animals; but in him they are sooner or later combined with reflection and foresight; they give rise to his apprehensions on the subject of property, and make him acquainted with that object of care which he calls his interest" (*Essay*, p. 11).

89. *Principles*, II, p. 371.

90. *Principles*, I, p. 254, p. 253.

91. *Principles*, I, p. 254.

92. *Principles*, I, p. 252. The examples Ferguson offered in this connection were Sparta and the Roman Republic.

93. *Principles*, I, p. 235.

94. "The laws made to secure the rights and liberties of the people, may serve as encouragements to population and commerce" (*Essay*, p. 136).

Progress and Commerce in Anglo-American Thought · 83

suit of commerce coupled with a vigorous defense of individual rights. "The growth of industry," he wrote, "the endeavours of men to improve their arts, to extend their commerce, to secure their possessions, and to establish their rights, are indeed the most effectual means to promote population."[95]

These sentiments cast grave doubt on J. G. A. Pocock's conclusions, which see a basic antagonism between commercial society and a polity of free men in Ferguson's philosophy. It is, I think, a distortion of Ferguson's thought to conclude that he shared the view that "commerce and culture were incompatible with virtue and liberty"[96] or, as Pocock wrote specifically of Ferguson, that "society as an engine for the production and multiplication of goods was inherently hostile to society as the moral foundation of personality."[97] Ferguson was neither distrustful of wealth nor did he believe that it invariably retarded social virtue and a free society.[98] The centrality of the notion of progress to Ferguson's thought bears repeating. The ascent of man toward perfection represents the primary motive force of human action, while, with respect to our social arrangements, progress takes the form of a transition from savagery to barbarism and, ultimately, to civilization.[99] Commercial societies, which Ferguson closely associated—if not completely identified—with civilization were, thus, no less natural, no less indicative of man's never-ending movement toward perfection, than were the more primitive social institutions they supplanted. "If the palace be

95. *Essay*, p. 140.

96. J. G. A. Pocock, *The Machiavellian Moment: Florentine Political Thought and the Atlantic Republican Tradition* (Princeton: Princeton University Press, 1975), p. 492. Although it is put forward in its most fully developed form in *The Machiavellian Moment*, Pocock's argument earlier appeared in "Civic Humanism and its Role in Anglo-American Thought," and "Machiavelli, Harrington and English Political Ideologies in the Eighteenth Century" in J. G. A. Pocock, ed., *Politics, Language and Time: Essays on Political Thought and History* (New York: Atheneum, 1971), pp. 80–103 and pp. 104–47. See also Pocock's *"The Machiavellian Moment* Revisited: A Study in History and Ideology," *Journal of Modern History*, LIII(1981):49–72, for a summary of the controversy surrounding his thesis. It is of some interest that Pocock has recently referred to the civic humanist interpretation of eighteenth-century Anglo-American political theory as simply a "paradigm," rather than as canonical description ("Cambridge Paradigms and Scotch Philosophers: A Study of the Relations Between the Civic Humanist and the Civil Jurisprudential Interpretation of Eighteenth-Century Social Thought," in Hont and Ignatieff, *Wealth and Virtue*, pp. 235–52).

Pocock's attempt to assimilate the writers of the Scottish Enlightenment into his civic humanist model has been questioned by earlier commentators. See James Moore, "Hume's Political Science and the Classical Republican Tradition," *Canadian Journal of Political Science*, X(1977):809–39, and, particularly, Edward J. Harpham, "Liberalism, Civic Humanism, and the Case of Adam Smith," *American Political Science Review*, LXXVIII(1984):764–74.

97. Pocock, *The Machiavellian Moment*, p. 501. Duncan Forbes has similarly noted: "It is precisely community that is likely to be a casualty in the progress of civilization" ("Adam Ferguson and the Idea of Community," in Douglas Young, *et al.*, *Edinburgh in the Age of Reason: A Commemoration* [Edinburgh: Edinburgh University Press, 1967] p. 43).

98. Indeed, Ferguson tended to regard wealth and civic virtue as directly linked: "The wealth," he commented, "the aggrandizement and power of nations, are commonly the effects of virtue; the loss of these advantages, is often a consequence of vice" (*Essay*, p. 206).

99. A useful analysis of Ferguson's theory of progress appears in Jules Delvaille, *Essai sur l'histoire de l'idée de progrès* (Paris: Alcan & Guillaumin, 1910), pp. 475–6.

84 · *Interpretation*

unnatural," Ferguson concluded, "the cottage is so no less; and the highest refinements of political and moral apprehension, are not more artificial in their kind, than the first operations of sentiment and reason."[100]

All this is not to deny that Ferguson dealt extensively with the harmful effects of the increasing division of labor that marked advanced commercial societies. These effects he regarded as possessing the potential of producing a permanent subordination of rank, thus allowing for the rise of despotism.[101] "Many mechanical arts," he wrote,

> require no capacity; they succeed best under a total suppression of sentiment and reason; and ignorance is the mother of industry as well as of superstition. Reflection and fancy are subject to err; but a habit of moving the hand, or the foot, is independent of either. Manufactures, accordingly, prosper most, where the mind is least consulted, and where the workshop may, without any great effort of imagination, be considered as an engine, the parts of which are men.[102]

The ever-greater specialization of labor, Ferguson feared, could lead to a system of stratification in which thinking itself might become the particular province of a privileged class:

> But if many parts in the practice of every art, and in the detail of every department, require no abilities, or actually tend to contract and to limit the views of the mind, there are others which lead to general reflections, and to enlargement of thought. Even in manufacture, the genius of the master, perhaps, is cultivated, while that of the inferior workman lies waste. The statesman may have a wide comprehension of human affairs, while the tools he employs are ignorant of the system in which they are themselves combined. The general officer may be a great proficient in the art of war, while the soldier is confined to a few motions of the hand and the foot. . . .
>
> The practitioner of every art and profession may afford matter of general speculation to the man of science; and thinking itself, in this age of separations, may become a peculiar craft.[103]

In elaborating the consequences of the division of labor, however, Ferguson did not conclude that it would inevitably prove to be a Trojan horse whose ultimate social effect would invariably be the destruction of a free and virtuous society. Although the division of labor might well place strains upon the social fabric and make possible a permanent subordination of the many by the few, it also facilitates the fullest expression of each individual's natural abilities and personal excellences and hence serves a particularly valuable moral and social purpose. "With the benefit of commerce, . . . [and the division of labor which naturally accompanies it]," Ferguson noted, "every individual is enabled to avail himself, to the utmost, of the peculiar advantage of his place; to work on the peculiar ma-

100. *Essay*, p. 8.
101. Ferguson's views respecting the dangers arising out of the division of labor are discussed at some length in Forbes, "Ferguson and the Idea of Community," pp. 40–7, and Ronald Hamowy, "Adam Smith, Adam Ferguson, and the Division of Labour," *Economica*, xxxv(1968):249–59.
102. *Essay*, pp. 182–83.
103. *Essay*, p. 183.

Progress and Commerce in Anglo-American Thought · 85

terials with which nature has furnished him; to humour his genius or disposition, and betake himself to the task in which he is peculiarly qualified to proceed."[104]

Ferguson's response to the question of whether the dangers inherent in commercial societies could be averted was unambiguous. So long as the members of the community take an active role in civic affairs, so long as they prevent the division of labor from embracing the more crucial aspects of political and military life,[105] it is possible to secure the nation against despotism. "It is difficult," he wrote,

> to tell how long the decay of states might be suspended by the cultivation of arts on which their real felicity and strength depend; by cultivating in the higher ranks those talents for the council and the field, which cannot, without great disadvantage, be separated; and in the body of a people, that zeal for their country, and that military character, which enable them to take a share in defending its rights.
>
> Times may come, when every proprietor must defend his own possessions, and every free people maintain their own independence.[106]

In sum, while it is true that commercial societies bring with them the risks of despotism in the form of an over-specialization of function and a permanent system of subordination, a decline into tyranny need not follow. The stifling of public involvement in the affairs of state—either through the throttling of individual capacity consequent on an extensive division of labor or out of an all-consuming concern solely for one's private wealth—is, in the end, what makes despotism possible. Encourage the populace to actively participate in the civic and military affairs of the nation and tyranny can be averted. Man's ability to uncover the laws that determine his condition[107] provides him the opportunity to avoid what might otherwise be regarded as that corruption to which all commercial societies must descend.

104. *Principles*, II, p. 424.

105. Ferguson was a strong supporter of a civilian army and had written tracts pointing out the serious dangers consequent on a professional military and calling for the establishment of a civilian militia. See his *Reflections Previous to the Establishment of a Militia* (London: R. & J. Dodsley, 1756), published anonymously. The benefits of a militia over a mercenary army, he contended, were several and obvious. While a professional military force could act as the tool of a government intent on depriving the citizens of their rights and subjecting them to despotic measures, a civilian militia would invariably thwart such designs. More importantly, the citizen who had abdicated from active civic and military involvement in his community could not but be a poor citizen, open to the depredations of a corrupt regime at home while incompetently protected by a mercenary army against attack from abroad.

While a number of his fellow Scots supported a variety of schemes for a militia which called for compulsory participation, the plan put forward by Ferguson in his *Reflections Previous to the Establishment of a Militia* appears to have favored voluntary involvement. His proposal called for legislation ending certain restraints on the use of arms, such as the Game Laws, in addition to permitting freeholders the right to arm one man. For a detailed discussion of the militia question in eighteenth-century Scotland, see John Robertson, *The Scottish Enlightenment and the Militia Issue* (Edinburgh: John Donald, 1985).

106. *Essay*, p. 227.

107. "Man is by nature an artist," Ferguson noted, "endowed with ingenuity, discernment, and will. These faculties he is qualified to employ on different materials; but is chiefly concerned to em-

86 · *Interpretation*

With respect to the dangers of despotism, commercial societies present no greater risks than do those more primitive communities that preceded them. "In the lowest state of commercial arts," Ferguson observed,

> the passions for wealth, and for dominion, have exhibited scenes of oppression, or servility, which the most finished corruption of the arrogant, the cowardly, and the mercenary, founded on the desire of procuring, or the fear of losing, a fortune, could not exceed. In such cases, the vices of men, unrestrained by forms, and unawed by police, are suffered to riot at large, and to produce their entire effects. Parties accordingly unite, or separate, on the maxims of a gang of robbers; they sacrifice to interest the tenderest affections of human nature. The parent supplies the market for slaves, even by the sale of his own children; the cottage ceases to be a sanctuary for the weak and the defenceless stranger; and rites of hospitality, often so sacred among nations in their primitive state, come to be violated, like every other tie of humanity, without fear or remorse.[108]

A number of commentators have confused Ferguson's fears regarding the dangers of political indifference with a basic animosity towards commercial activity. But the fact is that Ferguson offered a strong defense of commercial society throughout his writings.[109] Indeed, his distrust could with justice be said to center not on commercial society itself but on the various efforts by politicians to intervene in economic life with the end of improving it. These attempts, no matter how well-meaning, almost always resulted in hindering the production of wealth. "In matters of particular profession, industry, and trade," wrote Ferguson, "the experienced practitioner is the master, . . . When the refined politician would lend an active hand, he only multiplies interruptions and grounds of complaint."[110]

---

ploy them on himself: Over this subject his power is most immediate and most complete; as he may know the law, according to which his progress is effected, by conforming himself to it, he may, hasten or secure the result" (*Principles*, 1, p. 200).

108. *Essay*, p. 242.

109. Kettler has concluded of Ferguson's discussions of commerce that "in the final analysis and on the basis of the most central feature of the activist conception of virtue, Ferguson's position eventuated in a vindication of commercial society" (Kettler, *Thought of Adam Ferguson*, p. 236). And, with particular reference to Ferguson's *Essay*, Roy Harvey Pearce has observed that one reason for its popularity, especially among Americans, was Ferguson's unambiguous defense of commercial society over more primitive cultures, despite the social costs that might accompany civilization. "What generally emerges from Ferguson's *Essay*, and from others like it," he notes, "is a simple and clear demonstration from conjectural history of a proposition which Americans, in their feelings of pity and censure over the fate of the Indians, needed desparately to believe; that men in becoming civilized had gained much more than they had lost; and that civilization, the act of civilizing, for all of its destruction of primitive virtues, put something higher and greater in their place" (*The Savages of America: A Study of the Indian and the Idea of Civilization* [rev. ed.; Baltimore: The Johns Hopkins Press, 1965], p. 85).

110. *Essay*, p. 144. Consider also the following: "Men are tempted to labour, and to practise lucrative arts, by motives of interest. Secure to the workman the fruit of his labour, give him the prospects of independence or freedom, the public has found a faithful minister in the acquisition of

Progress and Commerce in Anglo-American Thought · 87

We live in an age dominated by sociology and politics, when moral philosophy and economics are less exciting and of less concern than they were two centuries ago. Accordingly, contemporary scholarship often tends to emphasize certain of Ferguson's observations relating to his fears of despotism at the expense of his conclusions respecting man's moral perfectability and of the value, both moral and economic, of the unhampered activities of the market. Nevertheless, these aspects of Ferguson's thought were of greater concern to him. In this sense, at least to his contemporaries, Ferguson shared the attributes of what one historian has labeled the "new-model man,"[111] having embraced a regime of commerce within a political system in which citizens were active participants in civic life.

From the standpoint of current scholarship in the social sciences, it would be hard to argue against the view that Ferguson's most significant and lasting contribution was his formulation of the theory of spontaneously-generated orders and the application of this theory to a whole range of complex social phenomena, including law and language. Of slightly lesser, but unquestionably enduring, consequence is Ferguson's analysis of the social effects of the increasing division of labor. However, it was not until the nineteenth century that these aspects of Ferguson's thought were fully appreciated. The eighteenth century was to derive from Ferguson's works more positive elements there discussed: the benefits of a society based on commerce, the need for a public-spirited and vigilant citizenry as a bulwark against tyranny, and the possibilities of unbounded progress towards moral perfection to which mankind naturally inclined.

---

wealth, and a faithful steward in hoarding what he has gained. The statesman in this, as in the case of population itself, can do little more than avoid doing mischief. It is well, if, in the beginnings of commerce, he knows how to repress the frauds to which it is subject. Commerce, if continued, is the branch in which men committed to the effects of their own experience, are least apt to go wrong" (*Essay*, p. 143).

111. Ralph Lerner, "Commerce and Character: The Anglo-American as New-Model Man," *William and Mary Quarterly*, 3d ser., XXXVI(1979):3–26.

2

Adam Smith, Adam Ferguson, and the Division of Labour

By Ronald Hamowy

John Rae, in his biography of Adam Smith, reports that when Adam Ferguson's *Essay on the History of Civil Society* was published in 1767, Smith accused Ferguson of "having borrowed some of his ideas without owning them",[1] to which Ferguson is said to have replied that he had borrowed nothing from Smith, but much from some unnamed French source "where Smith had been before him".

The nature of the dispute has never been fully reported, although we know that it was of sufficient importance to Smith to cause him to break off his close and long-standing friendship with Ferguson until Smith's fatal illness in 1790.[2] Several interpretations and speculative arguments have been offered concerning the nature of the dispute, despite the cloudiness of the issue and the lack of any more concrete evidence than that provided by Dr. Alexander Carlyle in his *Autobiography*[3] and repeated by Rae. Perhaps the most important, because the most widely accepted, of these is that proposed by the German critic, August Oncken, in an article published in 1909.[4]

Oncken suggests the following:

(1) The "French source" alluded to by Ferguson must have been either Quesnay or another of the Physiocrats, or Montesquieu. (2) It is unlikely that Ferguson was referring to any of the Physiocrats since he does not mention them in any of his writings, nor does his *Essay* reveal that he was influenced by the physiocratic spirit. (3) It is further unlikely that Ferguson was referring to an economist of this school since Smith had only that year come into contact with physiocratic thought and Ferguson must have been aware of this. (4) Therefore, the common connection to whom Ferguson must have been referring was Montesquieu. (5) The issue in dispute, continues Oncken, must almost certainly have been the division of labour, an idea common to both Ferguson's *Essay*[5] and Smith's writings, and one which would

---

[1] J. Rae, *Life of Adam Smith*, 1895, p. 65.

[2] *Ibid.*, p. 433.

[3] *The Autobiography of Dr. Alexander Carlyle of Inveresk*, London and Edinburgh, 1910, p. 299. "Smith had been weak enough", writes Carlyle, "to accuse him [Ferguson] of having borrowed some of his inventions without owning them. This Ferguson denied, but owned he derived many notions from a French author, and that Smith had been there before him."

[4] "Adam Smith und Adam Ferguson", *Zeitschrift für Socialwissenschaft*, vol. XII (1909), Part I, pp. 129–37; Part II, pp. 206–16. The bulk of Oncken's argument on the controversy appears in Part I.

[5] Ferguson devotes a full chapter to the question of the division of labour, in which he writes:

249

have been felt by Smith to have been of great enough importance to warrant that he be credited. (6) Further evidence concerning the issue involved comes from the fact that Smith, in the *Wealth of Nations*, does not credit Ferguson with the idea of the division of labour, although it was not published until nine years after the first appearance of Ferguson's *Essay*. (7) Edwin Cannan's researches[1] indicate that Smith's lecture notes (which circulated and could even be bought from some booksellers) contained the idea of the division of labour, as it later appeared in the *Wealth of Nations*, as early as 1763. And Oncken categorically declared that Ferguson utilized Smith's circulated notes when working on his *Essay*.[2] (8) Montesquieu does not raise the issue of the division of labour, so Ferguson was clearly unjustified in suggesting to Smith that his (Ferguson's) source was French. Ferguson took the idea of the division of labour from Smith. (9) There is evidence that Ferguson developed a bad conscience over this act of plagiarism, for the fourth (1773) and all subsequent editions of his *Essay* carry a footnote in which Ferguson adds a blurb for Smith's forthcoming "theory of national economy", the *Wealth of Nations*.[3]

The above, in summary, is Oncken's argument for the position that the issue in dispute between Smith and Ferguson—which occurred in 1767—concerned the idea of the division of labour which Smith, with some justification, claimed was taken from him without acknowledgment and which Ferguson, perhaps out of oversight, incorrectly suggested came jointly to them via Montesquieu. Oncken's argument, at least on the face of it, appears convincing and has led the latest commentator on Ferguson to agree that Smith's charges of plagiarism were not unfounded;[4] and one of the leading Smith scholars has reached

---

"The artist finds, that the more he can confine his attention to a particular part of any work, his productions are the more perfect, and grow under his hands in the greater quantities. Every undertaker in manufacture finds, that the more he can subdivide the tasks of his workmen, and the more hands he can employ on separate articles, the more are his expences diminished, and his profits increased. The consumer too requires, in every kind of commodity, a workmanship more perfect than hands employed on a variety of subjects can produce; and the progress of commerce is but a continued subdivision of the mechanical arts. . . .

By the separation of arts and professions, the sources of wealth are laid open; every species of material is wrought up to the greatest perfection, and every commodity is produced in the greatest abundance. . . ." *An Essay on the History of Civil Society* [Part IV, Section 1], Duncan Forbes, ed., Edinburgh, 1966, p. 181.

[1] Cf. Cannan's Introduction to Smith's *Lectures on Justice, Police, Revenue and Arms*, Edwin Cannan, ed., Oxford, 1896.

[2] ". . . dass Ferguson bei der Ausarbeitung seines 'Essay' eines der damals viel verbreiteten Vorlesungshefte der Smithschen Moralphilosophie benutzt hatte." *Op. cit.*, p. 136.

[3] *Essay, op. cit.*, p. 287.

[4] ". . . Smith . . . became enraged at the book [the *Essay*] because he believed that some crucial points had been plagiarized from his own work. . . . A German critic has attempted to adjudicate this controversy and has argued quite convincingly that Smith was in the right." David Kettler, *The Social and Political Thought of Adam Ferguson*, Columbus, Ohio, 1965, p. 74, n. 35.

a similar conclusion.[1] In point of fact, however, there seems little reason to suppose that—if, in fact, the argument between Smith and Ferguson was over the division of labour—Smith could be considered to have a legitimate complaint.

The same idea had, before Smith's time, been adopted by a number of writers who dealt with economic questions. It can, for example, be found in Hume's *Treatise on Human Nature* (1739) and in his *Political Discourses* (1752),[2] in James Harris' *Dialogue concerning Happiness* (1741),[3] in Mandeville's *Fable of the Bees* (1714—published in slightly different form in 1705 under the title of *The Grumbling Hive*),[4] and in an anonymous treatise on trade in 1701.[5] It is discussed extensively in the works of Sir William Petty, of which Schumpeter writes: "On division of labor ... we find all the essentials of what Adam Smith was to say of it, including its dependence upon the size of markets."[6] The benefits of territorial division of labour are discussed in contemporaneous mercantilist literature.[7] Nor did the idea of the division of labour

[1] "As far as can be judged from the scanty material available, ... Ferguson borrowed from Adam Smith's lectures without any acknowledgement." William Robert Scott, *Adam Smith as Student and Professor*, Glasgow, 1937, p. 119.

[2] "When every individual person labours a-part, and only for himself, his force is too small to execute any considerable work; his labour being employ'd in supplying all his different necessities, he never attains a perfection in any particular art; and as his force and success are not at all times equal, the least failure in either of these particulars must be attended with inevitable ruin and misery. Society provides a remedy for these *three* inconveniences. By the conjunction of forces, our power is augmented: By the partition of employments, our ability encreases: And by mutual succour we are less expos'd to fortune and accidents." *A Treatise on Human Nature*, T. H. Green and T. H. Grose, eds., 1878, II, p. 259.
There are several references to the idea of the division of labour in the *Political Discourses*. For example, Hume refers to the lack of any marked degree of urban specialization as an important contributing factor to the comparative poverty of the ancient world as compared with mid-eighteenth-century Europe. "Of the Populousness of Ancient Nations", in *Essays Moral, Political, and Literary*, T. H. Green and T. H. Grose, eds., 1889, I, pp. 381–443. Cf., also, Marcus Arkin, "The Economic Writings of David Hume—A Reassessment", *South African Journal of Economics*, vol. XXIV (1956), pp. 204–20; and Eugene Rotwein, ed., *David Hume: Writings on Economics*, Madison, Wis., 1955, pp. liv–xc.

[3] Dugald Stewart mentions Harris of Salisbury, *Dialogue concerning Happiness* [Part I, Section 12], together with Ferguson's *Civil Society* as works which anticipate Smith's writings on the division of labour. *Lectures on Political Economy*, vols. VIII and IX of *The Collected Works of Dugald Stewart*, Sir William Hamilton, ed., Edinburgh, 1855, VIII, p. 311.

[4] Mandeville makes reference to the division of labour in both parts of the treatise. His index includes the following entry: "Labour. The usefulness of dividing it and subdividing it". Cf. the 1924 reprint of *The Fable of the Bees*, F. B. Kaye, ed., Oxford, 1924. References to the division of labour occur in vol. I, pp. 356–58, and vol. II, pp. 141–2, 284 and 325.

[5] The author of *Consideration on the East India Trade*, who uses international specialization as the basis of his argument favouring a liberal economic policy. Cf. Marcus Arkin, "A Neglected Forerunner of Adam Smith", *South African Journal of Economics*, vol. XXIII (1955), pp. 299–314; and Joseph Schumpeter, *History of Economic Analysis*, New York, 1954, pp. 373–4.

[6] Schumpeter, *op. cit.*, p. 214. The division of labour is discussed in several of Petty's writings, but see particularly his *Political Arithmetick*, first published in 1690 but written and circulated much earlier.

[7] *Ibid.*, pp. 373–6.

escape the notice of classical writers, particularly Plato and Aristotle.[1]

Smith, we know, was familiar with the writings of most of these thinkers; certainly he knew Petty, Harris and Hume well.[2] How, then, can his anger with Ferguson be explained over the question of priority concerning the idea of the division of labour?

It is known that Smith was particularly sensitive to the possibility of having his ideas appropriated by some other author. In 1755, when delivering a paper before the Glasgow Economic Society in which he expounded his system of natural liberty, Smith publicly asserted his claim to the authorship of that system.[3] According to Dugald Stewart, Smith "was anxious to establish his exclusive right . . . to certain leading principles both political and literary . . . in order to prevent the possibility of some rival claims which he thought he had reason to apprehend, and to which his situation as a professor, added to his unreserved communications in private companies, rendered him peculiarly liable".[4] On this occasion, Smith manifested "a good deal of that honest and indignant warmth which is perhaps unavoidable by a man who is conscious of the purity of his intentions when he suspects that advantages have been taken of the frankness of his temper".[5, 6]

It is also reported[7] that when Robertson's *History of the Reign of Charles V* appeared in print in 1769, Smith and/or his friends levelled charges similar to those with which Ferguson was earlier confronted against Robertson, although no evidence survives of exactly what, in Robertson's work, was claimed as having originally come from Smith.

[1] *Ibid.*, p. 56. For an excellent discussion of the idea of the division of labour, as well as a general overview of the economic thought of classical authors, see Albert A. Trever, *A History of Greek Economic Thought*, Chicago, 1916.

[2] Schumpeter, *op. cit.*, p. 184. For a discussion of the similarity between Smith's Glasgow *Lectures* and the economic sections of Francis Hutcheson's work, and for a careful comparison of the economic writings of Smith and Hume, cf. W. L. Taylor. "Eighteenth Century Scottish Political Economy: The Impact on Adam Smith and his Work, of his Association with Francis Hutcheson and David Hume", *South African Journal of Economics*, vol. XXIV (1956), pp. 261–76, and Taylor, *Francis Hutcheson and David Hume as Predecessors of Adam Smith*, Durham, North Carolina, 1965.

[3] Rae, *op. cit.*, p. 63.

[4] Stewart, "Biographical Memoir of Adam Smith", in *Collected Works, op. cit.*, X, p. 68.

[5] Rae, *op. cit.*, pp. 63–4.

[6] Rae disposes of the contention of James Bonar that Smith's 1755 manifesto was directed against Ferguson. ". . . it is unlikely that Ferguson was the occasion of offence in 1755. Up till that year he was generally living abroad with the regiment of which he was chaplain, and it is not probable that he had begun his *History* [the *Essay*] before his return to Scotland, or that he had time between his return and the composition of Smith's manifesto to do or project anything to occasion such a remonstrance. Then he is found on the friendliest footing with Smith in the years immediately following the manifesto, and Stewart's allusion to the circumstances implies a graver breach than could be healed so summarily. Besides, had Ferguson been the cause of offence, Stewart would have probably avoided the subject altogether in a paper to the Royal Society, of which Ferguson was still an active member. [Stewart's biographical sketch, which contains the report of Smith's manifesto of 1755, was delivered before the Royal Society of Edinburgh in 1793, well before Ferguson's own death and while Ferguson was still actively participating in the Society's affairs.]" *Ibid.*, p. 65.

[7] Scott, *op. cit.*, pp. 100–1.

Rae's biography refers to the obituary notice of Smith published in the *Monthly Review* of 1790, where the author of the notice alleges that during this period "Smith lived in such constant apprehension of being robbed of his ideas that, if he saw any of his students take notes of his lectures, he would instantly stop him and say 'I hate scribblers'."[1] As Rae goes on to point out, such an attack is controverted by other evidence which suggests that Smith was, in fact, fairly permissive in allowing note-taking in his classes.[2] But the fact remains that he three times found it necessary to allude to the possibility of plagiarism: in 1755, in the manifesto delivered to the Glasgow Economic Society; in 1767, in a personal accusation levelled at Ferguson; and in 1769, in a charge against Principal Robertson. Further, he left not a few of his students with the impression that the threat of someone stealing his ideas was a serious worry to him, and Dr. Carlyle reports that he had "some little jealousy in his temper".[3]

What I hope to suggest is not that Smith was suffering from paranoia, but, rather, that he was peculiarly excitable about the idea of plagiarism —which might easily have led him to find it where none existed. That he seems to have been unjustified in claiming priority in 1755 has been persuasively argued by Schumpeter.[4] It seems clear that a similar case could be made for the incident with Ferguson in 1767.[5]

What, then, of Oncken's argument? That the issue in dispute between Smith and Ferguson was the idea of the division of labour seems likely, on the basis of some of the evidence furnished by Oncken. But there is no reason for believing that Ferguson took this idea from Smith—the notion of the division of labour was fairly commonly held at the time of the writing of the *Essay*—and it seems a pure act of fantasy, if, in fact, the dispute *did* occur in 1767, to suppose that Ferguson's 1773 footnote announcing Smith's forthcoming *Wealth of Nations* was done to assuage a guilty conscience. After all, Ferguson never felt badly towards Smith,

---

[1] Rae, *op. cit.*, p. 64.

[2] *Ibid.*

[3] Carlyle, *op. cit.*, p. 281.

[4] "Smith . . . indeed laid claim . . . to priority concerning the principle of Natural Liberty on the ground that he had taught it as early as 1749. By this principle he meant both a canon of policy—the removal of all restraints except those imposed by 'justice'—and the analytic proposition that free interaction of individuals produces not chaos but an orderly pattern that is logically determined: he never distinguished the two quite clearly. Taken in either sense, however, the principle had been quite clearly enunciated before, for example, by Grotius and Pufendorf. It is precisely for this reason that no charge of plagiarism can be made either against Smith or on his behalf. . . This does not exclude the possibility of course that, in stating it with greater force and fullness than anyone before him, Smith experienced subjectively all the thrill of discovery or even that, some time before 1749, he actually made the 'discovery' himself." Schumpeter, *op. cit.*, p. 185.

[5] Schumpeter concludes on the controversy between Smith and Ferguson that "there is hardly any reason to believe, as did Marx, that Smith owed any considerable debt to it [Ferguson's *Essay*] or, as others have held, that Ferguson owed much to Smith's lectures or conversation: the parallelisms that are adduced in support of either view concern ideas—on division of labor and taxation—which were common currency at that time and could have been drawn from a number of older authors". *Ibid.*, p. 184, n. 16.

even after their personal friendship had cooled, and always held his views in the highest regard.[1]

There is a further complication, however, which concerns the date of the dispute. There is some reason to doubt that it took place in 1767, rather than some much later year, despite Rae's report.[2] In 1772, for instance, Smith and Ferguson still appear to be on the best of terms. In a letter to William Pulteney, Smith mentions that he has recently spoken with Ferguson—about Pulteney's views on "the proper remedy for the disorders of the coin in Bengal".[3] In the same year, Hume reports in a letter to Smith that Ferguson has returned in good health from a recent trip and asks Smith to join them some time during the winter, indicating that the friendship between these three thinkers remained unbroken.[4]

Ferguson was still corresponding with Smith in the following year, 1773.[5] Further, Fay writes that a year's trip which Ferguson took and from which he returned in 1776 was taken "at Adam Smith's instance".[6] When Ferguson returned, the *Wealth of Nations* had already appeared and Ferguson penned a very warm letter to Smith concerning it, in which he writes: "I have been for some time so busy reading you, and recommending and quoting you to my students, that I have not had leisure to trouble you with letters. I suppppose that of all the opinions on which you have any curiosity, mine is among the least doubtful. . . . You are surely to reign alone on these subjects, to form opinions, and I hope, to govern at least the coming generations."[7] Ferguson again wrote to Smith in 1777, concerning Smith's part in recommending Ferguson to the tutorship of Lord Stanhope's ward, the Earl of Chesterfield.[8]

As late as 1779, in a letter to Lord Carlisle, Smith refers to "my friend Ferguson".[9] And during the same year, Ferguson in the company of Blair and Smith often visited with Princess Catherine Romanovna Dashkov, who was living in Edinburgh while her son was attending the University.[10]

We also know from Rae that Smith and Ferguson—in 1780—were

---

[1] "When it became evident that the sickness was to prove mortal", writes Rae, "Smith's old friend Adam Ferguson, who had been apparently estranged from him for some time, immediately forgot their coolness, whatever it was about, and came and waited on him with the old affection. 'Your friend Smith', writes Ferguson on 31st July 1790, announcing the death to Sir James Macpherson, Warren Hastings' successor as Governor-General of India—'your old friend Smith is no more. We knew he was dying for some months, and though matters, as you know, were a little awkward when he was in health, upon that appearance I turned my face that way and went to him without further consideration, and continued my attentions to the last'." *Op. cit.*, p. 433. These are not the actions of an embittered old man suffering from the burden of guilt for a harm done a once-close friend.
[2] *Ibid.*, p. 65. This date is accepted by Oncken, *op. cit.*, p. 129.
[3] Rae, *op. cit.*, p. 254.
[4] *Ibid.*, p. 258.
[5] *Ibid.*, p. 263.
[6] C. R. Fay, *Adam Smith and the Scotland of His Day*, Cambridge, 1956, p. 84.
[7] *Ibid.*
[8] Scott, *op. cit.*, p. 273. The letter is reprinted in full in Scott's book.
[9] Rae, *op. cit.*, p. 350.
[10] Robert M. Schnitz, *Hugh Blair*, Morningside Heights, New York, 1948, p. 64.

both active members of a weekly dining club which met every Friday in the Grassmarket in Edinburgh.[1] This would hardly be in keeping with the seriousness with which the participants took the dispute which ended their close friendship.

Herta Jogland, in her study of Ferguson, claims—on the basis of some of the evidence offered above—that there is no reason to suppose that the date of the dispute was 1767 rather than, say, 1784–1790.[2] Scott's suggestion[3] that the rupture between the two friends occurred in 1767 but was healed by 1777 cannot stand since we definitely know that Smith and Ferguson were distant just prior to Smith's death in 1790. We are left with the conclusion that the dispute probably occurred some time between 1780 and Smith's death in 1790. This re-dating of the dispute allows a consideration of other factors than those offered by Oncken in establishing the nature of the altercation between Smith and Ferguson.

The example of the division of labour which Smith uses in his Glasgow lectures and repeats in the *Wealth of Nations* concerns the number of operations employed in the manufacture of a pin. This is the same example employed by Ferguson in his *Principles of Moral and Political Science*[4] published in 1792, two years after Smith's death. However, the preparation of the manuscript of this work occupied much of Ferguson's time from 1781 until its publication,[5] and doubtless was under his consideration even a year or two before this. Inasmuch as both these men were members of the same dining club, it is likely that a discussion of Ferguson's lecture notes, which form the basis of the *Principles* and which he was in the process of preparing for publication, was brought up in conversation, at which point Smith might have made an allusion to Ferguson having got the idea of the division of labour from his Glasgow notes or from the *Wealth of Nations*—inasmuch as both Ferguson's and his own works use the manufacture of pins as the illustrative example. As we know, Ferguson responded to this accusation by suggesting that both he and Smith had got the idea from some "French source". What is this source?

---

[1] Rae, *op. cit.*, p. 334.

[2] "Nicht einmal der Zeitpunkt des Streites steht fest, denn auch der Behauptung August Onckens können anderslautende Daten entgegengehalten werden, wonach nicht das Jahr 1766 [*sic*] sondern die Jahre zwischen 1784 und 1790 dafür offen bleiben." Herta H. Jogland, *Ursprünge und Grundlagen der Soziologie bei Adam Ferguson*, Berlin, 1959, p. 22.

[3] Scott, *op. cit.*, p. 273, n. 5.

[4] "A fit assortment of persons, of whom each performs but a part in the manufacture of a *pin*, may produce much more in a given time, than perhaps double the number, of which each was to produce the whole, or to perform every part in the construction of that diminutive article." *Principles of Moral and Political Science*, Edinburgh, 1792, II, p. 424.

[5] "[Ferguson] had for many years no written lectures, but trusted to his mastery of the subject for the expression of his ideas on the spur of the moment. When his health gave way in 1781, however, he found it necessary to write out his course, which, during the leisure of his retirement, he corrected for the press and published in 1792." John Small, "Biographical Sketch of Adam Ferguson", *Transactions of the Royal Society of Edinburgh*, vol. XXIII, part III (1864), p. 643.

In point of fact, there is every indication that Smith took his example
—the manufacture of pins—from the *Encyclopédie*, where, in the
article *Épingle*, the description of the manufacture of a pin is reported
to consist of eighteen operations,[1] the same number of operations
reported by Smith in his Glasgow *Lectures*.[2] Cannan, who, in a footnote to the *Lectures*, offers the French article as Smith's source, adds
that "if Adam Smith had relied on an English authority, he might have
mentioned a larger number",[3] and goes on to cite Ephraim Chambers'
Cyclopaedia,[4] wherein the author reckons that there are "twenty-five
workmen" employed in distinct operations in making a pin. The
conclusion strongly suggests itself that Ferguson was alluding to this
article on pins by M. Delaire in the *Encyclopédie* to which we know
Smith had reference in the composition of his *Lectures*. Ferguson's
comment further suggests that he, too, referred to the same article as
the source of his example and had used it in his lectures.

In the light of the preceding evidence, then, the following theory of
the nature of the dispute seems most plausible.

(1) The dispute between Smith and Ferguson, as Oncken claims,
concerned the question of the division of labour. (2) It probably
occurred between 1780, when Ferguson began work on his lecture notes
for eventual publication, and 1785, when he retired from the Chair of
Moral Philosophy at the University of Edinburgh for reasons of health
and moved to the outskirts of the city[5]—most probably towards the
beginning of this period before his health had severely deteriorated and
he was still active at the dining club. (3) The dispute was occasioned by a
discussion of Ferguson's lecture notes, which he was in the process of
preparing for publication, and which illustrated the idea of the division
of labour with the same example as had been previously used by Smith.
(4) Smith accused Ferguson of having borrowed from his work without
crediting him. (5) Ferguson responded by claiming that Smith and he
took their example from the same French source. (6) The source to
which Ferguson was referring was an article on pins which had appeared
in the *Encyclopédie*. (7) The result was an argument bitter enough to
result in the breakup of their long friendship. This seems possible since
both men were, during this period, irascible and subject to jealousies.[6]

Concerning the question of who was "right" in the controversy, there
seems to be no doubt that a charge of plagiarism against Ferguson was
thoroughly unjustified, for reasons already offered. There is, equally, not
one whit of evidence that Smith took his views on the division of labour

---

[1] "Épingle", in vol. V of the *Encyclopédie* (1755), quoted by Cannan in Smith's
Lectures, op. cit., p. 164, n. 1.
[2] *Ibid.*, pp. 163–4.
[3] *Ibid.*, p. 164, n. 1.
[4] "Pin", in vol. II of the *Cyclopaedia*, 2nd ed., 1738; 4th ed., 1741, quoted by
Cannan, *ibid*.
[5] Small, *op. cit.*, p. 647.
[6] Henry Grey Graham, *Scottish Men of Letters in the Eighteenth Century*, 1901,
p. 117; Carlyle, *op. cit.*, p. 281.

from Ferguson's *Civil Society*, as has been contended by Marx and Lassalle.[1]

On one point, however, Ferguson surely can be granted priority, and this is on the sociological implications of the division of labour. Ferguson writes, in the same section of the *Essay* in which he discusses the material benefits arising out of the division of labour, of the psychological costs and the sociological consequences of the increasing subdivision of employment.

> Many mechanical arts, indeed, require no capacity; they succeed best under a total suppression of sentiment and reason; and ignorance is the mother of industry as well as of superstition. Reflection and fancy are subject to err; but a habit of moving the hand, or the foot, is independent of either. Manufactures, accordingly, prosper most, where the mind is least consulted, and where the workshop may, without any great effort of imagination, be considered as an engine, the parts of which are men.[2]

The result of ever-greater specialization in the economy will, Ferguson feels, lead to a system of social stratification and subordination in which thinking itself will, in time, become the particular province of one class of people only.

> But if many parts in the practice of every art, and in the detail of every department, require no abilities, or actually tend to contract and to limit the views of the mind, there are others which lead to general reflections, and to enlargement of thought. Even in manufacture, the genius of the master, perhaps, is cultivated, while that of the inferior workman lies waste. The statesman may have a wide comprehension of human affairs, while the tools he employs are ignorant of the system in which they are themselves combined. The general officer may be a great proficient in the knowledge of war, while the soldier is confined to a few motions of the hand and the foot. . . .
>
> The practitioner of every art and profession may afford matter of general speculation to the man of science; and thinking itself, in this age of separations, may become a peculiar craft.[3]

Ferguson goes on to spell out the political and sociological implications of this phenomenon.

> . . . the labourer, who toils that he may eat; the mechanic, whose art requires no exertion of genius, are degraded by the object they pursue, and by the means they employ to attain it. Professions requiring more

---

[1] Marx, in the *Capital*, refers to Ferguson in connection with the idea of the division of labour as Smith's "teacher" (*Capital* [Moscow, Foreign Languages Publishing House, 1961], I, p. 123, n.) and, later, as "the master of Adam Smith" (*ibid.*, p. 354). The same error can also be found in his *Poverty of Philosophy*, New York, International Publishers, 1963, where he writes of Smith as "a pupil of A. Ferguson", (p. 129). Lassalle, too, claims that Smith followed Ferguson's procedure in dealing with the question of the division of labour. Ferdinand Lassalle, *Herr Bastiat-Schulze von Delitzsch, der ökonomische Julian, oder Kapital und Arbeit*, Berlin, 1893, p. 75.

[2] *Essay, op. cit.*, pp. 182–3.

[3] *Ibid.*, p. 183.

knowledge and study; proceeding on the exercise of fancy, and the love of perfection; leading to applause as well as to profit, place the artist in a superior class, and bring him nearer to that station in which men are supposed to be highest; because in it they are bound to no task; because they are left to follow the disposition of the mind, and to take that part in society, to which they are led by the sentiments of the heart, or by the calls of the public.

. . . We look for elevation of sentiment, and liberality of mind, among those orders of citizens, who, by their condition, and their fortunes, are relieved from sordid cares and attentions. . . .

[Thus] in every commercial state, notwithstanding any pretensions to equal rights, the exaltation of a few must depress the many.[1]

Much of Ferguson's analysis formed the basis of Marx's later discussion of the division of labour and, indeed, Marx explicitly recognized Ferguson as one of the sources of his view.[2]

Adam Smith, on the other hand, does not discuss the sociological consequences of the division of labour in his earlier writings.[3] There is little evidence, I think, to support Jacob Viner's claim[4] that Smith had a clear notion of alienation as a consequence of the division of labour as early as 1755, a notion, Viner suggests, which came both to Smith and later to Ferguson from Rousseau. Smith, it is true, published a fairly lengthy letter in the *Edinburgh Review* of 1755[5] in which he discusses Rousseau's theory of the origin of property and the evils attendant on the introduction of this institution;[6] but Rousseau's broad conclusion that the advent of property and inequality in wealth marked the advent of a whole new psychology of man is considerably broader—and vaguer —than would warrant his being credited with the more specific and

[1] *Ibid.*, pp. 184–6.
[2] *Capital, op. cit.*, I, pp. 354–62.
[3] This is not, strictly speaking, true. Smith does, in his *Lectures*, touch on the possible confining effects the specialization of employment might have on the mind. There he writes: "Where the division of labour is brought to perfection, every man has only a simple operation to perform; to this his whole attention is confined, and few ideas pass in his mind but what have an immediate connexion with it. When the mind is employed about a variety of objects, it is somehow expanded and enlarged, and on this account a country artist is generally acknowledged to have a range of thoughts much above a city one." *Op. cit.*, p. 255. His discussion, however, is restricted to this one passage and in no way compares to Ferguson's broader and more systematic analysis. E. G. West has persuasively demonstrated that Smith's analysis of the division of labour in Book V of the *Wealth of Nations* can be understood as expressing a view which he held even as far back as his Glasgow lectures. "Adam Smith's Two Views on the Division of Labour", *Economica*, vol. XXXI (1964), pp. 23–32. However, there seems no reason to suppose that he had formulated his ideas on this subject with any greater precision or depth than is shown by the passage in the *Wealth of Nations*.
[4] "Guide to John Rae's *Life of Adam Smith*", in John Rae, *Life of Adam Smith*, "Reprints of Economic Classics", New York, 1965, pp. 35–6.
[5] "A Letter to the Authors of the *Edinburgh Review*", reprinted in *The Early Writings of Adam Smith*, J. Ralph Lindgren, ed., "Reprints of Economic Classics", New York, 1967, pp. 15–28.
[6] See J. J. Rousseau, *Sur l'origine de l'inégalité parmi les hommes*, vol. III of *Oeuvres complètes*, Bernard Gagnebin and Marcel Raymond, eds., Paris, 1964, pp. 171 ff. Smith, in his letter to the *Edinburgh Review*, quotes at length from this Discourse.

precise notion that the increasing subdivision of employment in society leads to a greater prevalence of a set of psychological attitudes which, when taken together, formed what Marx was later to term alienation.

It is really only with the appearance of the *Wealth of Nations* that Smith presents us with what might be called a sociological analysis relating the dynamics of capitalist production with a certain psychological stage of development. In Book V (Chapter 1, Part 3, Article 2) he writes:

> In the progress of the division of labour, the employment of the far greater part of those who live by labour, that is, of the great body of the people, comes to be confined to a few very simple operations, frequently to one or two. But the understandings of the greater part of men are necessarily formed by their ordinary employments. The man whose whole life is spent in performing a few simple operations; of which the effects too are, perhaps, always the same, or very nearly the same, has no occasion to exert his understanding, or to exercise his invention in finding out expedients for removing difficulties which never occur. He naturally loses, therefore, the habit of such exertion, and generally becomes as stupid and ignorant as it is possible for a human creature to become. The torpor of his mind renders him, not only incapable of relishing or bearing a part in any rational conversation, but of conceiving any generous, noble, or tender sentiment, and consequently of forming any just judgment concerning many even of the ordinary duties of private life.[1]

This is the extent of Smith's reference to the division of labour in a non-economic context and even here, it should be noted, his discussion is considerably limited in scope and offers none of the broader sociological and political implications which were suggested by Ferguson nine years earlier.

As a result, it can, I think, be legitimately argued that Ferguson, in dealing with the division of labour, can claim priority over Smith in offering, not an economic analysis of the question which was original with neither writer, but rather, the first methodical and penetrating sociological analysis, an analysis which was to have far-reaching consequences in intellectual history by contributing substantially to the sociological groundwork of Marxism. It is on this sociological point that the position of Marx and Lassalle, who point to Ferguson as Smith's forerunner, can be vindicated.

Stanford University.

[1] *Wealth of Nations*, Edwin Cannan, ed., New York, 1937, p. 734.

[3]

THE SCOTTISH ENLIGHTENMENT
AND THE
THEORY OF SPONTANEOUS ORDER

Introduction

PERHAPS THE SINGLE MOST SIGNIFICANT SOCIOLOGICAL CONTRIBUTION MADE by that group of writers whom we today regard as constituting the Scottish Enlightenment is the notion of spontaneously generated social orders. David Hume, Adam Smith, Adam Ferguson, Dugald Stewart, and a number of secondary eighteenth-century Scottish thinkers all incorporated the theory, to a greater or lesser extent, in their explanations of social phenomena. The theory, simply put, holds that the social arrangements under which we live are of such a high order of complexity that they invariably take their form not from deliberate calculation, but as the unintended consequence of countless individual actions, many of which may be the result of instinct and habit. The theory thus provides an explanation of the origin of complex social structures without the need to posit the existence of a directing intelligence. Rather, such structures come into being as a consequence of the aggregate of numerous discrete individual actions, none of which aims at the formation of coherent social institutions. Society is not the product of calculation but arises spontaneously, and its institutions are not the result of intentional design but of men's actions which have as their purpose an array of short-term private objectives.

It is important to underscore that this theory of spontaneous order, as—following Hayek[1]—I shall proceed to call it, does not simply contend that certain purposive social actions have unintended consequences. As Robert K. Merton has shown, this concept has been known to and discussed by every important contributor to the history of social thought.[2] Merton's notion of the "unanticipated consequences of purposive social action," however, differs in at least two important respects from that of the Scottish thinkers with whose theory we are concerned. The first distinction relates to the question of whether the individual actors, whose efforts taken in the aggregate result in certain unintended outcomes, invariably act purposively and with clear intent. In comparing Merton's juxtaposition of the deliberate nature of individual actions and the unintended character of their outcome

3

4 · THE SCOTTISH ENLIGHTENMENT

with the view held by the Scots, Louis Schneider has noted that the Scottish writers "are not invariably insistent that the individual action be clearly 'purposive.' It may shade off into the traditional, the ceremonial (or what is somewhat indeterminately called the 'instinctive'), while still having important uncontemplated social results."[3]

More importantly, Merton's concept is far broader than the doctrine of spontaneous order as it was employed by the Scottish Enlightenment thinkers. Merton is here joined by Duncan Forbes who, in one of his seminal essays on the nature of eighteenth-century Scottish thought, propounds what he calls "the law of the heterogeneity of ends"[4] to describe a similar principle of social change. In writing of the unanticipated consequences of certain acts, both Merton and Forbes appear to include the whole spectrum of unintended outcomes within the concept, regardless of their specific nature. The theory of spontaneous order, on the other hand, refers only to those acts the unanticipated results of which issue in complex social patterns. We would do well to stress this aspect of the theory, especially since the doctrine has sometimes been taken to be synonymous with the broader notion put forward by Merton and Forbes, when in fact it has reference to a considerably narrower range of unplanned effects.[5]

This is not to suggest that the Scottish thinkers did not recognize and offer up examples of both types of consequences. What made their contribution to social theory as revolutionary as it proved to be, however, was the proposition that social phenomena of a high degree of intricacy are not the product of intentional design. The originality of this theory is especially striking inasmuch as its conclusions are clearly counterintuitive. The argument from design, which has been so convincing to so many philosophers from Plato on, dictates that when we encounter any device or arrangement that exhibits extreme complexity, such as the institutions under which people live, then we are constrained to assume them to be the product of a designing intelligence.[6] This conclusion is explicitly rejected by the Scots, who denied that the rules and institutions which constitute society were artifacts, the conscious creation of a human agency. Rather, they were theorized to have emerged spontaneously, the unanticipated result of a myriad of human actions operating through a process of adaptive evolution.

Perhaps the clearest example of an undesigned and undirected social institution that exhibits a high degree of complexity is an unhampered market economy. However, the Scots did not limit their use of the principle of spontaneous order to explaining economic phenomena. It was also applied, at one point or another, to analyzing the system of moral rules under which we interact, the development of language, and the nature of the rules and institutions that make up the legal process. Proponents of a liberal society are thus particularly attracted to this doctrine, since under it, social order and individual liberty are apparently perfectly compatible.[7] *Dirigiste* systems, those that operate under central direction, are neither necessary nor, indeed, workable if society is to operate in a coherent and orderly fashion. It is, however, a mistake to suppose that all the social institutions that arise as the unintended outcome of human action are, by their nature, consistent with a free and open society. Indeed, the Scottish thinkers argued that government itself, including its form and structure, constitutes an example of an institution that evolves over time without conscious design.[8] Nor is there any assurance that governments that take their shape in this manner will provide the greatest amount of personal liberty. As Adam Ferguson observed in 1767:

> No constitution is formed by concert, no government is copied from a plan. The members of a small state contend for equality: the members of a greater, find themselves classed in a certain manner that lays a foundation for monarchy. They proceed from one form of government to another, by easy transitions, and frequently under old names adopt a new constitution. The seeds of every form are lodged in human nature; they spring up and ripen with the season. The prevalence of a particular species is often derived from an imperceptible ingredient mingled in the soil.[9]

Ferguson concluded that there is every reason to be skeptical of traditional histories that ascribe the founding of states to some Lycurgus-like legislator who possessed almost superhuman capabilities. "An author and a work, like cause and effect," he noted, "are perpetually coupled together. This is the simplest form under which we can consider the establishment of nations: and we ascribe to a previous design, what came to be known only by experience, what no human wisdom could foresee, and what, without the concurring humour and disposition of his age, no authority could enable an individual to execute."[10]

The view that the political and legal institutions of ancient states owed their structure to some legislator possessed of a godlike genius, such as a Lycurgus or a Romulus, was not an uncommon belief among eighteenth-century intellectuals, including the more radical French revolutionaries.[11] That it was within the power of the great legislators of any age not only to shape the institutions by which men are governed but to mold man's very nature can be found in thinkers as seemingly far apart as Rousseau and Burke.[12] The Scots, of course, rejected the notion that social patterns of any great intricacy, including the governmental arrangements under which societies operated, were the deliberate creations of any individual or group.

6 • THE SCOTTISH ENLIGHTENMENT

Indeed, the theory of spontaneous order as thus applied to the origin of political institutions has been regarded as one of the most important contributions to the advancement of the social sciences to emerge from the Scottish Enlightenment.[13]

One further introductory comment. The doctrine of spontaneous order falls squarely within that tradition in social theory commonly designated as antirationalist.[14] The epistemological underpinning of this theory rests on the notion that there exist certain social rules that are so complex that they are beyond the comprehension of any mind and hence are not discernible by reason. This view derives from David Hume, whose discussion of the origin and nature of justice in the *Treatise of Human Nature*[15] is of crucial importance to understanding this aspect of Scottish Enlightenment thought. It should be borne in mind, however, that Hume's claim that the rules that comprise justice are artificial does not entail that these rules are capricious. It has generally been assumed that if the rules by which society operates were not immediately deducible from self-evident principles, that is, if, in fact, they were regarded as the product of convention, then this amounted to a rejection of natural law. However, it has recently been convincingly argued that Hume's position is not inconsistent with a species of natural law theory, inasmuch as he regarded the rules of justice as grounded in man's common nature as a social animal born into a world of scarce resources.[16] Since the universe which we all enter is the same, the basic conditions that give rise to the rules of justice—what Hume called "the fundamental laws of nature"—are the same.[17] The writers of the Scottish Enlightenment who followed Hume were consequently able to explain the origin of intricate social patterns by analyzing them in terms of spontaneously generated orders while at the same time fitting themselves within the natural law tradition.

It should be noted at the outset that although the Scots were the first to elaborate the theory of spontaneous order as an explanatory device for complex social phenomena, the idea had been suggested by a number of other writers. Indeed, the germ of the doctrine can be found in the writings of Chuang Tzu who, as early as the fourth century B.C., commented on the oppressive nature of political and social institutions, which were incapable of responding to the diversity of people's preferences. Rather, in language that sounds surprisingly like the eighteenth century, Chuang Tzu claimed that "good order results spontaneously when things are let alone."[18]

A far clearer example of the notion that complex social patterns are the unintended result of men's action appears in Vico whose *Scienza Nuova* contains the following observation: "It is true that men have themselves made this world of nations . . . but this world without doubt has issued from a mind often diverse, at times quite contrary, and always superior to the particular ends that men had proposed to themselves; which narrow ends, made means to serve wider ends, it has always employed to preserve the human race upon this earth."[19] Several historians of ideas have argued that Vico deserves a particularly important place in the early history of the theory of spontaneous order. Duncan Forbes has referred to this passage as "the *locus classicus* of the law of the heterogeneity of ends."[20] And Friedrich Meinecke, in pointing to Ferguson's rejection of the Lycurgus myth and his conclusion that social institutions are not shaped by conscious design, remarked that Vico alone had earlier embraced views similar to those of Ferguson.[21] However influential Vico's ideas might have been in shaping eighteenth-century Scottish thought, however, it is clear that the fullest account of the doctrine prior to its systematic formulation by the Scots appears in the work of the Dutch social theorist, Bernard Mandeville.

Bernard Mandeville

Although Bernard Mandeville was, of course, not a Scotsman, his seminal contributions to the conception of spontaneous order and his extensive influence on Scottish thought[22] require that something be said of his social theory before we proceed to consider the Scottish writers themselves. Mandeville, a Dutch physician, migrated to England shortly after the Glorious Revolution, when he was in his midtwenties, and remained there until his death in January 1733 (1732 Old Style). His most important work, the *Fable of the Bees,* was first published in its original form in 1714, when it immediately became a *succès de scandale* for its defense of private vice.[23]

Mandeville contended that people were prompted to conduct themselves exclusively out of self-interest and that, when taken individually, their deeds showed none of the attributes we ordinarily associate with virtue. Our acts are motivated out of self-indulgence and the desire for personal gain and not out of a disinterested concern for the welfare of others. But though egoism thus rules mankind's actions, the unintended social effect is the prosperity of all. Our greed and rapaciousness give birth to the mechanism of the market, including the increasing division of labor,[24] which in turn leads to the creation of ever greater quantities of goods and services.

> Thus Vice nurs'd Ingenuity,
> Which join'd with Time and Industry,
> Had carry'd Life's Conveniencies,
> It's real Pleasures, Comforts, Ease,
> To such a Height, the very Poor
> Liv'd better than the Rich before.[25]

8 • THE SCOTTISH ENLIGHTENMENT

Production and commerce, Mandeville concluded, rested not on frugality but on prodigality and luxury, traits commonly regarded as morally evil. Yet national progress depended on these very vices. "Thus every Part was full of Vice,/Yet the whole Mass a Paradise"[26] The nature of Mandeville's economic theory has given rise to a major debate among critics of eighteenth-century thought. F. A. Hayek, among others, contends that Mandeville adopted an essentially laissez-faire attitude towards economic phenomena and that this view was consistent with other aspects of Mandeville's social theory, which reflected his adherence to the notion of spontaneously generated orders.[27] Jacob Viner, on the other hand, in his excellent introduction to Mandeville's *A Letter to Dion*,[28] has argued that Mandeville's mercantilist proclivities, the existence of which there can be no doubt, were decisive in determining Mandeville's attitude towards political intervention in the economy. Indeed, despite the conclusions reached by Kaye and others that Mandeville offered the first systematic account of the doctrine of laissez faire[29]—which was of decisive influence on Adam Smith[30]—Viner argued that

> Mandeville, in contrast to Adam Smith, put great and repeated stress on the importance of the role of government in producing a strong and prosperous society, through detailed and systematic regulation of economic activity.
>
> It is a common misinterpretation of Mandeville in this respect to read his motto, "Private Vices, Publick Benefits," as a laissez-faire motto, postulating the natural or spontaneous harmony between individual interests and the public good. The motto as it appeared on title pages of the *Fable of the Bees* was elliptical. In his text, Mandeville repeatedly stated that it was by "the skilful Management of the clever Politician" that private vices could be made to serve the public good, thus ridding the formula of any implication of laissez-faire.[31]

The intellectual historian takes issue with Professor Viner's interpretations at his own peril. However, in this instance, Hayek's account of Mandeville's attitude appears to be the correct one. As several commentators have observed, other than in the area of foreign trade, where Mandeville acknowledged the benefits of political intervention, Mandeville's economic views do not so much reflect the benefits of state action as provide a theory that points to the value of operating freely within a structure of general rules.[32]

Thus, when Mandeville writes that "Private Vices by the dextrous Management of a skilful Politician may be turned into Publick Benefits,"[33] Rosenberg argues that this sentiment is not a call for government interference in the economy. Rather, Mandeville is claiming that "the welfare of society has been most advanced by the introduction and diffusion of laws and institutions which best utilize man's basic passions and which channel his energies into socially useful activities."[34] This interpretation accords with that offered by Maurice Goldsmith, who observes that "the skillful politician is not a human being but a symbol of society, a system of rules into which individuals are fitted . . . on the basis of their natural capacities."[35] More important, evidence from the *Fable* itself strongly suggests that Mandeville's support for government intrusion in the marketplace was considerably circumscribed. Thus, with respect to the number of people employed in each of the various trades, he noted: "This Proportion as to Numbers in every Trade finds it self, and is never better kept than when no body meddles or interferes with it."[36] It is from this example, he observed, that we may learn "how the short-sighted Wisdom, of perhaps well-meaning People, may rob us of a Felicity, that would flow spontaneously from the Nature of every large Society, if none were to divert or interrupt the Stream."[37] Statements such as these are hardly consistent with the view that Mandeville advocated wholesale interference in market processes. As Rosenberg has concluded, Mandeville was indeed an interventionist, but of a peculiarly unique sort. "He intended that the ultimate result of these interventions would be the creation of a society which would 'run itself'—i.e. the work of the politician is not to repress man's egoistic impulses and action, but to provide the channels or grooves along which these impulses may be asserted."[38] Once the rules under which we operate have been set, men, by pursuing their private interests, will generate socially useful but unanticipated consequences.

This notion of spontaneous order pervades the *Fable*. Mandeville regarded the growth of social institutions and the advancement of knowledge as products of an evolutionary process that emerged as the unintended outcome of countless individual actions. Thus, when writing of the improvements that have taken place in the various arts and sciences, Mandeville observed that "it is almost inconceivable to what prodigious Height, from next to nothing, some Arts may be and have been raised by human Industry and Application, by the uninterrupted Labour, and joint Experience of many Ages, tho' none but Men of ordinary Capacity should ever be employ'd in them."[39] Similarly, Mandeville regarded "all the Laws, Prohibitions, Ordinances and Restrictions" that hinder one man from wronging another as the result of the same process. There is no need to assume that the laws under which we live are the invention of some particularly wise legislator. Rather, he observed, "there are very few, that are the Work of one Man, or of one Generation; the greatest part of them are the Product, the joynt Labour of several Ages."[40] Even with respect to the origin of language,

10 · THE SCOTTISH ENLIGHTENMENT

Mandeville adopted the view that the complex structure of speech and writing took their form by slow degrees and as the unintended result of actions aimed at far more limited goals.[41]

In sum, Mandeville's use of the theory of spontaneous order to explain the genesis and development of complex social patterns runs throughout his work and is applied to a multiplicity of institutions. Hayek, with some justification, has claimed that the central thesis of the *Fable*[42] is contained in Mandeville's observation that "we often ascribe to the Excellency of Man's Genius, and the Depth of his Penetration, what is in Reality owing to length of Time, and the Experience of many Generations, all of them very little differing from one another in natural Parts and Sagacity."[43] This notion appears to be Mandeville's most important legacy to the Scottish thinkers who followed him, despite the fact that they might well have been reluctant to concede the influence of any writer whose moral philosophy was grounded purely on egoism.

David Hume

Book III of Hume's *Treatise of Human Nature,* that portion of his masterwork that contains his discussion of the origin and nature of justice, was published in 1740, one year after the first two volumes of the *Treatise* appeared.[44] In it, he attempts an analysis of the relation between individual actions and the emergence of general rules of justice, and his conclusions reflect an evolutionary conception of their origin. For Hume, justice comes about through a spontaneously generated order; numerous individual actions, each motivated by self-love constrained by a sense of benevolence, have as their net effect a system of rules which, in the end, are crucial to preserving the public good.[45]

> If we examine all the questions, that come before any tribunal of justice, we shall find, that, considering each case apart, it wou'd as often be an instance of humanity to decide contrary to the laws of justice as conformable to them. Judges take from a poor man to give to a rich; they bestow on the dissolute the labour of the industrious; and put into the hands of the vicious the means of harming both themselves and others. The whole scheme, however, of law and justice is advantageous to society.[46]

The principle that the commands of justice serve the public good despite the fact that the public good is not the motive for their adoption emerges most clearly in Hume's discussion of the rules that give shape to property, right, and obligation.

If men had been endow'd with such a strong regard for public good, they wou'd never have restrain'd themselves by these rules; so that the laws of justice arise from natural principles in a manner still more oblique and artificial. 'Tis self-love which is their real origin; and as the self-love of one person is naturally contrary to that of another, these several interested passions are oblig'd to adjust themselves after such a manner as to concur in some system of conduct and behaviour. This system, therefore, comprehending the interest of each individual, is of course advantageous to the public; tho' it be not intended for that purpose by the inventors.[47]

In this manner, "the three fundamental laws of nature, *that of the stability of possession, of its transference by consent,* and *of the performance of promises,*"[48] arise. So inventive and imaginative is this approach to the origin of rules of just conduct that the careful reader of Hume cannot help but agree with Knud Haakonssen's observations. "To see justice in this way," Haakonssen writes, "as an unintended consequence of individual human actions, must be one of the boldest moves in the history of the philosophy of law. And it is as ingenious as it is bold. For it allows Hume to avoid any excessive rationalism, of a Hobbesian kind; although justice is a result of human activity, it is not deliberately constructed by men. And in this sense Hume avoids the pitfalls of legal positivism, and keeps the options open for some kind of 'natural law,' or basic law, standing above all positive law."[49]

Hume did not limit his application of the theory of spontaneously generated orders to the origin of justice. At one point in the *Treatise*, he remarked that one can also trace the evolution of money and language to the unanticipated consequences of a host of individual actions, each having separate and distinct goals. (In the absence of an explicit or implied "promise" or agreement, we must assume no concerted action or intent.) Like the rule concerning the stability of possession, which "arises gradually, and acquires force by a slow progression," so "are languages gradually establish'd by human convention without any promise. In like manner do gold and silver become the common measures of exchange, and are esteemed sufficient payment for what is of a hundred times their value."[50]

Hume's *Dialogues Concerning Natural Religion* displays an equally clear awareness of the notion of complex phenomena as the product of unintentional design. Hume there observed that an object possessing an intricate or elaborate pattern or serving an unusually complex purpose need not necessarily reflect that it was created by an intelligence fully aware of all aspects of its structure and function. This holds true as much for the artifacts fashioned by men as for the world itself. "Were this world ever so perfect a production," he wrote,

12 · THE SCOTTISH ENLIGHTENMENT

it must still remain uncertain, whether all the excellencies of the work can justly be ascribed to the workman. If we survey a ship, what an exalted idea must we form of the ingenuity of the carpenter, who framed so complicated, useful, and beautiful a machine? And what surprise must we entertain, when we find him a stupid mechanic, who imitated others, and copied an art, which, through a long succession of ages, after multiplied trials, mistakes, corrections, deliberations, and controversies, had been gradually improving? Many worlds might have been botched and bungled, throughout an eternity, ere this system was struck out: Much labour lost: Many fruitless trials made: And a slow, but continued improvement carried on during infinite ages in the art of world-making.[51]

This theme is reiterated at a later point in the *Dialogues* where Hume again rejected the notion that all ordered arrangements imply an orderer. To the question "How can order spring from any thing, which perceives not that order which it bestows?" Hume has one of his characters respond: "A tree bestows order and organization on that tree which springs from it, without knowing the order: an animal, in the same manner, on its offspring: a bird, on its nest: And instances of this kind are even more frequent in the world, than those of order, which arise from reason and contrivance."[52]

In addition to the *Dialogues*, elements of the theory of spontaneous order are also suggested in several of Hume's essays. Louis Schneider has called attention to the fact that in his essay on commerce, Hume raised the idea of employing the theory of indirection, according to which the actors are unaware of the aggregate effect of their individual actions, as a deliberate device to bring about a certain state of affairs.[53] For example, Hume noted that it is not possible to infuse "a passion for the public good" sufficient to act as a spur to industry, as was apparently the case in the ancient republics. Therefore, "it is requisite to govern men by other passions, and animate them with a spirit of avarice and industry, art and luxury." By such indirection, Hume contended, could one provide for the public welfare.[54] A similar sentiment respecting the beneficial but unintended consequences of uncoordinated human actions appears in Hume's *Enquiry*, where he discussed national rivalries. "As nature has implanted in every one a superior affection to his own country, we never expect any regard to distant nations, where a competition arises. Not to mention, that, while every man consults the good of his own community, we are sensible, that the general interest of mankind is better promoted, than by loose indeterminate views to the good of a species, whence no beneficial action could ever result, for want of a duly limited object, on which they never exert themselves."[55]

Finally, Hume's *History of England,* almost certainly the most widely read of Hume's works in the eighteenth century, makes a number of references to what Louis Schneider has felicitously called "the invisible hand of politics."[56] In writing of the history of the British government, Hume remarked on the value of providing a description of its early condition, wherein the reader is shown "the remote, and commonly faint and disfigured originals of the most finished and most noble institutions" and is instructed "in the great mixture of accident, which commonly concurs with a small ingredient of wisdom and foresight, in erecting the complicated fabric of the most perfect government."[57]

There can be no doubt that Hume made extensive use of the notion of spontaneous order in a variety of different contexts, including the growth of technical knowledge, the origin of rules of morality, and the evolution of political institutions. These, Hume held, all take their form gradually and by degrees and as the unintended result of human actions having as their object a range of disparate and more immediate ends. It is this aspect of Hume's political thought that has led Hayek to make the claim that "Hume gives us probably the only comprehensive statement of the legal and political philosophy which later became known as liberalism."[58] Although this is not the place to enter into any extended discussion of such a sweeping assertion, it is perhaps not inappropriate to observe that the adoption of liberal policies of the sort to which Hayek is referring did not require that one first accept the idea of spontaneously generated orders with respect to the origin and development of legal and political arrangements. Classical liberalism as it took shape over the course of the eighteenth and nineteenth centuries owed as much to nonevolutionary theories of government and law—such as Benthamite utilitarianism, which Hayek would most likely classify as a species of constructivist rationalism, and Lockean political philosophy, which is predicated on the doctrine of immutable rules of justice that are self-evidently true—as to the antirationalist theories elaborated by Hume and the other Scottish Enlightenment writers. Indeed, Hayek's own predilection for this approach to the genesis of political institutions should not blind us to the fact that this view, as Burke was later to prove, is consistent with a thoroughgoing legal and social conservatism.

Adam Smith

Probably the clearest exposition of the idea of spontaneous order as it related to economic phenomena is offered in the work of Adam Smith. It should be emphasized, however, that the theory that complex social patterns are self-coordinating and need no deliberate ordering applies as much to Smith's moral theory as to his analysis of the market.[59] Indeed, the former

14 · THE SCOTTISH ENLIGHTENMENT

stands logically prior to the latter, just as his *Theory of Moral Sentiments* precedes the *Wealth of Nations* and, in fact, appeared some seventeen years earlier. The general rules that comprise the moral fabric, Smith held, are the result of countless instances of moral evaluation made by large numbers of individuals over time. "We do not originally approve or condemn particular action because, upon examination, they appear to be agreeable or inconsistent with a certain general rule. The general rule, on the contrary, is formed, by finding from experience, that all actions of a certain kind, or circumstanced in a certain manner, are approved or disapproved of."[60] Thus, the laws of morality themselves are the unanticipated product of a multiplicity of moral judgments.

The active principle in determining our moral standards is sympathy, "our fellow-feeling with any passion whatever."[61] What Smith appears to mean by this is the ability all men have to place themselves in another's position and from thence to form a judgment of the situation they find themselves in.[62] The presence or absence of this sentiment explains our approbation or condemnation of any particular act. From these specific instances, rules of morality evolve and gradually come to be obeyed because, Smith added, men seek the approval of their fellow men or, in the case of rules relating to justice, because they also fear the punishment and the resentment of others that attend certain acts.

This is not to deny that man is also a self-regarding being, concerned with his own welfare. Indeed, it is for this reason that "mankind are disposed to sympathize more entirely with our joy than with our sorrow, that we make parade of our riches, and conceal our poverty."[63] A. S. Skinner has commented on this aspect of Smith's moral philosophy: "Smith often develops this theme within the context of broadly 'economic' aspirations, while reminding the reader that self-interested activities often have a 'social' reference."[64] Thus, the predisposition to sympathize with affluence serves the unintended but crucial purposes of promoting social stability[65] while encouraging the pursuit of wealth. And, although "the real satisfaction" great wealth provides will, upon sober reflection, appear "contemptible and trifling" in contributing to one's true happiness, the desire for riches unleashes enormous productive forces, which benefit all of mankind. "It is this deception," Smith wrote,

> which rouses and keeps in continual motion the industry of mankind. It is this which first prompted them to cultivate the ground, to build houses, to found cities and commonwealths, and to invent and improve all the sciences and arts, which enoble and embellish human life; which have entirely changed the whole face of the globe, have turned the rude forests of nature into agreeable

and fertile plains, and made the trackless and barren ocean a new fund of
subsistence, and the great high road of communication to the different nations
of the earth.[66]

Smith's theory of morality, one need hardly add, formed the underpinning of his analysis of justice.[67] Unlike Hume, however, Smith incorporated
into his theory of jurisprudence the concept of natural law, wherein men are
possessed of certain natural rights which are immediately demonstrable.[68]
The rights that Smith regarded as originating independently of any human
action are three: "A man merely as a man may be injured in three respects,
either 1st, in his person; or, 2dly, in his reputation; or 3dly, in his estate."[69]
Of these, however, the right one has in one's estate appears not to be
absolute but is dependent on the notion of property as it is understood by
others. As one commentator has put it, rightful possession, for Smith, "is a
historical question which must be answered differently for different periods
and different countries."[70] Indeed, Smith explicitly discussed the evolution
of the concept of property within the context of changes in society's primary
mode of production. "Before we consider exactly [the nature of occupation]
or any other methods by which property is acquired it will be proper to observe that the regulations concerning them must vary considerably according to the state or age society is in at that time. There are four distinct states
which mankind pass thro:—1st, the Age of Hunters; 2dly, the Age of Shep-
herds; 3dly, the Age of Agriculture; and 4thly, the Age of Commerce."[71]
Thus, even allowing for the fact that at certain points Smith wrote from the
perspective of an exponent of natural rights, we can still find strong evolutionary elements in his theory of justice, particularly with respect to the
development of rules of property and the emergence of civil government.
Indeed, in these respects, Smith seems far closer to Hume than to Grotius
and Pufendorf.[72]

Smith, like a number of his fellow Scots,[73] argued that societies evolved
through four stages, marked by the primary method whereby wealth is
produced.[74] The first of these stages, in which the predominant activities are
hunting and fishing, is one of universal poverty. Hence, such societies
"seldom possess any established magistrate or any regular administration of
justice."[75] The second stage, which Smith described as a shepherd society,
however, brings certain inequalities of fortune and consequently gives rise
to government. The relation between government and property in Smith's
schema is clear. Property constitutes one of the cardinal principles of justice
and justice, Smith held, "is the foundation of civil government."[76] "The first
and chief design of every system of government is to maintain justice; to
prevent the members of a society from incroaching on one anothers prop-

16 · THE SCOTTISH ENLIGHTENMENT

erty, or seizing what is not their own. The design here is to give each one the secure and peacable possession of his own property."[77]

The change from a pasturage economy to the age of agriculture, like the preceding transition from a society based on hunting, occurs by insensible degrees, as more and more people turn to the cultivation of land, partly as a consequence of the growth of population and the resultant pressure on the food supply. Property in land in turn promotes the division of labor and more extensive trade. Eventually agricultural societies evolve into commercial ones, in which trade becomes comprehensive and international and in which labor, recognizing no national borders, reaches the highest degree of specialization.[78]

These changes in the principal means by which wealth is produced, Smith argued, come about gradually as the unplanned result of innumerable individual actions, each having far more limited ends. The same evolutionary dynamic applies to the laws of property and to the structure of government, which reflect these alterations in the means of production. "It is easy to see," Smith wrote,

> that in these severall ages of society, the laws and regulations with regard to property must be very different. . . . When flocks and herds come to be reared property then becomes of a very considerable extent; there are many opportunities of injuring one another and such injuries are extremely pernicious to the sufferer. In this state many more laws and regulations must take place; theft and robbery being easily committed, will of consequence be punished with the utmost rigour. In the age of agriculture, they are not perhaps so much exposed to theft and open robbery, but then there are many ways added in which property may be interrupted as the subjects of it are considerably extended. The laws therefore tho perhaps not so rigorous will be of a far greater number than amongst a nation of shepherds. In the age of commerce, as the subjects of property are greatly increasd the laws must be proportionally multiplied. The more improved any society is and the greater length the severall means of supporting the inhabitants are carried, the greater will be the number of their laws and regulations necessary to maintain justice, and prevent infringements of the right to property.[79]

The moral rules by which we live, the laws relating to property which structure our notions of private possession, the very framework of our political institutions, all have a social origin; they are each the product of spontaneously generated orders shaped by the principle of evolution. But Smith did not limit the application of this doctrine to what has been called "theoretical or conjectural history,"[80] that is, to the broad outlines of the progress of society from its inception to the modern period. Duncan Forbes has shown how extensive Smith's use of the concept was when analyzing actual historical events.[81] Consider, for example, Smith's discussion of the unintended effects on the political power of the nobility of their consuming the whole of the value of their rents. As soon as they could exchange the whole surplus produce of their lands, they proceeded to consume it all. The effect was that they exchanged "the maintenance of a thousand men for a year, and with it the whole weight and authority which it could give them," for the most transient gratifications.[82] Thus, Smith concluded:

> A revolution of the greatest importance to the publick happiness, was in this manner brought about by two different orders of people [the nobility and the merchants from whom they bought the goods and services they desired], who had not the least intention to serve the publick. To gratify the most childish vanity was the sole motive of the great proprietors. The merchants and artificers, much less ridiculous, acted merely from a view to their own interest, and in pursuit of their own pedlar principle of turning a penny whenever a penny was to be got. Neither of them had either knowledge or foresight of that great revolution which the folly of the one, and the industry of the other, was gradually bringing about.[83]

Similarly, the power of the medieval Church was destroyed, not by reason, but by "the gradual improvements of arts, manufactures, and commerce" for which the clergy could exchange their produce. This, in turn, encouraged them to increase the rents imposed on their tenants, in return for which the clergy were forced to grant leases, thus conferring a degree of independence on their tenants that they never before possessed. "The ties of interest, which bound the inferior ranks of people to the clergy, were in this manner gradually broken and dissolved."[84] "The constitution of the church of Rome," Smith wrote,

> may be considered as the most formidable combination that ever was formed against the authority and security of civil government, as well as against the liberty, reason, and happiness of mankind. . . . Had this constitution been attacked by no other enemies but the feeble efforts of human reason, it must have endured forever. But that immense and well-built fabric, which all the wisdom and virtue of man could never have shaken, much less have overturned, was by the natural course of things, first weakened, and afterwards in part destroyed.[85]

Smith furnished an equally significant example of the creation of a spontaneously generated order—which also pointed to the value of competition—in his discussion of the historical development of the administration of

18 · The Scottish Enlightenment

justice in England. Smith noted that the fees that the courts imposed upon the litigants that appeared before them constituted the principal support of the various courts of justice. As a result, "each court endeavoured to draw to itself as much business as it could, and was, upon that account, willing to take cognizance of many suits which were not originally intended to fall under its jurisdiction." The effects of this gradual change were far-reaching.

> It came, in many cases, to depend altogether upon the parties before what court they would chuse to have their cause tried; and each court endeavoured by superior dispatch and impartiality, to draw to itself as many causes as it could. The present admirable constitution of the courts of justice in England was, perhaps, originally in a great measure, formed by this emulation, which antiently took place between their respective judges; each judge endeavouring to give, in his own court, the speediest and most effectual remedy, which the law would admit, for every sort of injustice.[86]

Smith applied the principle that complex social arrangements can take shape as the unanticipated consequence of a myriad of uncoordinated human actions (what Forbes is partially referrring to when he employs the term "the law of the heterogeneity of ends"[87]) to numerous historical events. Indeed, Forbes has remarked that, as in the example just given, "Adam Smith's deepest insight into historical happening serves as his strongest and best-known argument for *laissez-faire*."[88] Thus, Smith held that the division of labor evolved as the unintended result of our propensity to engage in the exhange of goods: "The division of labour, from which so many advantages are derived, is not originally the effect of any human wisdom, which foresees and intends that general opulence to which it gives occasion. It is the necessary, though very slow and gradual consequence of a certain propensity in human nature which has in view no such extensive utility; the propensity to truck, barter, and exchange one thing for another."[89]

Indeed, the structure of Smith's analysis of the production and distribution of wealth rests on the theory that the market constitutes a self-regulating mechanism that produces complex patterns without the need of an orderer. Hence the crucial importance to Smith's thought of such concepts as "natural justice" and "the invisible hand." Although Smith appears to have first employed the term "invisible hand" in a somewhat different context,[90] its earliest use with reference to economic phenomena occurs in the *Theory of Moral Sentiments* in the course of his discussion of the effects of the uneven distribution of wealth. The rich, he noted,

> consume little more than the poor, and in spite of their natural selfishness and rapacity, though they mean only their own conveniency, though the sole end

which they propose from the labours of all the thousands whom they employ, be the gratification of their own vain and insatiable desires, they divide with the poor the produce of all their improvements. They are led by an invisible hand to make nearly the same distribution of the necessities of life, which would have been made, had the earth been divided into equal portions among all its inhabitants, and thus without intending it, without knowing it, advance the interest of society, and afford means to the multiplication of the species."[91]

The term appears again in the *Wealth of Nations,* where Smith once more used it to describe the beneficial but unanticipated consequences of certain actions, in this instance, the individual's preference for domestic over foreign investment.

As every individual endeavours as much as he can both to employ his capital in the support of domestick industry, and so to direct that industry that its produce may be of the greatest value; every individual necessarily labours to render the annual revenue of the society as great as he can. He generally, indeed, neither intends to promote the publick interest, nor knows how much he is promoting it. By preferring the support of domestick to that of foreign industry, he intends only his own security; and by directing that industry in such a manner as its produce may be of the greatest value, he intends only his own gain, and he is in this, as in any other cases, led by an invisible hand to promote an end which was no part of his intention. Nor is it always the worse for the society that it was no part of it.[92]

Indeed, the very notion of an unfettered market is predicated on the idea that a socially beneficial ordered arrangement is likely to emerge out of the free actions of countless individuals, each aiming at the satisfaction of his own private ends. "By pursuing his own interest," Smith wrote, "he frequently promotes that of the society more effectually than when he really intends to promote it. I have never known much good done by those who affected to trade for the publick good. It is an affectation, indeed, not very common among merchants and very few words need be employed in dissuading them from it."[93]

Not only is a free market self-coordinating but, more important, intervention in its operation thwarts it in its function of maximizing the production of wealth, thus retarding social progress.

Every system which endeavours, either, by extraordinary encouragements, to draw towards a particular species of industry a greater share of the capital of the society than what would naturally go to it; or, by extraordinary restraints, to force from a particular species of industry some share of the capital which would otherwise be employed in it; is in reality subversive of the great purpose which it means to promote. It retards, instead of accelerating, the progress of society towards real wealth and greatness; and diminishes, instead of increasing, the real value of the annual produce of its land and labour.

All systems either of preference or of restraint, therefore, being thus completely taken away, the obvious and simple system of natural liberty establishes itself of its own accord. Every man, as long as he does not violate the laws of justice, is left perfectly free to pursue his own interest his own way, and to bring both his industry and capital into competition with those of any other man, or order of men. The sovereign is completely discharged from a duty, in the attempting to perform which he must always be exposed to innumerable delusions, and for the proper performance of which no human wisdom or knowledge could ever be sufficient; the duty of superintending the industry of private people, and of directing it towards the employments most suitable to the interest of the society.[94]

This classic affirmation of laissez-faire contains what is probably the clearest statement of the spontaneous order inherent in the marketplace that appears anywhere in Scottish Enlightenment literature.

The reader should not take this to suggest that Smith did not support government intervention, that is, the deliberate direction of economic and social life by the sovereign, in those areas where he felt utilitarian considerations dictated such interference. Indeed, Smith explicitly recognized three primary areas of government activity as consistent with his conception of natural liberty.

According to the system of natural liberty the sovereign has only three duties to attend to: three duties of great importance, indeed, but plain and intelligible to common understandings: first, the duty of protecting the society from the violence and invasion of other independent societies; secondly, the duty of protecting, as far as possible, every member of the society from the injustice or oppression of every other member of it, or the duty of establishing an exact administration of justice; and, thirdly, the duty of erecting and maintaining certain publick works and certain public institutions, which it can never be for the interest of any individual, or small number of individuals, to erect and maintain; because the profit could never repay the expence of any individual or small number of individuals, though it may frequently do much more than repay it to a great society.[95]

As important as is the protection of society from foreign invasion, however, it is logically inferior to Smith's second duty, the provision of justice, since it is the provision of justice which makes society possible in the first instance. "Society may subsist, though not in the most comfortable state, without beneficence; but the prevalence of injustice must utterly destroy it."[96] Thus, the most significant task which governments are required to undertake is the establishment of a legal framework, without which no market can function.

In addition to the provision of justice and of defense, Smith supported a number of specific governmental intrusions into the market, among them the regulation of paper money banking,[97] the compulsory registration of mortgages,[98] government participation in education,[99] control of the coinage,[100] taxes on the sale of liquor,[101] the granting of temporary monopolies to merchants engaged in enterprises of great risk aimed at establishing new branches of trade, patents, copyrights,[102] government stamps of quality on plate and on linen and woollen cloth,[103] and the establishment of a maximum rate of interest.[104] Yet, despite Smith's advocacy of these measures—together with others calling for the use of the taxing power as an instrument to achieve certain ends[105]—the overall thrust of Smith's argument is distrust of public intervention and in favor of laissez-faire. Although commentators have differed on the degree to which Smith was an exponent of an unfettered market,[106] one cannot but agree with Jacob Viner that "there is no possible room for doubt . . . that Smith in general believed that there was, to say the least, a strong presumption against government activity beyond its fundamental duties of protection against its foreign foes and maintenance of justice."[107] Indeed, all the exceptions notwithstanding, Smith's analysis of economic phenomena displayed a thoroughly sophisticated understanding of the market process, which in turn reflected the underlying importance of the notion of spontaneously generated orders to his social theory. As one commentator has noted: "The unifying feature of Smithian economics is the idea that relative price movements convey information to individuals about underlying resource scarcities in a way that coordinates their actions and leads them to (unintentionally) maximize the national product at each stage of economic development."[108]

One final example might be offered respecting the pervasiveness in Smith's thought of the idea that certain complex results are the unanticipated product of numerous discrete actions. In writing of "the great ends which Nature seems to have proposed in the formation of all animals," self-preservation and the propagation of the species, Smith observed that these ends have

> not been intrusted to the slow and uncertain determinations of our reason, to find out the proper means of bringing them about. Nature has directed us to the greater part of these by original and immediate instincts. Hunger, thirst, the passion which unites the two sexes, the love of pleasure, and the dread of pain, prompt us to apply those means for their own sakes, and without any consideration of their tendency to those beneficent ends which the great Director of nature intended to produce by them.[109]

Thus, embedded in the very structure of nature is the notion of achieving ends by indirection. Social arrangements of great complexity are arrived at as the unintended result of individual actions, each having disparate ends but, when taken together, creating a convoluted pattern. No plainer example of the use of the doctrine of spontaneous order occurs in Smith's noneconomic observations than in his discussion of the ends nature has proposed for mankind. "With regard to all those ends which, upon account of their peculiar importance, may be regarded, if such an expression is allowable, as the favourite ends of nature, she has constantly in this manner not only endowed mankind with an appetite for the end which she proposes, but likewise with an appetite for the means by which alone this end can be brought about, for their own sakes, and independent of their tendency to produce it."[110]

Adam Ferguson

Unlike Smith, Adam Ferguson wrote little on purely economic issues. Consequently, his writings contain fewer applications of the idea of spontaneous order than do Smith's. However, those that appear in Ferguson's two major works—his *Essay on the History of Civil Society* (1767) and his *Principles of Moral and Political Science* (1792)—are clear and sharply focussed. Thus, in discussing the nature of social institutions, Ferguson observed that their origin and development, far from being the product of deliberate calculation, were the result of an evolutionary process that gave shape to man's instincts and habits.

> The artifices of the beaver, the ant, and the bee, are ascribed to the wisdom of nature. Those of polished nations are ascribed to themselves, and are supposed to indicate a capacity superior to that of rude minds. But the establishments of men, like those of every animal, are suggested by nature, and are the result of instinct, directed by the variety of situations in which mankind are placed. Those establishments arose from successive improvements that were made, without any sense of their general effect; and they bring human affairs to a state of complication, which the greatest reach of capacity with which human nature was ever adorned, could not have projected; nor even when the whole is carried into execution, can it be comprehended in its full extent.[111]

Ferguson, in company with a number of his fellow Scots, held that societies progressed through certain clearly defined stages, which were a function of the primary means by which wealth was produced and of the property relationships that obtained at each stage of development. As Smith had similarly contended in his *Lectures on Jurisprudence*,[112] Ferguson regarded the development of private property—and of formal government which necessarily accompanies it—as a product of evolutionary forces. Like other institutions, property was an unanticipated consequence of countless individual actions over time, each aimed at distinct and separate ends. "It must appear very evident," Ferguson observed,

> that property is a matter of progress. It requires, among other particulars which are the effects of time, some method of defining possession. The very desire of it proceeds from experience; and the industry by which it is gained, or improved, requires such a habit of acting with a view to distant objects, as may overcome the present disposition either to sloth or to enjoyment. This habit is slowly acquired, and is in reality a principal distinction of nations in the advanced state of mechanic and commercial arts.[113]

The most primitive of precommercial societies, which Ferguson labelled "savage," were those based on hunting and fishing, in which private property was effectively unknown. In the absence of any clear notion of property, no formal system of subordination, that is, no government, can have arisen.[114] However, once property is introduced, as is the case in those societies that base their economies on agriculture or the herding of animals, a crude, often informal, system of laws and government emerges. Ferguson referred to this stage of development as "barbarian" and viewed it as a singular advance over savagery inasmuch as it provided the foundation for the property relationships and system of political subordination that marked commercial societies.[115] Commercial societies, in turn, although they might well strain the intimate social bonds that characterized more primitive societies, allowed for the broadest display of man's abilities and provided the conditions that permitted the fullest expression of his virtues. "The bulk of mankind," Ferguson observed,

> are, like other parts of the system, subjected to the law of their nature, and, without knowing it, are led to accomplish its purpose. While they intend no more than subsistence and accommodation, or the peace of society, and the safety of their persons and their property, their faculties are brought into use, and they profit by exercise. In mutually conducting their relative interests and concerns, they acquire the habits of political life; are made to taste of their highest enjoyments, in the affections of benevolence, integrity, and elevation of mind; and, before they have deliberately considered in what the merit or felicity of their own nature consist, have already learned to perform many of its noblest functions.
>
> Nature in this as in many other instances does not entrust the conduct of her works to the precarious views and designs of any subordinate agent.[116]

24 • THE SCOTTISH ENLIGHTENMENT

As Smith was later to do with such telling effect in the *Wealth of Nations*, Ferguson had recourse to the idea of spontaneously generated orders to explain particular historical events. Indeed, he went so far as to suggest that the rise and fall of nations came about, at least partially, as the unintended consequence of the efforts of men blind to the long-term effects of their actions.

> Among the circumstances which lead in the progress or decline of nations, that of political situation may be justly reckoned among the first or most important. And in this the most favourable conjuncture is sometimes obtained, or the reverse is incurred, with perfect blindness to the future, or ignorance of the consequences which are likely to follow. The parties would always better themselves: But they are often driving they know not whither. Thus the Barons of England, in times of high feudal aristocracy, knew not that the charters, which they extorted from their sovereign, were to become foundations of freedom to the people over whom they themselves wished to tyrannize. No more did the Roman people foresee, that the support they gave to Caesar, in reducing the senate, was in effect to establish a military despotism, under which they themselves were to forfeit all the advantages of a free nation.[117]

Nor did Ferguson limit his use of the concept of spontaneous order to the evolution of political arrangements. In an especially insightful observation, Ferguson noted that language constituted an ordered social structure that originated and developed without deliberate design. Indeed, it is a particularly apt example of a spontaneous formation which is shaped by the aggregate of numerous individual actions performed by actors no one of whom is even capable of fully understanding the complexity that language displays.

> Parts of speech, which, in speculation, cost the grammarian so much study, are in practice familiar to the vulgar. The rudest tribes, even the idiot, and the insane, are possessed of them: They are soonest learned in childhood; insomuch, that we must suppose human nature, in its lowest state, competent to the use of them; and, without the intervention of uncommon genius, mankind, in a succession of ages, qualified to accomplish in detail this amazing fabric of language, which, when raised to its height, appears so much above what could be ascribed to any simultaneous effort of the most sublime and comprehensive abilities.[118]

References to the idea of spontaneously generated orders are scattered throughout Ferguson's writings but are especially common in his *Essay*, in which he devoted a number of passages to discussing the prevalence of social institutions that arose independently of conscious reflection and deliberate intent. "Mankind, in following the present sense of their minds," he remarked, "in striving to remove inconveniencies, or to gain apparent and contiguous advantages, arrive at ends which even their imagination could not anticipate, and pass on, like other animals, in the track of their nature, without perceiving its ends."[119] Social formations of any degree of intricacy, he contended, whether political, legal, economic, linguistic, or otherwise, are the unanticipated product of human actions made by people unaware of the larger ends to which they are contributing. In a much-quoted comment, Ferguson noted:

> Like the winds, that come we know not whence, and blow whithersoever they list, the forms of society are derived from an obscure and distant origin; they arise, long before the date of philosophy, from the instincts, not from the speculations, of men. The croud of mankind, are directed in their establishments and measures, by the circumstances in which they are placed; and seldom are turned from their way, to follow the plan of any single projector.
>
> Every step and every movement of the multitude, even in what are termed enlightened ages, are made with equal blindness to the future; and nations stumble upon establishments, which are indeed the result of human action, but not the execution of any human design.[120]

Henry Home (Lord Kames), Gilbert Stuart, Thomas Reid, and John Millar

Less attention need be paid to these thinkers than to Hume, Smith, or Ferguson, not because they were, by some measure, lesser intellectuals (indeed, Reid can almost certainly be regarded as having made a greater contribution to the history of thought than can Ferguson), but because their observations regarding the idea of spontaneous order were neither as extensive nor as original as were those offered by the writers we have discussed.

Henry Home, Lord Kames, wrote extensively on a whole range of subjects from literary criticism to jurisprudence to farming. He was by training and profession an advocate and rose to occupy one of the highest judicial positions in Scotland when, in 1763, at the age of sixty-seven, he was appointed a Lord Commissioner of Justiciary, the supreme criminal court of Scotland.[121] Indeed, of Kames' seventeen books, nine concern the history and philosophy of law. In 1758, Kames published his *Historical Law-Tracts*, in which he first put forward a version of the four-stages theory of social

26 · THE SCOTTISH ENLIGHTENMENT

evolution—similar to that contained in Smith's Glasgow lectures of 1762–63[122]—and of the development of government and law. After outlining the various stages through which societies pass, based upon the principal mode of production then in effect, from hunting and fishing to the shepherd life to agriculture, Kames noted:

> In the first state of man, *viz.* that of hunting and fishing, there obviously is no place for government, except that which is exercised by the heads of families over children and domesticks. The shepherd life, in which societies are formed, by the conjunction of families for mutual defence, requires some sort of government, slight indeed in proportion to the slightness of the mutual connection. But it was agriculture which first produced a regular system of government. The intimate union among a multitude of individuals, occasioned by agriculture, discovered a number of social duties, formerly unknown. These behoved to be ascertained by laws, the observance of which must be enforced by punishment. Such operations cannot be carried on, otherwise than by lodging power in one or more persons, to direct the resolutions, and apply the force of the whole society. In short, it may be laid down as an universal maxim, that in every society, the advances of government towards perfection, are strictly proportioned to the advances of the society towards intimacy of union.[123]

Kames reiterated these views in the second (1758) edition of his *Essays on the Principles of Morality and Natural Religion,* where he again suggested that the four-stages theory could serve as an explanation of the emergence of a formal system of government and of property in land.[124] Unlike Smith, however, Kames explicitly rejected the notion that the concept of private property arose only during a particular stage of social development, as the product of evolutionary forces. Property, he contended, had its roots in the individual's natural and universal instinct to hoard and, consequently, existed prior to the establishment of any society. In taking issue with Hobbes on this question, Kames concluded:

> It appears clear, that the sense of property does not owe its existence to society. But in a matter of so great importance in the science of morals, I cannot rest satisfied with a successful defence. I aim at a complete victory, by insisting on a proposition directly opposite to that of my antagonist [Hobbes], *viz.* That society owes its existence to the sense of property; or at least, that without this sense no society ever could have been formed. In the proof of this proposition, we have already made a considerable progress, by evincing, that man by his nature is a hoarding animal, and loves to store for his own use.[125]

Despite Kames' rejection of the notion of property as a social artifact,[126] it is worthwhile to emphasize that he still regarded the development of government and law as subject to evolutionary changes, themselves the product of the unintended consequences of countless individual actions. There are examples of Kames' application of the doctrine of spontaneously generated orders throughout his writings, especially in his discussions of the evolution of law and manners.[127] Consider also his use of the theory of spontaneous order in his analysis of the role played by the "true and genuine principles of action," namely. love of life, self-love, the love of justice, gratitude, and benevolence,[128] in structuring people's activities.

> These several principles of action are ordered with admirable wisdom, to promote the general good, in the best and most effectual manner. We act for the general good, when we act upon these principles, even when it is not our immediate aim. The general good is an object too remote, to be the sole impulsive motive to action. It is better ordered, that, in most instances, individuals should have a limited aim, which they can readily accomplish. To every man is assigned his own task. And if every man do his duty, the general good will be promoted much more effectually, than if it were the aim in every single action.[129]

A particularly clear illustration of the theory of spontaneous order as applied to the development of legal and political institutions is provided by Gilbert Stuart, who, like Kames, was a serious student of the history of jurisprudence. Although he is reputed to have lived a life of dissipation and appears to have been wanting in principle and given to excesses, Stuart did manage to author a large number of articles and reviews and no less than five books before his death at the age of forty-four in 1786. The son of the professor of Latin and of Roman Antiquities at the University of Edinburgh, Stuart sought the professorship of public law at the University in 1779. In this he proved unsuccessful, despite the fact that the University had awarded him the degree of doctor of law ten years earlier for his *Historical Dissertation concerning the Antiquity of the English Constitution* (1768), a work of great scholarship and insight. As a consequence, Stuart was forced to make his living by review writing and editing and was associated, at one point or another. with several of the leading periodicals of the day. In addition to the *Historical Dissertation,* Stuart's major writings include *A View of Society in Europe* (1778) and *The History of Scotland from the Establishment of the Reformation till the Death of Queen Mary* (1782).

The most important of his works, certainly for our purposes, is his

28 · THE SCOTTISH ENLIGHTENMENT

Historical Dissertation, in which Stuart offers as unambiguous a statement of the doctrine of spontaneously generated orders as appears in the literature of the period.

> Historians, judging of rude times by the standard of a cultivated age, have frequently concluded, that the establishments which arise in society are the result of intention and design. They seek for legislators before legislators could exist; and, while the greatest ignorance and inexperience have prevailed, they fancy, that the most difficult of the sciences had approached to perfection.
>
> It is, however, by circumstance and accident that rules are discovered for the conduct of men; and society must have subsisted for ages, and its different appearances must have been often unfolded, before the wisdom of individuals could plan or project the arrangements of nations. The tumult and confusion which flow from intercourse and the social connections, suggest first the advantages of order. Regulations are then made, and forms of justice are invented. The actions and commerce of the species extend themselves, and new regulations are called for. Improvements follow on improvements; and schemes of government attain by degrees their utility and value.[130]

Thomas Reid, who held the chair of moral philosophy at Glasgow from 1764 until his retirement in 1780, although a philosopher of the first rank, is of only minor importance to students of the doctrine of spontaneous order. Reid's remarks on the subject, which appear most fully in his *Essays on the Active Powers of Man* (1788), deal with the role played by man's instinctive behavior in both preserving him physically and morally and in perpetuating the human species. In these respects, Reid's comments are not dissimilar to those earlier made by Smith in his *Theory of Moral Sentiments.* Both works touch on the notion of nature acting through indirection to achieve its ends, and both underscore the importance of instinct and habit in promoting man's well-being.

Instinct, Reid wrote, refers to "a natural, blind impulse to certain actions, without having any end in view, without deliberation, and very often without any conception of what we do."[131] An especially felicitous example of an impulse that results in particularly complex patterns is the activity of bees in constructing their honeycombs. Bees engaged in this task act as if they were familiar with the most abstruse laws of solid geometry,[132] yet, as we are aware, "they work most geometrically, without any knowledge of geometry. . . . When a bee makes its comb so geometrically," Reid remarked, "the geometry is not in the bee, but in the great Geometrician who made the bee."[133] Just as the bee is led towards accomplishing particular ends of which it clearly has no knowledge, so the actions of human beings are occasionally directed towards achieving certain results that are totally uncontemplated by the actors.

> By instinct and habit, man, without deliberation or will, is led to many actions, necessary for his preservation and well-being, which, without those principles, all his skill and wisdom would not have been able to accomplish.
>
> It may perhaps be thought, that his deliberate and voluntary actions are to be guided by his reason.
>
> But it ought to be observed, that he is a voluntary agent long before he has the use of reason. Reason and virtue, the prerogatives of man, are of the latest growth. They come to maturity by slow degrees, and are too weak, in the greater part of the species, to secure the preservation of individuals and communities, and to produce that varied scene of human life in which they are to be exercised and improved.
>
> Therefore, the wise Author of our being hath implanted in human nature many inferior principles of action, which, with little or no aid of reason or virtue, preserve the species, and produce the various changes and revolutions which we observe upon the theatre of life. . . .
>
> Reason, if it were perfect, would lead us to desire power, knowledge, and the esteem and affection of our fellow-men, as means of promoting our own happiness, and of being useful to others. Here again, Nature, to supply the defects of reason, hath given us a strong natural desire of those objects, which leads us to pursue them without regard to their utility.[134]

It is anomalous that John Millar, the staunchest proponent of Whig political principles of the various writers we have been considering, should have interpreted the theory of spontaneous order in its most deterministic sense when applying it to the evolution of social arrangements. Born in 1735, Millar was elected to the chair of civil law at the University of Glasgow at the age of twenty-six—only sixteen months after having been called to the bar—upon the recommendation of Lord Kames, whose son he had tutored, and of Adam Smith, under whom he had studied. Although regarded as a lecturer of great ability and originality, Millar authored only two large works during his career, his *Observations Concerning the Distinction of Ranks in Society* (1771; revised under the title *The Origin of the Distinction of Ranks* in 1779) and the *Historical View of the English Government: From the Settlement of the Saxons in Britain to the Accession of the House of Stewart* (1787).[135] In addition, Millar composed several pamphlets and articles in which he defended the principles of the French Revolution and attacked Pitt's foreign policy.[136]

Millar was a resolute spokesman for the doctrine of spontaneous order, which suffuses his two book-length studies and which he applied to the

30 · THE SCOTTISH ENLIGHTENMENT

whole range of social institutions. His student and friend Francis Jeffrey noted:

> It is perfectly evident to all who are acquainted with their writings, that [Millar's] speculations are all formed upon the model of those of Lord Kames and Dr Smith, and that his merit consists, almost entirely, in the accuracy with which he surveyed, and the sagacity with which he pursued the path which they had the merit of discovering. It was one great object of both those original authors, to trace back the history of society to its most simple and universal elements,—to resolve almost all that has been ascribed to positive institution into the spontaneous and irresistible development of certain obvious principles,—and to show with how little contrivance or political wisdom the most complicated and apparently artificial schemes of policy might have been erected. This is very nearly the precise definition of what Mr Millar aimed at accomplishing in his lectures and his publications.[137]

Indeed, like Smith and Kames before him, Millar also adopted the four-stages theory of social development, in which the institutions under which modern society operates are seen as the products of an evolutionary process based primarily upon changes in the method by which wealth is produced.

> A nation of savages who feel the want of almost every thing requisite for the support of life, must have their attention directed to a small number of objects, to the acquisition of food and clothing, or the procuring shelter from the inclemencies of the weather; and their ideas and feelings, in conformity to their situation, must, of course, be narrow and contracted. Their first efforts are naturally calculated to increase the means of subsistence, by catching or ensnaring wild animals, or by gathering the spontaneous fruits of the earth; and the experience, acquired in the exercise of these employments, is apt, successively, to point out the methods of taming and rearing cattle, and of cultivating the ground. According as men have been successful in these great improvements, and find less difficulty in the attainment of bare necessities, their prospects are gradually enlarged, their appetites and desires are more and more awakened and called forth in pursuit of the several conveniencies of life; and the various branches of manufacture, together with commerce, its inseparable attendant, and with science and literature, the natural spring of ease and affluence, are introduced, and brought to maturity. By such gradual advances in rendering their situation more comfortable, the most important alterations are produced in the state and condition of a people; their numbers are increased; the connections of society are extended; and men, being less oppressed with their own wants, are more at liberty to cultivate the feelings of humanity: property, the great source of distinction among individuals, is established; and the various rights of mankind, arising from their multiplied

connections, are recognized and protected: the laws of a country are thereby rendered numerous; and a more complex form of government becomes necessary, for distributing justice, and for preventing the disorders which proceed from the jarring interests and passions of a large and opulent community.[138]

This lengthy quotation offers an excellent summary of the four-stages theory, which Millar and those before him regarded as revealing the evolutionary order that nations followed in their progress from savagery to commercial society. And, as Millar made clear, the guiding principle that transmuted the various social arrangements prevalent at each stage of development to a different and higher level is the doctrine of spontaneous order. A particularly good example of Millar's use of the doctrine surrounds his discussion of the origin and nature of law. Law, Millar concluded, was an especially apt illustration of an institution which took its form not as the conscious creation of a designing intelligence but as the result of a gradual process of change produced by the interaction of numerous individuals over time.

By the successive litigation of individuals, and by the continued experience and observation of judges, the science of law grows up in society, and advances more and more to a regular system. Particular decisions become the foundation of general rules, which are afterwards limited by particular exceptions; and these exceptions being also generalized, and reduced into different classes, are again subjected to future limitations. From a few parent stems, there issue various branches; and these are succeeded by subordinate ramifications; diminishing gradually in size, while they increase in number; separated from each other by endless divisions and subdivisions; exhibiting a great multiplicity and variety of parts, uniformly and regularly adjusted; and which may, therefore, be easily and readily traced through all their different connexions.[139]

Millar was quite prepared to extend the notion that legal arrangements were the unintended consequences of human action to the particulars of English constitutional history and his *Historical View of the English Government* is filled with examples of the application of the doctrine. Thus, with specific reference to the separation of the judicial from the executive power in England, Millar, echoing a similar observation made by Smith in his *Wealth of Nations,* remarked:

A distinguished political author[140] has pointed out the separation of the judicial power from the king's prerogative, as one of the great sources of the liberty enjoyed by the subjects of Britain. To those who speculate upon the conduct of human affairs, it is amusing to discover, that this important regulation was neither introduced from any foresight of its beneficial consequences, nor extorted from the monarch by any party that were jealous of his power; but was merely the suggestion of indolence; and was adopted by the king, in common with other feudal superiors, to relieve them from a degree of labour and attention which they did not chuse to bestow. It was, in reality, a consequence of the general progress of society by which employments of every sort, both liberal and mechanical, have been distributed among different individuals, and have become the object of separate professions and trades.[141]

Dugald Stewart

We need concern ourselves with only one more writer, and then primarily because of the great influence he was to have on nineteenth-century thought. Dugald Stewart, as original a thinker as he might have been, was, at least in this area of speculation, much more a borrower than an innovator. He had an intimate knowledge of the works of all the writers we have been considering and knew most of them personally. A student of Ferguson's and of Reid's, Stewart wrote biographical essays of both Reid and Adam Smith. More importantly, he had adopted the basic outlines of Ferguson's social and moral philosophy and of Smith's political and economic principles, including their conclusions respecting the evolution of social institutions, early in his education. These he transmitted to his students in his lectures at the University of Edinburgh, where he held the chair of moral philosophy from 1785, upon the retirement of Ferguson, until 1810, when for reasons of health he was forced to turn the actual teaching duties associated with the professorship over to a younger man. There seems little doubt that Stewart's economic views contributed substantially to the importance the theory of spontaneous order played in his thought. As his biographer has noted, Stewart was a confirmed proponent of an unfettered market, "advocating the freest scope for individual interest and effort, and the unrestricted exchange of the products of national industry." His defense of laissez-faire, in turn, constituted the chief corollary of his "general doctrine of the propriety of fully recognizing individual instincts and tendencies as normal social forces, and consequently of abstaining from legislative interference wherever it can be shown that natural principles are in themselves sufficient to realise the end which the proposed act of legislation seeks."[142]

The doctrine of spontaneous order appears throughout Stewart's writings. In addition to extensive quotations on the issue from Ferguson, Smith, and others, Stewart applied the concept to a wide range of social institutions. Thus, he concurred in the view that "in every society . . . which, in consequence of the general spirit of its government, enjoys the blessings of tranquillity and liberty, a great part of the political order which we are apt to ascribe to legislative sagacity, is the natural result of the selfish pursuits of individuals."[143] Similarly, in endorsing Smith's observations on the importance of distinguishing between certain social ends and the mechanisms by which these ends are consummated, Stewart noted that "what we call the Political Order, is much less the effect of human contrivance than is commonly imagined."[144] And again: "Neither would I wish it to be understood, that governments have, in general, taken their rise from political wisdom. On the contrary, almost every one of which we have any account has been the gradual result of time and experience, of circumstances and emergencies."[145] What obtains for government and the structure of law in society also holds true for languages: "*These*, as well as governments," Stewart maintained, "are the gradual result of time and experience, and not of philosophical speculation."[146]

These examples are doubtless sufficient to point to the importance the notion of spontaneous order played in Stewart's thinking. Equally significant, Stewart's philosophical reputation insured that these views would receive the widest attention. The only lectures to be offered on political economy at any British university in the 1790s were those presented by Stewart at the University of Edinburgh.[147] As a consequence, Stewart's influence on the development of this discipline was considerable. Among his students were Francis Horner (who was to coauthor the Bullion Report), Sydney Smith, Francis Jeffrey (later Lord Jeffrey, the first editor of the *Edinburgh Review*), Henry Brougham (Lord Brougham), George Joseph Bell (who was later elected to the chair of Scots law at the University of Edinburgh), Henry Reeve (the translator of Tocqueville), Henry John Temple (Viscount Palmerston), Lord John Russell, and James Mill (the economist and political theorist).[148] The eminence to which these men would rise in their respective fields and the intellectual influence they themselves were to wield assured that the theory of spontaneously generated orders entered the mainstream of nineteen-century economic and social theory.

Conclusion

It has at times been assumed that the theory played only a minor role in early nineteenth-century social thought. But this conclusion rests on a misreading of the doctrine which, when interpreted in a deterministic sense, is compatible with, among others, Marx's philosophy of history. Indeed, John Millar's use of the notion of spontaneous order adumbrated the

34 · THE SCOTTISH ENLIGHTENMENT

Marxist conception of the development of social institutions as necessarily the product of forces over which people have almost no conscious control. His student and friend Francis Jeffrey remarked on Millar's views, that

> it was the leading principle . . . of all his speculations on law, morality, government, language, the arts, sciences, and manners—that there was nothing produced by arbitrary or accidental causes; that no great change, institution, custom, or occurrence, could be ascribed to the character or exertions of an individual, to the temperament or disposition of a nation, to occasional policy, or peculiar wisdom or folly; every thing, on the contrary, he held, arose spontaneously from the situation of the society, and was suggested or imposed irresistibly by the opportunities or necessities of their condition.[149]

The antirationalist aspects of the theory are thus quite consistent with the view that we are ultimately impotent to improve the social arrangements in which we find ourselves. A social theory which appears compatible with the broadest possible individual freedom thus can also provide a theoretical justification for the most restrictive political and legal arrangements. The Scottish thinkers whom we have been considering appear to have been unaware of the full import of this implication.

Indeed, there is a strong traditionalist aspect to the doctrine of spontaneously generated orders which appears to have made it particularly attractive to conservative writers. Thus, the theory is adumbrated by Bishop Bossuet in 1681 as an elaboration of the commonly held Christian notion: "Homo proponet et Deus disponit."[150] Bossuet noted that those who govern us

> achieve more less than they plan, and their intentions have always led to unforseen consequences. They neither control the configuration of circumstances that was bequeathed to them by past centuries, nor can they foresee the course of the future, much less control that course. . . . In a word, there is no human power which does not unintentionally serve other ends than its own. God alone can subject everything to his will. That is why every event is unexpected if we perceive only its specific causes; and yet the world goes forward in a foreordained sequence.[151]

The conservative and antirationalist implications of the doctrine are especially evident in Burke's writings, in which he argues with great force that our social institutions—and particularly our political and legal arrangements—are so intricate that they fall beyond the capacity of our reason to comprehend them.[152] Burke's social theory embraces the essential characteristics of the notion of spontaneous order, that the social arrangements in which people find themselves are not the consequence of conscious design, but evolve through slow degrees over many generations and thus serve an infinity of ends.

> The states of the Christian world have grown up to their present magnitude in a great length of time, and by a great variety of accidents. They have been improved to what we see them with greater or less degrees of felicity and skill. Not one of them has been formed upon a regular plan or with any unity of design. As their constitutions are not systematical, they have not been directed to any *peculiar* end, eminently distinguished, and superseding every other. The objects which they embrace are of the greatest possible variety, and have become in a manner infinite.[153]

The criterion of a specific institution's value, therefore, is not its "reasonableness," which might well deceive us into destroying that which has great merit, but its age. As Burke argued:

> In states there are often some obscure and almost latent causes, things which appear at first view of little moment, on which a very great part of its prosperity or adversity may most essentially depend. The science of government being therefore so practical in itself, and intended for such practical purposes, a matter which requires experience, and even more experience than any person can gain in his whole life, however sagacious and observing he may be, it is with infinite caution that any man ought to venture upon pulling down an edifice, which has answered in any tolerable degree for ages the common purposes of society, or on building it up again, without having models and patterns of approved utility before his eyes.[154]

The theory of spontaneous order, thus construed, inevitably militates against any program of comprehensive reform. If the social arrangements we have inherited are the result of a slow evolutionary process brought about by trial and error and if the reason embedded in these arrangements is beyond our comprehension, then we must accept them despite our ignorance of their purpose or our inability to appreciate their value. Even institutions that appear to be socially injurious or patterns that initially seem undesirable are theoretically exempt from sudden and extensive change. Thus, suttee in India, the binding of feet in China, slavery in the southern states, all could claim the protective shield of tradition and of the wisdom Burke would have argued was contained in these traditional institutions.[155]

The full impact of this conservative bias was clearly not appreciated by the Scottish philosophers, who tended to stress the spontaneous nature of nongovernmental arrangements such as moral rules, language, and the

36 · THE SCOTTISH ENLIGHTENMENT

economy, and who often used the theory to attack political intervention. It does not seem to have occurred to men like Smith or Dugald Stewart that the doctrine of spontaneous order, which was compatible with a minimum of government intrusion and which served as the philosophical underpinning of their argument for the removal of obstacles to free trade, could equally serve to render immune from reform the invasive arrangements of government that had persisted for any length of time. However, it was not until the French Revolution and the political writings that appeared in reaction to this world-historical event that the traditionalist elements contained in the theory of spontaneously generated orders were fully elaborated.[156]

NOTES

1. Hayek appears to have first made use of the notion, with primary reference to economic phenomena, in F. A. Hayek, "The Use of Knowledge in Society," *American Economic Review* 35 (1945): 519–30; reprinted in *Individualism and Economic Order* (London: Routledge & Kegan Paul, 1949), 77–91. The earliest discussion in Hayek's writings of the principle in which he explicitly employs the term "spontaneous order" seems to have occurred in *The Constitution of Liberty* (Chicago: University of Chicago Press, 1960), 160–61.

In his recent study of Hayek, John Gray asserts that Hayek's concept of spontaneous order consists of three distinct elements: (1) that social patterns arise through an invisible hand; (2) that our knowledge of the social world is primarily embodied in our practical abilities; and (3) that our institutions evolve through a species of natural selection (*Hayek on Liberty* [Oxford: Basil Blackwell, 1984], 33–34). Regardless of whether this description of Hayek's theory is a fair one, it should be made clear that the term as employed in this paper has reference solely to the first of these elements.

2. Robert K. Merton, "The Unanticipated Consequences of Purposive Social Action," *American Sociological Review* 1 (1936): 894.

3. Louis Schneider, "Introduction," in *The Scottish Moralists on Human Nature and Society*, ed. Louis Schneider (Chicago: University of Chicago Press, 1967), xxx(n.).

4. Duncan Forbes, "'Scientific' Whiggism: Adam Smith and John Millar," *Cambridge Journal* 7 (1954): 643–70.

5. Robert Nozick appears to fall somewhere between the Scots and Hayek, on the one hand, and Merton and Forbes, on the other. He defines "invisible-hand explanations" (his term for the principle of spontaneously generated orders) as those wherein "some overall pattern or design, which one would have thought had to be produced by an individual's or group's successful attempt to realize the pattern, instead was produced and maintained by a process that in no way had the overall pattern or design 'in mind'" (*Anarchy, State, and Utopia* [New York: Basic Books, 1974], 18). Most of the illustrations he presents of this type of explanation deal with highly complex social phenomena, and the reader is at first tempted to believe that Nozick intends to confine the use of the term solely to actions that issue in intricate social arrangements. However, he then offers as an example of this explanation one which seeks to explain why the United States did not respond to the evidence it apparently had suggesting that Japan was on the verge of launching an attack on Pearl Harbor (p. 21). It is difficult to see how the response or lack of one to this information falls under the rubric of a "pattern or design," as opposed simply to an event or sequence of events.

6. The relation between invisible-hand explanations and the argument from design is touched on in Edna Ullmann-Margalit, "Invisible-Hand Explanations," *Synthese* 39 (1978): 263–91.

7. Among the leading exponents of this view are F. A. Hayek, Karl R. Popper, and Michael Polanyi. See F. A. Hayek, "Kinds of Rationalism" (1965) and "The Results of Human Action but not of Human Design" (1967) in *Studies in Philosophy, Politics and Economics* (Chicago:

40 · NOTES TO PAGES 5–6

University of Chicago Press, 1967), 82–95, 96–105, and the three volumes comprising his *Law, Legislation and Liberty:* vol. 1, *Rules and Order* (Chicago: University of Chicago Press, 1973); vol. 2, *The Mirage of Social Justice* (Chicago: University of Chicago Press, 1976); and vol. 3, *The Political Order of a Free People* (Chicago: University of Chicago Press, 1979). Popper touches on the question of the unintended consequences of men's actions and their connection with a free society in "The Poverty of Historicism," *Economica,* part 2, new ser., 11 (1944): 122–23; reprinted in *The Poverty of Historicism* (London: Routledge & Kegan Paul, 1960), 65–66; *The Open Society and Its Enemies,* 4th ed., 2 vols. (1945; rpt. Princeton: Princeton University Press, 1962), 2: 93, 323–24; and "Prediction and Prophecy in the Social Sciences" (1948), in *Conjectures and Refutations: The Growth of Scientific Knowledge* (New York: Basic Books, 1962), 336–46. Polanyi discusses the relation between individual liberty and spontaneously attained social order in "Manageability and Social Tasks," in *The Logic of Liberty: Reflections and Rejoinders* (Chicago: University of Chicago Press, 1951), 154–200.

8. See, for example, Adam Smith, *Lectures on Jurisprudence,* ed. R. L. Meek, D. D. Raphael, and P. G. Stein (Oxford: Clarendon Press, 1978), Report of 1762–63 [iv. 3–7], 200–202.

9. Adam Ferguson, *An Essay on the History of Civil Society,* ed. Duncan Forbes (Edinburgh: Edinburgh University Press, 1966), 123 (hereafter cited as *Essay*).

10. Ferguson, *Essay,* 123. Even despotism itself, Ferguson held, emerged as the unintended consequence of actions whose goal was unrelated to this end (*Essay,* 268).

11. See Harold T. Parker, *The Cult of Antiquity and the French Revolutionaries: A Study in the Development of the Revolutionary Spirit* (Chicago: University of Chicago Press, 1937), passim, esp. 146–70.

12. Jean Jacques Rousseau observed of the legislator that he must be able to change human nature and to alter man's very constitution in *Du contrat social* [II.vii] (*Oeuvres complètes,* ed. Bernard Gagnebin and Marcel Raymond, ["Bibliothèque de la Pléiade"; Paris: Librairie Gallimard, 1964], 3: 381–82). Even Edmund Burke at one point atypically wrote of "the wise legislators of all countries, who aimed at improving instincts into morals, and at grafting the virtues on the stock of the natural affections" ("Letters on a Regicide Peace" [Letter I: "On the Overtures of Peace" (1796)], in *The Works and Correspondence of the Right Honourable Edmund Burke,* 8 vols. [London: Francis & John Rivington, 1852], 5: 301).

13. Forbes, "Introduction," in Ferguson, *Essay,* xxiv.

14. Norman Barry, "The Tradition of Spontaneous Order," *Literature of Liberty* 5 (1982): 9, and F. A. Hayek, "Kinds of Rationalism," in *Studies in Philosophy, Politics and Economics,* 82–95. Hayek regards the term "antirationalism" as subject to misunderstanding and prefers to differentiate between two varieties of rationalism, the first of which he associates with Descartes and which he terms "constructivist rationalism." It is this species of rationalism that Hayek concludes is incompatible with the theory of spontaneous order.

15. Hume's examination of the nature of justice is contained in Book III, part ii, of the *Treatise.* The edition I have used is that edited by P. H. Nidditch (Oxford: Clarendon Press, 1978). This section of the *Treatise* has been the subject of detailed analysis. See Jonathan Harrison, *Hume's Theory of Justice* (Oxford: Clarendon Press, 1981).

16. "What Hume put before his contemporaries . . . was an exclusively secular because exclusively empirical . . . version of the fundamental principles of natural law, an attempt to lay the foundations of a science of morality and law in a science of man which had no need of the religion hypothesis" (Duncan Forbes, *Hume's Philosophical Politics* [Cambridge: Cambridge University Press, 1975], 68). Meinecke had noted as early as 1936 that what he regarded as one of Hume's most significant failings was his refusal to abandon totally the concept of natural law (Friedrich Meinecke, *Werke,* vol. 3, *Die Entstehung des Historismus,* ed. Carl Hinrichs [Munich: R. Oldenbourg Verlag, 1959], 195).

17. For Hume, "artificial phenomena are the result of the intervention of 'thought and reflexion' and . . . they, paradoxically, are natural in the sense that they exist with the same necessity as everything else in the world—which, of course, means that they are brought about by natural causes. . . . He explicitly refers to [this position] the first time he discusses the

distinction between natural and artificial in connection with moral qualities" (Knud Haakonssen, *The Science of a Legislator: The Natural Jurisprudence of David Hume and Adam Smith* [Cambridge: Cambridge University Press, 1981], 22).

18. The statement appears in Joseph J. Spengler, *Origins of Economic Thought and Justice* (Carbondale: Southern Illinois University Press, 1980), 57. The standard history of Chinese political and social theory describes Chuang Tzu's position as one in which "each person should pursue his own predilections; that is to say, others should not interfere with me. By . . . asserting that the world and the self should not interfere with or impose upon each other, one is led to the ideal of non-governing, and to the political method of 'letting the world alone'" (Kung-chuan Hsiao, *A History of Chinese Political Thought*, vol. 1, *From the Beginnings to the Sixth Century A. D.*, trans. F. W. Mote [Princeton: Princeton University Press, 1979], 306).

19. *The New Science of Giambattista Vico*, trans. Thomas Goddard Bergin and Max Harold Fisch, rev. ed. (Ithaca: Cornell University Press, 1984), 425 (par. 1108). The original reads: "Perché pur gli uomini hanno essi fatto questo mondo di nazioni . . . ma egli é questo mondo, senza dubbio, uscito da una mente spesso diversa ed alle volte tutta contraria e sempre superiore ad essi fini particolari ch 'essi uomini si avevan proposti; de' quali fini ristretti fatti mezzi per servire a fini più ampi, gli ha sempre adoperati per conservare l 'umana generazione in questa terra (*La Scienza Nuova*, ed. Fausto Nicolini, 3 vols. [Bari: Gius. Laterza & Figli, 1911–16], 3: 1048).

20. "'Scientific' Whiggism: Adam Smith and John Millar," 658.

21. In discussing Ferguson, Meinecke noted: "Die Einrichtungen der Gesellschaft, sagte er, sind dunklen und entfernten Ursprungs und entstehen aus natürlichen Trieben, nicht aus den Spekulationen der Menschen. Wie im Finstern tappen die Menschen an Anstalten hinan, die nicht beabsichtigt sind, sondern Erfolg ihrer Tätigkeit sind. . . . Roms und Spartas Verfassung, diese Lieblingsobjekte pragmatischer Staatsbetrachtung, beruhten für ihn nicht auf den Entwürfen einzelner Personen, sodern auf Situation und Genius des Volkes. Vico war einst einsam mit solchen Gedanken vorangegangen" (*Die Entstehung des Historismus*, 262–63).

22. Mandeville was familiar to, among others, Hume, Smith, and Ferguson, who all cited him. The significance of his connection to the Scottish Enlightenment writers is mentioned by Schneider, "Introduction," in *The Scottish Moralists*, xv(n.) and Barry, "The Tradition of Spontaneous Order," 16–17. Hayek observes of Mandeville that "almost everybody read him and few escaped infection" (F. A. Hayek, "Dr. Bernard Mandeville" [1967], in *New Studies in Philosophy, Politics, Economics and the History of Ideas* ([London: Routledge & Kegan Paul, 1978], 252). See also Alfred Espinas, "La troisième phase de la dissolution du mercantilisme," *Revue Internationale de Sociologie* 10 (1902): 162.

23. In 1705, Mandeville published a poem of some twenty-six pages, entitled *The Grumbling Hive: or, Knaves Turn'd Honest*. Some nine years later, Mandeville added a lengthy prose commentary to this earlier work and reissued it, again anonymously, under the title the *Fable of the Bees: or, Private Vices, Publick Virtues*. The work, which soon became notorious, went through several editions and was finally joined by a second volume in 1729. The standard edition is that edited by F. B. Kaye, 2 vols. (Oxford: Clarendon Press, 1924). All references to the *Fable of the Bees* (hereafter cited as *Fable*) that follow are to the Kaye edition.

24. Dugald Stewart, who studied moral philosophy at Glasgow under Thomas Reid, Smith's successor in that chair, and among whose writings is a biographical sketch of Adam Smith, suggested that Smith was directly influenced by Mandeville's discussion of the division of labor (Dugald Stewart, *Lectures on Political Economy*, vol. 1, *The Collected Works*, ed. Sir William Hamilton, 11 vols. [Edinburgh: Thomas Constable, 1854–60; facsimile reprint, Westmead: Gregg International Publishers, 1971], 8: 323). Indeed, the term "division of labor" itself appears to have been invented by Mandeville (Kaye, "Introduction," in Mandeville, *Fable*, 1: cxxxv).

25. Mandeville, *Fable*, 1: 26.

26. Mandeville, *Fable*, 1: 24.

27. Hayek, "Dr. Bernard Mandeville," 250. Hayek was anticipated in this view by Nathan Rosenberg, "Mandeville and Laissez-Faire," *Journal of the History of Ideas* 26 (1963): 183–96.

See also Alfred F. Chalk, "Mandeville's *Fable of the Bees:* A Reappraisal." *Southern Economic Journal* 33 (1966): 1–16, in which the author stresses Mandeville's contributions to the idea of the spontaneous development of social institutions while conceding his interventionist economic policies.

28. (Augustan Reprint Society publication 41 [Berkeley: University of California, William Andrews Clark Memorial Library, 1953]): 1–15; reprinted in Jacob Viner, *The Long View and the Short: Studies in Economic Theory and Policy* (Glencoe, Ill.: The Free Press, 1958), 332–42.

29. Kaye, "Introduction," in Mandeville, *Fable*, 1: xcviii–ciii; Alfred F. Chalk, "Natural Law and the Rise of Economic Individualism in England," *Journal of Political Economy* 59 (1951): 347. See also Albert Schatz, "Bernard de Mandeville: Contribution à l'étude des origines du libéralisme économique," *Vierteljahrschrift für Social- und Wirtschaftsgeschichte* 1 (1903): 434–80.

30. The position is a common one. See, for example, Kaye, "Introduction," in Mandeville, *Fable*, 1: cxxxiv–cxxxv, and Hayek, "Dr. Bernard Mandeville," 258. H. B. Acton has pointed out the similarity of context in which the notion of the invisible hand is first employed by Smith in his *Theory of Moral Sentiments* with the views earlier expressed in Mandeville's *Fable* (H. B. Acton, "Distributive Justice, the Invisible Hand and the Cunning of Reason," *Political Studies* 20 [1972]: 426–27).

31. Viner, "Introduction to Bernard Mandeville, *A Letter to Dion (1732)*," 341.

32. This reading is consistent with the little that is known of Mandeville's attitude towards contemporary politics. See H. T. Dickinson, "The Politics of Bernard Mandeville," in *Mandeville Studies: New Explorations in the Art and Thought of Dr. Bernard Mandeville (1670–1733)*, ed. Irwin Primer (The Hague: Martinus Nijhoff, 1975), 80–97.

33. Mandeville, *Fable*, 1: 369.

34. Rosenberg, "Mandeville and Laissez-Faire," 188.

35. M. M. Goldsmith, "Public Virtue and Private Vices: Bernard Mandeville and English Political Ideologies in the Early Eighteenth Century," *Eighteenth Century Studies* 9 (1976): 510.

36. Mandeville, *Fable*, 1: 299–300.

37. Mandeville, *Fable*, 2: 353. Both this quotation and the one preceding it are cited by Kaye and Hayek as decisive evidence that Mandeville had strong free-market leanings.

38. Rosenberg, "Mandeville and Laissez-Faire," 189. But see Thomas A. Horne, who argues that Mandeville was a thoroughgoing mercantilist who regarded economic individualism with little sympathy (*The Social Thought of Bernard Mandeville: Virtue and Commerce in Early Eighteenth-Century England* [London: Macmillan Press, 1978], 51–75).

39. Mandeville, *Fable*, 2: 141.

40. Mandeville, *Fable*, 2: 321–22.

41. See F. B. Kaye, "Mandeville on the Origin of Language," *Modern Language Notes* 39 (1924): 136–42.

42. Hayek, "Dr. Bernard Mandeville," 260.

43. Mandeville, *Fable*, 2: 142.

44. It bears repeating that Hume was only twenty-nine years old when the final volume of the *Treatise* first appeared in print.

45. In comparing Mandeville's use of the theory of spontaneous order with Hume's, Haakonssen notes: "Mandeville uses the idea in a rather general way, without too much attention to the details of the links between the individual causes and the over-all effect. . . . But the particular boldness in Hume is that he uses it in accounting for one of the traditionally most central, and in a way most 'sacred,' elements in social life, namely fundamental law itself, our very 'sense of justice'" (*The Science of a Legislator*, 21).

46. Hume, *Treatise* [III.iii.1], 579. Hume's ms. amendment to the first edition adds "and to every Individual" after "society" (672). Hume concluded similarly in his *Enquiry* that the benefit resulting from justice and fidelity "is not the consequence of every individual single act; but arises from the whole scheme or system, concurred in by the whole, or the greater part of the society. General peace and order are the attendants of justice or a general abstinence from the possession of others. But a particular regard to the particular right of one individual citizen

may frequently, considered in itself, be productive of pernicious consequences. The result of the individual acts is here, in many instances, directly opposite to that of the whole system of actions; and the former may be extremely hurtful, while the latter is, to the highest degree, advantageous. Riches, inherited from a parent, are, in a bad man's hand, the instrument of mischief. The right of succession may, in one instance, be hurtful. Its benefit arises only from the observance of the general rule" ("Appendix III: Some Farther Considerations With Regard to Justice," *An Enquiry Concerning the Principles of Morals* [hereafter cited as *Enquiry*], in *Essays Moral, Political, and Literary*, ed. T. H. Green and T. H. Grose, 2 vols., new ed. [London: Longmans, Green, 1882], 2: 273; facsimile reprint, vols. 3, 4 of David Hume, *The Philosophical Works* [Darmstadt: Scientia Verlag Aalen, 1964]).

47. Hume, *Treatise* [III.ii.6], 529.

48. Hume, *Treatise* [III.ii.6], 526.

49. Haakonssen, *The Science of a Legislator*, 21. For an extended discussion of the concept of spontaneous order in Hume's writings, see F. A. Hayek, "The Legal and Political Philosophy of David Hume," in *Hume*, ed. V. C. Chappell (Notre Dame: University of Notre Dame Press, 1968), 335–60.

50. Hume, *Treatise* [III.ii.2], 490. See also Hume, *Enquiry* [Appendix III], 2: 275.

51. Hume, *Dialogues Concerning Natural Religion*, ed. Norman Kemp Smith (Library of Liberal Arts, Indianapolis: Bobbs-Merrill, 1947) [part V]: 167.

52. Hume, *Dialogues* [part VII], 179. Hayek has suggested that in this work Hume adumbrated the notion of the evolution of biological organisms ("Legal and Political Philosophy of Hume," 356). "It is in vain," Hume noted, "to insist upon the uses of the parts in animals or vegetables, and their curious adjustment to each other. I would fain know how an animal could subsist, unless its parts were so adjusted? Do we not find, that it immediately perishes whenever this adjustment ceases, and that its matter corrupting tries some new form?" And in the following paragraph: "No form . . . can subsist, unless it possess those powers and organs, requisite for its subsistence: Some new order or economy must be tried, and so on, without intermission; till at last some order, which can support and maintain itself, is fallen upon" (*Dialogues* [part VIII], 185).

53. Schneider, "Introduction," *The Scottish Moralists*, xxxvi.

54. Hume, "Of Commerce," in *Essays Moral, Political, and Literary*, 1: 294–95.

55. Hume, *Enquiry* [V.ii], 2: 212 (n.).

56. Schneider, "Introduction," *The Scottish Moralists*, xxxv.

57. David Hume, *The History of England From the Invasion of Julius Caesar to the Revolution in 1688*, 6 vols. (Indianapolis: Liberty Classics, 1983–85), 2: 525.

58. Hayek, "The Legal and Political Philosophy of David Hume," 340.

59. See Haakonssen, *The Science of a Legislator*, 61–63.

60. Adam Smith, *The Theory of Moral Sentiments*, ed. D. D. Raphael and A. L. Macfie (Oxford: Clarendon Press, 1976) [III.4.8], 159 (hereafter cited as *Moral Sentiments*).

61. Smith, *Moral Sentiments* [I.i.1.5], 10.

62. See T. D. Campbell, *Adam Smith's Science of Morals* (London: George Allen & Unwin, 1971), 94–106.

63. Smith, *Moral Sentiments* [I.iii.2.1], 50.

64. Andrew S. Skinner, *A System of Social Science: Papers Relating to Adam Smith* (Oxford: Clarendon Press, 1979), 57.

65. "Upon this disposition of mankind, to go along with all the passions of the rich and powerful, is founded the distinction of ranks, and the order of society" (Smith, *Moral Sentiments* [I.iii.2.3.], 52).

66. Smith, *Moral Sentiments* [IV.1.10], 183–84.

67. Smith contended that "the rules of justice are the only rules of morality which are precise and accurate" (*Moral Sentiments* [VII.iv.1], 327). And at another point, he claimed that in terms of their precision, accuracy, and indispensability, "the rules of justice may be compared to the rules of grammar" (*Moral Sentiments* [III.6.11], 175). W. F. Campbell sees in this analogy a significant departure from the rationalist theories of natural law in favor of a more

44 · NOTES TO PAGE 15

evolutionary conception of justice. Unlike the laws of mathematics, which have "an absolute-ness and an a priori fixity, an independence from human will," to which Smith *might* have compared the rules of justice, the rules of grammar differ from society to society. "However," continues Campbell, "for any person living in a concrete society, the rules of grammar are fixed, and one can live with a long-run certainty that they will not be changed tomorrow. The rules of justice are established by a similar process; like grammar they are established by a slow process of social consensus, they are fixed for long periods of time without alteration, thus permitting individuals to make long-range plans without worrying about their being switched overnight" (W. F. Campbell, "Adam Smith's Theory of Justice, Prudence, and Beneficence," in *Adam Smith: Critical Assessments*, ed. John Cunningham Wood, 4 vols. [London: Croom Helm, 1984], 1: 353–54. [This article originally appeared in the *American Economic Review* 57 (1967): 571–77]).

68. "Smith based his discussion of rights on the work of the classical natural rights theorists, Grotius, Pufendorf and, in particular, his own teacher and predecessor in the Glasgow Chair [of Moral Philosophy], Francis Hutcheson" (Peter G. Stein, "Adam Smith's Theory of Law and Society," in *Classical Influences on Western Thought, A. D. 1650–1870*, ed. R. R. Bolgar, Proceedings of the Third International Conference on the Classical Influences on Western Thought, King's College, Cambridge, March 1977 [Cambridge: Cambridge University Press, 1979], 264).

69. Smith, *Lectures on Jurisprudence*, Report of 1762–63 [i.12], 8.

70. Haakonssen, *The Science of a Legislator*, 105. For an extended discussion of this aspect of Smith's thought, see Peter Stein, *Legal Evolution: The Story of an Idea* (Cambridge: Cambridge University Press, 1980), 29–50.

71. Smith, *Lectures on Jurisprudence*, Report of 1762–63 [i.26–27], 14.

72. "If identity of views is proved by expressed admiration," T. D. Campbell concludes, "there is more reason to say that Smith followed Hume in his attack on the natural law tradition. . . . Smith denies that reason plays a central part in human behavior in general and in moral judgment in particular. This shows in his rejection of casuistry, his argument against utility as the ground of approbation and his repeated insistence that reason cannot provide a motivational basis for morality. In jurisprudence his main interest lies in describing the content of positive law and explaining its origin and development. In so far as this is carrying on the tradition of *ius gentium*, it does so in the most empirical meaning of this concept" (T. D. Campbell, *Adam Smith's Science of Morals*, 58). See also H. J. Bittermann, "Adam Smith's Empiricism and the Law of Nature," in *Adam Smith: Critical Assessments*, 1: 190–235. (Bittermann's article originally appeared in two parts in the *Journal of Political Economy* 48 [1940]: 487–520, 703–34).

73. See particularly Sir John Dalrymple, *Essay Towards a General History of Feudal Property in Great Britain* (London: A. Millar, 1757); Henry Home, Lord Kames, *Historical Law-Tracts*, 2 vols. (Edinburgh: A. Kincaid and J. Bell, 1758) and the second edition of his *Essays on the Principles of Morality and Natural Religion* (Edinburgh: R. Fleming and A. Donaldson, 1758); William Robertson, *History of America*, 2 vols. (London: W. Strahan, 1777); and John Millar, *The Origin of the Distinction of Ranks*, 3d ed. (London: John Murray, 1779). A slightly altered version of the four-stages theory appears in Adam Ferguson, *An Essay on the History of Civil Society* (London: A. Strahan and P. Caddell, 1767).

74. The development of the four-stages doctrine and its role in shaping Marx's sociology is dealt with in Ronald L. Meek, "The Scottish Contribution to Marxist Sociology," in *Democracy and the Labour Movement: Essays in Honour of Dona Torr*, ed. John Saville (London: Lawrence and Wishart, 1954), 84–102. (This essay has been reprinted in somewhat modified form in Ronald L. Meek, *Economics and Ideology and Other Essays: Studies in the Development of Economic Thought* [London: Chapman and Hall, 1967], 34–50.) Meek's analysis has since been expanded to encompass the French as well as the Scottish proponents of the four-stages theory. See his "Smith, Turgot, and the 'Four-Stages' Theory," *History of Political Economy* 3 (1971): 9–27 (reprinted in *Adam Smith: Critical Assessments*, 4: 142–55), and particularly his *Social Science and the Ignoble Savage* (Cambridge: Cambridge University Press, 1976).

75. Adam Smith, *An Inquiry into the Nature and Causes of the Wealth of Nations*, ed. R. H. Campbell and A. S. Skinner, 2 vols. (Oxford: Clarendon Press, 1976) [V.i.b.2], 2: 709.
76. Smith, *Lectures on Jurisprudence*, Report dated 1766 [5], 398.
77. Smith, *Lectures on Jurisprudence*, Report of 1762–63 [i.1], 5. In the *Wealth of Nations*, Smith noted that the inequality of fortune that emerges in the age of pasturage "introduces some degree of that civil government which is indispensably necessary for its own preservation; and it seems to do this naturally, and even independent of the consideration of that necessity" [V.i.b.12] 2: 715).
78. Smith, *Lectures on Jurisprudence*, Report of 1762–63 [i.30–32], 15–16.
79. Smith, *Lectures on Jurisprudence*, Report of 1762–63 [i.32–35], 16. At one point Smith seems to have subscribed to Locke's view of property rights: "The property which every man has in his own labour, as it is the original foundation of all other property, so it is the most sacred and inviolable" (*Wealth of Nations* [I.x.c.12], 1: 138). But see Haakonssen's analysis of this statement within the context in which it appears in Smith's work (*The Science of a Legislator*, 106).
80. The term was coined by Dugald Stewart and refers to "a particular sort of inquiry, which, so far as I know, is entirely of modern origin, and which seems, in a peculiar degree, to have interested Mr. Smith's curiosity. Something very similar to it may be traced in all his different works, whether moral, political, or literary; and on all these subjects he has exemplified it with the happiest success" (Stewart, "Account of the Life and Writings of Adam Smith, LL.D.," in *Biographical Memoirs of Adam Smith, LL.D., William Robertson, D.D., Thomas Reid, D.D.*, in *The Collected Works*, 10: 33–34).
81. Forbes, "'Scientific' Whiggism: Adam Smith and John Millar," 655–57.
82. Smith, *Wealth of Nations* [III.iv.10], 1: 418–19.
83. Smith, *Wealth of Nations* [III.iv.17], 1: 422.
84. Smith, *Wealth of Nations* [V.i.g.25], 2: 803–4.
85. Smith, *Wealth of Nations* [V.i.g.24], 2: 802–3.
86. Smith, *Wealth of Nations* [V.i.b.21], 2: 720.
87. The term, as Forbes notes, originally appeared in Herman Huth, "Soziale und Individualistische Auffassung im 18. Jahrhundert, vornehmlich bei Adam Smith und Adam Ferguson," *Staats- und Sozialwissenschaftliche Forschungen* (Leipzig: Duncker und Humblot, 1907), 158, who wrote of "das Gesetz der Heterogonie der Zwecke."
88. Forbes, "'Scientific' Whiggism: Adam Smith and John Millar," 653.
89. Smith, *Wealth of Nations* [I.ii.1], 1: 25. In an interesting essay concerning Smith's advice respecting public policy, T. D. Campbell and I. S. Ross have noted that Smith, as is the case here, repeatedly "attempts to demonstrate the unintended utilitarian consequences of non-utilitarian motivations" ("Adam Smith's Utilitarian Policy Advice," *Journal of the History of Ideas* 42 [1981]: 76).
90. The term appears in Smith's "History of Astronomy" [III.2], which was most likely written before the *Theory of Moral Sentiments*. See Alec Macfie, "The Invisible Hand of Jupiter," *Journal of the History of Ideas* 32 (1971): 595–99.
91. Smith, *Moral Sentiments* [IV.1.10], 184–85.
92. Smith, *Wealth of Nations* [IV.ii.9], 1: 456.
93. Smith, *Wealth of Nations* [IV.ii.9], 1: 456.
94. Smith, *Wealth of Nations* [IV.ix.50–51], 2: 687. Smith apparently formulated at least a portion of his theory of natural liberty at least twenty-five years prior to the publication of the *Wealth of Nations*. Dugald Stewart cited a portion of a manuscript presented by Smith in 1755, in which Smith referred to the fact that the opinions there expressed were treated at length in a series of lectures delivered at Glasgow at least six years earlier. The portion quoted by Stewart reads: "Man is generally considered by statesmen and projectors as the materials of a sort of political mechanics. Projectors disturb nature in the course of her operations in human affairs; and it requires no more than to let her alone, and give her fair play in the pursuit of her ends, that she may establish her own designs. . . . Little else is requisite to carry a State to the highest degree of opulence from the lowest barbarism, but peace, easy taxes, and a tolerable administration of justice; all the rest being brought about by the natural course of things. All

46 · NOTES TO PAGES 20–22

governments which thwart this natural course, which force things into another channel, or which endeavour to arrest the progress of society at a particular point, are unnatural, and to support themselves are obliged to be oppressive and tyrannical" (Stewart, "Account of the Life and Writings of Adam Smith," in *The Collected Works*, 10: 68).

95. Smith, *Wealth of Nations* [IV.ix.51], 2: 687–88.

96. Smith, *Moral Sentiments* [II.II.3.3], 86.

97. Smith, *Wealth of Nations* [II.ii.89–94], 1: 322–24.

98. Smith, *Wealth of Nations* [V.ii.h.17], 2: 863.

99. Smith, *Wealth of Nations* [V.i.f.48–50], 2: 781–82.

100. Smith, *Wealth of Nations* [IV.vi.19], 2: 551.

101. Smith, *Wealth of Nations* [V.ii.g.4], 2: 853.

102. Smith, *Wealth of Nations* [V.i.e.30], 2: 754.

103. Smith, *Wealth of Nations* [I.x.c.13], 1: 138–39.

104. Smith, *Wealth of Nations* [II.iv.15], 1: 357.

105. For extended discussions of Smith's views respecting the legitimate functions of government, especially with respect to the economy, see Viner, "Adam Smith and Laissez-Faire," in *Adam Smith: Critical Assessments*, 1: 143–67 (reprinted from the *Journal of Political Economy*, 35 [1927]: 198–232), and Skinner, *A System of Social Science*, 209–37.

106. See, for example, Viner, "Adam Smith and Laissez-Faire," in *Adam Smith: Critical Assessments*, 1: 143–67; James M. Buchanan, "Public Goods and Natural Liberty," in *The Market and the State: Essays in Honour of Adam Smith*, ed. Thomas Wilson and Andrew S. Skinner (Oxford: Clarendon Press, 1976), 271–86; and E. G. West, "Adam Smith's Public Economics: A Re-evaluation," *Canadian Journal of Economics* 10 (1977): 1–18 (reprinted in *Adam Smith: Critical Assessments*, 1: 640–55).

107. Viner, "Adam Smith and Laissez-Faire," in *Adam Smith: Critical Assessments*, 1: 157.

108. Laurence S. Moss, "The Economics of Adam Smith: Professor Hollander's Reappraisal," in *Adam Smith: Critical Assessments*, 4: 211 (reprinted from *History of Political Economy* 8 [1976]: 564–74).

109. Smith, *Moral Sentiments* [II.i.5.10], 77–78.

110. Smith, *Moral Sentiments* [II.i.5.10], 77. Consider also the following observation: "In every part of the universe we observe means adjusted with the nicest artifice to the ends which they are intended to produce; and in the mechanism of a plant, or animal body, admire how every thing is contrived for advancing the two great purposes of nature, the support of the individual, and the propagation of the species. But in these, and in all such objects, we still distinguish the efficient from the final cause of their several motions and organizations. The digestion of the food, the circulation of the blood, and the secretion of the several juices which are drawn from it, are operations all of them necessary for the great purposes of animal life. Yet we never endeavour to account for them from those purposes as from their efficient causes, nor imagine that the blood circulates, or that the food digests of its own accord, and with a view or intention to the purposes of circulation or digestion. The wheels of the watch are all admirably adjusted to the end for which it was made, the pointing of the hour. All their various motions conspire in the nicest manner to produce this effect. If they were endowed with a desire and intention to produce it, they could not do it better. Yet we never ascribe any such desire or intention to them, but to the watch-maker, and we know that they are put into motion by a spring, which intends the effect it produces as little as they do. But though, in accounting for the operations of bodies, we never fail to distinguish in this manner the efficient from the final cause, in accounting for those of the mind we are very apt to confound these two different things with one another. When by natural principles we are led to advance those ends, which a refined and enlightened reason would recommend to us, we are very apt to impute to that reason, as to their efficient cause, the sentiments and actions by which we advance those ends, and to imagine that to be the wisdom of man, which in reality is the wisdom of God. Upon a superficial view, this cause seems sufficient to produce the effects which are ascribed to it; and the system of

human nature seems to be more simple and agreeable when all its different operations are in this manner deduced from a single principle" (Smith, *Moral Sentiments* [II.ii.3.5], 87). This distinction between Nature's ends and the mechanisms by which these ends are accomplished is quoted approvingly by Stewart in his *Elements of the Philosophy of the Human Mind*, vol. 2, in *The Collected Works*, 3: 351–52.

111. Ferguson. *Essay*, 182.

112. "Among hunters," Smith remarked, "there is no regular government. . . . The appropriation of herds and flocks, which introduced an inequality of fortune, was that which first gave rise to regular government. Till there be property there can be no government, the very end of which is to secure wealth, and to defend the rich from the poor" (Smith, *Lectures on Jurisprudence*, Report dated 1766 [19–20], 404).

The relation between property and government among the Scottish Enlightenment thinkers is ably discussed in Roy Pascal, "Property and Society: The Scottish Historical School of the Eighteenth Century," *Modern Quarterly* (London) 1 (1938): 167–79. See also Paul Bowles. "The Origin of Property and the Development of Scottish Historical Science," *Journal of the History of Ideas* 46 (1985): 197–209. Bowles argues that with Smith, the Scottish thinkers abandoned the view that property had its basis in natural law in favor of the view that property, like other social institutions, emerged as the product of evolutionary forces.

113. Ferguson. *Essay*, 82.

114. Ferguson. *Essay*, 81–96.

115. Ferguson. *Essay*, 96–107.

116. Ferguson. *Principles of Moral and Political Science; Being Chiefly a Retrospect of Lectures Delivered in the College of Edinburgh*, 2 vols. (Edinburgh: W. Creech, 1792) [I.iii.1], 1: 201 (hereafter cited as *Principles*).

117. Ferguson. *Principles* [I.iii.13], 1: 313–14.

118. Ferguson. *Principles* [I.i.4], 1: 43. Dugald Stewart twice quoted this passage in his own discussions of the nature of language. See Stewart's *Dissertation: Exhibiting the Progress of Metaphysical, Ethical, and Political Philosophy, Since the Revival of Letters in Europe* (1815–1821), in *The Collected Works*, 1: 365, and *Elements of the Philosophy of the Human Mind*, vol. 3. in *The Collected Works*, 4: 27.

119. Ferguson. *Essay*, 122.

120. Ferguson. *Essay*, 122.

121. The definitive biography of Kames is that by Ian S. Ross, *Lord Kames and the Scotland of his Day* (Oxford: Clarendon Press, 1972). See also W. C. Lehmann, *Henry Home, Lord Kames, and the Scottish Enlightenment: A Study in National Character and the History of Ideas* (The Hague: Martinus Nijhoff, 1971), and Arthur E. McGuinness, *Henry Home, Lord Kames* (New York: Twayne Publishers, 1970). McGuinness' brief study confines itself to three of Kames' works, his *Essays on the Principles of Morality and Natural Religion*, the *Elements of Criticism*, and the *Sketches on the History of Man*.

122. On the question of priority to the notion, together with its broader implications, as between Kames and Smith, Meek notes: "What the question . . . at issue really comes down to . . . is simply whether Smith had also been employing the theory . . . in (or before) the mid-1750s, and, if so, whether details of his analysis were likely to have come to the notice of Kames. The answer to both these questions seems to me very probably to be 'yes'" (*Social Science and the Ingnoble Savage*, 107).

Kames adumbrated his discussion of the connection between the principal forms of property that marked successive earlier societies and the evolution of a formalized civil structure as early as the mid-1740s, in his essay "Touching the Hereditary and Indefeasible Right of Kings." He there noted that "while Acorns were the Food of Man, and Water his Drink, there was neither Use nor Appetite for Society. Accordingly we find Mankind originally in every Corner of the Earth living in scattered Habitations, with little Intercourse, except among the Members of the same Family. The Culture of Corn laid the Foundation of a more extensive Intercourse, because thereby mutual Alliance became necessary. When Arts were invented, and Industry

48 · Notes to Pages 26–29

increased, it was found convenient to herd together in Towns and Villages. From this closser [sic] Connection one Evil sprung, Opposition of Interests, formally rare; which at first was the Occasion of Quarrels and Bloodshed, and afterwards of frequent Appeals to Men of Weight and Probity. In Time the Necessity of fixed Judges to determine Differences being discovered, the Election of these Judges, which could not otherways be than popular, was the first Step to Government" (Appendix, *Essays upon Several Subjects concerning British Antiquities* [Edinburgh: A. Kincaid, 1747]: 194–95). Although not published until 1747, these essays were composed in 1745 and, like so many of Kames' works, were originally published anonymously.

123. Kames, *Historical Law-Tracts*, 2d ed. (Edinburgh: A. Kincaid and J. Bell, 1761), 50–51 (n.).

124. [Henry Home, Lord Kames,] *Essays on the Principles of Morality and Natural Religion*, 2d ed. (London: C. Hitch and L. Hawes, 1758; facsimile reprint, Hildesheim: Georg Olms Verlag, 1976), 77–78 (hereafter cited as *Essays*).

125. [Kames], *Essays*, 81.

126. "Nothing can be more evident, than that relying upon the sense of property, and the prevalence of justice, a few individuals ventured at first to unite for mutual defence and mutual support; and finding the manifold comforts of such a state, that they afterwards gradually united into larger and larger societies" ([Kames], *Essays*, 82).

127. See Lehmann, *Henry Home, Lord Kames*, 177–94.

128. [Kames], *Essays*, 64–66.

129. [Kames], *Essays*, 66.

130. [Gilbert Stuart], *An Historical Dissertation concerning the Antiquity of the English Constitution* (Edinburgh: A. Kincaid and J. Bell, 1768): 222–23.

131. Thomas Reid, *Essays on the Active Powers of Man*, in *Philosophical Works*, ed. Sir William Hamilton, 8th ed., 2 vols. (Edinburgh: J. Thin, 1895; facsimile reprint, Hildesheim: Georg Olms Verlagsbuchhandlung, 1967) [III.i.2], 2: 545 (hereafter cited as *Essays*.).

132. James Burnett, Lord Monboddo (1714–99), one of the lesser but more fascinating writers of the Scottish Enlightenment, had made a similar point in 1782. Schneider has called attention to the parallels between Reid's views and the following observation. "I believe," wrote Monboddo, "nobody will maintain . . . that [the bee] knows the rules of Geometry, by which it makes its hexagons, and joins them together in such a way, that, with the least expence of materials, it makes its cells contain the greatest quantity of honey possible. . . . It is therefore admitted that the Bee is no Geometer. . . . The Bee, however, acts by Intelligence, though she has it not herself, but by an Intelligence much superior to the human, no less Intelligence than the Divine. Nor ought we to be surprised that a Being not intelligent should act intelligently: For it often happens, even among us who have Intelligence, that we act by an Intelligence superior to our own, doing what we are directed to do by men wiser than we, without knowing for what purpose we act. And this I say is the case of every well governed society, where by far the greater part of the subjects act by rules, of which they do not understand the reason" (*Antient Metaphysics: or, the Science of Universals*, 6 vols. [Edinburgh: J. Balfour, 1779–1799; facsimile reprint, New York: Garland Publishing, 1977], 2 (1782): 299–300. Consider also the following: "The bee . . . forms here hexagon cells as accurately as if she had been instructed by Euclid; yet it is impossible to believe, that she understands geometry, and knows the rules by which she works, or even the end for which she works. It is therefore only instinct" ([James Burnett, Lord Monboddo], *Of the Origin and Progress of Language*, vol. 1, 2d ed. [Edinburgh: J. Balfour, 1774; facsimile reprint, New York: Garland Publishing, 1970]: 412. [The first edition of volume one of the work originally appeared in 1773, while the sixth and final volume was published in 1792.]).

Monboddo's life and works are discussed at some length in William Knight, *Lord Monboddo and Some of His Contemporaries* (London: John Murray, 1900), and E. L. Cloyd, *James Burnett, Lord Monboddo* (Oxford: Clarendon Press, 1972).

133. Reid, *Essays* [III.i.2], 2: 546–47.

134. Reid, *Essays* [III.ii.3], 2: 558.

135. Millar was able to extend the period covered by his study of the historical development of the English constitution to the Glorious Revolution but the additions did not appear in published form before his death. In 1803, the full work, including the earlier published portion, appeared in print and the subtitle was altered to *From the Settlement of the Saxons in Britain to the Revolution of 1688.*

136. See John Craig, "An Account of the Life and Writings of John Millar," in John Millar, *The Origin of the Distinction of Ranks: or, An Inquiry into the Circumstances which Give Rise to Influence and Authority in the Different Members of Society*, 4th ed. (Edinburgh: William Blackwood, 1806), i–cxxxiv. (This is the only edition to which Craig's "Life" is prefixed.) See also William C. Lehmann, *John Millar of Glasgow, 1735–1801: His Life and Thought and his Contribution to Sociological Analysis* (Cambridge: Cambridge University Press, 1960), 9–86.

137. [Craig's *Life of Millar*], *Edinburgh Review* 9 (1806–7): 84.

138. Millar, *Distinction of Ranks*, 3–4. (Lehmann's *John Millar of Glasgow* contains a complete reprinting of Millar's *Distinction of Ranks*; the quotation can be found on p. 176.)

139. The quotation is taken from Essay VII, "The Principles of Law and Government" (subjoined to Millar's *An Historical View of the English Government: From the Settlement of the Saxons in Britain to the Revolution of 1688*, ed. John Craig and James Mylne, 4 vols. [London: Mawman, 1803], 4: 266–310; reprinted in Lehmann, *John Millar of Glasgow*, 345).

140. The reference is to the Swiss legal theorist Jean Louis De Lolme (1740–1806), whose *Constitution de l'Angleterre* was published in 1771.

141. John Millar, *An Historical View of the English Government: From the Settlement of the Saxons in Britain to the Accession of the House of Stewart* (London: A. Strahan and T. Cadell, 1787) [I.xii], 222.

142. John Veitch, "A Memoir of Dugald Stewart," in Stewart, *The Collected Works*, 10: xlix.

143. *Elements of the Philosophy of the Human Mind*, vol. 1, in *The Collected Works*, 2: 227.

144. *Elements of the Philosophy of the Human Mind*, vol. 2, in *The Collected Works*, 3: 333.

145. *Lectures on Political Economy*, vol. 2, in *The Collected Works*, 9: 419.

146. *Lectures on Political Economy*, vol. 2, in *The Collected Works*, 9: 423.

147. Veitch, "A Memoir of Dugald Stewart," in Stewart, *The Collected Works*, 10: li. One historian has remarked of the late eighteenth century that "in no earlier period would young English aristocrats like the future Lords Lansdowne and Melbourne have been sent to Scottish universities. The most obvious example of Scottish cultural influence is the *Edinburgh Review*, but Political Economy was, at least till Ricardo, a distinctly Scottish export and was disseminated by Scots like James Mill and McCulloch" (J. W. Burrow, *Evolution and Society: A Study in Victorian Social Theory* [Cambridge: Cambridge University Press, 1966], 15 [n.]). Both Lansdowne and Mill were students of Stewart's.

148. Veitch, "A Memoir of Dugald Stewart," in Stewart, *The Collected Works*, liv–lv (n.), lviii–lxix (n.), and James McCosh, *The Scottish Philosophy: Biographical, Expository, Critical, From Hutcheson to Hamilton* (London: Macmillan, 1875; facsimile reprint, Hildesheim: Georg Olms Verlagsbuchhandlung, 1966), 283.

149. ["Millar's *View of the English Gove*"], *Edinburgh Review* 3 (1803–4): 157.

150. Robert Brown has called attention to Bossuet's statement and has suggested that it constitutes a link between the common Christian notion that man proposes while God disposes and the theory of the invisible hand. See his *The Nature of Social Laws: Machiavelli to Mill* (Cambridge: Cambridge University Press, 1984), 67–68.

151. Jacques-Bénigne Bossuet, *Discourse on Universal History*, trans. Elborg Forster (Chicago: University of Chicago Press, 1976), 375. The original reads: "[Tous ceux qui gouvernent] font plus ou moins qu'ils ne pensent, et leurs conseils n'ont jamais manqué d'avoir des effets imprévus. Ni ils ne sont maîtres des dispositions que les siècles passés ont mises dans les affaires, ni ils ne peuvent prévoir le cours que prendra l'avenir, loin qu'ils le puissent forcer . . . En un mot, il n'y a point de puissance humaine qui ne serve malgré elle à d'autres desseins que les siens. Dieu seul sait tout réduire à sa volonté. C'est pourquoi tout est surprenant, à ne regarder

que les causes particulières, et néanmoins tout s'avance avec une suite réglée" (*Discours sur l'Historie Universelle*, in *Oeuvres de Bossuet*, 43 vols. [Versailles: J. A. Lebel, 1815–19], 35: 558–59).

152. "We are afraid to put men to live and trade each on his own private stock of reason: because we suspect that the stock in each man is small, and that the individuals would do better to avail themselves of the general bank and capital of nations and of ages" (Burke, *Reflections on the Revolution in France* [1790], in *Works and Correspondence*, 4: 222).

For a particularly insightful discussion of this aspect of Burke's thought, see J. G. A. Pocock, "Burke and the Ancient Constitution—a Problem in the History of Ideas," *The Historical Journal* 3 (1960): 125–43.

153. "Letters on a Regicide Peace" (Letter II: "On the Genius and Character of the French Revolution as it Regards Other Nations" [1796]), in *Works and Correspondence*, 5: 339 (Burke's italics).

154. *Reflections on the Revolution in France*, in *Works and Correspondence*, 4: 200. Burke's conclusions appear to have issued from the seventeenth-century notion, shaped by the British common-law theorists, that the English constitution was a product of custom rather than of reason. Burke's views are especially similar to those put forward by Sir Matthew Hale, Chief Justice of the King's Bench, in Hale's reply to Hobbes' *Dialogue of the Common Laws*. At one point Hale remarks: "Againe it is a reason for me to preferre a Law by wch a Kingdome hath been happily governed four or five hundrd yeares then to adventure the happiness and Peace of a Kingdome upon Some new Theory of my owne tho' I am better acquainted wth the reasonableness of my owne theory then wth that Law. Againe I have reason to assure myselfe that Long Experience makes more discoveries touching conveniences or Inconveniences of Laws then is possible for the wisest Councill of Men att first to foresee. And that those amendmts and Supplemts that through the various Experiences of wise and knowing men have been applyed to any Law must needs be better suited to the Convenience of Laws, then the best Invention of the most pregnant witts not ayded by Such a Series and tract of Experience" ("Reflections by the Lrd. Cheife Justice Hale on Mr. Hobbes His Dialogue of the Lawe," reprinted as an appendix to W. S. Holdsworth, *A History of English Law*, vol. 5, 2d ed. [London: Methuen, 1937]: 504). First published posthumously in 1715, there is some evidence that Hale's reply was composed shortly before February 1673.

Hale's contributions to the doctrine of the ancient constitution in British legal thought as well as the relation of this theory to Burke's views is analyzed by J. G. A. Pocock, "Burke and the Ancient Constitution," and in his *The Ancient Constitution and the Feudal Law: A Study of English Historical Thought in the Seventeenth Century* (Cambridge: Cambridge University Press, 1957), 148–81, 229–51.

155. Compare F. A. Hayek, who writes of "the necessity in any complex society in which the effects of anyone's action reach far beyond his possible range of vision, of the individual submitting to the anonymous and seemingly irrational forces of society" ("Individualism: True and False," in *Individualism and Economic Order*, 24). At another point Hayek refers to "that higher, superindividual wisdom which, in a certain sense, the products of spontaneous social growth may possess" (*Constitution of Liberty*, 110).

156. See Samuel Coleman, "Is There Reason in Tradition?," in *Politics and Experience: Essays Presented to Professor Michael Oakeshott on the Occasion of his Retirement* ed. Preston King and B. C. Parekh (Cambridge: Cambridge University Press, 1968), 239–82.

Appendix: Works by the Scottish writers discussed in this essay[1]

The following bibliography is limited to those editions of the works of the various Scottish writers discussed in this monograph that were published prior to approximately a decade following the death of the author. The one exception concerns the posthumous appearance of a work, in which case the facts of its first publication are given.

Although every attempt has been made to construct a complete bibliography within these limits, it is possible that some editions and particularly certain translations have escaped notice. Facts of publication, including the publisher and number of volumes or pages, of each work are shown where this information was available.

Adam Ferguson (1723–1816)

1746   *A Sermon [on 2 Sam. ix. 12] Preached in the Ersh Language to His Majesty's Highland Regiment of Foot, Commanded by Lord John Murray, at their Cantonment at Camberwell, on the 18th Day of December 1745, Being Appointed as a Solemn Fast.* London: Printed for A. Millar. [23 p.]

1756   [**Anonymous**]. *Reflections Previous to the Establishment of a Militia.* London: Printed for R. and J. Dodsley, in Pall Mall. [53 p.]

1757   [**Anonymous**]. *The Morality of Stage Plays Seriously Considered.* Edinburgh. [29 p.]

1760   *Of Natural Philosophy: For the Use of Students in the College of Edinburgh.* Edinburgh. [36 p.]

Attributed to Ferguson. The only extant copy, in the University of Edinburgh Library, is missing the title-page.

1761   [**Anonymous**]. *The History of the Proceedings in the Case of Margaret, Commonly Called Peg, Only Lawful Sister of John Bull, Esq.* London: Printed for W. Owen, near Temple Bar. [188 p.]

Actually published in December 1760. While this satire has traditionally been ascribed to Adam Ferguson, in 1982 David Raynor issued a new edition of the work attributing its authorship to David Hume (*Sister Peg: A Pamphlet Hitherto Unknown by David Hume* [Cambridge: Cambridge University Press, 1982]). Most critics, however, have concluded that the evidence Raynor marshals is insufficient to support the view that Hume did in fact compose the essay.

1761 2nd edition. London: Printed for W. Owen, near Temple Bar. [iv + 188 p.]

There also appears to be a variant of this edition in 86 pages.

1769 *The History of John Bull, with large explanatory notes; as also of the proceedings in the case of Margaret, commonly called Peg, only lawful sister to John Bull, Esq., with a complete key.* Edinburgh: Printed by David Willison. [200 p. + 106 p.]

Part 1 consists of John Arbuthnot's "Law is a Bottomless Pit," while Part 2 originally appeared as "The History of the Proceedings in the Case of Margaret."

1776 *Law is a Bottomless Pit; or the History of John Bull: Published from a Manuscript found in the Cabinet of the Famous Sir H. Polesworth, in the Year 1712.* London: Printed for M. Cowper, Paternoster Row. [200 p. + 106 p.]

As in the edition of 1769, "Sister Peg" appears as Part 2 of the work.

1766 **[Anonymous]. *Analysis of Pneumatics and Moral Philosophy. For the Use of Students in the College of Edinburgh*. Edinburgh: Sold by A. Kincaid & J. Bell. [55 p.]**

1767 *An Essay on the History of Civil Society*. Edinburgh: Printed for A. Millar and T. Caddel [*sic*] in the Strand, London; and A. Kincaid and J. Bell, Edinburgh. [vii + 430 p.]

1767 Dublin: Printed by Boulter Grierson. [viii + 416 p.]

1768 2nd edition, corrected. London: Printed for A. Millar and T. Cadell, in the Strand and A. Kincaid and J. Bell, Edinburgh. [vii + 430 p.]

1768 3rd edition, corrected. London: Printed for A. Millar and T. Cadell in the Strand and A. Kincaid and J. Bell, Edinburgh. [vii + 464 p.]

1773 4th edition, revised and corrected. Printed for T. Caddel [*sic*] in the Strand and A. Kincaid, W. Creech and J. Bell, Edinburgh. [vii + 466 p.]

1782 5th edition. Printed for T. Cadell, in the Strand, and W. Creech and J. Bell, Edinburgh. [vii + 468 p.]

1789 A new edition. Basil: Printed for J.J. Tourneisen, Paris, sold by Pissot. [vi + 424 p.]

1791 Basil. Tourneisen.

1793 6th edition. Printed for T. Cadell, in the Strand, and W. Creech and Bell and Bradfute, at Edinburgh. [vii + 468 p.]

1809	7th edition. Boston: Hastings, Etheridge and Bliss. [vii + 464 p.]
1814	7th edition. Edinburgh: Printed for Bell & Bradfute. [vii + 468 p.]
1819	8th edition. Philadelphia: Published by A. Finlay. [viii + 506 p.]

Translations: *French*

1783	*Essai sur l'histoire de la société civile*. Translated from the English by M. [Claude-François] Bergier. Revised, with annotations and an introduction by [Alexandre-Joseph] Meunier. Paris: La veuve Desaint. [2 vols.]
1796	New edition. Paris: Volland.

German

1768	*Versuch über die Geschichte der bürgerlichen Gesellschaft*. Translated by Christian Friedrich Jünger. Leipzig: Bey Johann Friedrich Junius. [viii + 437 p.]

Italian

1791–92	*Saggio sopra la storia di società civile di Adamo Ferguson*. Translated from the English by M. Bergier and then from the French into Italian by Tommaso Cerato. Venice: nella Stamperia Turra. [2 vols.]
1807	*Saggio circa la storia di civile società di Adamo Ferguson*. Translated by [Pietro] Antoniutti. Venice: della Tipografia Santini, Andrea. [viii + 256 p.]

Russian

1817–18	Ferguson, Adam. *Opyt istorii grazhdanskogo obshchestva*. S angliiskogo perevel Ivan Timkovskii. Ch. 1–3. St. Petersburg: v tipografii Gvardeiskogo shtaba. [3 vols.]

Swedish

1790	*Försök till Historien om borgerligt Samhälle*. Translated from the English by Peter Jacob Hjelm. Wysgeerige: tryckt hos Johan A. Carlbohm. [vi + 588 p.]

1769	***Institutes of Moral Philosophy***. Edinburgh: Printed for A. Kincaid and J. Bell. [xvi + 319 p.]

1773   2nd edition, revised and corrected. Edinburgh: A. Kincaid & W. Creech, and J. Bell. Sold in London, by S. Crowder, R. Baldwin, E. & C. Dillies and T. Cadell. [xvi + 294 p.]

1785   3rd edition, enlarged. Edinburgh: J. Bell and W. Creech. Sold in London, by S. Crowder, R. Baldwin, E. & C. Dillies and T. Cadell. [xvi + 317 p.]

1786   A new edition, revised and corrected. Mentz, Frankfurt: Printed for J.F. Schiller; and sold by Varrentrapp junior and Wenner. [v + 206 p.]

1800   A new edition, enlarged. Basil: Printed and sold by James Decker, Paris. Sold by Levrault Frères, Quai Malaquai. [xii + 242 p.]

1815   A new edition. Mainz: Kupferberg.

1828   2nd edition. Madras. [xvi + 294 p.]

Translations: French

1775   *Institutions de philosophie morale.* [Translated by E.S.P. Reverdil.] Geneva: Chez C. Philabert et B. Chirol. [xx + 256 p.]

German

1772   *Grundsätze der Moralphilosophie.* Translated and with a commentary by Christian Garve. Leipzig: In der Dyckischen Buchhandlung. [420 p.]

1787   Frankfurt and Leipzig. [viii + 280 p.]

Italian

1790   *Istituzioni di Filosofia morale.* Venice: Nella Stamperia Graziosi a S. Apollinaire. [xvi + 240 p.]

Russian

1804   *Nachal'nye osnovanija nravstvennoi filosofii.* Translated from the German by A. Briantsev. Moscow: Moskovskom' Universitete.

1776   [Anonymous]. *Remarks on a Pamphlet Lately Published by Dr. Price, intitled "Observations on the Nature of Civil Liberty, the principles of government, and the justice and policy of the war with America, &c," in a Letter from a Gentleman in the Country to a Member of Parliament.* London: T. Cadell. [61 p.]

| 1776 | Dublin: Printed for Messrs. Whitestone, Sheppard, Potts, J. Hoey, W. Colles, Moncrieffe, Walker, Jenkin, W. Wilson, Mills, Gilbert, Hallhead, and Talbot. [72 p.] |

There exists an anonymous pamphlet of some 76 pages carrying the title *Remarks on Dr. Price's Observations on the Nature of Civil Liberty* (London: Printed for G. Kearsley, 1776) but this is not the same publication and should not be confused with Ferguson's essay.

1783 *The History of the Progress and Termination of the Roman Republic.* London: W. Strahan and T. Cadell; and W. Creech, in Edinburgh. [3 vols.]

1783	Dublin: Printed for Price, Whitestone, Colles, Moncrieffe, Jenkin, O. Walker, Exshaw, Beatty, White, Burton, Byrne, Cash, and Sleater. [3 vols.]
1791	Basil: Printed and sold by J.J. Tourneisen. [6 vols.]
1799	New edition, revised and corrected. Edinburgh: Bell & Bradfute; and G.G. & J. Robinson, London. [5 vols.]
1805	New edition, revised and corrected. Edinburgh: Bell & Bradfute. [5 vols.]
1805	1st American edition. Philadelphia: Printed for the proprietors, Wm. Poyntell & Co. [3 vols.]
1811	Philadelphia: Moses Thomas, No. 118, Chestnut Street. [3 vols.]
1813	New edition, revised and corrected. Edinburgh: Bell & Bradfute. [5 vols.]
1824	Philadelphia: Thomas Wardle. [493 p.]
1825	New edition, revised and corrected. Edinburgh: Bell & Bradfute. [5 vols.]
1825	University edition. London: Jones & Co. [viii + 469 p.]
1827	London: Jones & Co. [vii + 480 p.]
1829	University edition. London: Jones & Co. [viii + 480 p.]

Translations: *French*

| 1784–91 | *Histoire des progrès et de la chûte de la République romaine.* Translated by Jean Nicolas Démeunier et Jacques Gibelin. Paris: De l'imprimerie de P.G. Simon et N.H. Nyon l'aîné, Imprimeur du Parlement de Nyon. [7 vols.] |
| 1810–11 | *Histoire de la République romaine.* Translated by M. Breton. [volumes 19 to 28 of the *Bibliothèque historique à l'usage des jeunes gens*]. Paris: F. Schoell. [10 vols.] |

German

1784–86   *Geschichte des Fortganges und Unterganges der Römischen Republik.* Translated from the English by Christian Daniel Beck. Leipzig: M.G. Weidmanns erben und Reich. [3 vols.]

Italian

1793   *Ricerche storiche e critiche sulle cause dei progressi e del decadimento della republica romana.* Venice: Antonio Zatta e figli. [8 vols.]

1792   *Principles of Moral and Political Science: Being Chiefly a Retrospect of Lectures Delivered in the College of Edinburgh.* Printed for A. Strahan and T. Cadell, London; and W. Creech, Edinburgh. [2 vols.]

1805   *Essays on the Intellectual Powers, Moral Sentiment, Happiness and National Felicity.* [Parsons and Galignani's British Library No. 30]. Paris: Parsons and Galignani. [72 p.]

Apparently an unauthorized edition of selections from Ferguson's *Principles.*

Translations: French

1796, 1805   T.E. Jessop (*A Bibliography of David Hume and of Scottish Philosophy from Francis Hutcheson to Lord Balfour* [New York: Russell & Russell, 1966]: 122) notes that extracts of Ferguson's *Principles* appeared in French in the serial *Bibliothèque britannique, ou Receuil extrait des ouvrages anglais périodiques. Sciences et arts*, published in Geneva: vols. II (1796): 1–19; XXVIII (1805): 21–36 and 145–65; and XXIX (1805): 153–75.

1821   *Principes de la science morale et politique, ou Résumé des leçons données au collège d'Édimbourg.* Translated from the English by A.D. Paris: Kleffer. [2 vols.]

German

1796   *Ausfürliche Darstellung der Gründe der Moral und Politik.* Translated from the English by K.G. Schreiter. Zürich: Bey Orell, Gessner, Füssli und Comp. [xx + 576 p.]

1801   "Minutes of the Life and Character of Joseph Black, M.D.," *Transactions of the Royal Society of Edinburgh*, 5 (1801): 101–17.

1817   *Biographical Sketch, or Memoir, of Lieutenant-Colonel Patrick Ferguson, originally intended for the British Encyclopædia.* Edinburgh:

Printed for J. Moir. [35 p.]

Several libraries report the date of publication as 1816.

1960 **"'Of the Principle of Moral Estimation: A Discourse Between David Hume, Robert Clerk, and Adam Smith'; an unpublished MS by Adam Ferguson,"** Ernest Campbell Mossner, ed., *Journal of the History of Ideas*, 21 (1960): 222–32.

Mossner notes that this essay was probably written in 1761.

1965 **"Adam Ferguson's 'Dialogue on a Highland Jaunt' with Robert Adam, William Cleghorn, David Hume, and William Wilkie,"** Ernest Campbell Mossner, ed., in *Restoration and Eighteenth-Century Literature*, Carroll Camden, ed., Chicago: University of Chicago Press. 297–308.

Mossner notes that it is impossible to determine whether the dialogue was a work of fiction or an account of an actual event. Nor can one reliably date the essay. One of its participants, William Cleghorn, died in 1754, while the paper on which the dialogue is written is watermarked 1799.

1986 *The Unpublished Essays of Adam Ferguson*. Winifred M. Philip, ed., Kilberry, Argyll: Published by the Editor, W.M. Philip. [3 vols.]

The three volumes that comprise this collection are a typed transcription of Ferguson's unpublished essays in the Archives of the University of Edinburgh. Their contents are as follows:

Volume I:	Of Happiness and Merit
	On Wisdom
	Of the Distinctions which Mankind Experience or Apprehend in the Nature of Things, to Direct Them in What They Pursue or Avoid
	Of the Freedom of Wit and Humour, and Their Value as a Test of Rectitude and Truth
	Of the Distinctions on Which we Act in Human Life
	Of the Intellectual System
	Of the Sciences of Which the Subject is Mind
	Of the First Law of Living Nature: Preserve Thyself
	Of Liberty and Necessity
	Of the Things That Are or May Be
	Of the Different Aspects of Moral Science
Volume II:	On Perfection and Happiness
	What May be Affirmed or Apprehended of the Supreme Creative Being
	Of History and Its Appropriate Stile
	Of the Comparative Form of Being
	Reputed Pleasures of Imagination
	Of Cause and Effect, Ends and Means, Order, Combination, and Design
	Of the French Revolution with Its Actual and Still Impending Consequences in Europe

Of the Separation of Departments, Professions, and Tasks
Resulting from the Progress of Arts in Society

Of the Categories

Of the Principle of Moral Estimation: David Hume, Robert
Clerk, Adam Smith

Volume III: Of Statesmen and Warriours

An Excursion in the Highlands: Discourse on Various
Subjects

Of the Categories of Constituents of Discourse and Fabrick
of Thought

Waking Dreams

Of the Distinction on Which it is the Lot of Man to Deliberate

Of Good and Evil. Perfection and Defect

Of Things That Are or May Be – Part One

Of Things That Are or May Be – Part Two

Of Nature and Art

Of the Laws of Nature in the Department of Active Man

Of the Intellectual or Conscious Powers: Conceptive,
Cognitive, and Spontaneous

Characteristics of Man's Nature

1987   **"Adam Ferguson and the Division of Labour,"** Yasuo Amoh, ed. *Kochi University Review of Social Science*, 29 (July 1987): 71–85.

1990   **"Memorial Respecting the Measures to be Pursued on the Present Immediate Prospect of a Final Separation of the American Colonys [*sic*] from Great Britain,"** Yasuo Amoh, ed., *Kochi University Review of Social Science*, 37 (March 1990): 81–7.

The language of the document suggests that it was written sometime after April 1779.

1991   **"Adam Ferguson's Rules of War,"** Jane Bush Fagg and Yasuo Amoh, eds., *Eighteenth-Century Scotland: The Newsletter of the Eighteenth-Century Scottish Studies Society*, no. 5 (Spring 1991): 10–13.

1996   *Collection of Essays*. Edited, with an introduction, by Yasuo Amoh. Kyoto: Rinsen Book Co. [xxxi + 333 p.]

The essays in this collection are the same as those published in typescript by Prof. Winifred Philip ten years earlier. They are as follows:

1. Of Perfection and Happiness
2. What May Be Affirmed or Apprehended of the Supreme Creative Being
3. Of History and Its Appropriate Style
4. Of Statesmen and Warriors
5. An Excursion Into the Highlands: Discourse on Various Subjects
6. Of Happiness and Merit
7. Distinction of Value and Its Source in Existence

8. Of the Comparative Forms of Being
9. Reputed Pleasures of Imagination
10. On Wisdom
11. Of the Categories or Constituents of Discourse and Fabrick of Thought
12. Of the Distinctions Which Mankind Experience or Apprehend in the Nature of Things to Direct Them in What They Pursue or Avoid
13. Of Cause and Effect, Ends and Means, Order, Combination and Design
14. Of the French Revolution With its Actual and Still Impending Consequences in Europe
15. Of the Separation of Departments, Professions and Tasks Resulting from the Progress of Arts in Society
16. Of the Freedom of Wit and Humour and Their Value as a Test of Rectitude and Truth
17. Waking Dreams
18. Of the Distinctions on Which We Act in Human Life
19. Of the Categories
20. Of the Distinctions on Which It Is the Lot of Man to Deliberate
21. Of the Intellectual System
22. Of the Sciences of Which the Subject is Mind
23. Of Good and Evil, Perfection and Defect
24. Of the First Law of Living Nature: *Preserve Thyself*
25. Of the Principle of Moral Estimation: David Hume, Robert Clerk, Adam Smith
26. Of Liberty and Necessity
27. Of the Things That Are or May Be – Part One
    Of the Things That Are or May Be – Part Two
28. Of Nature and Art
29. Of the Different Aspects of Moral Science
30. Of the Laws of Nature in the Department of Active Man
31. Of the Intellectual or Conscious Powers: Conceptive, Cognitive and Spontaneous
32. Characteristics of Man's Nature

In addition, Prof. Amoh has included three brief appendices by Ferguson:

1. A Little Boy
2. Epitaph
3. Memorial Respecting the Measures to be Pursued on the Present Immediate Prospect of a Final Separation of the American Colonys [*sic*] from Great Britain

David Hume (1711–76)

1739–40 [Anonymous]. *A Treatise of Human Nature: Being an Attempt to Introduce the Experimental Method of Reasoning into Moral Subjects.*

1739   *Vol. I: Of the Understanding*. London: Printed for John Noon, at the White Hart, near Mercer's Chapel, in Cheapside. [viii + 475 p.]

1739   *Vol. II: Of the Passions*. London: Printed for John Noon, at the White Hart, near Mercer's Chapel, in Cheapside. [iv + 318 p.]

1740   *Vol. III: Of Morals*. London: Printed for Thomas Longman, at the Ship in Paternoster Row. [viii + 310 p.]

Translations: German

1790–92   *Über die Menschliche Natur*. Translated from the English by Ludwig Heinrich von Jakob. Halle: Bei Hemmerde und Schwetschke. [3 vols.]

1740   [Anonymous]. *An Abstract of a Book lately Published; Entituled, A Treatise of Human Nature, &c, wherein the chief argument of that Book is farther illustrated and explained*. London: Printed for C. Borbet. [xxxii + 32 p.]

1741   [Anonymous]. *Essays, Moral and Political*. Vol. I. Edinburgh: Printed by R. Fleming and A. Alison for A. Kincaid, bookseller, and sold at his shop above the Cross. [viii + 187 p.]

Comprising the following essays:

1. Of the Delicacy of Taste and Passion
2. Of the Liberty of the Press
3. Of Impudence and Modesty
4. That Politicks May be Reduc'd to a Science
5. Of the First Principles of Government
6. Of Love and Marriage
7. Of the Study of History
8. Of the Independency of Parliament
9. Whether the British Government Inclines More to Absolute Monarchy or to a Republick
10. Of Parties in General
11. Of the Parties in Great Britain
12. Of Superstition and Enthusiasm
13. Of Avarice
14. Of the Dignity of Human Nature
15. Of Liberty and Despotism

1742   2nd edition, corrected. Edinburgh: Printed for A. Kincaid, near the Cross. [viii + 189 p.]

1742   [Anonymous]. *Essays, Moral and Political*. Vol. II. Edinburgh: Printed for A. Kincaid, near the Cross, by R. Fleming and A. Alison. [vi + 205 p.]

Comprising the following essays:

16. Of Essay Writing
17. Of Eloquence
18. Of Moral Prejudices
19. Of the Middle Station of Life
20. Of the Rise and Progress of the Arts and Sciences
21. The Epicurean
22. The Stoic
23. The Platonist
24. The Sceptic
25. Of Polygamy and Divorces
26. Of Simplicity and Refinement
27. A Character of Sir Robert Walpole

1748   3rd edition, corrected, with additions. London: Printed for A. Millar, over against Catherine Street in the Strand; and A. Kincaid in Edinburgh. [iv + 312 p.]

Comprises essays 1 to 15, as in the 2nd edition, in addition to essays 17 and 20 to 26, to which are added the three essays (28 to 30) that first appeared in the supplementary volume of 1748. Essay 27 appears as an extended footnote to essay 4.

1753   4th edition, corrected, with additions. London: Printed for A. Millar, in the Strand; and A. Kincaid and A. Donaldson, Edinburgh. [270 p.]

See **Vol. I,** *Essays and Treatises on Several Subjects* (1753–56).

1772   "Of Impudence and Modesty" [essay 3], "Of Love and Marriage" [essay 6] and "Of avarice" [essay 13) reprinted in Anonymous, ed., *The Beauties of the Magazines, and other periodical works*. London: Richard and Urquhart. [2 vols.]

Translations: French

1769   "Les quatres philosophes" [essays 21 through 24], translated by J.B. Mérian, in Vol. I of J.F. Dreux du Radier, ed., *Le temple du bonheur, ou receuil des plus excellens traités sur le bonheur.* [3 vols.] [Paris]: A. Bouillon et se trouve à Paris.

1770   New edition, reviewed, corrected and enlarged. [4 vols.] Paris: A. Bouillon.

1779   "'L'épicurien,' traduit des *Essais* de M. Hume," in *Nouveaux mélanges de poésies grecques*. Amsterdam: Chez la veuve Merkus; Paris: Chez Mérigot le jeune. [xi + 242 p.]

    1783   Amsterdam: Chez la veuve Merkus; Paris: Chez Mérigot le jeune. [xi + 242 p.]

German

1768   *Die vier Philosophen* [essays 21 through 24]. Glogau: Bey Christian Friedrich Günthern. [111 p.]

1788–89   *Beiträge zur Beförderung der Menschenkenntniß, besonders in Rücksicht unserer moralischen Natur.* Edited by Karl Friedrich Pockels. Berlin: Vieweg. [2 vols.]

Contains essays 12 and 28 through 30.

1745   **[Anonymous].** *A Letter from a Gentleman to his Friend in Edinburgh, Containing Some Observations on a Specimen of the Principles Concerning Religion and Morality, Said to be Maintain'd in a Book Lately Publish'd, intituled, a Treatise of Human Nature, &c.* Edinburgh: [T.L. Lumisden and J. Robertson]. [34 p.]

1748   **[Anonymous].** *A True Account of the Behavior and Conduct of Archibald Stewart, Esq.; late Lord Provost of Edinburgh, in a letter to a friend.* London: Printed for M. Cooper, at the Globe in Paternoster Row. [iv + 51 p.]

Todd [William Todd, ed., *Hume and the Enlightenment: Essays Presented to Ernest Campbell Mossner* (Edinburgh: University Press, 1974): 192] shows four variants for this edition.

1748   *Three Essays, Moral and Political.* London: Printed for A. Millar; over against Catherine Street in the Strand; and A. Kincaid in Edinburgh. [60 p.]

Comprising the following essays:

28.   Of National Characters
29.   Of the Original Contract
30.   Of Passive Obedience

The first of Hume's published works to bear his name.

Translations: French

1770   *Variétés Angloises.* London: Chez J.B. [300 p.]

The collection contains Hume's essays "Of National Characters" (no. 28) and "Of the Liberty of the Press" (no. 2). Place of publication is in fact either Paris or Brussels.

1748   *Philosophical Essays Concerning Human Understanding.* London: Printed for A. Millar, opposite Katharine Street, in the Strand. [iv + 256 p.]

Comprising the following essays:

Of the Different Species of Philosophy
Of the Origin of Ideas
Of the Connexions of Ideas

Sceptical Doubts Concerning the Operations of the Understanding
Sceptical Solution of These Doubts
Of Probability
Of the Idea of Power or Necessary Connexion
Of Liberty and Necessity
Of the Reason of Animals
Of Miracles
Of the Practical Consequences of Natural Religion
Of the Academical or Sceptical Philosophy

1750   2nd edition, with additions and corrections. London: Printed for A. Millar. [iii + 259 p.]

The title of the last essay was changed to "Of a Particular Providence and a Future State."

1751   2nd edition, with additions and corrections. London: Printed for M. Cooper, at the Globe in Paternoster Row. [iii + 259 p.]

1753   2nd edition, with additions and corrections. London: Printed for A. Millar, in the Strand. [iii + 259 p.]

1756   3rd edition, with additions and corrections. London: Printed for A. Millar, in the Strand. [250 p.]

See **Vol. II,** *Essays and Treatises on Several Subjects* (1753–56).

1758   *An Enquiry Concerning Human Understanding.* In *Essays and Treatises on Several Subjects.* A new edition; London: Printed for A. Millar, in the Strand and for A. Kincaid and A. Donaldson, at Edinburgh. [viii + 539 p.]

Translations: French

1758   *Essais philosophiques sur l'entendement humain, par Mr. Hume. Avec les quatre philosophes du même auteur.* Translated by Jean-Bernard Mérian. Amsterdam: Chez J.H. Schneider. [2 vols.]

This is a translation of the edition of the *Philosophical Essays Concerning Human Understanding* that had been published as volume 2 (1756) of the first edition of the *Essays and Treatises on Several Subjects.* It is accompanied by a translation of essays 21 through 24.

1761   2nd edition. Amsterdam: Chez J.H. Schneider. [340 p.]

German

1755   *Philosophische Versuche über die menschliche Erkenntniss.*

Translated by J.G. Sulzer. Hamburg: Bey G.C. Grund und A.H. Holle. [374 p.]

This is a translation of the edition of the *Philosophical Essays Concerning Human Understanding* that had been published as volume 2 (1756) of the first edition of the *Essays and Treatises on Several Subjects*.

1793   *Untersuchung über den menschlichen Verstand neu übersezt von M.W.G.M. Tennemann nebst einer Abhandlung über den philosophischen Skepticismus von Herrn Professor Reinhold in Jena.* Jena: 1793. [lii + 380 p.]

1751   [Pseudonymous: Zerobabel MacGilchrist]. *The Petition of the Grave and Venerable Bellmen (or Sextons) of the Church of Scotland, to the Hon. House of Commons.* Edinburgh. [Broadside, 2 p.]

1751   *An Enquiry Concerning the Principles of Morals.* London: Printed for A. Millar, over against Catherine Street. [viii + 253 p.]

1753   *Some Late Opinions Concerning the Foundations of Morality, Examined in a Letter to a Friend.* London: Printed for R. Dodsley and M. Cooper. [46 p.]

This collection contains excerpts from David Hume's *Enquiry Concerning the Principles of Morals*; Henry Home, Lord Kames, *Essays on the Principles of Morality and Natural Religion*; and James Balfour, *Delineation of the Nature and Obligation of Morality.*

1753   2nd edition. London: Printed for A. Millar, in the Strand. [ii + 256 p.]

See **Vol. III, *Essays and Treatises on Several Subjects*** (1753–56).

1752   *Political Discourses.* Edinburgh: Printed by R. Fleming, for A. Kincaid and A. Donaldson. [ii + 304 p.]

Comprising the following essays:

31.   Of Commerce
32.   Of Luxury
33.   Of Money
34.   Of Interest
35.   Of the Balance of Trade
36.   Of the Balance of Power
37.   Of Taxes.
38.   Of Public Credit
39.   Of Some Remarkable Customs
40.   Of the Populousness of Antient Nations
41.   Of the Protestant Succession

42.   Idea of a Perfect Commonwealth.

1752   2nd edition. Edinburgh: Printed by R. Fleming, for A. Kincaid
           and A. Donaldson. [vi + 304 p.]

1753   2nd edition. Edinburgh: Printed for A. Kincaid and A. Donaldson.
           [270 p.]

1754   3rd edition, with additions and corrections. Edinburgh: Printed
           by Sands, Murray & Cochran for A. Kincaid & A. Donaldson.
           [lv + 270 p.]

1754   See *Essays and Treatises on Several Subjects* (1753–56).

1787   "On the Balance of Trade" [essay 35], "On the Jealousy of
           Trade" [essay 47] and "On the Balance of Power" [essay 36]
           appended to a reprint of Josiah Tucker, *Brief Essay on the
           Advantages and Disadvantages which Respectively Attend
           France and Great Britain, with Regard to Trade*. London:
           Printed for John Stockdale. [96 p.]

Translations: *Dutch*

1764   *Wysgeerige en staatkundige verhandelingen, van den heere
           David Hume*. Amsterdam: Kornelis van Tongerlo. [xii + 436 p.]

French

1754   *Discours politiques*. Translated from the English by [Eléasar]
           de M[auvillon]. Amsterdam: Chez J. Schreuder et Pierre
           Mortier, le jeune. [1 vol. in a 4 vol. set]

           Contents: All 12 discourses. This work, which includes the
           political disquisitions of a number of authors, appeared in five
           volumes, of which Hume's Essays are contained in volume 1.
           [Other contributors: Pierre-André O'Heguerty (1700–63):
           "Essai sur les intérêts du commerce maritime"; François Véron
           Duverger de Forbonnais (1722–1800): "Considérations sur les
           finances d'Espagne; Henry St. John, Viscount Bolingbroke
           (1678–1751): "Réflexions politiques sur l'état présent de
           l'Angleterre"; Richard Cantillon (d. 1734): "Essai sur la nature
           du commerce"; Ange Goudar (1720–91): "Intérêts de la France
           mal entendus".]

           The essays by Hume are:

           1.   Du commerce
           2.   Du luxe
           3.   Sur l'argent
           4.   De l'intérêt
           5.   Sur la balance du commerce

6. De la balance du pouvoir
7. Sur les impôts
8. Sur le crédit public
9. Sur quelques coutumes remarquables
10. Sur le nombre d'habitans parmi quelques nations anciens
11. Sur la succession protestante
12. Idée d'une république parfaite

1756–57   Amsterdam: Chez J. Schreuder et Pierre Mortier le jeune. [4 vols.]

It appears that this collection was published to complement Hume's writings on economic issues.

1754   *Discours politiques.* Translated from the English by l'Abbé J.B. LeBlanc. Amsterdam: et se vend à Paris, chez M. Lambert. [2 vols.]

Contents: The 12 discourses plus an essay by Bolingbroke ["Some Reflections on the Present State of the Nation"] and a survey of contemporary essays on economics. The work was in fact published in Paris.

> 1755   New edition. Dresden: Chez Groell, Libraire & Marchand d'Estampes. [2 vols.]
>
> Contents: Same as in the edition of 1754.

1761   Amsterdam: J.S. Schreuder & Pierre Mortier. [iv + 355 p.]

1765   *Essais sur la commerce; le luxe; l'argent; l'intérêt de l'argent; les impôts; le crédit public et la balance du commerce.* Traduction nouvelle, avec des Réflexions du Traducteur. Et Lettre d'un Négociant de Londres, . . . contenant des Réflexions sur les impôts auxquels son assujetties les denrées de première nécessité, & sur la conséquence dont ils peuvent être relativement à la main-d'oeuvre dans les manufactures d'Angleterre. Amsterdam. [288 p.]

1766   *Essais sur la commerce; le luxe; l'argent; l'intérêt de l'argent; les impôts; le crédit public et la balance du commerce.* Traduction nouvelle, avec des Réflexions du Traducteur. Et Lettre d'un Négociant de Londres, . . . contenant des Réflexions sur les impôts auxquels son assujetties les denrées de première nécessité, & sur la conséquence dont ils peuvent être relativement à la main-d'oeuvre dans les manufactures d'Angleterre. Traduite sur la seconde édition, imprimée à Londres en 1765. Amsterdam. [288 p.]

1767   *Essais sur la commerce; le luxe; l'argent; l'intérêt de l'argent; les impôts; le crédit public et la balance du commerce,* et lettre d'un négociant de Londres, a un de ses amis contenant des

Réflexions sur les impôts auxquels son assujetties les denrées de première nécessité, & sur la conséquence dont ils peuvent être relativement à la main-d'oeuvre dans les manufactures d'Angleterre. Translated from the 2nd edition. A new translation [by Mlle de la Chaux]. À Paris: À Lyon: Chez Saillant, rue S. Jean-de-Beauvais; Chez Aimé Delaroche, aux Halles de la Grenette. [ix + 288 p.]

Translations of essays 31 to 35 and 37 to 38. The Bibliothèque Nationale shows the bibliographical information for this edition as above. The National Library of Scotland catalogue, however, lists the publication date as 1766 and the place of publication as Amsterdam.

1769   *Discours politiques*. Amsterdam: Chez J. Schreuder. [viii + 324 p.]

Contains Hume's political discourses, Henry St. John Bolingbroke's, "Réflexions politiques sur l'état présent d'Angleterre," and two essays by François Véron Duverger de Forbonnais: "Considerations sur les finances d'Espagne" and "Réflexions sur la necessité de comprendre l'étude du commerce."

German

1766   *Über die Handlung, die Manufacturen, und die andern Quellen des Reichtums und die Macht eines Staates*. Leipzig: A.H. Hollens witwe. [v + 392 p.]

Italian

1764   *Saggi morali e politici*. Amsterdam.

1767   *Saggi politici sopra il commercio/Political Discourses on Commerce*. Translated by Matteo Dandolo. [Text in English and Italian, on opposite pages.] Venice: Appresso Giammaria Bassaglia e Luigi Pavini. [2 vols.]

    1774   2nd edition. Tradotti dall'inglese col'aggiunta di un discorso preliminare sul commercio di Sicilia di D. Isidoro Bianchi, socio della Reale Accademia della Scienze di Siena. Venice e Palermo: presso Andrea Rapetti q. Antonio. [xii + 128 p.]

1769   *Saggio sul commercio relativamente alla primaria sua bas l'agricultura*. [Translated by P.M. Scottoni.] Venezia: Si vende dal Librajo Alvise Milocco. [xii + 298 p.]

1772   *Del lusso. Discorso cristiano con un dialogo filosofico*. Bassano.

Russian

1776   *Nauka k poznaniiu roskoshi.* Sochinennaia na anglinskom iazyke g. professorom Davidom Giumom; A s originala frantsuzskago perevel na rossiiskii iazyk leib-gvardii Preobrazhenskago polku furier ilmperatorskago Moskovskogo universiteta student Fedor Levchenkov. St. Petersburg: Tip. Mor. Kadet. Korpusa.

The essay "Refinement of the Arts," translated from the French translation by Fedor Levchenkov, officer of the Preobrazhenskii Regiment and a student at Moscow Imperial University.

Swedish

1791   *Smärre afhandlingar l allmänna hushållningen, af David Hume, Esquire. Oversåttning ifrån fista engelska uplagan af år 1772. I. Samlingen.* Stockholm: tryckt hos Johan A. Carlbohm. [iv + 198 p.]

1752   **[Anonymous].** *Scotticisms.* [Edinburgh]: [R. Fleming and A. Donaldson]. [6 p.]

1770   Edinburgh. [6 p.]

1753   ***Essays and Treatises on Several Subjects.*** [4 vols.]

1753   **Vol. I: *Containing Essays, Moral and Political.*** 4th edition, corrected, with additions. London: Printed for A. Millar, in the Strand; and A. Kincaid and A. Donaldson, in Edinburgh. [iv + 331 p.]

Twenty-six essays as in the 1748 edition.

1753   **Vol. II: *Philosophical Essays Concerning Human Understanding.*** 2nd edition, with additions and corrections. London: Printed for A. Millar, in the Strand. [259 p.]

1753   **Vol. III: *Containing An Enquiry Concerning the Principles of Morals.*** London: Printed for A. Millar, in the Strand. [256 p.]

1753   **Vol. IV: *Containing Political Discourses.*** 2nd edition. Edinburgh: Printed for A. Kincaid and A. Donaldson. [304 p.]

1753–56   *Essays and Treatises on Several Subjects.* [4 vols.]

1753   Vol. I: *Containing Essays, Moral and Political.* 4th edition, corrected, with additions. London: Printed for A. Millar, in the Strand; and A. Kincaid and A. Donaldson, Edinburgh. [iv + 331 p.]

A further edition of the *Essays, Moral and Political*, whose contents are the same as that in the 3rd edition, published in 1748.

1756   Vol. II: *Containing Philosophical Essays Concerning Human Understanding*. 3rd edition, with additions and corrections. London: Printed for A. Millar, in the Strand. [250 p.]

A further edition of the *Philosophical Essays Concerning Human Understanding*, whose contents are the same as that of the 2nd edition, published in 1753.

1753   Vol. III: *Containing an Enquiry Concerning the Principles Of Morals*. 2nd edition. London: Printed for A. Millar, in the Strand. [256 p.]

A further edition of the *Enquiry Concerning the Principles of Morals*, whose contents are the same as that of the 1st edition of 1751.

1754   Vol. IV: *Containing Political Discourses*. 3rd edition, with additions and corrections. London: Printed for A. Millar; and A. Kincaid and A. Donaldson, in Edinburgh. [270 p.]

A further edition of the *Political Discourses*, whose contents are the same as that of the 2nd edition of 1752.

1758   A new edition; London: Printed for A. Millar, in the Strand; and for A. Kincaid and A. Donaldson, at Edinburgh. [viii + 539 p.]

Contains *Essays, Moral, Political and Literary*, Parts I and II (Part I: 26 essays comprising nos. 1 through 15, 17, 20 through 26 and 28 [essay 15 is retitled "Of Civil Liberty"], and nos. 45 and 46 from the *Four Dissertations*. Part II: the 12 essays comprising the *Political Discourses* [essays 21 through 42], and nos. 29 and 30 from the supplementary volume of 1748; *An Enquiry Concerning Human Understanding* (the *Philosophical Essays Concerning Human Understanding* of 1748) "Dissertation on the Passions" (no. 44), "Natural History of Religion" (no. 43) and *An Enquiry Concerning the Principles of Morals*.

1760   A new edition. London: Printed for A. Millar, in the Strand; and A. Kincaid and A. Donaldson, in Edinburgh. [4 vols.]

Comprising: Vol. I: *Essays, Moral, Political and Literary*, Part I (iii + 395 p.); Vol. II: *Essays, Moral, Political and Literary*, Part II (iv + 379 p.); Vol. III: *Enquiry Concerning Human Understanding* (299 p.); Vol. IV: *Enquiry Concerning the Principles of Morals* (v + 352 p.). Contents: As in the edition of 1748, except that essay 32 is retitled "Of Refinement in the Arts" and two new essays – previously bound in separately in the 1758 edition – are added:

47.   Of the Jealousy of Trade
48.   Of the Coalition of Parties

1764   New edition. London: Printed for A. Millar, in the Strand; and A. Kincaid and A. Donaldson, at Edinburgh. [2 vols.]

Contents: Omits essays 3, 6 and 7. Volume II includes both the *Enquiry Concerning Human Understanding* and the *Enquiry Concerning the Principles of Morals*, plus the *Natural History of Religion.*

1767   A new edition. London: Printed for A. Millar; and A. Kincaid and A. Donaldson, at Edinburgh. [2 vols.]

Contents: Same as the edition of 1764.

1768   A new edition. London: Printed for A. Millar, A. Kincaid, J. Bell and A. Donaldson, in Edinburgh, and sold by T. Cadell in the Strand. [2 vols.]

Contents: Same as in the edition of 1764.

1770   A new edition. London: Printed for T. Cadell (successor to Mr. Millar) and A. Kincaid and A. Donaldson, at Edinburgh. [4 vols.]

Contents: As in the edition of 1764, except that essay 13 and the extended note on Walpole appended to essay 4, have been deleted.

1772   New edition. London: Printed for T. Cadell; and A. Kincaid and A. Donaldson, at Edinburgh. [2 vols.]

Contents: Same as the edition of 1770.

1774   New edition. Dublin: Printed for J. Williams. [2 vols.]

Contents: Same as the edition of 1770.

1777   A new edition. London: Printed for T. Cadell in the Strand; and A. Donaldson & W. Creech, Edinburgh. [2 vols.]

Contents: As in the edition of 1770, except that a new essay has been added:

49.   Of the Origin of Government.

1779   A new edition. Dublin: Printed by J. Williams. [2 vols.]

Contents: Same as the edition of 1777.

1784   A new edition. London: Printed for T. Cadell; A. Donaldson and W. Creech, at Edinburgh. [2 vols.]

Contents: Same as the edition of 1777.

1788   A new edition. London: Printed for T. Cadell; C. Elliot, T. Kay and C. Elliot, Edinburgh. [2 vols.]

Content: Same as the edition of 1777.

1782   *The Beauties of Hume and Bolingbroke.* London: Printed for J. Kearsly [*sic*]. [xxxii + 262 p.]

The volume contains selections from Hume's essays.

Translations: French

1758–60   *Œuvres philosophiques de D. Hume.* [Translated by J.B. Mérian and J.B.R. Robinet.] Amsterdam: J.H. Schneider. [5 vols.]

    1758   Vols. I and II: *Essais philosophiques sur l'entendement humain. Avec les quatre philosophes* [essays 21 through 24]. Translated by J.B. Mérian. Preface by J.H.S. Formey.

    1759   Vol. III: *Histoire naturelle de la religion.* Avec un examen critique et philosophique de cet ouvrage. Translated by J.B. Mérian. [viii + 180 p.]

        Also issued by the publisher, Schneider, as a separate volume.

    1759   Vol. IV: *Dissertations sur les passions, sur la tragédie, sur la règle du goût.* Translated by J.B. Mérian. [139 p.]

        Also issued by the publisher, Schneider, as a separate volume.

    1760   Vol. V: *Essais de morale, ou Recherches sur les principes de la morale.* Translated by J.B.R. Robinet.

1759   *Œuvres philosophiques de M. D. Hume.* [Translated by J.B. Mérian]. Amsterdam: J.H. Schneider. [2 vols.]

    The title is misleading. The edition is limited to the first two volumes of the 1758–60 edition, containing *Essais philosophiques sur l'entendement humain. Avec les quatre philosophes* [essays 21 through 24].

1759–64   *Œuvres philosophiques de M. Hume.* [Translated by J.B. Mérian and J.B. Robinet.] 2nd edition. Amsterdam: J.H. Schneider. [5 vols.]

    1759   Vol. I: *Histoire naturelle de la religion, avec un examen critique et philosophique de cet ouvrage.*

    1759   Vol. II: *Dissertation sur les passions, sur la tragédie, sur la régle du goût.*

    1764   Vol. I: *Essais moraux et politiques.* [493 p.]

        Contents: The 26 essays of the 1748 edition.

    1761   Vol. II: *Essais philosophiques sur l'entendement humain.* [340 p.]

        Contents: As in volumes I and II of the 1758–60 edition, omitting "the four philosophers."

    1759   Vol. III: *Histoire naturelle de la religion.* Avec un examen critique et philosophique de cet ouvrage. [180 p.]

        Contents: As in volume III of the edition of 1758–60.

1759   Vol. IV: *Dissertations sur les passions, sur la tragédie, sur la règle du goût.* [120 p.]

Contents: As in volume IV of the edition of 1758–60.

1760   Vol. V: *Essais de morale, ou Recherches sur les principes de la morale.* [312 p.]

Contents: As in volume V of the edition of 1758–60.

1764   *Œuvres philosophiques de M. Hume.* [Translated by J.B. Mérian and J.B. Robinet.] New edition. Amsterdam: J.H. Schneider. [6 vols.]

Vol. I: *Les huits premiers essais sur l'entendement humain.*
Vol. II: *Les quatre derniers essais sur l'entendement humain et les quatre philosophes.*
Vol. III: *Histoire naturelle de la religion.*
Vol. IV: *Les dissertations sur les passions, sur la tragédie et sur la règle du goût.*
Vol. V: *Les recherches sur les principes de la morale.*
Vol. VI: *Les essais moraux et politiques.*
Publication information variously given as "À Londres: Chez David Wilson."

1767   *Pensées philosophiques, morales, critiques, littéraires et politiques de M. Hume.* [Translated by J.A.J. Desboulmiers.] London [Paris]: et se trouve chez la veuve Duchesne. [xii + 416 p.]

Contains a selection from the essays.

1788   *Œuvres philosophiques de M. D. Hume.* New edition. London [Paris]. [7 vols.]

Contents: The same as the edition of 1758–60 except that the contents are ordered differently. In addition, vol. 7 contains Hume's essays on political economy entitled *Les Essais sur les Commerce*, seven of the political discourses translated by Mlle de la Chaux that appeared in 1752.

German

1754–56 *Vermischte Schriften.* [Translated by H.A. Pisatorius and J.C. Sulzer.] Hamburg and Leipzig: Bey Georg Christian Grund und Adam Heinrich Holle. [4 vols.]

1754   Vol. I: *Über die Handlung, die Manufacturen, und die andern Quellen des Reichtums und die Macht eines Staates.* [Translation of the *Political Discourses*.] [392 p.]

1755   Vol. II: *Philosophische Versuch über die menschliche Erkenntnis.* [Translation of *Philosophical Essays Concerning Human Understanding*.] [374 p.]

1756   Vol. III: *Sittenlehre der Gesellschaft.* [Translation of *Enquiry Concerning the Principles of Morals.*] [280 p.]

1756   Vol. IV: *Moralische und politische Versuche.* [Translation of *Essays, Moral, Political and Literary.*] [380 p.]

1766   Leipzig: Bey Adam Heinrich Hollens Witwe. [4 vols.]

1767   *Abriss des gegenwärtigen natürlichen und politischen Zustandes von Grossbritannien.* Ein vollständiges Handbuch für Reisende. Nebst einer umständlichen Nachricht von der Handlung, den Staatsverhält nissen und dem Interesse dieses Reiches. [Selections from *Essays and Treatises on Several Subjects.*] Copenhagen: Johann Gottlob Rothe. [iv + 404 p.]

1754   ***The History of Great Britain*. Vol. I: *Containing the Reigns of James I and Charles I*.** Edinburgh: Printed by Hamilton, Balfour and Neill. [vi + 473 p.]

1755   *The History of Great Britain.* Vol. I: *Containing the Reign of James I and part of Charles I.* Dublin: Printed for John Smith. [v + 433 p.]
And
The History of Great Britain. Vol. II: *Containing the continuation of the reign of Charles I.* Dublin: Printed for John Smith. [iv + 276 p.]

1759   2nd edition, corrected. London: A. Millar. [viii + 464 p.]

1762   *The History of Great Britain.* Vol. I: *Containing the Reign of James I and part of Charles I.* Dublin: Printed for Sarah Cotter, Bookseller, under Dick's Coffee-House. [v + 433 p.]
And
The History of Great Britain. Vol. II: *Containing the continuation of the reign of Charles I.* Dublin: printed for Sarah Cotter, Bookseller, under Dick's Coffee-House. [iv + 276 p.]

1770   *Important Extracts Respecting the Life and Reign of Charles I.* [n.p.] [79 p.]

1757   ***The History of Great Britain*. Vol. II: *Containing the Commonwealth, and the Reigns of Charles II and James II*.** London: Printed for A. Millar, opposite Catherine Street, in the Strand. [v + 459 p.]

1757   *The History of Great Britain.* Vol. III: *Containing the Commonwealth and part of the reign of Charles II.* Dublin: Printed for John Smith. [ii + 368 p.]
And
The History of Great Britain. Vol. IV: *Containing part of Charles II and the reign of James II.* Dublin: Printed for John Smith. [vi + 354 p.]

1759   2nd edition, corrected. London: A. Millar. [vi + 457 p.]

1762   *History of Great Britain.* Vol. III: *Containing the Commonwealth and part of the reign of Charles II.* Dublin: Printed for Sarah Cotter, Bookseller, under Dick's Coffee-House in Skinner Row. [368 p.]
And
History of Great Britain. Vol. IV: *Containing part of Charles II and the Reign of James II.* Dublin: Printed for Sarah Cotter, Bookseller, under Dick's Coffee-House in Skinner Row. [354 p.]

Translations: French

1760   *Histoire de la maison de Stuart sur le trône d'Angleterre.* [Translated by (l'Abbé) A[ntoine] F[rançois] Prévost d'Exiles.] London. [3 vols.] Printed in Amsterdam.

1761   London. [6 vols.] Probably printed in Paris.

1763   Amsterdam. [6 vols.] In fact printed in Paris. This edition was also published in two volumes.

1766   London. [6 vols.] Probably printed in Paris.

1783   *Histoire de la maison de Stuard [sic], sur le trône d'Angleterre.* London: et se trouve à Paris, chez la veuve Desaint [et] Nyon, l'aîné, et fils, libraire. [2 vols.] Printed in Paris.

1788   London: et se trouve à Paris, chez la veuve Desaint [et] Nyon, l'aîné, et fils, libraire. [6 vols.] Printed in Paris.

German

1762–63   *Geschichte von Grossbritannien.* Vol. I: Die der Regierungen Jakobs I. und Carls I. enthält. Vol. II: Der das gemeine Wesen und die Regierungun Carls II and Jakobs II, enthält. [Translated by J.J. Dusch.] Breslau: Goschorsky. [2 vols.]

1757   ***Four Dissertations.*** London: Printed for A. Millar, in the Strand. [ix + 240 p.]

Comprising the following essays:

43.   The Natural History of Religion
44.   Of the Passions
45.   Of Tragedy
46.   Of the Standard of Taste

1755   *Vier Abhandlungen.* Translated by Friedrich Gabriel Resewitz. Querdlingburg and Leipzig: Bey Andreas Franz Biesterfeld. [xvi + 280 p.]

1. Die natürliche Geschichte der Religion
2. Von den Leidenschaften
3. Vom Trauerspiel
4. Von der Grundregel des Geschmacks

1759 Querdlingburg and Leipzig: Bey Andreas Franz Biesterfeld. [xvi + 280 p.]

Apparently a reprinting of the 1755 edition.

1759 *The History of England Under the House of Tudor*. London: Printed for A. Millar, in the Strand. [2 vols.: viii + 739 p.]

1759 *The History of England Under the House of Tudor: Comprehending the reigns of K. Henry VII. K. Henry VIII. K. Edward VI. Q. Mary, and Q. Elizabeth*. Dublin: Printed for Sarah Cotter, Bookseller. [3 vols.]

1762 Dublin: Printed for Sarah Cotter, Bookseller, under Dick's Coffee-House in Skinner Row. [3 vols.]

1764 London: Printed for A. Millar. [2 vols.]

1792 *The History of the Reign of Henry the Eighth*. London: Printed by D. Brewman. [viii + 191 p.]

According to the British Library, this essay was issued with volume IV of *The Historical Magazine*.

1793 *The History of the Reign of Edward the Sixth*. London: Printed by D. Brewman. [iv + 52 p.]

According to the British Library, this essay was issued with volume IV of *The Historical Magazine*.

Translations: *French*

1763 *Histoire de la maison de Tudor sur le trône d'Angleterre*. Translated by [Octavie Guichard Durey de Meinières], [formerly] Madame B[elot]. Amsterdam. [6 vols.]

Printed in Paris. This and subsequent 18th-century French editions were apparently also issued in two volumes.

1763 *Histoire d'Angleterre, contenant la maison de Tudor*. Translated from the English by [Octavie Guichard Durey de Meinières], [formerly] Madame B[elot]. Amsterdam. [6 vols.]

Printed in Paris.

1768 *Histoire d'Angleterre, contenant la maison de Tudor*. Translated from the English by [Octavie Guichard Durey de Meinières], [formerly] Madame B[elot]. London. [6 vols.]

In fact printed in Amsterdam.

1783   *Histoire d'Angleterre, contenant la maison de Tudor.* Translated from the English by [Octavie Guichard Durey de Meinières], [formerly] Madame B[elot]. London [i.e. Paris], et se trouve à Paris, chez la veuve Desaint, Nyon l'aîné, libraire. [6 vols.]

    Variously titled *Histoire de la maison de Tudor sur le trône d'Angleterre, depuis le regne de Henri VII jusqu'à l'avènement de Jacques 1er.*

1762 The History of England from the Invasion of Julius Caesar to the Accession of Henry VII. London: Printed for A. Millar, in the Strand. [2 vols.]

The National Library of Scotland notes that volume I in fact appeared in 1761.

1762   Dublin: Printed for George and Alexander Ewing. [4 vols.]

1762   Dublin: Printed for Sarah Cotter, under Dick's Coffee-House in Skinner Row. [4 vols.]

Translations: *French*

    The three translations below were all alternately titled *Histoire d'Angleterre, contenant la maison de Plantagenet* and were issued in either two or six volumes.

1765   *Histoire de la maison de Plantagenet sur le trône d'Angleterre, depuis l'invasion de Jules César jusqu'à l'avènement de Henri VII.* Translated by [Octavie Guichard Durey de Meinières], [formerly] Madame B[elot]. Amsterdam [Paris]. [6 vols.]

1769   *Histoire de la maison de Plantagenet sur le trône d'Angleterre, depuis l'invasion de Jules César jusqu'à l'avènement de Henri VII.* Translated from the English by [Octavie Guichard] Madame B[elot]. Amsterdam. [2 vols.]

1783   *Histoire de la maison de Plantagenet sur le trône d'Angleterre, depuis l'invasion de Jules César jusqu'à l'avènement de Henri VII.* Translated by [Octavie Guichard Durey de Meinières], [formerly] Madame B[elot]. London: et se trouve à Paris, chez la veuve Desaint. Nyon l'aîné, libraire. [2 vols.]

German

1767–71 *Geschichte von England von dem Einfalle des Julius Cäsar bis auf die Thronbesteigung Heinrichs des VII.* Translated from the English [by J.J. Dusch]. Breslau: Bey Johann Ernst Meyer. [4 vols.]

[1761]–1762 The History of England from the Invasion of Julius Caesar to the Revolution of 1688. A new edition, corrected. London: Printed for A. Millar, in the Strand. [6 vols.]

Vol. I: The Anglo-Saxons, William the Conqueror, William Rufus, Henry I, Stephen, Henry II, Richard I and John.

Vol. II: Henry III, Edward I, Edward II, Edward III, Richard II, Henry IV, Henry V, Henry VI, Edward IV, Edward V and Richard III.

Vol. III: Henry VII, Henry VIII, Edward IV, Mary.

Vol. IV: Elizabeth.

Vol. V: James I, Charles I.

Vol VI: The Commonwealth, Charles II, James II.

1762 Dublin: Printed for George and Alexander Ewing. [11 vols.]

1762–64 New edition. London: Printed for A. Millar. [6 vols. in 3]

1763 A new edition, corrected. London: Printed for A. Millar in the Strand. [8 vols.]

1767 A new edition with corrections and some additions. London: Printed for A. Millar, and sold by T. Cadell, over against Catherine Street, in the Strand. [8 vols.]

   Also published in an edition of six volumes.

1769 A new edition, corrected, to which is added a complete index. Dublin: Printed for James Williams. [8 vols.]

1770 A new edition, corrected. Dublin. Printed for James Williams, in Skinner Row. [8 vols.]

1770 A new edition, corrected. London: Printed for T. Cadell (successor to A. Millar), in the Strand. [8 vols.]

1771 A new edition with corrections, and some additions, by the author; also a complete index. [Robert Bell, bookseller at the late Union library, in Third Street, Philadelphia, America]: Printed for the subscribers. [8 vols.]

1772 A new edition, corrected, to which is added a complete index. Dublin: Printed for James Williams, in Skinner Row. [8 vols.]

1773 A new edition, corrected. London: Printed for T. Cadell, in the Strand. [8 vols.]

1773 A new edition, corrected. To which is added a complete index. London: Printed for A. Millar. [8 vols.]

Both 1773 editions are listed in the catalogue of the National Library of Scotland.

1775–76 A new edition, corrected. To which is added a complete index. Dublin: Printed for the United Company of Booksellers. [8 vols.]

1776 *The History of England from the Invasion of Julius Caesar to the Abdication of James the Second, 1688.* A new edition, with the author's last corrections and improvements. To which is prefixed a short account of his life, written by himself. Philadelphia: Lippincott. [6 vols.]

1776   A new edition, with the author's last corrections and improvements. To which is prefixed a short account of his life, written by himself. New York: John B. Alden. [6 vols.]

1776   A new edition, with the author's last corrections and improvements. To which is prefixed a short account of his life, written by himself. Philadelphia: Porter and Coates. [5 vols.]

1777   A new edition, with the author's last corrections and improvements. London: Printed for T. Cadell. [8 vols.]

1777   A new edition, with corrections and some additions. London: Printed for A. Millar. [2 vols.]

1778   A new edition, with the author's last corrections and improvements. To which is prefixed a short account of his life, written by himself. London: Printed for T. Cadell, in the Strand. [8 vols.]

1780   A new edition, corrected. To which is added a complete index. Dublin: Printed by James Williams, in Skinner Row. [8 vols.]

1782   A new edition, with the author's last corrections and improvements. To which is prefixed a short account of his life, written by himself. London: Printed for T. Cadell, in the Strand. [8 vols.]

1786   A new edition, with the author's last corrections and improvements. To which is prefixed a short account of his life, written by himself. London: Printed for T. Cadell, in the Strand. [8 vols.]

Translations: Dutch

1769–74   *Historie van Engeland van den inval van Julius Caesar tot de staets-verandering in 't jaer 1688, of komste van Willem III, op den troon; in agt deelen.* Rotterdam: by Losel, Bosch, Smithof, Burgvliet, Arrenberg en Beman. [8 vols.]

French

1770   *Le Génie de M. Hume, ou analyse de ses ouvrages, dans laquelle on pourra prendre une idée exacte des mœurs, des usages, des coutumes, des lois, & du Gouvernement du peuple Anglois.* London [Paris]: et se trouve à Paris: Vincent, Impr.-libraire. [viii + 472 p.]

1781   *Histoire d'Angleterre, depuis l'invasion de Jules César, jusqu'à l'évasion de Jacques II.* Augmentée d'une critique de cette histoire par M. [Joseph] Towers, & de la suite jusqu'à l'avènement de Georges III au trône. Yverdon. [19 vols.]

1783   *Histoire d'Angleterre*: Vols. 1–2: *Histoire de la maison Plantagenet*; Vols. 3–4: *Histoire de la maison Tudor*; Vols. 5–6: *Histoire de la maison de Stuard.* Paris: La veuve Desaint, Libraire et Nyon l'aîné, libraire. [6 vols.]

1789   *Histoire d'Angleterre, depuis l'invasion de Jules César, jusqu'à la chute des Stuarts en 1688.* Translated from the English by [Octavie Durey de Meinières], [formerly] Madame B[elot], avec des notes. Paris. [18 vols.]

German

1774   *Das Genie des Hrn Hume. Oder Sammlung der vorzüglichsten Grundsätze dieses Philosophen, welche zugleich einen genauen Begriff der Sitten, Gebrauche Gewohnheiten, Gesteze und der Regierunsform der Englischen Nation wie auch einige hauptzüge ihrer Geschichte und einige kurze anakdoten berühmter Männer enthält.* Edited and translated by Johann Gottfried Bremer. Leipzig: Bey Christian Gottlob Hilschern. [xiv + 348 p.]

1786–88   *Geschichte der Großbritannien.* Translated from the English. Frankenthal: Gedruckt bei Ludwig Bernhard Friedrich Gegel. [20 vols.]

1759   [Anonymous]. **Letter to the author of the** *Critical Review* **[regarding the** *Epigoniad* **of W. Wilkie].** *Critical Review*, 7 (April 1759): 323–34.

1766   [Anonymous]. *Exposé Succinct de la Contestation Qui S'est Élevée entre M. Hume et M. Rousseau, Avec les Pièces Justificatives*. [The English portions of this account translated by J.B.A. Suard.] London. [xvi + 127 p.]

1766   London [i.e., Yverdon: Printed for F.-B. De Felice]. [xii + 177 p.]

Pages 133 to 177 are devoted to the following: "Le rapporteur de bonne-foi ou examen sans partialité & sans prétention du différend survenu entre M. Hume & M. Rousseau de Genéve." This appears to be a pirated edition.

1766   *Exposé Succinct de la Contestation Qui S'est Elevée entre M. Hume et M.J.J. Rousseau, Avec les Pièces Justificatives. Auquel on a joint le Docteur Pansophe, ou letter de M. Voltaire.* London [Paris]. [xiv + 132 p.]

1767   *Recueil de pièces sur le démêlé de M. Hume, et M.J.J. Rousseau contenant l'Exposé succinct, la Justification de J.J. Rousseau, le Docteur Pansophe, le Jugement de l'auteur des Affiches sur*

> *ce démêlé: avec une lettre de M. Freron, tome septième de l'Année littéraire sur le même sujet.* Translated by J.B.A. Suard. London. [xii + 92 p.]
>
> Actually printed in Paris.

Translations: English

> 1766   *A Concise and Genuine Account of the Dispute Between Mr. Hume and Mr. Rousseau: With the Letters that Passed Between Them During Their Controversy. As also the Letters of the Hon. Mr. Walpole and Mr. D'Alembert, Relative to this Extraordinary Affair.* Translated from the French. London: Printed for T. Becket and P.A. De Hondt, near Surry Street, in the Strand. [viii + 95 p.]
>
> 1777   *Three Letters to Jean Jacques Rousseau, 19 June–22 July 1766.* [n.p.]
>
> Reported in the British Library. Without publication place or date and almost certainly pirated.
>
> 1777   *Original Letters of David Hume, Relative to J.J. Rousseau.* [n.p.]
>
> Reported in the British Library. Without publication place or date and almost certainly pirated.

Italian

> 1767   *Esposizione della contestazione insorta fra il signor Davide Hume e il signor Gian Jacopo Russo con la Scritture loro Giustificative ed una Dichiarazione agli editori del signor d'Alembert.* Translated from the French. Venice: appresso Luigi Pavini. [96 p.]
>
> Rousseau's Christian name is variously spelled as Jacopo or Giacopo.

1772   **"Of Impudence and Modesty," "Of Love and Marriage," and "Of Avarice,"** [essays 3, 6 and 13] in volume 1 of ***The Beauty of the Magazines, and other periodical works, selected for a series of years, consisting of essays, moral tales, characters and other fugitive pieces, in prose***. London: Richardson and Urquhart. [2 vols.]

Essays 3 and 6 had ceased being reprinted with the 1758 edition of Hume's *Essays. Moral, Political and Literary*, while essay 13 was omitted from the 1770 and subsequent editions.

1777   *The Life of David Hume, Esq. Written by Himself*. London: Printed for W. Strahan and T. Cadell, in the Strand. [iv + 62 p.]

> 1777   London: Printed for W. Strahan and T. Cadell, and sold in Dublin by Alex Kelburn. [iv + 36 p.]

1777   *To which is added, a letter from Adam Smith, LL.D. to William Strahan, Esq.* Dublin: Printed for J. Williams. [vi + 26 p.]

1778   *The Life of David Hume, Esq., The Philosopher and Historian.* Philadelphia: Printed and sold by Robert Bell, next door to St. Paul's Church, in Third Street. [ii + 62 p.]

1778   Hume's autobiographical essay is contained in Philip Morin Freneau. ed. *Miscellanies for sentimentalists.* Philadelphia: Printed and sold by Robert Bell. [425 p.]

Translations: French

1777   *Vie de David Hume, écrite par lui-même.* Translated by Jean-Baptiste Antoine Suard. London. [viii + 61 p.]

A variant shows this essay released in an edition of 37 pages. Additionally, the place of publication is fictitious. The essay was almost certainly published in either Switzerland or France.

Italian

178?   *Vita di David Hume, scritta de lui medesimo.* Translated from the English and containing Adam Smith's letter to William Strahan. [n.p.: n.p.]

The Cambridge University Library is unable to offer greater precision regarding the date or facts of publication.

Latin

1787   *Davidis Humei, Scoti, summi apud suos philosophi, de vita sua acta liber singularis: nunc primum latinè redditus.* Translated by David Dalrymple. Edinburgh. [ii + 12 p.]

Russian

1781   *Zhizn' Davyda Gumma, opisannaia in samim.* Translated by Ivan Morkov. Moscow: [Senatskaia tip.] u F. Gippiusa. [54 p.]

1777   **[Anonymous].** *Two Essays.* London. [41 p.]

An unauthorized publication of Hume's essays **"Of Suicide"** and **"Of the Immortality of the Soul."** These essays were originally intended for inclusion in the 1757 *Dissertations* but were withdrawn at the last moment. They were actually printed and a few sets were bound in with the 1757 volume before Hume apparently decided to withhold the essays from publication. A copy of the *Dissertations* in the National Library of Scotland contains the essay "On Suicide" together with the replacement Dissertation Four, "Of the Standard of Taste."

1783   *Essays on Suicide and the Immortality of the Soul, ascribed to the late David Hume, Esq. Never before published. With remarks, intended as an antidote to the poison contained in these performances, by the editor. To which is added, Two letters on suicide, from Rosseau's [sic] Eloisa.* London: Printed for M. Smith, and sold at booksellers in Piccadilly, Fleet Street and Paternoster Row. [iv + 107 p.]

1784   *Essay on the immortality of the soul; shewing the fallacy and malignity of a sceptical one, lately published, together with such another on suicide; and both ascribed, by the editor, to the late David Hume, Esq.* London: T. Spilsbury. [xiii + 45 p.]

1789   *Essays on suicide and the immortality of the soul, by the late David Hume, Esq. With remarks by the editor. To which is added, two letters on suicide, from Rousseau's Eloisa.* A new edition, with considerable improvements. London: Printed for G. Kearsley, and sold by the booksellers in Piccadilly, Fleet Street and Paternoster Row. [iv + 189 p.]

1799   *Essays on Suicide and the Immortality of the Soul. With remarks by the editor. To which are added, two letters on suicide, from Rousseau's Eloisa.* A new edition. Basil: Printed for the Editor of the Collection of English Classics. Sold by James Decker. [vi + 124 p.]

Translations: French

1770   The two essays were printed surreptitiously, without attribution of authorship, as sections x and xi in volume 2 of the *Recueil Philosophique, ou Mélange de pièces sur la religion et la morale* [*par différents auteurs*]. London. [2 vols.]

The translation of these two essays is customarily attributed to Baron d'Holbach, whose own essays adjoin them. The National Library of Scotland states that the work was actually printed in Amsterdam by M.M. Rey and published by J.A. Naigeon.

1785   *Essai sur le suicide.* Translated from the English. [n.p.: n. p.] [23 p.]

1779   *Dialogues Concerning Natural Religion*. [London]. [152 p.]

1779   2nd edition. London. [264 p.]

1782   *To which is added, Divine benevolence asserted; and vindicated from the objections of ancient and modern sceptics. By Thomas Balguy.* Dublin: Printed by John Exshaw. [iv + 175 + v + 125 p.]

Translations: *French*

1779 *Dialogues sur la religion naturelle. Ouvrage posthume de David Hume, Ecuyer.* Edinburgh. [viii + 292 p.]

   Jessop notes that this edition was probably printed and published in France or Holland.

 German

1781 *Gespräche über natürliche Religion. Nebst einem Gespräch über den Atheismus von Ernst Platner.* To which is added a discussion of atheism by Ernst Platner. Translated from the English by K.G. Schreiter. Leipzig. In der Weygandschen Buchhandlung. [iv + 396 p.]

1780 ***The Works of David Hume, containing the History of England, from the invasion of Julius Caesar to the Revolution of 1688; Essays Moral, Political and Literary, with last corrections.*** Dublin: Printed for J. Williams. [10 vols.]

   Comprising the 1779 edition in two volumes of Hume's *Essays and Treatises on Several Subjects* and the 1780 edition in eight volumes of *The History of England.*

1795 **Letter from David Hume, Esq. to the Author of the *Delineation of the Nature and Obligation of Morality*.** Edinburgh. [5 p.]

   The letter is dated 15 March 1753 and is directed to James Balfour.

1846 **"The Descent on the Coast of Brittany in 1746, and the Causes of Its Failure,"** in John Hill Burton, *Life and Correspondence of David Hume* (2 vols.; Edinburgh: William Tait, 1846): 1: 441–56.

1846 **"Of the Authenticity of Ossian's Poems,"** in John Hill Burton, *Life of Hume*, 1: 471–80.

1958 **"Hume at La Flèche, 1735; An Unpublished Letter edited by Ernest Campbell Mossner,"** in *The University of Texas Studies in English*, 37 (1958).

   1958 *Hume at La Flèche, 1735; An Unpublished Letter edited by Ernest Campbell Mossner. Reprinted in* The University of Texas Studies in English, *37 (1958). Austin, Texas.*

1967 **A Letter from a Gentleman to His Friend in Edinburgh, 1745.** Ernest Campbell Mossner and John V. Prince, eds., Edinburgh: Edinburgh University Press. [xxv + 42 p.]

Henry Home, Lord Kames (1696–1782)

1728 *Remarkable Decisions of the Court of Session, From 1716 to 1728.* Edinburgh: Printed by Mr. Tho. Ruddiman. [iv + 287p.]

1790   2nd edition. Edinburgh: Bell & Bradfute, and W. Creech. [iv + 209 p.]

1732   **[Anonymous].** *Essays on Several Subjects in Law* **[sciz. jus tertii, beneficium cedenarum actionum, vinco vincentem, prescription.]** Edinburgh: Printed by R. Fleming and Company, and sold at Mr. James McEven's shop. [iv + 164 p.]

1741   *The Decisions of the Court of Session, from its First Institution [17 May 1532] to the Present Time: Abridged and digested under proper heads in Form of a Dictionary.* Edinburgh: Printed by Richard Watkins, for himself. Alexander Kincaid and Robert Fleming. Sold by the said Alexander Kincaid. [2 vols.]

    1774   *The Decisions of the Court of Session, from its institution till the year 1764, with several decisions since that period, arranged under proper titles, in the form of a dictionary.* London: Printed for the editor, and sold by E. and C. Dilly, and Charles Elliot, Edinburgh. [5 vols.]

    1791   2nd edition. Printed for Bell & Bradfute, William Creech and Watson, Elder and Co. [2 vols.]

1747   **[Anonymous].** *Essays on Several Subjects Concerning British Antiquities* **[viz. I. Introduction of the feudal law into Scotland. II. Constitution of Parliament. III. Honour. Dignity. IV. Succession or descent.]** [With an appendix upon hereditary and indefeasible right.] Edinburgh: Printed for A. Kincaid. [iv + 217 p.]

    1749   2nd edition. London: M. Cooper. [iv + 217 p.]

    1763   3rd edition, with additions and alterations. Edinburgh: Printed for A. Kincaid and J. Bell. [iv + 216 p.]

    1795   *An Essay on the Hereditary and Indefeasible Right of Kings.* Composed in the year 1745. Edinburgh. Printed for Thomas Maccliesh & Co. [24 p.]
           1797   Edinburgh. [24 p.]

    1797   Edinburgh: Printed for T. Maccliesh & Co. [iv + 98 p.]

1751   **[Anonymous].** *Essays on the Principles of Morality and Natural Religion.* Edinburgh: Printed for R. Fleming, for A. Kincaid and A. Donaldson. [vi + 394 p.]

    1753   *Some Late Opinions Concerning the Foundations of Morality, Examined, in a Letter to a Friend.* London: Printed for R. Dodsley and M. Cooper. [46 p.]

           This collection contains excerpts from David Hume's *Enquiry Concerning the Principles of Morals*; Henry Home, Lord Kames's, *Essays on the Principles of Morality and Natural*

Religion; and James Balfour's, *Delineation of the Nature and Obligation of Morality.*

1758	2nd edition, with alterations and additions. London: Printed for C. Hitch & L. Hawes, R. & J. Dodsley, J. Rivington & J. Fletcher, and J. Richardson. [vi + 309 p.]
1779	Several essays added concerning the proof of a deity. Corrected and improved, in a 3rd edition. Edinburgh: Printed for John Bell and John Murray, London. [x + 380 p.]

Translations: *German*

1768	*Versuche über die ersten Gründe der Sittlichkeit und der natürlichen Religion.* Translated by C.G. Rautenberg. Brunswick: J.C. Meyer. [2 vols.]
1786	Vienna: Trattnern. [2 vols.]

1754 **"Of the Laws of Motion," in *Essays and Observations, Physical and Literary*. Read before a Society in Edinburgh** (the Philosophical Society of Edinburgh) 1: [1754]: 1–69.

1756 **[Anonymous].** *Objections against the Essays on Morality and Natural Religion Examined.* Edinburgh. [64 p.]

Ian Ross reports that Kames published this pamphlet in December 1756 in order to re-establish himself with the orthodox wing of the Kirk. There is evidence that he was aided in writing the essay by Hugh Blair and Robert Wallace.

1757 *Decisions of the Court of Session from the Month of November 1735 to the Month of July 1744.* Printed for G. Hamilton & J. Balfour. [ii + 460 p.]

1791	Edinburgh: Bell & Bradfute. [464 p.]

1757 **[Anonymous].** *Statute Law of Scotland, Abridged. With Historical Notes.* Edinburgh: Printed by Sands, Donaldson, Murray and Cochran. For A. Kincaid and A. Donaldson. [vi + 453 p.]

1769	2nd edition. Edinburgh: Printed for A. Kincaid and J. Bell. [vi + 465 p.]

1758 **[Anonymous].** *Historical Law tracts.* Edinburgh: Printed for A. Millar, London; and A. Kincaid & J. Bell, Edinburgh. [2 vols.]

1761	2nd edition. Edinburgh: Printed for A. Kincaid, His Majesty's printer, for A. Millar, London; and A. Kincaid and J. Bell in Edinburgh. [xv + 463 p.]
1776	3rd edition, with additions and corrections. Edinburgh: Printed for T. Cadell, London; and J. Bell and W. Creech, Edinburgh. [xvi + 471 p.]

1792   4th edition, with additions and corrections. Edinburgh: Printed for T. Cadell, London; and Bell & Bradfute and W. Creech, Edinburgh. [xvi + 487 p.]

Translations: French

1766   *Essais historiques sur les loix*. Translated from the English by Mathieu-Antoine Bouchaud, with notes and commentary by the translator. Paris: Chez vente libraire au bas de la Montagne de Ste Genevieve; De l'imprimerie de Quillau. [xi + 391 p.]

A translation of Kames's essays on the "History of the Criminal Law" and the "History of Property," to which a third essay, by the translator, "Observation sur le troisième chef de la loi de Cincia," is added.

1760   **[Anonymous].** ***Principles of Equity***. Edinburgh: Printed by Alexander Kincaid. For A. Millar, London; and A. Kincaid and J. Bell, Edinburgh. [xviii + 289 p.]

1767   2nd edition, corrected and enlarged. Edinburgh: Printed for A. Millar, London; and A. Kincaid and J. Bell, Edinburgh. [x + 375 p.]

1778   3rd edition. Edinburgh: Printed for J. Bell and W. Creech, Edinburgh; and T. Cadell, London. [2 vols.]

Translations: German

1778   *Untersuchung über die moralischen Gesetze der Gesellschaft.* Translated from the English by Johann Christian Macher. Leipzig: im Verlage der Dyckischen Buchhandlung. [96 p.]

1761   **[Anonymous].** ***Introduction to the Art of Thinking***. Edinburgh: Printed for A. Kincaid and J. Bell. [x + 202 p.]

1764   2nd edition, enlarged with additional maxims and illustrations. Edinburgh: Printed for A. Kincaid and J. Bell. [x + 282 p.]

1775   3rd edition, enlarged with additional maxims and illustrations. Edinburgh: Printed for W. Creech. [x + 311 p.]

1789   4th edition, enlarged with additional maxims and illustrations. Edinburgh: Printed for William Creech and T. Cadell, London. [x + 311 p.]

1762   **[Anonymous].** ***Elements of Criticism***. Edinburgh: Printed for A. Millar, London; and A. Kincaid and J. Bell, Edinburgh. [3 vols.]

1762   Dublin: Printed by Sarah Cotter. [2 vols.]

1763   2nd edition, with additions and improvements. Edinburgh:

Printed for A. Millar, London; and A. Kincaid and J. Bell, Edinburgh. [3 vols.]

1765   3rd edition, with additions and improvements. Edinburgh: Printed for A. Millar, London; and A. Kincaid and J. Bell, Edinburgh. [2 vols.]

1769   4th edition, with additions and improvements. Edinburgh: Printed for A. Millar and T. Caddel [*sic*], London; and A. Kincaid and J. Bell, Edinburgh. [2 vols.]

1772   5th edition, with additions and improvements. Dublin: Printed for Charles Ingham. [2 vols.]

1774   5th edition. Edinburgh: Printed for A. Kincaid & W. Creech and J. Bell, Edinburgh; and W. Johnston and T. Cadell, London. [2 vols.]

1785   6th edition, with the author's last corrections and additions. Edinburgh: Printed for John Bell and William Creech; and for T. Cadell and G. Robinson, London. [2 vols.]

1788   7th edition, with the author's last corrections and additions. Edinburgh: Printed for John Bell and William Creech; and for T. Cadell, G.G.J. and J. Robinson, London. [2 vols.]

Translations: *German*

1763   *Grundsätze der Critik*. En drei theilen. Translated from the English by Johann Nicolaus Meinhard. Leipzig: Dyckischen Handlung. [3 vols.]

1772   Leipzig: Dyckischen Handlung. [2 vols.]

1775   Frankfurt and Leipzig. [2 vols.]

1785–86   Vienna: Gedruckt bey Johann Thomas Edlen von Trattnern. [2 vols.]

1790   Leipzig: Dyckischen Buchhandlung. [3 vols.]

1790   Vienna: F.A. Schrämbl. [3 vols.]

1766   **[Anonymous].** *Progress of Flax-Husbandry in Scotland*. Edinburgh: Printed by Sands, Murray, and Cochran. [31 p.]

1766   *Remarkable Decisions of the Court of Session, From 1730 to 1752*. Edinburgh: A. Kincaid and J. Bell. [viii + 284 p.]

1771   **"Observations upon the Foregoing Paper Concerning Shallow Ploughing," in *Essays and Observations, Physical and Literary*. Read before a Society in Edinburgh** (the Philosophical Society of Edinburgh), 3: [1771]: 68–79.

1771   *"On Evaporation,"* in *Essays and Observations, Physical and Literary.* **Read before a Society in Edinburgh** (the Philosophical Society of Edinburgh), 3: [1771]: 80–99.

1774   **[Anonymous]** *Sketches of the History of Man.* Edinburgh: Printed for W. Creech, Edinburgh, and for W. Strahan and T. Cadell, London. [2 vols.]

> 1774–75   Dublin: Printed for J. Williams. [4 vols.]

The author's name is given as Henry Home, Lord Kaims. According to the catalogue of the National Library of Scotland, volumes 1 and 2 are dated 1775, while volumes 3 and 4 are dated 1774.

> 1775   Dublin: Printed for the United Company of Booksellers. [4 vols.]

> 1776   *Six Sketches on the History of Man.* [Partial reprinting. Containing, the progress of men as individuals. I. The diversity of men, and of languages. II. Of food and population. III. Of property. IV. The origin and progress of commerce. V. The origin and progress of arts. VI. The progress of the female sex. With an appendix, concerning the propagation of animals, and the care of their offspring.] Philadelphia: Sold by R. Bell, in Third Street and R. Aitken, in Front Street. [vi + 262 p.]

> 1778   Considerably improved in a 2nd edition. Edinburgh: Printed for W. Strahan and T. Cadell, London; and for William Creech, Edinburgh. [4 vols.]

> 1779   Considerably improved in a 3rd edition. Dublin: Printed for James Williams. [2 vols.]

> 1788   Another edition, considerably enlarged by the last additions and corrections of the author. Edinburgh: Printed for A. Strahan and T. Cadell, London; and for William Creech, Edinburgh. [4 vols.]

> 1789   *Curious Thoughts on the History of Man.* Chiefly abridged or selected from the celebrated works of Lord Kaimes [*sic*], Lord Monboddo, . . . by the Rev. John Adams. London: Printed for G. Kearsley. [xi + 359 p.]
>
> > 1790   Dublin: Printed by William Porter, for P. Wogan, P. Byrne, B. Dornin and W. Jones. [xi + 299 p.]

Translations: German

> 1774–75   *Versuche über die Geschichte des Menschen.* Translated from the English by Anton Ernst Klausing. Leipzig: Bey Johann Friedrich Junius. [2 vols.]

> 1783–84   Leipzig: Bey Johann Freidrich Junius. [2 vols.]

> 1787   Vienna: Gedruckt bey Johann Thomas Edlen Trattnern. [2 vols.]

1790   Vienna: Gedruckt für F.A. Schrämbl. [3 vols.]

1776   [Anonymous]. *The Gentleman Farmer. Being an Attempt to Improve Agriculture by Subjecting it to the Test of Rational Principles.* Edinburgh: Printed for W. Creech, Edinburgh; and T. Cadell, London. [xxiv + 409 p.]

   1779   Dublin: Printed by James Williams. [xxiv + 375 p.]

   1779   2nd edition, with considerable additions. Edinburgh: Printed for John Bell. [xxviii + 438 p.]

   1788   3rd edition, with the author's last corrections and additions. Edinburgh: Printed for John Bell and G.G.J. and J. Robinson, London. [xxxi + 438 p.]

1777   [Anonymous]. *Elucidations Respecting the Common and Statute Law of Scotland.* Edinburgh: Printed for William Creech and sold, in London, by T. Cadell. [xvi + 421 p.]

**1780   ** *Select Decisions of the Court of Session, From the Year 1752 to the Year 1768.* Edinburgh: Printed by Neill and Company, for John Bell. [xvii + 351 p.]

1781   [Anonymous]. *Loose Hints Upon Education: Chiefly Concerning the Culture of the Heart.* Edinburgh: Printed for John Bell; and John Murray, London. [xi + 381 p.]

   1782   Dublin: Printed by T. Henshall, for S. Price, W. & H. Whitestone, T. Walker, J. Beatty, R. Burton, and P. Byrne. [vi + 256 p.]

   1782   2nd edition, enlarged. Edinburgh: Printed for John Bell. Geo. Robinson, Paternoster Row, and John Murray, London. [xi + 419 p.]

Ian Simpson Ross, in his study of Kames [*Lord Kames and the Scotland of His Day* (Oxford: Clarendon Press, 1972)], reports the following two works by Kames of which I can find no record: a 1764 edition of *The Decisions of the Court of Session, from its First Institution to the Present Time: Abridged and digested under proper Heads in Form of a Dictionary* and a 1778 edition of *Statute Law of Scotland, Abridged. With Historical Notes.*

John Millar (1735–1801)

**1760   ** *Disputatio Juridica ad Tit. 3 Lib. xxvi Pand. De confirmando tutore vel curatore.* Edinburgh: Edinburgh University Library.

   Millar's Bar Examination.

1771   [Anonymous]. *A Course of Lectures on Government; Given Annually in the University.* Glasgow. [8 p.]

**1771   ** *Observations Concerning the Distinction of Ranks in Society.* London: Printed for W. and J. Richardson, for John Murray, no. 32 Fleet Street, opposite St. Dunstan's Church. [xv + 242 p.]

1771   Dublin: Printed by T. Ewing. [xiv + 240 p.]

1773   2nd edition, greatly enlarged. London: Printed for John Murray. [xxii + 312 p.]

1779   *The Origin of the Distinction of Ranks; or, An Enquiry into the Circumstances Which Give Rise to Influence and Authority in the Different Members of Society.* 3rd edition, corrected and enlarged. London: J. Murray. [viii + 362 p.]

1779   3rd edition. Glasgow: Andrew Foulis. [viii + 362 p.]

1781   3rd edition, corrected and enlarged. London: J. Murray. [viii + 362 p.]

1793   Basil: Printed and sold by J.J. Tourneisen. [iv + 284 p.]

1806   4th edition, corrected, to which is prefixed, *An Account of the Author*, by John Craig, esq. Edinburgh: Printed for W. Blackwood, and Longman, Hurst, Rees, and Orme, London. [cxxiv + 296 p.]

Translations: French

1773   *Observations sur les commencemens de la société.* Translated by Jean Baptiste Antoine Suard. Amsterdam: Chez Arkstée et Meerkus. [xxiv + 423 p.]

The edition carries a fictitious imprint and was in fact published in Paris.

1778   *Observations sur la distinction des rangs dans la société.* Translated by Jean Baptiste Antoine Suard. Amsterdam: et se trouve à Paris: Chez Pissot. [xxiv + 423 p.]

Another edition of the 1773 translation with a change in title.

German

1772   *Bemerkungen über den Unterschied der Stände in der Bürgerlichen Gesellschaft.* Leipzig: Bey Engelhart Benjamin Schwickert. [237 p.]

1798   *Aufklärungen über Ursprung und Fortschritte des Unterschieds der Stände und des Ranges, in Hinsicht auf Kultur und Sitten bei den vorzüglichsten Nationen.* Translated by Johann Bergk. Leipzig: Weygand. [viii + 392 p.]

1783   *Disputatio Juridica ad Tit. 1 Lib. xliv Digest: De exceptionibus, praescriptionibus, et praejudiciis.* Edinburgh.

1787   *An Historical View of the English Government, from the Settlement of the Saxons in Britain to the Accession of the House of Stewart.* London: Printed for A. Strahan and T. Cadell, and J. Murray. [vii + 565 p.]

1789	Dublin: Printed by Zachariah Jackson, for Grueber and M'Allister. [vi + 506 p.]
1790	Dublin: Printed for J. Jones. [vi + 506 p.]
1790	London: Printed for the Company of Booksellers. [vi + 506 p.]
1790	2nd edition. London: Printed for A. Strahan and T. Cadell, and J. Murray. [vii + 565 p.]

1803   *An Historical View of the English Government, from the Settlement of the Saxons in Britain to the Revolution of 1688. To which are Subjoined Some Dissertations Connected with the History of Government, from the Revolution to the Present Time.* Edited by John Craig and James Mylne. London: Printed for J. Mawman. [4 vols.]

The first two volumes are an unaltered reprinting of the two volumes of the 2nd edition.

1804	London: Printed for J. Mawman. [4 vols.]
1812	London: Printed for J. Mawman. [4 vols.]

Translations: *German*

1819–21   *John Millar's Historische Entwickelung der englischen Staatsverfassung.* Translated by Karl Ernst Schmid. Jena: In Commission bei August Schmid. [3 vols.]

1796   [Pseudonymous]. *Letters of Crito, on the Causes, Objects, and Consequences of the Present War.* Edinburgh: Printed for J. Johnstone and sold at the office of the *Scots Chronicle.* [x + 109 p.]

Fifteen letters originally published in the *Scots Chronicle* from May to September 1796.

1796   Edinburgh: Printed for J. Johnstone; London: Printed for J. Debrett. [x + 109 p.]

1796   [Pseudonymous]. *Letters of Sidney on inequality of property*: to which is added a treatise on *The Effects of War on Commercial Prosperity.* Ten letters published serially in the *Scots Chronicle*, from August to October 1776.

William C. Lehmann, *John Millar of Glasgow, 1735–1801: His Life and Thought and His Contributions to Sociological Analysis* (Cambridge: University Press, 1960), maintains that these letters were in fact among Millar's pseudonymous writings.

1796   To which is added eight additional letters, in a pamphlet dedicated to the Earl of Lauderdale. Edinburgh: Printed and sold at the office of the *Scots Chronicle,* and by J. Debrett,

London: Messrs. J. Elder, J. Robertson and W. Berry, Edinburgh; Messrs. Brash & Reid and Cameron and Murdoch, Glasgow. [iv + 115 p.]

James Burnett, Lord Monboddo (1714–99)

1737   **Disputatio juridica, ad Tit. 2. Lib. VI. Pand. de publiciana in rem actione: quam, ... pro advocati munere consequendo, publicae disquisitioni subjicit Jacobus Burnet.** Edinburgh: Thomas Ruddiman. [iv + 8 p.]

1768   **Preface to *An Account of a Savage Girl Caught Wild in the Woods of Champagne*.** Written by Madam H.-T. [de la Condamine] and translated by William Robertson, Edinburgh: Printed for A. Kincaid and J. Bell. [xviii + 63 p.]

    1796   Aberdeen: Printed by Burnett and Rettie, and sold by John Burnett, bookseller. [xix + 64 p.]

    1797   Reprinted in Monboddo's *Antient Metaphysics*.

1773–92   **[Anonymous].** *Of the Origin and Progress of Language*.

1773   **Vol. I**: Edinburgh: Printed for A. Kincaid and W. Creech, and T. Cadell, London.

    1774   2nd edition. Edinburgh: Printed for J. Balfour; and T. Cadell, London.

1774   **Vol. II**: Edinburgh: Printed for J. Balfour; and T. Cadell, London.

    1809   2nd edition, including an Appendix containing the ms additions made on the author's copy of this volume. Edinburgh: Printed for Alex Smellie; for Cuthell and Martin, Holborn, London. [xi + 588 p.]

    Added to the 2nd edition of volume 2 were the following dissertations: 1. Of the formation of the Greek language; 2. Of the sound of the Greek language; 3. Of the composition of the ancients; and particularly of that of Demosthenes.

1776   **Vol. III**: Edinburgh: Printed for J. Balfour; and T. Cadell, London.

    1786   2nd edition. London: Printed for T. Cadell; and J. Balfour, Edinburgh.

1787   **Vol. IV**: Edinburgh: Printed for J. Bell; and T. Cadell, London.

1789   **Vol. V**: Edinburgh: Printed for J. Bell; and T. Cadell, London.

1792   **Vol. VI**: Edinburgh: London: Printed for Bell and Bradfute; and T. Cadell in the Strand. [vi + 473 p.]

Translations: German

> 1784–85 *Des Lord Monboddo Werk von dem Ursprunge und Fortgange der Sprache.* Translated by E.A. Schmid, with an introduction by Johann Gottfried von Herder. Riga: Bey Johann Friedrich Hareknoch. [2 vols.]

1779–99 [Anonymous]. *Antient Metaphysics, or the Science of Universals.*

> **1779** **Vol. I:** *The Science of Universals.* With an Appendix Containing an Examination of Sir Isaac Newton's Philosophy. Edinburgh: Printed for J. Balfour; and T. Cadell, London.

> **1782** **Vol. II:** *The Science of Universals.* Containing a Further Examination of the Principles of Sir Isaac Newton's Astronomy. London: Printed for T. Cadell.

> **1784** **Vol. III:** *The History and Philosophy of Men.* London: Printed for T. Cadell.

> **1795** **Vol. IV:** *The History of Man.* Edinburgh: Printed for Bell & Bradfute.

> **1797** **Vol. V:** *The History of Man in the Civilized State.* Edinburgh: Printed for Bell & Bradfute.

> **1799** **Vol. VI:** [God]. Edinburgh: Printed for J. Balfour; and T. Cadell, London.

> 1789 *Curious Thoughts on the History of Man.* Chiefly abridged or selected from the celebrated works of Lord Kaimes [*sic*], Lord Monboddo, . . . by the Rev. John Adams. London: Printed for G. Kearsley. [xi + 359 p.]

>> 1790 Dublin: Printed by William Porter, for P. Wogan, P. Byrne, B. Dornin and W. Jones. [xi + 299 p.]

1789 **"Advertisement"** to John Brown, *Letters upon the Poetry and Music of the Italian Opera, Addressed to a Friend.* Edinburgh: Bell & Bradfute. [xx + 141 p.]

> 1791 2nd edition. London: T. Cadell.

1829 **"Decisions Collected by Lord Monboddo,"** in M.P. Brown, ed., *General Synopsis of the Decisions of the Court of Session.* 5 vols. Edinburgh: William Tait. 5: 651–941.

Thomas Reid (1710–96)

1748 **"An Essay on Quantity, Occasioned by Reading a Treatise in Which Simple and Compound Ratios are Applied to Virtue and Merit,"** in *Philosophical Transactions of the Royal Society*, 45 (1748): 505–20.

1764   *An Inquiry into the Human Mind, on the Principles of Common Sense.* Edinburgh: Printed for A. Millar, London; and A. Kincaid and J. Bell, Edinburgh. [xvi + 541 p.]

> 1764   Dublin: Alexander Ewing. [xii + 316 p.]
>
> 1765   2nd edition, corrected. Edinburgh: Printed for A. Millar, London; and A. Kincaid and J. Bell, Edinburgh. [xvi + 383 p.]
>
> 1769   3rd edition, corrected. London: Printed for T. Cadell (successor to A. Millar) and T. Longman, London; and A. Kincaid and J. Bell, Edinburgh. [xvi + 383 p.]
>
> 1779   3rd edition. Dublin: Printed for R. Marchbank, for the Company of Booksellers. [xii + 316 p.]
>
> 1785   4th edition, corrected. London: Printed for T. Cadell in the Strand, London: and J. Bell and W. Creech, Edinburgh. [xvi + 488 p.]
>
> 1801   5th edition. Edinburgh: Bell & Bradfute and W. Creech, and for T. Cadell, jun. and W. Davies, London, by A. Neill. [xvi + 478 p.]
>
> 1804   6th edition. Glasgow: Gray, Maver & Co.; London: Vernor & Hood. [viii + 407 p.]
>
> 1806   6th edition. Glasgow: Gray, Maver. [viii + 407 p.]

Translations: *French*

> 1768   *Recherches sur l'entendement humain d'après les principes du sens commun.* Amsterdam: Chez Jean Meyer. [2 vols.]

German

> 1782   *Untersuchungen über den menschlichen Geist den Grundsätzen des gemeinen Menschenverstandes.* Leipzig: Schwickertschen Verlage. [397 p.]

1774   **"A Brief Account of Aristotle's Logic, with Remarks,"** in [Henry Home, Lord Kames], *Sketches of the History of Man.* 2 vols. Edinburgh: Printed for W. Creech, Edinburgh and for W. Strahan and T. Cadell, London. 2: 168–241.

Reid's essay on Aristotle's logic was included in subsequent editions of Kames's *Sketches.* (1774–75, 1775, 1776, 1778, 1779, 1788, 1789, 1796). See, for example, the 3rd edition of the *Sketches* (1779), "considerably improved," 2 vols. Dublin: Printed for James Williams, where Reid's comments appear at 2: 184–262. The 4th edition of the *Sketches* (1788), "considerably enlarged by the last additions and corrections of the author,"

4 vols.; Edinburgh: Printed for A. Strahan and T. Cadell, London and William Creech, Edinburgh, carries Reid's essay at 3: 309–432.

    1806   *Analysis of Aristotle's Logic with Remarks*. 2nd edition. Edinburgh: Printed for William Creech; and sold by J. Murray, Fleet Street, London. [v + 149 p.]

1775–76 **[Anonymous] Review of Joseph Priestley's** *Hartley's Theory of the Human Mind*, in *Monthly Review*, 53 (1775): 380–90 and 54 (1776): 41–7.

1785 *Essays on the Intellectual Powers of Man*. Edinburgh: Printed for J. Bell, and G.G.J. & J. Robinson, London. [xii + 766 p.]

    1786   Dublin: Printed for L. White. [2 vols.]

1788 *Essays on the Active Powers of Man*. Edinburgh: Printed for J. Bell, Parliament Square; and G.G.J. & J. Robinson, London. [vii + 493 p.]

    1790   Dublin: Printed for P. Byrne and J. Milliken. [vii + 465 p.]

Both works were given the combined title:

    1786–90 *Essays on the Intellectual and Active Powers of Man*. Dublin: Printed for L. White. [3 vols.]

    1790   Dublin: Printed for P. Byrne and J. Milliken. [3 vols.]

    1793   Philadelphia: Printed by William Young, bookseller, no. 25, Second Street, corner of Chestnut Street. [2 vols.]

    1803   *Essays on the Powers of the Human Mind*. To which is prefixed "An Account of the Life and Writings of the Author" [by Dugald Stewart]. Edinburgh: Printed for Bell & Bradfute. Sold by G. & J. Robinson, London. [3 vols.]

    1808   Edinburgh: Printed for Bell & Bradfute, Edinburgh; Longman, Hurst, Rees & Orme, J. Murray and T. Hamilton, London. [3 vols.]

    1812   To which is prefixed "An essay on quantity, and an analysis of Aristotle's logic." Edinburgh: Printed for Bell & Bradfute, sold by F.C. & J. Rivington, Longman, J. Murray and T. Hamilton, London. [3 vols.]

1794 **"Observations on the Danger of Political Innovation, from a Discourse Delivered on the 28th November 1794 before the Literary Society in Glasgow College,"** *Glasgow Courier*, 18 December 1794.

    1796   Reprinted in [R. Cleghorn], *Sketch of the Character of the late Thomas Reid, D.D., Professor of Moral Philosophy in the University of Glasgow*. Printed in the *Courier* Office for J. McNayr & Co. [16 p.]

1799 **"A Statistical Account of the University of Glasgow,"** in Sir John Sinclair, ed. *Statistical Account of Scotland*. 21 vols.; Edinburgh: Printed and sold by W. Creech and also sold by J. Donaldson, 1791–99. 21 (Appendix): 1–50.

1803   *The Works of Thomas Reid*. Edinburgh: Printed for Bell & Bradfute, by A. Neill and Co. [4 vols.]

The contents are as follows:

Vol. I: "An Account of the Life and Writings of Thomas Reid," by Dugald Stewart; and the 5th edition (1801) of Reid's *An Inquiry into the Human Mind, on the Principles of Common Sense.*

Vols. II, III, IV: The 1803 edition, in three volumes, of the *Essays on the Powers of the Human Mind.*

> 1812   A new edition. Edinburgh: Bell & Bradfute. [4 vols.]
>
> The contents are as follows:
>
> Vol. I: The 7th (1814) edition of Reid's *An Inquiry into the Human Mind, on the Principles of Common Sense.*
> Vols. II, III, IV: The 1812 edition, in three volumes, of the *Essays on the Power of the Human Mind.*

> 1813–15   With "An Account of his Life and Writings." With notes by the American editors. Dugald Stewart, ed. Charlestown, Mass.: Samuel Etheridge, Jun'r. [4 vols.]
>
> The biographical essay attached to Reid's works was written by Dugald Stewart.

1937   *Philosophical Orations of Thomas Reid, Delivered at Graduation Ceremonies in King's College, Aberdeen, 1753, 1756, 1759, 1762*. Edited from the Birkwood Manuscripts by Walter Robson Humphries. Aberdeen: The University Press. [47 p.]

The text of Reid's orations are in Latin.

Translations: English

> 1989   *The Philosophical Orations of Thomas Reid, Delivered at Graduation Ceremonies in King's College, Aberdeen, 1753, 1756, 1759, 1762*. Translated by Shirley Darcus Sullivan and edited by D.D. Todd. Monograph in the *Journal of the History of Philosophy*. Carbondale: Southern Illinois University Press.
>
> The four orations concern themselves with the laws of philosophy and with the human intellect.

1973   *Thomas Reid's Lectures on the Fine Arts*. Transcribed from the original manuscript. Peter Kivy, ed., The Hague: Martinus Nijhoff. [viii + 57 p.]

These comments are divided into "Mind and Body" and "Taste and the Fine Arts."

1981   *Thomas Reid's Lectures on Natural Theology*. Transcribed from student notes, edited, and with an introduction by Elmer H. Duncan. Washington, D.C.: University Press of America. [xxxxviii + 129 p.]

1982   **"Thomas Reid's '*Curâ Primâ* on Common Sense,'"** David Fate Norton, ed., in Louise Marcil-Lacoste, *Claude Buffier and Thomas Reid: Two Common-Sense Philosophers*. Kingston: McGill-Queen's University Press. 179–208.

1990   *Practical Ethics: Being Lectures and Papers on Natural Religion, Self-Government, Natural Jurisprudence, and the Law of Nations*. Edited from the manuscripts by Knud Haakonssen. Princeton: Princeton University Press. [xii + 556 p.]

Contents:

1. Introductory Lecture
2. Duties to God
3. Duties to Ourselves: Prudence, Temperance, Fortitude
4. Duties to Others: Justice
5. Duties to Others: Individuals in Private Jurisprudence
6. Duties to Others: Individuals in Oeconomical Jurisprudence
7. Duties to Others: Individuals in Political Jurisprudence
8. Duties to Others: States
9. Supplement to Duties to Ourselves
10. Natural Law and Natural Rights
11. Property
12. Succession
13. On Dissolution of Obligations and On Interpretation
14. Oeconomical Jurisprudence
15. Social Contract as Implied Contract
16. Political Jurisprudence
17. Rights and Duties of States
18. Some Thoughts on the Utopian System

1996   *Thomas Reid on the Animate Creation: Papers Relating to the Life Sciences*. Paul Wood, ed., University Park, Pennsylvania: Pennsylvania State University Press. [xiv + 274 p.]

The collection contains a transcription of Reid's notes on "Natural History," "Physiology," and "Materialism."

2001   **"Of Power,"** in *The Philosophical Quarterly*, 51 (2001): 1–12.

2005   *Thomas Reid on Logic, Rhetoric, and the Fine Arts: Papers on the Culture of the Mind*. Alexander Broadie, ed., University Park, Pennsylvania: Pennsylvania State University Press.

Adam Smith (1723–90)

1748   **[Anonymous]. Preface to [William Hamilton of Bangour].** *Poems on Several Occasions*. Glasgow: Printed and sold by Robert and Andrew Foulis.

        1758   2nd edition. Glasgow: Printed and sold by Robert and Andrew Foulis.

The 1758 edition also contains a brief dedication that appears to have been written by Smith.

1755   **[Anonymous]. Review of Johnson's** *Dictionary of the English Language*, in *Edinburgh Review*, 1 (1755): 61–73.

      1755   Reprinted in *The Scots Magazine*, 17 (November, 1755): 539–44.

1756   **[Anonymous]. Letter to the Authors of the** *Edinburgh Review* [recommending that the *Review* take continuing note of the literature of the Continent], in *Edinburgh Review*, 2 (1756): 63–79.

1759   *The Theory of Moral Sentiments*. London: Printed for A. Millar; and A. Kincaid and J. Bell, in Edinburgh. [xii + 551 p.]

      1761   2nd edition. London: Printed for A. Millar, in the Strand; and A. Kincaid and J. Bell, Edinburgh. [viii + 436 p.]

      1767   3rd edition. To which is added a dissertation on the origin of languages. London: Printed for A. Millar; and A. Kincaid and J. Bell in Edinburgh, and sold by T. Cadell. [viii + 478 p.]

      1774   *or, An Essay Towards an Analysis of the Principles by Which Men Naturally Judge Concerning the Conduct and Character, First of their Neighbours, and Afterwards of Themselves. To which is added a dissertation on the origin of languages.* 4th edition. London: Printed for W. Strahan, J. & F. Rivington, W. Johnston, T. Longman; and T. Cadell and W. Creech at Edinburgh. [viii + 478 p.]

      1777   *or, An Essay Towards an Analysis of the Principles by Which Men Naturally Judge Concerning the Conduct and Character, First of their Neighbours, and Afterwards of Themselves. To which is added a dissertation on the origin of languages.* 6th edition [*sic*]. Dublin. Printed for J. Beatty and C. Jackson, no. 32, Skinner Row. [vii + 426 p.]

      1781   *or, An Essay Towards an Analysis of the Principles by Which Men Naturally Judge Concerning the Conduct and Character, First of their Neighbours, and Afterwards of Themselves. To which is added a dissertation on the origin of languages.* 5th edition. London: Printed for W. Strahan, J. & F. Rivington, T. Longman and T. Cadell; and W. Creech at Edinburgh. [viii + 478 p.]

      1790   *or, An Essay Towards an Analysis of the Principles by Which Men Naturally Judge Concerning the Conduct and Character, First of their Neighbours, and Afterwards of Themselves. To which is added a dissertation on the origin of languages.* 6th edition, with considerable additions and corrections. London: Printed for A. Strahan and T. Cadell, and W. Creech and J. Bell & Co. at Edinburgh. [2 vols.]

1792   *or, An Essay Towards an Analysis of the Principles by Which Men Naturally Judge Concerning the Conduct and Character, First of their Neighbours, and Afterwards of Themselves. To which is added a dissertation on the origin of languages.* 7th edition. London: A. Strahan and T. Cadell; and W. Creech and J. Bell & Co., Edinburgh. [2 vols.]

1793   *or, An Essay Towards an Analysis of the Principles by Which Men Naturally Judge Concerning the Conduct and Character, First of their Neighbours, and Afterwards of Themselves. To which is added a dissertation on the origin of languages.* New edition. Basil: Printed and Sold by J.J. Tourneisen. [2 vols.]

1793   *or, An Essay Towards an Analysis of the Principles by Which Men Naturally Judge Concerning the Conduct and Character, First of their Neighbours, and Afterwards of Themselves. To which is added a dissertation on the origin of languages.* New edition. [Leith]: Printed by A. Allardice. [vii + 528 p.]

1797   *or, An Essay Towards an Analysis of the Principles by Which Men Naturally Judge Concerning the Conduct and Character, First of their Neighbours, and Afterwards of Themselves. To which is added a dissertation on the origin of languages.* 8th edition. London: Printed for A. Strahan; and T. Cadell jun. and W. Davies (successors to Mr. Cadell); and W. Creech and J. Bell & Co. at Edinburgh. [2 vols.]

Translations: French

1764   *Métaphysique de l'âme; ou, Théorie des sentimens moraux.* Translated from the English by M[arc Antoine Eidous]. Paris: Chez Briasson, rue S. Jacques, à la Science. [2 vols.]

1798   *Théorie des sentimens moraux, ou Essai analytique sur les principes des jugemens que portent naturellement les hommes, d'abord sur les actions des autres, et ensuite sur leurs propres actions: suivi d'une dissertation sur origine des langues.* Translated from English by M[arc Antoine Eidous] and [Marie-Louise-Sophie] de Grouchy, Marquise de Condorcet. Paris: F. Buisson. [2 vols.]

Dated "An 6 de la République." The edition also contains a translation of eight letters on sympathy by Smith, translated by Condorcet.

1774   *Théorie des sentimens moraux.* A new translation from the English by l'abbé Blavet. Paris: Chez Valade. [2 vols.]

1782   2nd edition. Paris: Laporte. [2 vols.]

German

1770   *Theorie der moralischen Empfindungen.* Translated from the 3rd English edition [by Christian Günter Rautenberg]. Brunswick: Meyerischen Buchhandlung. [576 p.]

1791–95   *Theorie der Sittlichen Gefühle.* Translated by Ludwig Theobul Kosegarten. Leipzig: In der Gräffschen Buchhandlung, C.F. Solbrig. [2 vols.]

1794   *Theorie der Sittlichen Gefühle, Zusätze.* Translated by Ludwig Theobul Kosegarten. Leipzig: In der Gräffschen Buchhandlung.

Contains the revisions and corrections Smith made to the 1790, 6th edition, of the *Theory of Moral Sentiments.*

1771   **"Considerations Concerning the First Formation of Languages, and the Different Genius of Original and Compounded Languages," in *The Philological Miscellany; Consisting of Select Essays.*** London: Printed for the Editor and Sold by T. Beckett and P.A. Dehondt. I: 440–79.

1767   Reprinted in *The Theory of Moral Sentiments.* 3rd edition. London: Printed for A. Millar; and A. Kincaid and J. Bell, Edinburgh. 437–78.

This essay was included in subsequent editions of Smith's *Moral Sentiments.*

Translations: French

1796   *Considérations sur la première formation des langues, et le différent génie des langues originales et composées.* Translated by [A.M.H. Boulard]. Paris: Baillio et Colas. [80 p.]

1796   *Dissertation sur l'origine des langues.* Translated by A.M.H. Boulard. Paris.

1776   **An Inquiry into the Nature and Causes of the Wealth of Nations.** London: W. Strahan and T. Cadell. [2 vols.]

1776   Dublin: Printed for Messrs. Whitestone, Chamberlaine, W. Watson, Potts, S. Watson. [3 vols.]

1778   2nd edition. London: W. Strahan and T. Cadell. [2 vols.]

1784   ***Additions and Corrections to the First and Second Editions of Dr. Adam Smith's Inquiry into the Nature and Causes of the Wealth of Nations.*** London. [79 p.]

1784   3rd edition, with additions. London: W. Strahan and T. Cadell. [3 vols.]

1785   4th edition, with additions. Dublin: Printed for W. Colles, R. Moncrieffe, G. Burnet, W. Wilson, C. Jenkin, L. White, H. Whitestone, P. Byrne, J. Cash, W. McKenzie. [2 vols.]

1786   4th edition. London: Printed for A. Strahan and T. Cadell. [3 vols.]

1789   5th edition. London: A. Strahan and T. Cadell, in the Strand. [3 vols.]

1789   A new edition. Philadelphia: Printed for Thomas Dobson, at the stone house, no. 41, S. Second Street. [3 vols.]

1791   6th edition. London: Printed for A. Strahan and T. Cadell. [3 vols.]

1791   Basil: Printed for J.J. Tourneisen and J.L. Legrand. [4 vols.]

1793   5th edition, with additions [*sic*]. Dublin: Printed by William Porter, for G. Burney, L. White, W. Wilson, P. Byrne, W. McKenzie, J. Moore, and W. Jones. [2 vols.]

1793   7th edition. London: A. Strahan and T. Cadell. [3 vols.]

1796   A new edition. Philadelphia: Printed by Thomas Dobson, at the stone house, no. 41, S. Second Street. [3 vols.]

1796   8th edition. London: Printed for A. Strahan and T. Cadell jun. and W. Davies (successors to Mr. Cadell). [3 vols.]

1797   ***A complete analysis, or abridgement of Dr. Smith's Inquiry into the Nature and Causes of the Wealth of Nations***. Jeremiah Joyce, ed., Cambridge: Printed by Benjamin Flower: for J. Deighton and J. Nicholson; also G.G. and J. Robinson, W.H. Lunn and T. Conder, London; and J. March, Norwich. [iv + 290 p.]

    1804   2nd edition. Cambridge: Printed by and for B. Flower. [324 p.]

1799   9th edition. London: Printed for A. Strahan and T. Cadell jun. and W. Davies. [3 vols.]

1800   London: Ward, Lock and Tyler. [cvi + 780 p.]

1801   6th edition, with additions. Printed by N. Kelly for P. Wogan. [2 vols.]

Translations: *Danish*

1779–80   *Undersøgelse om National-Velstands Natur og Aarsag.* Translated from the English by Frants Dræbye. Copenhagen: Gyldendal. [2 vols.]

Dutch

1796   *Naspeuringen over de Natuur en Oorzaken van den Rijkdom
        der Volkeren.* Translated by Dirk Hoola van Nooten.
        Amsterdam. [311 p.]

        The following account of this translation is taken from his "Note
        on Dutch Editions" of the works of Adam Smith in Tribe's
        Critical Bibliography:

> The translation as published contains only Chapters I–X of Book
> One, but runs over 300 pages due to the notes. [The translator]
> nevertheless had completed a full annotated translation. It proved
> however very difficult to find a publisher for the work and in the
> end he was forced to publish the first part at his own cost, expecting
> to continue publication if sales were sufficient. But they were not.
> It is estimated that only two hundred copies were printed, of which
> only one copy can be found in a Dutch library, at Leiden. (pp. 391–
> 92)

French

1778   *Fragment sur les colonies en général, et sur celles des Anglois
        en particulier.* Translated from the English [by Elie Salomon
        François Reverdil]. Basil: Jean Jacques Flick. [viii + 170 p.]

        A translation of Book iv, chapter vii, "Of Colonies," of the
        Wealth of Nations.

        1778   Lausanne: Chez la Société Typographique. [viii +
                170 p.]

1778–79 *Recherches sur la nature et les causes de la richesse des nations.*
        Translated from the English by M***. The Hague. [4 vols.]

        1789   *Recherches très-utiles sur les affaires présentes, le
                les causes de la richesse des nations.* Amsterdam.
                [4 vols.]

                Published anonymously.

1781   *Recherches sur la nature et les causes de la richesse des nations.*
        Translated by l'abbé [Jean-Louis] Blavet. Paris. [3 vols.]

        According to the University of London Library, this translation
        had previously appeared in the 1779–80 issues of the *Journal
        d'Agriculture, des Arts et du Commerce* (23 monthly parts from
        February 1779 to December 1780), before appearing in book
        form in 1781. See also item 20 in the "Main Bibliography:
        Chronological" in Keith Tribe, ed., *A Critical Bibliography of
        Adam Smith* (London: Pickering & Chatto, 2002): 230.

        1781   Yverdon: F.B. De Felice. [6 vols.]

1784–88   Extracts from the Blavet translation of the *Richesse des nations* in the four-volume *Encyclopédie méthodique: Économie politique et diplomatique.* Paris. Pancoucke.

1786   London and Paris: Poinçot. [6 vols.]
According to Tribe, this is the first book form of the *Wealth of Nations* available in France.

1788   London: et se trouve à Paris: Duplain. [2 vols.]

1800–01   Paris: de l'imprimerie de Laran. [4 vols.]
The translator's name is given as "citoyen Blavet" and the date of publication as "l'an 9 de la République."

The translation was revised with the assistance of Abraham Guyot and based in part on changes made by Smith to the 3rd edition of the treatise.

1790   A summary of Smith's *Recherches sur la nature et les causes de la richesses des Nations*, in vols. III [pp. 108–216] and IV [pp. 1–115] of *Bibliothèque de l'homme publique, ou Analyse raisonnée des principaux ouvrages français et étrangers sur la politique en général, la législation, les finances, la police.* Jean-Antoine-Nicolas de Caritat, Mis de Cordorcet, Charles de Peyssonnel (fils), et Isaac-René-Guy La Chapelier, eds. Paris: Buisson. 28 vols. in 14.

Tribe notes that this summary was based on the new Roucher translation up to Book VI, chapter 1, after which it relied on the Blavet version.

1790–91   *Recherches sur la nature et les causes de la richesse des nations.* Translated from the 4th English edition by M. [Jean Antoine] Roucher. With a volume devoted to commentaries by M. Le Marquis de Condorcet. Paris. Chez Buisson, Libraire, rue Haute-Feuille, Hôtel de Coetlosquet, no. 20. [4 vols.]

The fifth volume of this edition, projected to contain Condorcet's notes, appears not to have been published.

1791   New edition. Avignon: Fortia d'Urban, Chez J.J. Niel. [4 vols.]

The edition is supplemented by introductory comments and notes. A promised translation of Xenophon's "Economics" is not included.

1792   Neuchâtel, Switzerland: L. Fouche-Borel. [5 vols.]

1794   2nd edition, revised and substantially corrected. Paris: Chez Buisson. [5 vols.]

Marked as published in Year 3 of the Republic. Tribe

notes that Roucher is reported to have completed the revisions to his translation during the ten months that he was awaiting the guillotine.

1802   *Recherches sur la nature et les causes de la richesse des nations.* A new translation by Germain Garnier. Paris: Henri Agasse. [5 vols.]

Year 10 of the Republic. With a preface by the translator, containing a summary of Smith's economic views, a comparison between Smith's ideas and those of the French economists, and a comparison of the wealth of France with that of England.

German

1776–78   *Untersuchung über der Natur und Ursachen von Nationalreichthümern.* Translated from the English by [Johann Friedrich Schiller and Christian August Wichmann]. Leipzig: Bey Weidmanns Erben und Reich. [2 vols.]

A third volume, published in 1792, contains a translation by Christian August Wichmann of Smith's *Additions and Corrections to the First and Second Editions of the Wealth of Nations.*

1779   *Historische und politische Betrachtungen über die Colonien besonders in Rücksicht auf die Englische-Amerikanischen.* Bern: In der Hallerschen Buchhandlung. [152 p.]

A translation of Book IV, chapter 7, of the *Wealth of Nations.* The translation appears to have also been issued by the same publisher under the title *Abhandlung über die Colonien überhaupt und die Amerikanischen besonders* in the same year. Tribe's *Critical Bibliography* gives the publisher as Beat Ludwig Walthard in Bern.

1792   *Untersuchung über der Natur und Ursachen von Nationalreichthümern.* Leipzig: Weidmannischen Buchhandlung. [140 pp.]

The third volume of the Schiller translation of 1776–78, containing the "Additions and Corrections to the First and Second Editions of Dr. Smith's *Inquiry into the Nature and Causes of the Wealth of Nations*". The gap between its release and that of the earlier volumes is accounted for by the fact that sales of the complete edition were lower than hoped.

1794–96   *Untersuchung über der Natur und Ursachen von Nationalreichthums.* Translated from the English by Christian Garve. Breslau: bei Wilhelm Gottlieb Korn. [4 vols.]

1796–99   Frankfurt. [4 vols.]

1799   2nd edition. Breslau and Leipzig: W.G. Korn. [3 vols.]

To which is appended Dugald Stewart's *Account of the Life and Writings of Adam Smith.*

1796   *Handbuch der Staatswirthschaft zum Gebrauche bey akademischen Vorlesungen: nach Adam Smith's Grundsätzen ausgearbeitet.* Abridged by Georg Sartorius. Berlin: Johann Friedrich Unger. [xxxxix + 234 p.]

An abridged edition of Smith's *Wealth of Nations.*

1800–04   *Über Nationalindustrie und Staatswirthschaft. Nach Adam Smith bearbeitet.* Berlin: Heinrich Frölich. [3 vols.]

The author, August Ferdinand Lueder, originally set out to condense Smith's treatise but by adding a substantial amount of historical material, he actually extended the work.

Italian

1781   "Observations on the Potato," in S.A.D. Tissot, *Dissertazione del signor Tissot sul pane, sull'economia, e cultura de'grani, e sul pane di pomi di terra etc., in confutazione di una dissertazione del Signor Linguet contro l'uso del pane, e del grano. Si aggiunge la dissertazione medesima tradotta dal francese, con note, etc / [del signor Linguet] ; Ed altri trattati del Sign. Antonio Matani, e del Sig. Parmentier sulla panizazione, e sul pane di pomi di terra &c.* Napoli: Presso Giuseppi Maria Procelli con licenza de'superiori.

The collection contains a translation of Smith's observations on the potato (pp. 147–51) from *The Wealth of Nations.*

1782   S.A.D. Tissot, *Del Pane e della economica e coltura de' grani. Dissertazioni del Signor Tissot in confutazione d'un opuscolo de Signor Linguet contro l'uso del pane, del grano: aggiuntovi l'opuscolo stresso con altri trattari sulla panizzazione e sul pane di pomi di terra etc.* Venice: G. Bassagnia.

1792   Venice: Presso Giacomo Carcani. 112–16.

1790–91   *Ricerche sulla Natura, e la cagioni della Recchezzo della Nazioni.* Naples: Guiseppe Policarpo Merande. [3 vols.]

The University of London Library reports a five-volume version of this edition.The translation, according to Tribe, is based on the Blavet French translation.

Russian

1802–06   *Izsliedovanie svoistva I prichin bogatstva narodov.* Translated by N. Politkovskii. [St. Petersburg]: Tipografii Gosudarstvennoi Meditsinskoi Kollegii. [4 vols.]

Spanish

1792   *Compendio de la obra inglesa intitulada Riqueza de la Naciones, hecho por el Marques de Condorcet, y traduicido al castellano convarias adiciones del original, por Don Carlos Martinez de Irujo.* Madrid: En la Imprenta Real. [xii + 296 p.] A translation of the Blavet/Roucher condensation of Smith's *Wealth of Nations* that had appeared in the *Bibliothèque de l'homme publique* in 1790. While Condorcet did not contribute to the translation he lent his name to the work, which restores to the text a summary of Smith's Digression on the Bank of Amsterdam and omits his criticism of the Catholic clergy.

   1803   Madrid: La Imprenta Real. [xi + 300 p.]

   1814   Palma de Mallorca: Impr. de Miguel Domingo. [xii + 264 p.]

1794   *Investigacíon de la Naturaleza y Causas de la Riqueza de la Naciones.* Translated by Josef Alonso Ortiz. Valladolid: En la Oficina de la Viuda y Hijos de Santander. [4 vols.]

   1805–06   2nd edition, greatly expanded and corrected. Valladolid. En la Oficina de la Viuda y Hijos De Santander. [4 vols.]

Swedish

1797–1801   *Läsning I blandade ämnen.* Georg Adlersparre, ed. Stockholm: tryckt hos Henrik A Nordstöm.

   These constitute a series of selections from *The Wealth of Nations* that appeared in the above periodical over the course of the four years shown. The contents are as follows: no. 25/26 pp. 43–72, Om jordbruks-systemet I en rikshushållning, samt om economisterne I Frankrike; af Adam Smith – no. 25/26 pp. 92–114. Om handelsbalancen; af Adam Smith – no. 27/28 pp. 57–62, Om pappers-myntet I Norr-Amerikanska kolonierne; af Adam Smith – no. 27/28 pp. 93–120, Om jordbrukets förfall I Europa, efter Romerska väldets undergång; af Adam Smith – no. 29/31 pp. 137–45, Om krono-jord; af Adam Smith – no. 36/38 pp. 145–77, Om beskattning; af Adam Smith.

1800   *Handbok för Statshushållningen efter Adam Smiths Grundsattser*. Författad af Georg Sartorius. Stockholm: Tryckt I Kumblinska Tryckeriet. [iv + 230 p.]

A Swedish translation by Johan Holmsbergsson of Georg Sartorius's abridgement of Adam Smith's *Wealth of Nations*.

1800   *Undersökning om Kongl. stora sjö- och gränse-tullar, samt acciser och små-tuller med Flera consumtions-afgifter*. Translated by Erik Erl. Bodell. Stockholm: C. Deleen o J.G. Forsgren. [89 p.]

A translation of a section of Book V, chapter 2: "Of the Sources of the General or Public Revenue of the Society."

1777   Letter to William Strahan, November 9, 1776 [on Hume's last illness]. Appended to *The Life of David Hume, Esq., Written by Himself*. London: Printed for W. Strahan and T. Cadell. 37–62.

1777   *The Life of David Hume, Esq., Written by Himself. To which is added, a letter from Adam Smith, LL.D. to William Strahan, Esq*. Dublin: printed for J. Williams. [vi + 26 p.]

1777   London: Printed for W. Strahan and T. Cadell, and sold in Dublin by Alex Kelburn. [iv + 36 p.]

1788   *Letter from Adam Smith, LL.D., to William Strahan, Esq*. [London]. [17 p.]

Translations: French

1777   Reprinted in *La Vie de David Hume, écrite par lui-même*. Translated by Jean-Baptiste Antoine Suard. London.

The place of publication is fictitious. The essay was almost certainly published in either Switzerland or France.

Italian

1777   "Lettera del Sig. Adamo Smith al Sig. Strahan riguardo al Sig. Davide Hume," *Giornale enciclopedico*, 6 June 1777. Venice. 39–43.

178?   *Vita di David Hume, scritta de lui medesimo*. Translated from the English and containing Adam Smith's letter to William Strahan. [n.p.: n.p.]

The Cambridge University Library is unable to offer greater precision regarding the date or facts of publication. Keith Tribe, *A Critical Bibliography of Adam Smith* (London: Pickering & Chatto, 2002), p. 382, refers to the following, which might possibly be the same work: *Vita di David Hume scitta da lui*

*stesso, aggiunta una lettera di Adamo Smith 9 Novembre 1776
circa la morte e il carattere del suo amico Londra 1792 Ed.*,
translated by Pietro Antoniutti, privately printed [probably by
Tipografia di Andrea Santini], Venice, 1820.

Latin

1788   *Adami Smithi, LL.D. ad Gul. Strahanum armigerum de rebus
novissimis Davidis Humei, epostola.* Translated by Sir David
Dalrymple. Edinburgh. [iv + 17 p.]

Parallel English and Latin texts, with the Latin in verse, the
English in prose.

Russian

1781   Reprinted in *Zhizn' Davyda Gumma, opisannaia in samim.*
Translated by Ivan Morkov. Moscow: [Senatskaia tip.] u
F. Gippiusa. 33–54.

1795   ***Essays on Philosophical Subjects***. [To which is prefixed an account of the
life and writings of the author, by Dugald Stewart, F.R.S.E.] Edited by
Joseph Black and James Hutton. London: Printed for T. Cadell, jun. and
W. Davies (successors to Mr. Cadell); and W. Creech, Edinburgh. [xcv +
244 p.]

The collection contains the following essays:

1. The Principles which Lead and Direct Philosophical Enquiries
   Illustrated by the History of Astronomy
2. The Principles which Lead and Direct Philosophical Enquiries
   Illustrated by the History of the Ancient Physics
3. The Principles which Lead and Direct Philosophical Enquiries
   Illustrated by the History of the Ancient Logics and Metaphysics
4. Of the Nature of that Imitation which Takes Place in What are Called
   the Imitative Arts.
5. Of the Affinity Between Certain English and Italian Verses
6. Of the External Senses

1795   Dublin: Printed for Mssrs. Wogan, Byrne, J. Moore, Colbert,
Rice, W. Jones, Porter and Folingsby. [cxxiii + 332 p.]

1799   Basil: Printed for the Editors of the *Collection of English
Classics.* Sold by James Decker. [cxviii + 313 p.]

1799   Strasbourg: Sold by F.G. Levrault, printer and bookseller. [cxviii
+ 313 p.]

1800   Basil.

Translations: *French*

1797   *Essais philosophiques, précédés d'un précis de sa vie et de ses écrits par Dugald Stewart.* Translated by Pierre Prévost. Paris: Chez H. Agasse. [283 + 316 p.]

A translation of the essays on philosophical subjects, prefixed by a translated *Account of the Life and Writings of Adam Smith*, by Dugald Stewart, and by the translator's reflections on Smith's posthumous works. Published in year 5 of the Republic.

1896   ***Lectures on Justice, Police, Revenue, and Arms, Delivered in the University of Glasgow by Adam Smith.*** Edwin Cannan, ed., Oxford: Clarendon Press. [xxxix + 293 p.]

These notes constitute Smith's lectures on jurisprudence delivered in 1763–64 and transcribed by a student, possibly for sale, in 1766.

1963   ***Lectures on Rhetoric and Belles Lettres, Delivered in the University of Glasgow by Adam Smith.*** London: Thomas Nelson & Sons. [xl + 205 p.]

1978   ***Lectures on Jurisprudence.*** R.L. Meek, D.D. Raphael and P.G. Stein, eds., Oxford: Oxford University Press.

This edition contains a newly-discovered set of notes covering Smith's lectures on jurisprudence that were delivered in the 1762–63 session. (The volume also includes a reprinting of the 1766 report, originally published in 1896.)

Dugald Stewart (1753–1828)

1792   ***Elements of the Philosophy of the Human Mind. Vol. I.*** London: Printed for A. Strahan and T. Cadell. [xii + 566 p.]

    1793   Philadelphia: Printed for William Young. [xi + 500 p.]

    1795   Philadelphia: Printed for William Young. [500 p.]

    1802   2nd edition, corrected. London: Printed for T. Cadell and W. Davies, and W. Creech, Edinburgh. [xii + 587 p.]

    1808   Brattleborough, Vt.: Published by William Fessenden, bookseller. [viii + 496 p.]

    1808   3rd edition, corrected. London: Printed for T. Cadell and W. Davies, and W. Creech, Edinburgh. [xii + 585 p.]

    1811   4th edition, corrected. London: Printed for T. Cadell and W. Davies, in the Strand, and W. Creech, Edinburgh. [xii + 585 p.]

    1813   3rd American edition, corrected. Brattleborough, Vt.: William Fessenden. [viii + 509 p.]

1814   5th edition. London: Printed for T. Cadell and W. Davies, in the Strand, and W. Creech, Edinburgh. [xii + 585 p.]

1816   London: T. Cadell and W. Davies.

1818   6th edition. London: Printed for T. Cadell and W. Davies and A. Constable and Co., Edinburgh.

Translations: *French*

1798   Extracts of Volume I of the *Elements* appeared in French translation in the *Bibliothèque britannique* [*ou Recueil extrait des ouvrages anglais périodiques et autres; des memoires et transactions des societés et académies de la Grande Bretagne, d'Asie, d'Afrique, d'Amérique.*] Geneva. 8: 409–34.

1808   *Élémens de la philosophie de l'esprit humain.* Translated by Pierre Prévost. Geneva: J.J. Paschaud. [2 vols.]

German

1793–94   *Anfangsgründe der Philosophie über die menschliche Seele.* Translated by Samuel Gottlieb Lange. Berlin: F. Mauer. [2 vols.]

1814   ***Elements of the Philosophy of the Human Mind.* Vol. II**. Edinburgh: Archibald Constable & Co., and Cadell and Davies, London. [xiv + 554 p.]

1814   New York: Eastburn, Kirk & Co., at the Literary Rooms, Corner of Wall and Nassau Streets.

1816   2nd edition. Edinburgh: Printed for George Ramsay and Company for Archibald Constable & Co., and Cadell and Davies, London.

1818   New York: James Eastburn & Company. [2 vols.]

1821   3rd edition. Edinburgh: Printed by T. Allan for Constable, and Cadell and Davies, London. [xv + 595 p.]

1822   4th edition. Edinburgh.

Translations: *French*

1825   *Elémens de la philosophie de l'esprit humain.* Translated from the English [by J.R. Farcy]. Geneva: J.J. Paschaud.

The following editions of ***Elements of the Philosophy of the Human Mind*** contain both volumes **I** and **II**.

1814   With references, sectional heads, synoptical table of contents and translations of the numerous Greek, Latin and French quotations by G.N. Wright. London: W. Tegg. [xi + 602 p.]

1818	From the latest London edition. New York: James Eastburn & Co. [2 vols.]
1818	Boston: Printed and published by Wells and Lilly. [2 vols. in 1]
1821	Albany: Websters and Skinners. [2 vols. in 1]
1821	Revised edition. Boston: Wells and Lilly [2 vols. in 1]
1822	Albany: E. & E. Hosford. [2 vols. in 1]
1827	Albany: Websters and Skinners. [2 vols.]
1829	Cambridge: Hilliard and Brown. [2 vols.]
1833	Cambridge: James Monroe and Company. [2 vols.]
1836–37	Boston: J. Munroe and Company. [2 vols. in 1]
1837	New edition, with notes and life of the author. London: Baynes & Son, 54 Paternoster Row, E. Johnson, J. and J. Thornton, John Cumming, A.C. Baynes, 57 Church Street. [xii + 447 p.]

1827   *Elements of the Philosophy of the Human Mind.* **Vol. III**. *To which are annexed Additions to Vol. 1.* London: Printed for A. Strahan and T. Cadell; Edinburgh: W. Creech. [vi + 521 + 46 p.]

1827	*To which are annexed Additions to Vol. 1.* London: Murray.
1827	Philadelphia: Carey, Lee & Carey.

1793   **[Anonymous]**. ***Outlines of Moral Philosophy. For the Use of Students in the University of Edinburgh***. Edinburgh: W. Creech; London: T. Cadell. [xiv + 302 p.]

1801	2nd edition, enlarged. Edinburgh: Printed for W. Creech; sold by T. Cadell, jun. and W. Davies. [xvi + 324 p.]
1808	3rd edition, corrected. Edinburgh: Printed for W. Creech; sold by T. Cadell, jun. and W. Davies. [xvi + 323 p.]
1818	4th edition. Edinburgh: Archibald Constable and Co. [xvi + 320 p.]
1829	5th edition. Edinburgh: Cadell & Co. [xvi + 320 p.]

Translations: *French*

1826	*Esquisses de philosophie morale.* Translated from the 4th English edition by Théodore-Simon Jouffroy. Paris: A. Johanneau. [clv + 236 p.]
1829	*Esquisses de philosophie morale.* Translated from the 4th English edition by Théodore-Simon Jouffroy. Louvain: F. Michel. [ii + 172 pp.]

1833   *Esquisses de philosophie morale*. Translated from the 4th English edition by Théodore-Simon Jouffroy. Paris: A. Johanneau. [clv + 207 p.]

Italian

1821   *Compendio di filosofia morale*. Translated from the 4th English edition by Pompeo Ferrario. Padua: Tipographia della Minerva. [257 p.]

1793   **"Account of the Life and Writings of Adam Smith," [Read Before the Society on 21 January and 18 March 1793]** *Transactions of the Royal Society of Edinburgh*, 3 (1794): 55–137.

1793   Reprinted in Adam Smith. *The Theory of Moral Sentiments: or, An Essay Towards and Analysis of the Principles by which Men Naturally Judge Concerning the Conduct and Character, First of Their Neighbours, and Afterwards of Themselves: To Which is Added, A Dissertation on the Origin of Languages.* [Leith]: Printed by A. Allardice. [viii + 432 + 96 p.]

1794   *Account of the Life and Writings of Adam Smith, from the Transactions of the Royal Society of Edinburgh.* Edinburgh: Royal Society of Edinburgh. [85 p.]

1795   Reprinted in Adam Smith. *Essays on Philosophical Subjects, to which is prefixed an Account of the Life and Writings of the Author.* London: T. Cadell jun. and W. Davies; and W. Creech, Edinburgh. [xcv + 244 p.]

1795   Reprinted in Adam Smith. *Essays on Philosophical Subjects.* Dublin: Printed for Messrs. Wogan, Byrne, J. Moore, Colbert, Rice, W. Jones, Porter and Folingsby. [cxxiii + 332 p.]

1799   Reprinted in Adam Smith. *Essays on Philosophical Subjects.* Basil: Printed for the Editor of the *Collection of English Classics*; sold by James Decker, Printer and bookseller. [313 p.]

1799   Reprinted in Adam Smith. *Essays on Philosophical Subjects.* Strasbourg: Sold by F.G. Lavrault. [cxviii + 313 p.]

1811–12 Reprinted in Vol. 5 of *The Works of Adam Smith, LL.D. and F.R.S. of London and Edinburgh; one of the Commissioners of his Majesty's Customs in Scotland, and formerly Professor of Moral Philosophy in the University of Glasgow: With an account of his life and writings.* London: Printed for T. Cadell and W. Davies. [5 vols.]

1812   Reprinted in *The Works of Adam Smith, with an Account of his Life and Writings.* London: Printed for T. Cadell and W. Davies. [5 vols.]

1817   Reprinted in Adam Smith. *Theory of Moral Sentiments, or, An essay towards an analysis of principles.* From the last [eleventh] English edition. Boston: Wells and Lilly. [2 vols. in 1]

1818   Reprinted in Adam Smith. *An Inquiry into the Nature and Causes of the Wealth of Nations.* New edition, with additions. Hartford: Published by Cooke & Hale. [2 vols.]

1835–39   Reprinted in Adam Smith. *An Inquiry into the Nature and Causes of the Wealth of Nations.* London: C. Knight. [6 vols.]

1835–40   Reprinted in Adam Smith. *An Inquiry into the Nature and Causes of the Wealth of Nations.* London: Charles Knight & Co. [4 vols.]

Translations: French

1797   Adam Smith. *Essais philosophiques. Précédés d'un précis de sa vie et de ses écrits par Dugald Stewart.* Translated by P. Prévost. Paris: Chez H. Agasse. [2 vols.]

German

1799   Adam Smith. *Untersuchung über die Natur und die Ursachen des Nationalreichthüms; mit Stewart's Nachricht von dem Leben und den Schriften.* Translated by Christian Garve. Breslau: W.G. Korn. [3 vols.]

1810   Adam Smith. *Untersuchung über die Natur und die Ursachen des Nationalreichthüms; mit Stewart's Nachricht von dem Leben und den Schriften des Autors verm. unveränderte Ausg.* Translated by Christian Garve. Breslau: W.G. Korn. [3 vols.]

1814   Adam Smith. *Untersuchung über die Natur und die Ursachen des Nationalreichthüms; mit Stewart's Nachricht von dem Leben und den Schriften des Autors verm. unveränderte Ausg.* 3rd edition. Translated by Christian Garve. Vienna: B.P. Bauer. [3 vols.]

1801   *Account of the Life and Writings of William Robertson, D.D., F.R.S.E., late principal of the University of Edinburgh, and Historiographer to His Majesty for Scotland.* [**Read before the Royal Society of Edinburgh, 1796.**] London: Printed by A. Strahan, Printers Street, for T. Cadell, jun., and W. Davies in the Strand and E. Balfour, Edinburgh. [iv + 307 p.]

1801   [Anonymous]. *Account of the Life and Writings of William Robertson.* London: Printed by A. Strahan for T. Cadell, jun. and W. Davies in the Strand and E. Balfour, Edinburgh. [iv + 202 p.]

1802   2nd edition. London: Printed for A. Strahan, Printers Street, for T. Cadell, jun., and W. Davies in the Strand and E. Balfour, Edinburgh. [iv + 307 p.]

1802   Reprinted in William Robertson. *The History of Scotland During the Reigns of Queen Mary and King James VI until His Accession to the Crown of England* [with a review of the Scottish history previous to that period and an appendix containing original papers]. 16th edition. London: Printed by A. Strahan for T. Cadell and W. Davies. [3 vols.]

1804   Reprinted in William Robertson. *The History of Scotland During the Reigns of Queen Mary and King James VI until His Accession to the Crown of England.* 17th edition. Edinburgh: J. Robertson. [3 vols.]

1809   Reprinted in William Robertson. *The History of Scotland During the Reigns of Queen Mary and King James VI until His Accession to the Crown of England.* 18th edition. London: Printed for T. Cadell. [3 vols.]

1811   Reprinted in William Robertson. *The History of Scotland During the Reigns of Queen Mary and King James VI until His Accession to the Crown of England: With a Review of the Scottish History Previous to that Period: and an Appendix Containing Original Papers.* 1st American edition from the 16th London edition, with the author's last emendations and additions, to which is prefixed an account of the life and writings of the author. Philadelphia: Published by J. Bioren and T.L. Plowman, A. Fagan, printer. [2 vols.]

1812   Reprinted in William Robertson. *The History of Scotland During the Reigns of Queen Mary and King James VI until His Accession to the Crown of England.* 19th edition. London: Printed for T. Cadell and W. Davies. [3 vols.]

1812   Reprinted in *The Works of William Robertson, D.D., to which is prefixed an account of his life and writings by Dugald Stewart.* London: Printed for T. Cadell and W. Davies, F.C. and J. Rivington. [12 vols.]

1817   Reprinted in William Robertson. *The History of Scotland During the Reigns of Queen Mary and King James VI Until His Accession to the Crown of England: With a Review of the Scottish History Previous to that Period: and an Appendix Containing Original Papers.* 20th edition. London: Printed for T. Cadell and W. Davies. [3 vols.]

1817   Reprinted in *The Works of William Robertson, to which is prefixed an account of his life and writings.* A new edition. London: Printed for T. Cadell and W. Davies. [12 vols.]

1821 Reprinted in *The Works of William Robertson, to which is prefixed an account of his life and writings*. A new edition. London: Printed for T. Cadell; F.C. and J. Rivington. [10 vols.]

1822 Reprinted in [William] *Robertson's Works*. Albany: E. and E. Hosford. [8 vols.]

1822 Reprinted in William Robertson. *The History of Scotland During the Reigns of Queen Mary and King James VI Until His Accession to the Crown of England: With a Review of the Scottish History Previous to that Period: and an Appendix Containing Original Papers*. Albany: E. and E. Hosford. [2 vols.]

1824 Reprinted in *The Works of William Robertson, D.D., with an account of his life and writings*. London: Whitmore and Fenn. [8 vols.]

1825 Reprinted in *The Works of William Robertson, D.D.* Oxford: Published by Talboys and Wheeler; London: W. Pickering. [8 vols.]

1827 Reprinted in *The Works of William Robertson, D.D., to which is prefixed an account of his life and writings*. London: Printed for T. Cadell. [8 vols.]

1830 Reprinted in *The Works of William Robertson, To which is prefixed, An Account of the Life and Writings of the Author*. Edinburgh: Thomas Nelson and Peter Brown. [2 vols.]

1831 Reprinted in *The Works of William Robertson, To which is prefixed, An Account of the Life and Writings of the Author*. Edinburgh: Thomas Nelson and Peter Brown. [2 vols.]

1831 Reprinted in *The Works of William Robertson, To which is prefixed, An Account of his Life and Writings*. New edition in one volume. Edinburgh: Printed for T. Cadell. [1,170 p.]

1831 Reprinted in *The Works of William Robertson, D.D., to which is prefixed an account of his life and writings, by Dugald Stewart*. London: Joseph Ogle Robinson. [lviii + 1,184 p.]

1835 Reprinted in *The Works of William Robertson, D.D., to which is prefixed an account of the life and writings of the author*. London: Frederick Westley and A.H. Davis; printed for J.R. and C. Childs. [lviii + 1,184 p.]

1839 Reprinted in William Robertson. *The History of the Discovery and Conquest of America*. [With a memoir of the author from that of Dugald Stewart.] London: Printed for Scott, Webster and Geary. [xlviii + 551 p.]

1839   Reprinted in *The Works of William Robertson, to which is prefixed an account of the life and writings of Dugald Stewart.* Edinburgh: T. Nelson. [2 vols.]

1840   Reprinted in *The Works of William Robertson, D.D., to which is prefixed an account of his life and writings, by Dugald Stewart.* London: W. Ball. [lviii + 1,184 p.]

1840   Reprinted in William Robertson. *Works. To which is prefixed an account of the life and writings of the author.* London: Printed for T. Cadell. [8 vols.]

Translations: *French*

1806   *Essais historiques sur la vie et les ouvrages de William Robertson, auteur des Histoires d'Ecosses, de Charles V, et d'Amerique.* Translated by Jean Gilbert Ymbert. Paris: L. Collin. [xx + 214 p.]

1802   *Account of the Life and Writings of Thomas Reid*, D.D., F.R.S. Edin., late Professor of Moral Philosophy in the University of Glasgow [Read before the Royal Society of Edinburgh, 1796.] Edinburgh: Printed by Adam Neill and Company. [164 p.]

1800–10   Reprinted in Thomas Reid. *The Works, Now Fully Collected, With Selections From his Unpublished Letters.* London: Longman. [2 vols.]

1803   Edinburgh: Printed by William Creech, and Longman and Rees, London. [222 p.]

1803   Reprinted in *The Works of Thomas Reid, with an account of his life and writings by Dugald Stewart.* New edition. Edinburgh: Printed for Bell & Bradfute by A. Neill and Co. [4 vols.]

1803   Reprinted in Thomas Reid. *Essays on the Powers of the Human Mind.* Edinburgh: Printed for Bell & Bradfute. 1: i–clxiv. [3 vols.]

1813–15   Reprinted in *The Works of Thomas Reid, with an account of his life and writings.* Charlestown: Printed and published by Samuel Etheridge, Jun'r. [4 vols.]

1822   Reprinted in *The Works of Thomas Reid, with an account of his life and writings by Dugald Stewart.* New York: E. Duyckinck, Collins and Hannay and R. and W.A. Bartow. [3 vols.]

1822   Reprinted in *The Works of Thomas Reid, with an account of his life and writings.* New York: Published by N. Bangs and T. Mason, for the Methodist Episcopal Church. [3 vols.]

Translations: French

1828–36   *Œuvres complètes de Thomas Reid, chef d'école écossaise, publiées par M. Théodore-Simon Jouffroy, avec les Fragments de M. Royer-Collard et une introduction de L'éditeur.* Paris: V. Masson. [6 vols.]

Volume I contains "La vie de Reid, par Dugald Stewart."

1836   *Vie de Reid.* Paris: V. Masson. [118 p.]

Extracted from *Œuvres complètes de Thomas Reid.*

1837   Reprinted in *Œuvres posthumes de M. F[rançois]. Thurot. Leçons de grammaire de logique. Vie de Reid.* Paris: Hachette. [xxxviii + 528 p.]

The book carries the following notation: "Cet ouvrage n'a été qu'a cent quatre-vingt exemplaires."

1805   **[Anonymous].** ***A Short Statement of Some Important Facts Relative to the Late Election of a Mathematical Professor in the University of Edinburgh; Accompanied with Original Papers and Critical Remarks.*** Edinburgh: Printed by Murray & Cochrane. [ii + 127 p.]

1805   2nd edition. Edinburgh: Printed by Murray & Cochrane, and sold by William Creech and Archibald Constable & Co. [ii + 127 p.]

1805   3rd edition. Edinburgh: Printed by Murray & Cochrane, and sold by W. Creech. [ii + 139 p.]

1806   A revised version of the 3rd edition appeared in the *Edinburgh Review*, VII (1806): 113–34.

1806   The 3rd edition, reprinted in *Tracts, Historical and Philosophical, Relative to the Important Discussions which Lately Took Place Between Members of the University and the Presbytery of Edinburgh, Respecting the Election of Mr. Leslie to the Professorship of Mathematics in that University.* Edinburgh. [2 vols.]

1806   ***Postscript to Mr. Stewart's Short Statement of Facts Relative to the Election of Professor Leslie.*** Edinburgh: Printed by Murray & Cochrane, and sold by W. Creech. [48 p.]

1806   2nd edition. Edinburgh: Mundeld, Doig & Stevenson. [48 p.]

1806   Reprinted in *Tracts, Historical and Philosophical, Relative to the Important Discussions which Lately Took Place Between Members of the University and the Presbytery of Edinburgh, Respecting the Election of Mr. Leslie to the Professorship of Mathematics in that University.* Edinburgh. [2 vols.]

1810   *Philosophical Essays.* Edinburgh: Printed by George Ramsay and Company, for Wm. Creech and Archibald Constable and Company, Edinburgh; T. Cadell and W. Davies, Strand, John Murray, Fleet Street, and Constable, Hunter, Park and Hunter, London. [lxxvi + 590 p.]

> 1811   1st American edition. Philadelphia; New York: Printed for Anthony Finley; Whiting and Watson. [xii + 580 p.]
>
> 1816   2nd edition. Edinburgh: Printed for G. Ramsay and Co., for Archibald Constable and Co. [xii + 615 p.]
>
> 1818   3rd edition. Edinburgh: Printed for Archibald Constable and Company; Longman, Hurst, Rees, Orme and Brown, J. Murray. [xii + 615 p.]

> *Translations*: French
>
> 1828   *Essais philosophiques sur les systèmes de Locke, Berkeley, Priestley, Horne-Tooke, etc.* [Translated from the English by Charles Huret.] Paris: A. Johanneau. [xv + 387 p.]
>
> The translation is limited to Part I of the *Philosophical Essays*.

1811   *Biographical Memoirs of Adam Smith, LL.D., of William Robertson, D.D., and of Thomas Reid, D.D. Read Before the Royal Society of Edinburgh. Now Collected into One Volume, with Some Additional Notes.* Edinburgh: Printed by G. Ramsay and Co., for W. Creech, Bell and Bradfute, and A. Constable and Co., Edinburgh; F. and C. Rivington, Otridge and Son, London. [x + 532 p.]

1815   "Some Account of a Boy Born Blind and Deaf, Collected From Authentic Sources of Information; With a Few Remarks and Comments," *Transactions of the Royal Society of Edinburgh*, 7 (1815): 1–78.

> 1815   *Some Account of a Boy Born Blind and Deaf, Collected from Authentic Sources of Information; With a Few Remarks and Comments. From the Translations of the Royal Society of Edinburgh.* Edinburgh: Royal Society of Edinburgh. [78 p.]

1815–21   "Dissertation First: Exhibiting a General View of the Progress of Metaphysical, Ethical, and Political Philosophy Since the Revival of Letters in Europe," in the *Supplement to the Fourth, Fifth, and Sixth Editions of the Encyclopedia Britannica*. Edinburgh: Archibald Constable & Co. I: 1–166 and V: 1–257. [6 vols.]

The dissertation originally appeared in two parts, the first in 1815, the second in 1821.

> 1817   Boston: Wells & Lilly. [260 p.]
>
> Part 1 of Stewart's *Dissertation*.

1817   Boston: Wells & Lilly. [260 + 197 p.]

Part 1 of Stewart's *Dissertation*, together with John Playfair, *Dissertation Second: Exhibiting a General View of the Progress of Mathematical and Physical Science Since the Revival of Letters in Europe.*

1817–22   *A General View of the Progress of Metaphysical, Ethical, and Political Philosophy Since the Revival of Letters in Europe.* Boston: Wells & Lilly. [2 vols.]

Parts 1 and 2 of Stewart's *Dissertation.*

1821   Boston: Wells & Lilly. [2 vols.]

Parts 1 and 2 of Stewart's *Dissertation.*

1822   *A General View of the Progress of Metaphysical, Ethical, and Political Philosophy Since the Revival of Letters in Europe.* In two Dissertations. Boston: Wells & Lilly. [390 p.]

Both parts 1 and 2 of Stewart's *Dissertation.* Also released in a two-volume edition.

1835   *A General View of the Progress of Metaphysical, Ethical, and Political Philosophy Since the Revival of Letters in Europe* [bound together with John Playfair, *Dissertation the third: exhibiting a general view of the progress of mathematical and physical science, since the revival of letters in Europe*]. Edinburgh. [2 vols. in 1]

Parts 1 and 2 of Stewart's *Dissertation.*

1835   *Dissertations on the History of Metaphysical and Ethical, and Mathematical and Physical Science.* Edinburgh: Adam and Charles Black. [vii + 711 p.]

Translations: *French*

1820–23   *Histoire abrégée des sciences métaphysiques, morales et politiques, depuis la renaissance des lettres.* Translated by J.A. Buchon. Paris: F.G. Levrault. [3 vols.]

1827   ***The Collected Works of Dugald Stewart****. Sir William Hamilton, ed. Philadelphia: Carey, Lee & Carey. [11 vols.]

Vol. I: Dissertation: Exhibiting the Progress of Metaphysical, Ethical, and Political Philosophy, Since the Revival of Letters in Europe.
Vol. II, III, IV: Elements of the Philosophy of the Human Mind . . . to which is prefixed the introduction and part first of the outlines of moral philosophy.
Vol. V: Philosophical Essays.

Vol. VI, VII: The Philosophy of the Active and Moral Powers of Man . . . to which is prefixed part second of the outlines of moral philosophy.

Vol. VIII, IX: Lectures on Political Economy . . . to which is prefixed part third of the outlines of moral philosophy.

Vol. X: Biographical Memoirs of Adam Smith, William Robertson, Thomas Reid. To which is prefixed a Memoir of Dugald Stewart, with selections of his Correspondence . . . by J. Veitch.

Vol. XI: Translations of the Passages in Foreign Languages Contained in the Collected Works of Dugald Stewart.

General Index.

1828   Dugald Stewart. *Works*. Edinburgh: W. Creech. [7 vols.]

Vol. I: *Outlines of Moral Philosophy*. 3rd edition, corrected (1808).

Vol. II, III: *Elements of the Philosophy of the Human Mind*. 3rd edition, corrected. (1808–21).

Vol. IV: *Philosophical Essays*. 3rd edition. (1818).

Vol. V, VI: *The Philosophy of the Active and Moral Powers of Man*. (1828).

Vol. VII: *Account of the Life and Writings of Thomas Reid*. (1803).

1829   *Works of Dugald Stewart*. Cambridge, Mass.: Hilliard and Brown. [7 vols.]

Vol. I, II: *Elements of the Philosophy of the Human Mind*.

Vol. III: *Elements of the Philosophy of the Human Mind* (continued); *Outlines of Moral Philosophy*.

Vol. IV: *Philosophical Essays*.

Vol. V: *The Philosophy of the Active and Moral Powers of Man*.

Vol. VI: *Dissertation Exhibiting a General View of the Progress of Metaphysical, Ethical, and Political Philosophy, Since the Revival of Letters in Europe*.

Vol. VII: *Account of the Life and Writings of Adam Smith; Account of the Life and Writings of William Robertson; Account of the Life and Writings of Thomas Reid; Tracts Respecting the Election of Mr. Leslie to the Professorship in Mathematics in the University of Edinburgh*.

Translations: French

1829   *Œuvres de Dugald Stewart*. Translated by Théodore Jouffroy, Charles Huret and J.A. Buchon. Brussels: Librarie Philosophique. [5 vols.]

Vol. I: *Esquisses de philosophie morale*.

Vol. II: *Essais philosophiques sur les systèmes de Locke, Berkeley, Priestley, Horne-Tooke*.

Vol. III, IV, V: *Histoire abrégée des sciences métaphysiques, morales et politiques, depuis la Renaissance des lettres.*

1828 *The Philosophy of the Active and Moral Powers of Man*. Edinburgh: Printed for Adam Black. [2 vols.]

1828 Boston: Wells & Lilly. [2 vols.]

Translations: *French*

1834 *Philosophie des facultés actives et morales de l'homme.* Translated by Dr. Léon Simon. Paris: A. Johanneau. [2 vols.]

1855–56 *Lectures on Political Economy*. Volumes 8 and 9 of *The Collected Works of Dugald Stewart*. Sir William Hamilton, ed. 11 vols. Edinburgh: Thomas Constable and Co. [2 vols.]

Gilbert Stuart (1742–86)

Stuart was a prolific contributor to the newspapers and journals of the period, authoring numerous articles for, among others, the *Monthly Review*, the *English Review* and the *Political Herald Review*, which he edited during 1785–86. In addition, Stuart was co-owner and chief writer during the four-year existence of the *Edinburgh Magazine and Review* (1773–76). No attempt has been made to include Stuart's many shorter essays and reviews on a wide variety of subjects in the bibliography that follows. Indeed, such a task would be a daunting one. Rather, the works listed below are, in the main, confined to Stuart's book-length monographs. (A listing of Stuart's reviews and essays in the *Edinburgh Magazine* appears in Robert Kerr, *Memoirs of the Life, Writings, and Correspondence of William Smellie* [2 vols.; Edinburgh: Printed for John Anderson, 1811]: 1: 403–8.)

1768 [**Anonymous**]. *An Historical Dissertation Concerning the Antiquity of the English Constitution*. Edinburgh: Printed for A. Kincard and J. Bell; and for W. Sanby, J. Dodsley, E. Dilly and T. Cadell, London. [xii + 290 p.]

1770 2nd edition, corrected. London: T. Cadell, successor to Mr. Millar and A. Kincaid and J. Bell, Edinburgh. [xvi + 290 p.]

1771 2nd edition, corrected. London: T. Cadell, successor to Mr. Millar and A. Kincaid and W. Creech, Edinburgh. [xvi + 290 p.]

1778 London: T. Cadell.

1798 Edinburgh.

Translations: *French*

1794 *Dissertation historique sur l'ancienne constitution des Germains, Saxons, et habitans de Grande-Bretagne; ouvrage* contenant des recherches sur l'ancienneté des jurés et des délibérations des communes. Paris: Chez Maradan. [254 p.] "L'an 4 de la République."

German

1779   *Historische Abhandlung von dem Alterthum der Englischen Staatsverfassung.* Translated from the second English edition. Lübeck: Bey Christian Gottfried Donatius. [vi + 246 p.]

1776   **"Discourse Concerning the Laws and Government of England,"** prefixed to the 2nd edition of Francis Stoughton Sullivan, *Lectures on the Constitution and Laws of England: With a Commentary on Magna Carta and Illustrations of Many of the English Statutes.* London: Printed for E. and C. Dilly. [xxxii + 415 p.]

1776   2nd edition, to which authorities are added. London: Printed for Edward and Charles Dilly and Joseph Johnson. [xxxii + 415 p.]

1777   London: Printed for Edward and Charles Dilly and Joseph Johnson. [xxxii + 415 p.]

1790   2nd edition. Dublin: Printed by Graisberry and Campbell, for W. Jones. [xlii + 570 p.]

1777   *Faction Displayed or, a Genuine Relation of the Representation of the Trades, and the Late Political Contentions in the City of Edinburgh.* Edinburgh. [25 p.]

1778   *A View of Society in Europe, in its Progress from Rudeness to Refinement; or Inquiries Concerning the History of Law, Government, and Manners.* Edinburgh: Printed for John Bell; and J. Murray, London. [xx + 433 p.]

1778   Dublin. Printed for W. Whitestone, W. Colles, J. Hoey, W. Wilson, J. Williams, T. Walker. [xvi + 445 p.]

1782   2nd edition. London: Printed for J. Murray. [xx + 433 p.]

1783   2nd edition. London: J. Murray. [xx + 433 p.]

1792   2nd edition. Edinburgh: Printed for J. Robertson. [viii + 441 p.]

1797   New edition. Basil: Printed and sold by J.J. Tourneisen. [xii + 315 p.]

Translations: French

1789   *Tableau des progrés de la societé en Europe, ouvrage contenant des recherches sur l'origine des gouvernmens, les variations des mœurs et du système féodal.* [Translated from the English by A.M.H. Boulard.] Paris: Maradan, libraire, Hôtel de Châteauvieux, rue Saint-André-des-Arcs. [2 vols.]

German

1779   *Abriss des gesellschftlichen Zustandes in Europa, in seinem*
            Fortgange von Rohigkeit zu Verfeinerung, oder Untersuchungen
            die Geschichte der Gesetze, der Regierungsform und der Sitten
            betreffend. Liepzig: M.G. Weidmanns Erben und Reich. [xvi +
            414 p.]

1779   ***Observations Concerning the Public Law and the Constitutional***
            History of Scotland; With Occasional Remarks Concerning English
            Antiquity. Edinburgh: Printed for W. Creech; and J. Murray, London. [xxii
            + 395 p.]

1780   ***The History of the Establishment of the Reformation of Religion in***
            Scotland. London: Printed for J. Murray; and J. Bell, at Edinburgh. [iv +
            265 p.]

Translations: *German*

1786   *Geschichte der Reformation in Schottland.* Translated from the
            English [by Leopold Ludwig Brunn]. Altenburg: In der
            Richterschen Buchhandlung. [xvi + 244 p.]

1782   ***The History of Scotland from the Establishment of the Reformation till***
            the Death of Queen Mary. London: Printed for J. Murray and J. Bell at
            Edinburgh. [2 vols.]

            1782   Dublin: Printed for W. Gilbert, T. Walker, J. Beatty, R. Burton,
                        J. Exshaw, P. Byrne and J. Cash. [2 vols.]

            1782   A new edition. London: C. Dilly. [2 vols.]

            1783   *To Which are Annexed, Observations Concerning the Public*
                        Law and the Constitution of Scotland. 2nd edition. London:
                        Printed for J. Murray. [2 vols.]

            1783–84   *To Which are Annexed, Observations Concerning the Public*
                        Law and the Constitution of Scotland. 2nd edition. London:
                        Printed for J. Murray and G. Robinson. [2 vols.]

1782   **[Anonymous].** ***Critical Observations Concerning the Scottish Historians***
            Hume, Stuart, and Robertson: Including an Idea of the Reign of Mary
            Queen of Scots, as a Portion of History, Specimens of the Histories of
            this Princess, by Dr. Stuart and Dr. Robertson, and a Comparative View
            of the Merits of these Rival Historians. London: Printed for T. Evans. [ii
            + 53 p.]

            The National Library of Scotland attributes the pamphlet to Gilbert Stuart
            who attacked "the eminent historian William Robertson and his *History of*
            Scotland, comparing Robertson unfavourably with himself and David

Hume. Stuart had been an unsuccessful candidate for the professorship of public law at Edinburgh University and attributed his failure to the influence of Robertson. He subsequently 'pursued that historian with undying hatred' (DNB)."

Note

1. The bibliography that follows was constructed by consulting a number of written sources and a variety of library catalogues available on the World Wide Web, most importantly WorldCat and COPAC. WorldCat, provided by the Online Computer Library Center, allows simultaneous searches of every major academic library in the United States and Canada and a number of others in different parts of the globe while COPAC constitutes a union catalogue for almost all the major university research libraries in the United Kingdom and Ireland, plus the National Library and the National Library of Scotland. In addition, I have examined the holdings of the Bibliothèque Nationale in Paris, the Biblioteca Nazionale Centrale di Roma, the Deutsche Bibliothek Leipzig, the Karlsruhe Virtueller Katalog, a meta-catalogue of German research libraries, and the Östreichischer Bibliothekenverbund Gesamtkatalog, a union catalogue of Austrian research libraries. Finally, I am indebted to the Slavic Research Service at the University of Illinois at Urbana-Champaign, whose staff were unfailingly helpful in tracking down relevant citations in Russian, and to the research librarians at the National Library of Scotland, the Edinburgh University Library, and the Harvard University Library, whose efforts were crucial in explaining some of the bibliographic anomalies that were encountered.

    Among the books consulted were: T.E. Jessop, *A Bibliography of David Hume and of Scottish Philosophy from Francis Hutcheson to Lord Balfour* (New York: Russell and Russell, 1966) [reprint of the 1938 edition]; William B. Todd, "David Hume: A Preliminary Bibliography," in William B. Todd, ed., *Hume and the Enlightenment: Essays Presented to Ernest Campbell Mossner* (Edinburgh: The University Press, 1974): 189–205; *David Hume and the* [*sic*] *Eighteenth Century British Thought: An Annotated Catalogue* (Centennial Publication of Chuo University; Tokyo: Chuo University Library, 1986); Ian Simpson Ross, *Lord Kames and the Scotland of His Day* (Oxford: Clarendon Press, 1972); William C. Lehmann, *John Millar of Glasgow, 1735–1801* (Cambridge: University Press, 1960); Jane B. Fagg, "Introduction," in Vincenzo Merolle, ed., *The Correspondence of Adam Ferguson* (2 vols.; London: William Pickering, 1995): **I**: xx–cxl; E.L. Cloyd, *James Burnett: Lord Monboddo* (Oxford: Clarendon Press, 1972); and, Keith Tribe, *A Critical Bibliography of Adam Smith* (London: Pickering and Chatto, 2002).

4

Two Whig views of the American Revolution: Adam Ferguson's response to Richard Price

What this essay seeks to show is that late-eighteenth-century Whig thought was able to accommodate two different approaches to political philosophy that differed both in their epistemological roots and in their approach to the origins of government and the nature of political institutions while at the same time arriving at similar conclusions regarding what constitutes a free and open society. It is indicative of the wide range of views that Whig doctrine could accommodate both Adam Ferguson and Richard Price, two thinkers whose views diverged in so many particulars, but continued to be regarded as staunch Whigs and, depending on the particulars, as allies of the colonial cause. Indeed, Ferguson and Price put forward two distinct strands of late-eighteenth-century Whig ideology that were to continue on into nineteenth-century classical liberal thought. Ferguson's views, like those of Hume and Burke, reflected a theory of liberty for the most part based on the development of British traditions and institutions that evolved and took their shape from countless individual actions over centuries, each of which contributed to establishing a free society but none deliberately designed with that end in view. Price's political philosophy, on the other hand, was far more rationalist and was predicated on the notion that the ends for which political society existed and the particular institutions that conduced to those ends were open to reason and that it was possible to deliberately design the political arrangements under which we lived to maximize individual liberty. F.A. Hayek has made much of this distinction, maintaining that the political presuppositions embraced by Ferguson can alone give rise to a regime of liberty and that Price's rationalistic philosophy inevitably leads to authoritarianism.[1] As I hope to show, however, this claim is seriously deficient with respect to eighteenth-century Whig doctrine and to the arguments put forward in support of the American Revolution.

At the time Richard Price published his *Observations on the Nature of Civil Liberty, the Principles of Government, and the Justice and Policy of War with America* in 1776 he had already gained a reputation as one of the most ardent defenders of civil and religious liberty and republican values in Great Britain. The son of a Congregationalist minister, Price was born in the parish of Llangeinor in Glamorgan, Wales, in 1723. At the age of 17, Price entered Coward's Academy in Tenter Ailey, Moorfields, where he studied under John Eames, a friend and disciple of Isaac Newton. It was doubtless while a student at the Academy that Price gained his lifelong interest in mathematics and his philosophical rationalism. While Price rejected his father's harsh puritanism, he appeared quite early in his education to have determined to prepare for the ministry and was ordained a Non-Conformist minister in 1744. His church at Newington Green, a center of Dissent for a number of years, soon became a magnet for reformers and radicals, among them Mary Wollstonecraft, John Howard, Benjamin Franklin,

John Adams, and Adam Smith. Price's principal philosophical work, *A Review of the Principal Questions and Difficulties in Morals* was published in 1758 and it was this work that resulted in his being awarded a Doctorate of Divinity by Marischal College, Aberdeen, in 1769. Price's "discourse on the love of our country," a ringing defense of the revolutionary events in France preached in November 1789, provided the immediate stimulus not only for Burke's *Reflections* but for a huge number of responses. In 1791, the year in which he died, Price became a founding member of the Unitarian Society.

The *Observations*, prepared in the winter of 1775–76, made its appearance on 8 February and became an immediate success. Several thousand copies were sold within a few days of its publication, 60,000 copies by the close of 1776. The work ran into five editions within five weeks and into 12 editions within the year.[2] No one interested in the affairs of the empire was ignorant of its contents. The essay prompted the Council of the City of London to award Price its highest honour, the Freedom of the City, for laying bare "those pure principles of which alone the supreme legislative authority of Great Britain over her colonies can be justly or beneficially maintained."[3] The essay was quickly republished across the Atlantic, with editions appearing in Boston, New York, Charleston, and Philadelphia.[4] And while its effect on the pro-independence forces was not nearly as great as was that of Thomas Paine's *Common Sense*, the *Observations* did contribute to the arsenal at the disposal of those seeking a separation from Great Britain.

Price's pamphlet was regarded as so significant a challenge both to the government's position on America and to the arguments put forward by those who accepted the authority of Parliament to tax the colonies that it gave birth to a profusion of responses. The government's policy was ardently defended by, among others, Josiah Tucker, John Fletcher, and the Methodist John Wesley.[5] Dr. John Shebbeare, who was regularly paid by the government to defend its positions and who had previously been pilloried for libel, penned one of the most scurrilous of the replies, while Burke's response was one of the mildest, calling for conciliation with the rebellious colonies while not repudiating the abhorrent Declaratory Act,[6] which had been enacted during the administration of the Marquis of Rockingham, with whom Burke was associated.[7]

One of the most measured of the published rebuttals was that written by Adam Ferguson, the Scottish philosopher and Professor of Pneumatics and Moral Philosophy at the University of Edinburgh. Ferguson's sympathies, like those of many other Scottish men of letters, were with the British government, whose understanding of the constitutional relationship of the American colonies to the authority of Westminster was regarded as consistent with both British tradition and British law.[8] Ferguson had earlier shown some sensitivity to the colonial cause and had condemned the Stamp Act as politically inept and foolish. In a letter to John MacPherson, probably written in 1772, he noted that "I think Greenevilles Stamp Act a very unlucky affair for this Countrey. It has brought on a disspute in which this Mother Countrey as it is very properly called has made a very shabby figure, And I am affraid cannot mend the matter."[9] Even as late as the beginning of 1776 Ferguson, while convinced of the legality of the government's position, expressed concern that Britain would not be able to extricate itself from the impasse it had arrived at with the colonies. These speculations were occasioned by his having received a copy of James MacPherson's pamphlet "on the Rights of this Countrey against the Claims of America." [10] "I have never had any doubt on any of the rights Established in this Pamphlet," Ferguson maintained. "The only Question with me was what this Countrey in Wisdom ought to do in the Situation at which the Colonys were Arrived. This Question becomes every Day more complicated & more difficult." [11]

It appears that as early as 1772 Ferguson had been approached by the Administration to publish his views on the American crisis, doubtless in the expectation that the high reputation in which he was held by educated colonists might work to blunt their increasing hostility towards Britain. As one of the leading figures of the Scottish Enlightenment, Ferguson was well-known and his work highly respected. Indeed, the Scottish Enlightenment, as one historian has noted, "was probably the most potent single tradition in the American Enlightenment. From Hutcheson to Ferguson, including Hume and Adam Smith, came a body of philosophical literature that aroused men from their dogmatic slumbers on both sides of the Atlantic." [12]

Scottish moral philosophy was decisively established in America through the mediation of John Witherspoon, who arrived in the colonies from Scotland to take up the position of president of Princeton (then known as the College of New Jersey) in 1768. Witherspoon, one of the more outspoken Evangelical ministers in the Church of Scotland, brought with him an intimate knowledge of the work of the leading Scottish writers, which he kept current and attempted to impart to his students. Thus, Ferguson's *Essay on the History of Civil Society*, Ferguson's principle treatise, appears among the works comprising Witherspoon's recommended reading list for his course in political theory. [13] A student of Witherspoon's, James Madison was especially receptive to Ferguson's writings, [14] but Madison was certainly not alone among Americans in having studied Ferguson. Data presented by Lundberg and May indicate that between 1777 and 1813 the *Essay* appeared in no less than 22 percent of the American library catalogues and booksellers' lists examined. [15] Jefferson had been introduced to the works of the major Scottish thinkers when a student at William and Mary College, [16] and among the items listed in the catalogue of books sold to the Library of Congress in 1815 was a copy of the *Essay*. [17]

In New England the effects of Scottish philosophy in shaping the American Enlightenment were even more profound than in the South. Scottish thought was to prove crucial in temporalizing Calvinist doctrine and replacing it with secular conceptions of history and progress. As one intellectual historian has observed, one can only imagine the effect of sentiments such as these on minds steeped in a Puritan theology that viewed man as entirely dependent on God, whose earthly magistrates we are obligated to obey. [18] It was Adam Ferguson who gave this sweeping secularization its best expression: "We speak of art as distinguished from nature," he wrote,

> but art itself is natural to man. He is in some measure the artificer of his own frame, as well as his fortune, and is destined, from the first age of his being, to invent and contrive. . . . If we are asked therefore, Where the state of nature is to be found? we may answer, It is here, and it matters not where we are understood to speak in the island of Great Britain, at the Cape of Good Hope, or the Straits of Magellan. . . . If the palace be unnatural, the cottage is so no less; and the highest refinements of political and moral apprehension, are not more artificial in their kind, than the first operations of sentiment and reason. [19]

When the first shots were fired at Lexington in April 1775 Ferguson was almost 52 years old and had held the chair of philosophy at the University of Edinburgh for 11 years. He was born at Logierait, Perthshire, on the border of the Scottish Highlands, on 20 June 1723, the youngest child of the parish minister. Having received his early education at the parish school and the local grammar school, he was sent to the University of St Andrews in 1738, where he gained a reputation for classical scholarship. Ferguson took his MA degree in 1742 and, in the same year, entered the Divinity Hall at St Andrews. Soon thereafter he transferred to Edinburgh University and in 1745, after having completed only three years of the required six-year course of study in theology, he was offered the deputy chaplaincy of the Black Watch Regiment, largely, it appears, because of his knowledge of Gaelic. In July 1745 he was ordained in the Scottish Kirk and raised to the rank of principal chaplain He remained with his regiment until 1754, at which time he resigned his commission and quit the clerical profession.

With the help of his friend David Hume, Ferguson was appointed to the post of Keeper of the Advocates Library, Edinburgh, in 1757, having succeeded Hume to that office (and thus providing Ferguson with access to one of the best libraries in Europe). Following the death of the professor of natural philosophy at the University of Edinburgh, and again through the intercession of, among others, David Hume, Ferguson was named to that chair in 1759; five years later, in 1764, he transferred to the chair of pneumatics and moral philosophy, which he held until his retirement in 1785. It was during his tenure as professor of moral philosophy that three of his four most important works were published: the *Essay on the History of Civil Society*, in 1767; the *Institutes of Moral Philosophy*, a synopsis of his lectures on moral philosophy, in 1769, and the *History of the Progress and Termination of the Roman Republic*, in five volumes, in 1783.[20]

While Ferguson's political sympathies were decidedly Whiggish, it is likely that Ferguson's views on American independence were in part shaped by the economic loss that would likely follow a change in Scottish commercial relations with the colonies. More important, Ferguson saw no diminution in the liberties of Scottish people in the wake of the Act of Union of 1707; in this he reflected the votes cast by most Scottish members of Parliament who regarded the arguments put forward by the British government as constitutionally correct. Ferguson regarded the American position on taxation as without merit.[21] The notion that England should underwrite the costs of garrisoning an army in North America to protect the colonists while being blocked from taxing the beneficiaries of this policy struck Ferguson as nonsensical. Having received the benefits of subjects, it followed that the colonists were subject to the duties of subjects. It is true that England had profited from its trade with America but this held equally true of America in its trade with the mother country. Indeed, the laws of nature clearly provided that one body politic could legally submit itself to the authority of and to contribute to the supplies of another, as was the case, Ferguson maintained, with the American colonies in its relation with the Parliament of Great Britain.

These conclusions, well known to the authorities, prompted the North Administration in 1772 to approach Ferguson with a view to publishing a pamphlet in support of the government's policies in North America. To this suggestion, Ferguson, in writing to

Sir John Macpherson,[22] declined, noting that "I could come under no Obligations which I am affraid the Step of your Friendship Suggests would seem to Promise." [23] Ferguson adds that, while he will not write a pamphlet, "I will continue to write you what occurs to me" and noted that he would have no objection to his comments being brought to the attention of Lord Grafton.[24]

In 1776 Ferguson was again approached, this time by Sir John Dalrymple, who had at first suggested that Ferguson participate in a plan to contribute regularly to a weekly journal defending the government's policies but this scheme appears never to have been implemented. However, Dalrymple was successful in gaining for Ferguson a handsome government stipend at the beginning of 1776. Dalrymple argued that Ferguson had been a faithful adherent of Administration policy on numerous occasions, especially with regard to the colonies. However, his support, unlike that of so many of his colleagues, had never been acknowledged with some favor or another and as a consequence, according to Dalrymple, Ferguson had begun to grow somewhat bitter. As a consequence, he was awarded a grant of £200 per annum, conferred on him on 23 January 1776 by the King's Warrant under the Privy Seal of Scotland.[25]

The effect of this subsidy appears to have been immediate. Price's *Observations* appeared in early February and Ferguson quickly began work on a rejoinder to the essay, which he sent to the government to be used as they wished. On behalf of the government, Sir Grey Cooper, who held the post of Secretary of the Treasury, instructed the publisher William Strahan in Edinburgh to print Ferguson's essay[26] and it was soon republished by a group of printers in Dublin.[27] The pamphlet appeared under the title *Remarks on a Pamphlet Lately Published by Dr. Price, Intitled Observations on the Nature of Civil Liberty, the Principles of Government, and the Justice and Policy of the War With America, etc., In a Letter from a Gentlemen in the Country to a Member of Parliament.* It sold for one shilling[28] and was very well-received, being quoted at length in the *Critical Review* and the *Monthly Review*, two of the leading magazines of the day. Even Price referred to its author as "one even of the most candid as well as the ablest of my opponents." [29]

Ferguson's attitude towards the colonies appeared to have hardened following publication of his *Remarks*. Again writing to John Macpherson, on 27 October 1777, Ferguson expressed the hope that British forces, "for our own Credit, [would inflict on] that people . . . a sound drubbing." Once having done so, however, Ferguson supported the removal of British troops from the rebellious colonies inasmuch as their upkeep would be beyond the financial capacities of the colonies to sustain. He writes:

> I protest that if we had news to morrow that Howe had beat Washington and Burgoyne Arnold the use I would make of it would be to leave America with contempt. For it looks as if no Calamity would force them to Submission & if it did their Submission is not worth haveing. Their whole resource for any Visi[ble] time to Come will not pay the Army that ke[eps] them in Submission. So I am partial enough to Great Britain to wish them to the bottom of the Sea.[30]

What occasioned this mean-spiritedness and led Ferguson to such a foolish miscalculation regarding the colonies' economic capacities is impossible to say. He continued in the same vein three months later, when, after outlining a military campaign that he felt would prove sufficient to subdue the rebellion, he noted: "In our Way to this Object the Rebels may be induced to prefer accommodation to the Continuance of Such A War. But Lord have mercy on those who expect any Good in this business without Sufficient Instruments of Terror in one hand & of Moderation and justice in the Other."[31] Having been selected to join the Commission appointed to seek some accommodation with the colonies, Ferguson felt it expedient to moderate his views somewhat prior to setting sail to America in early 1778. He noted in yet another letter to John Macpherson that he hoped the Administration would signal to the colonies that they had no intention of invading American liberties and that they supported the establishment of a general parliament for America.[32]

In the fall of 1777, General John Burgoyne, who had led an invasion force from Canada with the intention of linking up with the British army in New York City, suffered a decisive defeat at Saratoga and on 17 October Burgoyne and his whole army surrendered to General Horatio Gates. The news of Burgoyne's defeat caused a sensation across the Atlantic. The French government set in train formal diplomatic efforts to recognize America's independence and the British government, in an effort to be as conciliatory as possible, abruptly reversed its policies. In February the North Administration introduced bills in Parliament repealing all acts of which the colonies complained passed since 1763. At the same time a commission was struck whose purpose was to enter into negotiations with the Americans to grant to the colonies anything they wished[33] provided they remain loyal to the Crown.

The commissioners were appointed by George III, who personally had little hope that they would prove successful. As its head, the Crown appointed Frederick Howard, fifth Earl of Carlisle, and its membership comprised William Eden (later Lord Auckland), a close friend of Lord North, and George Johnstone, who had been appointed the first governor of West Florida in 1763.[34] It was Johnstone, an old friend of Ferguson, who was responsible for inviting Ferguson to accompany the Commission to America.[35] Upon arriving at Philadelphia in June, the Commission appointed Ferguson its secretary and immediately attempted to enter into negotiations with several members of Congress.[36] These proved a complete failure, nor was the Commission any more successful in prevailing upon Washington to grant Ferguson a passport through the American lines to treat directly with Congress.[37] Having been defeated at reaching agreement with the colonies short of recognizing their independence and withdrawing all British troops, the Commission returned home in late 1778. Ferguson continued to occupy himself with Commission business until the spring of the following year, at which point he resumed his chair at the University.[38]

Despite having spent six months in the colonies, Ferguson's sentiments regarding the colonial cause had not softened since having written in reply to Price two years earlier. Indeed, if the Manifesto and Proclamation issued by the Conciliation Commission in October 1778, of which Ferguson was one of the authors,[39] is any indication, Ferguson's animus towards the colonists had deepened in the wake of America's alliance with France, a nation, it was argued, that traditionally opposed freedom of conscience and that held religious toleration, which Englishmen took for granted, in contempt.[40] A treaty with France, the Manifesto observed, would convert the existing hostilities between those sharing a common heritage into a world struggle. In light of this, it went on, self-preservation would justify England's destruction of the colonies.[41] Thomas Paine was especially offended by the Manifesto's claim that France was the "natural enemy" of both England and America and devoted a good part of *The Crisis*, No. 6 to criticizing Ferguson for his use of the notion "natural enemies," which Paine characterized as a meaningless barbarism.[42]

Richard Price, it need hardly be added, was not moved to alter his views in light of America's alliance with France although he appears to have shared Ferguson's aversion to a treaty between a people dedicated to establishing a free society and a nation as closely tied to its feudal past as was France. In early 1778, he had published a new edition of his *Observations* to which he appended a second essay replying to his numerous critics. This second pamphlet, which first appeared in February 1777 under the title *Additional Observations on the Nature and Value of Liberty*, was issued with the *Observations* in January 1778, as *Two Tracts on Civil Liberty*, to which he added a general introduction and supplement.[43] Price's introductory observations pointed to the need to hasten a resolution of the conflict with the colonies by acceding to their demands, a comment prompted by his belief that an American–French alliance was imminent.[44] Indeed, once the alliance was concluded Price saw even less reason to deny the United States its independence. "France," he wrote,

> has acknowledged the independence of America. Every power in Europe is ready to do it. All *real* authority is gone; and it cannot be expected that by any *nominal* authority we can bind them to anything that interferes with their interest. In these circumstances, all hesitation about yielding independence to them seems unreasonable.[45]

A reading of Price's *Observations* and Ferguson's response naturally raises the question, in which ways did these two writers, who shared so much of the Whig tradition and who were both highly regarded for their political insights by so many colonists, differ from each other in their assessment of the events in America? In this regard it will prove useful to contrast Price and Ferguson with respect to the philosophical differences that bore most decisively on their views of the American crisis.

Epistemology and its relation to ethics

As F.A. Hayek has pointed out, Ferguson and Price are particularly good exemplars of the two distinct liberal traditions of which he writes, the one empirical and unsystematic, the other speculative and rationalistic. And even though Hayek refers to the first as English and the second as French, he concedes that both views were embraced by intellectuals on both sides of the Channel and especially by Englishmen like Price who regarded the French Revolution with enthusiasm.[46]

While Locke was clearly a major influence in shaping Price's views, the underlying epistemology that shaped Price's political philosophy differs markedly. In his *A Review of the Principal Questions in Morals*, first published in 1758, Price maintains that certain ideas, for example those having to do with identity and causation, are simply not derivable from our sensory experiences but rather are known through rational intuition. Equally, our intellectual perceptions of right and wrong, our notions of moral rightness, follow immediately from our understanding and, once having been intuited, are appealable to nothing more fundamental. Among these immutable and objective truths of which the mind is aware are our duty to God and our sense of justice. And justice, in turn, entails the duty to respect property, which includes an individual's life, limbs, faculties, and goods.[47] Alongside this view, Price also asserted that utility and benevolence constituted legitimate criteria for judging the rightness of an act. At the point at which these several principles of morals might conflict, Price asserts, reason will dictate which principle has priority.

It is this epistemological foundation that underlies Price's discussion of civil liberty in the *Observations*.[48] When Price notes that civil liberty entails that every man act as his own legislator (that is, that each of us participates in some capacity or another in determining the rules that govern us)[49] and that no community can rightfully assume authority over a person or his property without adequate representation, he regarded these claims as deductively true. It is, Price would contend, in the nature of free societies that those who live in them have the right to legislate for themselves, since as truly free agents their dispositions are such that they would legislate correctly.

Ferguson's approach to ethics varies considerably from that of Price. His *Essay*, while apparently a work in conjectural sociology, was regarded by Ferguson as primarily an extension of his researches into moral philosophy, the starting point for which, he believed, was the study of the way man functions, both as an individual and in conjunction with others. He regarded all aprioristic notions of man's nature as unsatisfactory and maintained that the only adequate method of gaining information about the principles of ethics was by studying man within the context of his history. "Before we can ascertain the rules of morality for mankind," he wrote, "the history of man's nature, his dispositions, his specific enjoyments and sufferings, his condition and future prospects, should be known."[50] Indeed, Ferguson insisted, we are as capable of gaining real knowledge about the nature of human beings and the laws governing how they are to be treated as we are about the physical universe.

This, coupled with Ferguson's belief in the inevitable moral progress of the human species, led him to conclude that it was possible to define the ends towards which man ought to move and, indeed, was moving, as he approaches a more perfect condition. An empirical investigation of man's nature would provide the facts from which we are able to determine what his ends are. "Our knowledge of what any nature ought to be," he observed, must be derived from our knowledge of its faculties and powers and the attainment to be aimed at must be of the kind which these faculties and powers are fitted to produce."[51]

The sharply divergent epistemological presuppositions that shaped the arguments that Price and Ferguson put forward account in part for Ferguson's criticisms of Price's notions of liberty, one of whose divisions Price characterizes as our "power of following our own sense of right and wrong." Ferguson notes that were we to accept this definition, then it follows that any constraint whatever on our behavior constitutes a species of slavery. However, Price is here claiming that we are morally unfree to the extent that we are prevented from complying with our sense of what is right; this formulation, when applied to civil liberty, leads inexorably to the conclusion that to be truly free entails our being able to legislate for ourselves. As one commentator has observed, Ferguson's response that this interpretation would empower thieves and pickpockets to make their own laws, misses the point since what Price is claiming is that it is in the nature of things that in a truly free society all its citizens, as morally free agents, would act rationally, in keeping with rectitude and virtue.[52] Further,

Ferguson argues that, inasmuch as the great end of government is to secure to each of us our persons and our property by restraining others from invasive acts, it follows that liberty as Price understands the term, that is, the absence of any restraint, is inconsistent with peace and civil society. But, again, Price's argument has reference to external restraints on truly free agents, whose choices would already be restrained by their moral sense.

It is true that Price later concedes that freedom is consistent with "limitations on our licentious actions and insults to our persons, property, and good name," but, Ferguson argues, Price has recourse to this amendment only after having been shown that his earlier formulation is far too broad. Interestingly, Price's addendum serves to bring his notion of liberty into line with that offered by Locke and reflects Ferguson's own conception of personal liberty as not so much a power but the security of our rights.[53] Doing what we please, Ferguson argues, is not what liberty is about. Rather, being free to act as we choose, circumscribed by the rights of others and secure in our right to so act, is the defining characteristic of a truly free society. In point of fact this seems to be very close to what Price is suggesting.

Thus it appears that both Price and Ferguson, by completely divergent routes and despite differing epistemological underpinnings, arrive at similar conclusions respecting the nature of liberty. Independent of exactly how rights are defined, both Price and Ferguson agree that a free society is one, in Ferguson's words, "which secures to us the possession of our rights, while it restrains us from invading the rights of others."[54]

Rights

Price had defended America in its controversies with the Crown since their inception. Indeed, he regarded the cause of the colonies as the cause of all free English people and saw in colonial resistance to the depredations of the North Administration the best hope that freedom would be preserved in Britain. The colonists, Price maintained, in fighting the English battle for liberty, were preserving a future asylum for those seeking freedom.[55]

The concept of liberty Price puts forward in the *Observations*, borrows heavily from Locke and differs only in minor particulars.[56] While he was prepared to put forward utilitarian arguments in support of certain political ends, Price does not rest his case for freedom on any doctrine of utility but bases it firmly on a foundation of natural rights whose principles are eternally valid. Price divides liberty into four aspects, physical, moral, religious, and civil, all of which reflect some notion of self-direction. Physical liberty entails the power to act as an agent free from physical restraint; moral liberty consists in the power to conduct oneself in accord with one's sense of right or wrong; religious liberty lies in being able to choose those beliefs and modes of worship that conform to the dictates of one's conscience; and civil liberty refers to the community's power to govern itself by laws of its own making.

Price's understanding of rights is purely Lockean. Rights, he maintains, derive from our nature as human beings and are inalienable. They are to be understood in their negative designation only, prohibiting certain actions on the part of others directed at the rights holder, that is, one's right to something entails that others may not intervene should the rights holder attempt to exercise it. It does not entail that others are positively obligated to help the rights holder to exercise it. My right to my life denotes that I may do all within my power consistent with the rights of others to keep myself alive (that is, that I am under no obligation not to prevent myself from dying) and that others are prohibited from intervening should I attempt to preserve my life. Thus, when Price writes of religious liberty, that it is the power of acting as we choose with respect to our religious beliefs,[57] he notes that inasmuch as we each possess the same inalienable right to this liberty, no one may use this right in such a way that he encroaches on the equal liberty of others. Price argues that this is self-evidently true since were it not, then "there would be a contradiction in the nature of things, and it would be true that every one had a right to enjoy what every one had a right to destroy."[58] However, my right does not imply any positive duty on the part of others that they help save me. The right to one's life does not connote that one will be free from disease nor that it is incumbent on others to do all they can to prevent one from dying, but only that they not actively intervene to kill you. Even under circumstances where two people are confronted with conditions such that one man's life is contingent on the other's death, neither may raise his hand against the other under pain of violating this right, despite the fact that both will die. Or, put more simply, my right to something, say my liberty or my life, entails only prohibitions on others and not positive commands.

All civil government, Price maintains, both originates with the people and exists to advance their happiness by securing these rights.[59] Those governments that operate on principles at variance with this debase the natural ends of government and enslave their citizens. Free governments, furthermore, are the only kind that are favorable to human improvement. Since the essential function of government to insure that we may peaceably enjoy our rights and since this conduces most to our happiness, nations that are administered in conformity with other ends pervert the natural and inherent equality with which God has endowed each of us.

Ferguson's conception of rights is at sharp variance with that offered by Price. Just as notions of private property evolve as societies develop from the rudest to the most polished, so it is with rights, whose primary function is to secure property and thus insure our liberty. These rights evolve over time and owe their origin to the inequalities of station and the attempts to curb the abuse of power that arise as societies advance from savagery to civilization. This subordination of rank that marks all societies except the most primitive is, Ferguson writes, natural and salutary. "It is a common observation," he notes:

> that mankind were originally equal. They have indeed by nature equal rights to their preservation, and to the use of their talents; but they are fitted for different stations; and when they are classed by a rule taken from this circumstance, they suffer no injustice on the side of their natural rights. It is obvious, that some mode of subordination is as necessary to men as society itself; and this, not only to attain the ends of government, but to comply with an order established by nature.[60]

Unlike Price, Ferguson rejects the idea that our rights and the personal liberty that they allow are natural and attach to us by virtue of our humanity, independent of our history. In fact, he argues, they take their specific form from the totality of events that shape our past and differ in particulars as society evolves. He observes:

Liberty, in one sense, appears to be the portion of polished nations alone. The savage is personally free, because he lives unrestrained, and acts with the members of his tribe on terms of equality. The barbarian is frequently independent from a continuance of the same circumstance, or because he has courage and a sword. But good policy alone can provide for the regular administration of justice, reconstitute a force in the state, which is ready on every occasion to defend the rights of its members.

The distinction between Price and Ferguson on the issue of rights emerges most clearly in Ferguson's *Remarks* where he juxtaposes Price's appeal to the concept of natural universal rights to the historical obligations and privileges that in law determined the relation of the colonists to Great Britain. "The Doctor is pleased to say," Ferguson writes, "that the question of right, with all liberal inquirers, ought to be, not what jurisdiction over them, precedents, statutes, and charters give, but what reason and equity, and the rights of humanity give."[61] Ferguson expressed amazement at this approach to politics, which, he felt, could only lead to expressions of private interest and opinion, depriving one of the fixed landmarks provided by Britain's history of precedents, statutes, and charters.

In any case, Ferguson did not regard liberty as dependent on the presence of abstract rights. Rather, the crucial determinant of a free society was the stability of those institutions that guaranteed our ability to enjoy what rights we in fact had. Throughout his writings Ferguson emphasizes the singular importance of the security of property, without which justice and liberty would be impossible. It is the preservation of our property and station that makes society possible and secures to each of us the rights that we have acquired. Indeed, the paramount function of government is to insure to its citizens this security. "Liberty consists in the security of the citizen against every enemy," Ferguson maintained in his *Principles*,

> whether foreign or domestic, public or private, from whom, without any provision being made for his defence, he might be exposed to wrong or oppression of any sort: And the first requisite, it should seem, towards obtaining this security, is the existence of an effective government to wield the strength of the community against foreign enemies, and to repress the commission of wrongs at home.[62]

Ferguson's views on the prescriptive rights to which all Englishmen were heir certainly reflected the arguments embraced by Americans at the start of the conflict but as the struggle intensified it was Price's reiteration of the Lockean notion of natural rights that struck the colonists as more appropriate and that pervaded the colonial arguments against the Crown in the later stages of the struggle. Finally it was not the prescriptive rights of Englishmen but Locke's conception of man's innate rights that found its most eloquent expression in the Declaration of Independence.

The nature of empire

Price and Ferguson approach the question of the nature of empire with clearly different presuppositions. It seems clear that Ferguson conceives of the empire covering the home islands and the American colonies as a unitary political structure comprising one people bound together by the same laws, customs, and traditions. He observes that the colonies, by virtue of having been part of the British empire, are subject to the sovereignty of the mother country and to its legislature.[63] Price, on the other hand, offers a conception of empire that is clearly federative, with each constituent unit independent of the others with regard to its internal affairs and all paying loyalty to the same sovereign. For Price, the logic of contemporary circumstances appears to have shaped his views on the relation of one aggregation of free people to another. "An empire," Price maintains,

> is a collection of states or communities united by some common bond or tie. If these states have each of them free constitutions of government and, with respect to taxation and internal legislation, are independent of the other states but united by compacts or alliances or subjection to a great council representing the whole, or to one monarch entrusted with the supreme executive power, in these circumstances the empire will be an empire of freemen. If, on the contrary, like the different provinces subject to the Grand Seignior, none of the states possess any independent legislative authority but are all subject to an absolute monarch whose will is law, then is the empire an empire of slaves.[64]

It is worth noting that Price, together with almost all the English radicals who were sympathetic to the colonial cause, originally opposed American independence and hoped that some reconciliation with Great Britain would prove possible. Indeed, the primary purpose of his *Observations on the Nature of Civil Liberty*, which was published before the States declared their independence, was to prevail upon the British government to moderate its policies in such a way as to re-establish an imperial connection. Price's proposal would, if adopted, provide the necessary machinery to safeguard the rights and liberties of Americans while maintaining a political link between British North America and Great Britain.[65]

Ferguson's notion of the British empire of the eighteenth century is far more traditional.[66] Having expanded its territory and having originally populated these new areas with its own people who carried with them British law, the empire constituted nothing more than a geographical extension of the original state whose ultimate political authority remained where it was previously lodged. In fact, the colonies, economic satellites of the mother country, had as their primary function the generation of wealth for Britain. The mere expansion of territory, Ferguson would have maintained, was not sufficient justification for the creation of separate, constituent sovereignties, each independent of the others and reliant on the central authority only on issues touching the whole. The history of mankind, Ferguson contended, reflects this motive to empire, a desire to extend the limits of the existing state and uniting the whole under one central power while severely limiting the degree of self-government in the provinces.

In America's case especially, justice demanded that the colonies contribute to the upkeep of this centralized empire inasmuch as they were the recipients of the most essential benefits the mother country could extend to them, by securing their property from domestic and foreign assault and by providing them with an outlet for their goods.[67] Britain's relation to her colonies was indeed particularly generous[68] and it was incumbent on the American colonies to indemnify her for the expenses that the central authority had determined had been incurred on their behalf.

It is interesting that in his *Essay* Ferguson called attention to the dangers that adhere in too extensive an empire, the effect of which is to deprive us of a stage on which men of political integrity and sagacity can play a role. "When we reason in behalf of our species," Ferguson writes, although we may lament the abuses which sometimes arise from independence, and opposition of interest; yet, whilst any degrees of virtue remain with mankind, we cannot wish to croud, under one establishment, numbers of men who may serve to constitute several; or to commit affairs to the conduct of one senate, one legislative or executive power, which, upon a distinct and separate footing, might furnish an exercise of ability, and a theater of glory, to many.[69]

Despite this caution, however, he remained committed to supporting the conflict with the colonies until Britain was successful in reestablishing its North American empire. At some point following the return of the Carlisle Commission to Plymouth in December 1778 Ferguson penned a memorial regarding American independence in which he maintained that "the danger and the consequences of this separation are so great as to justify every tryal that can be made to prevent it."[70]

In the event, the success of the American cause put an end to the empire as Ferguson conceived it and transformed its essential nature from one of political dominion to one of economic penetration. It has recently been noted:

> British statesmen in the late eighteenth century were sometimes given to musing that a world-wide network of commerce was preferable to an Empire of rule over land and people. Some historians have argued that a "revulsion against colonization," accentuated by the quarrel that led to the loss of most of Britain's dominions in North America and coinciding with the rise of industrialization, brought about a shift away from an empire of rule to the pursuit of trade and influence throughout the world. Trade, it has been argued, came to be preferred to dominion.[71]

State of nature and government by contract

No issues make clearer the distinction between Ferguson's conception of political institutions as the products of evolution and of spontaneously generated growth and Price's notion of these institutions as the deliberate product of human design than their views on the state of nature and the social contract. Price, like Locke, holds that political authority derives and, indeed, can only derive, from the people. Men have no more natural an obligation to obey their government than they do their neighbor. The obligation to conform to the dictates of the civil magistrate stems solely from the freely extended consent of the person governed, without which one cannot become the subject of another or be constrained by law not of one's making. As Price argues:

> All civil government, as far as it can be denominated *free*, is the creature of the people. It originates with them. It is conducted under their direction; and has in view nothing but their happiness. All its different forms are no more than so many different modes in which they chuse to direct their affairs, and to secure the quiet enjoyment of their rights. In every free state every man is his own Legislator. All *taxes* are free gifts for public services. All *laws* are particular provisions or regulations established by COMMON CONSENT for gaining protection and safety. And all *Magistrates* are Trustees or Deputies for carrying these regulations into execution.[72]

Indeed, in one significant area Price goes significantly further than does Locke in leaving greater power in the hands of the people. Locke's social contract, like those of most other political theorists who invoke the notion, is such that it empowers its signers to determine the form of political authority that will prevail together with its duration and its limits. Once having established the terms of the original social contract, however, those bound by its terms are forever constrained to observe its provisions unless the magistrate violates his obligations. They hold no residual power to change the form of government, having ceded such a right when removing themselves from the state of nature. Price, on the other hand, maintained that ultimate sovereignty over the form and style of government was never surrendered and remained in the keeping of those who were governed throughout. The political sovereignty of the people is continuous and may be exercised as and when they see fit.[73]

Price's arguments supporting the colonists' demands for a change in the civil magistracy are thus even stronger than those that would have been put forward by Locke. Not only had the civil magistrate, in the form of the Royal Court and the various Administrations responsible for American policy since the end of the French and Indian War, violated the terms of the original contract whereby the English colonists who settled in the New World were guaranteed their rights, but it was also the case that the American people wished to reorder their political institutions to better reflect their needs and wishes, which they had every right to do. Despite the fact that the history of the relationship between Great Britain and her American colonies was an oppressive and despotic one, the colonists were under no obligation to prove that the British magistracy had breached the contract it had entered into with its subjects to protect their rights. It was sufficient that they wished to replace the political authority of the mother country with one more in keeping with their welfare.

Unlike Price, Ferguson rejected the notion that civil society and government are artifacts, creations of some original contract whereby free and equal beings living independently in some natural state devoid of political authority came together to confer their natural rights and powers on a newly-designated sovereign. Committed to approaching the study of man and society scientifically, that is, to describing man as he is actually observed, Ferguson rejected the notion of "man in the state of nature," in the sense of man before the advent of society. "Mankind are taken in groupes," he wrote, "as they have always subsisted." That society is coeval with man is confirmed by the fact that the individual is the bearer of social dispositions and that regardless of where we find man, we find him gathered together with others.[74]

Ferguson rejected the social contract theory as a valid account of the origins of government with many of the same arguments earlier offered by Hume.[75] The establishment of formal rules enforceable by a permanent political institution emerge, claimed Ferguson, not from the desire to create a stronger social union, but rather in response to the abuses that arise from an imperfect distribution of justice. Ferguson held that a system of formal political arrangements did not rest on consent but was gradually shaped to meet the interests of justice with respect to securing private property.[76] It is a useless analytical tool, he claimed, to posit the idea of universal consent to what was, in fact, the gradual emergence of formalized rules of action which took their origin in earlier modes of behavior. "What was in one generation a propensity to herd with the species," Ferguson observed, "becomes, in the ages which follow, a principle of national union. What was originally an alliance for common defence, becomes a concerted plan of political force."[77]

Ferguson does, however, make use of the term "state of nature," but he confines its use to his ethics rather than to his political theory. He regarded a progression towards excellence or perfection as the governing principle of all moral life. Thus, at one and the same time, Ferguson enunciated a law of perfection that offered an explanation both for individual morality and for social progress. For Ferguson, the natural development of the individual and the species towards perfection describes the "state of nature." Any point that lies along this continuum of development is as much man's "state of nature" as is any other point.[78] In his major work on moral philosophy, Ferguson noted:

> The state of nature or the distinctive character of any progressive being is to be taken, not from its description at the outset, or at any subsequent stage of its progress; but from an accumulative view of its movement throughout. The oak is distinguishable from the pine, not merely by its seed leaf; but by every successive aspect of its form; by its foliage in every successive season; by its acorn; by its spreading top; by its lofty growth; and the length of its period. And the state of nature, relative to every tree in the wood, includes all the varieties of form or dimension through which it is known to pass in the course of its nature.[79]

Commerce

Despite the fact that both Price and Ferguson were aware of the advantages to be derived from commerce, in the case of neither writer was their support unreserved. While the nature of their fears regarding an unrestrained commercial society were similar, Price was particularly fearful that a substantial increase in luxury might pose a fatal threat to liberty. This is not to suggest that Price advocated an austere and frugal lifestyle as alone compatible with a free and independent nation. He appears to have been aware of the benefits that accrued to Great Britain from its flourishing trade with the American colonies. "This trade," he maintained,

> was not only thus an increasing trade, but it was a trade in which we had no rivals, a trade certain, constant, and uninterrupted, and which, by the shipping employed in it, and the naval stores supplied by it, contributed greatly to the support of that navy which is our chief national strength. Viewed in these lights it was an object unspeakably important. But it will appear still more so if we view it in its connexions and dependencies. It is well known that our trade with Africa and the West-Indies cannot easily subsist without it. And, upon the whole, it is undeniable that it has been one of the main springs of our opulence and splendour and that we have, in a great measure, been indebted to it for our ability to bear a debt so much heavier than that which, fifty years ago, the wisest men thought would necessarily sink us.[80]

Despite these sentiments, however, Price's preferences were clear. He saw in a society that devoted itself primarily to commerce and the acquisition of wealth a source of servility and venality that would inevitably lead to corruption and the loss of liberty. With respect to the decline in trade with Britain on the American colonies Price noted, "having all the necessaries and chief conveniencies of life within themselves they have no dependence upon [their pre-Revolutionary trade], and the loss of it will do them unspeakable good, by preserving them from the evils of luxury and the temptations of wealth and keeping them in that state of virtuous simplicity which is the greatest happiness."[81] These views are particularly surprising inasmuch as Price was fully aware of the benefits of international trade in encouraging tolerance among diverse communities and in fostering peaceful relations between states, a sentiment raised to a principle of liberal ideology in the following century. "Foreign trade," he wrote, has, in some respects, the most useful tendency. By creating an intercourse between distant kingdoms it extends benevolence, removes local prejudices, leads every man to consider himself more as a citizen of the world than of any particular state, and, consequently, checks the excesses of that love of our country which has been applauded as one of the noblest, but which, really, is one of the most destructive principles in human nature. Trade also, by enabling every country to draw from other countries conveniencies and advantages which it cannot find within itself, produces among nations a sense of mutual dependence, and promotes the general improvement.[82]

Yet, despite Price's economic sophistication[83] he repeatedly viewed America as exempt from these benefits. Indeed, immediately following the passage just quoted, Price wrote that "There is no part of mankind to which these uses of trade are of less consequence than the American states."[84] And, in a letter to Ezra Stiles written after the war's conclusion, he observed that "it may be best for the United States that their rage for foreign trade should be checked, and that they should be oblig'd to find all they want within themselves, and to be satisfy'd with the simplicity, health, plenty, vigour, virtue and happiness which they may derive from agriculture and internal colonization."[85] Price appears to have believed that men in an agrarian society, who were under no compulsion to act in their narrow self-interest and whose connections with one's fellow men and with the community were deeper, were more likely to defend their rights against domestic and foreign invasion. Price expanded on these views in 1785 when he returned to the subject of American independence:

Better infinitely will it be for them to consist of bodies of plain and honest farmers, than of opulent and splendid merchants. Where in these states do the purest manners prevail? Where do the inhabitants live most on an equality and most at their ease? Is it not in those inland parts where agriculture gives health and plenty, and trade is scarcely known? Where, on the contrary, are the inhabitants most selfish, luxurious, loose, and vicious, and at the same time most unhappy? Is it not along the sea coasts and in the great towns where trade flourishes and merchants abound? So striking is the effect of these different situations on the vigour and happiness of human life, that in the one, population would languish did it receive no aid from emigration, while in the other, it increases to a degree scarcely ever before known.[86]

Ferguson was far more positive in his assessment of the benefits of commerce than was Price, despite what he regarded as its potential dangers. He was prepared to concede that commercial societies, which he equated with societies based on the principle of private property, would inevitably display an uneven distribution of wealth. But this inequality, he argued, served the function of acting as a spur to industry and an incentive to the labor of the great mass of the population,[87] the ultimate effect of which would serve to encourage the production of ever-greater quantities of wealth, thus benefitting all members of the community. "The object of commerce is wealth," wrote Ferguson, and "in the progress, as well as in the result of commercial arts, mankind are enabled to subsist in growing numbers; learn to ply their resources, and to wield their strength, with superior ease and success."[88]

He further argued that active participation in commercial life encouraged men in the exercise of a host of virtues, including industry, sobriety, frugality, justice, even beneficence and friendship.[89] Although Ferguson contended that civilization was not invariably accompanied by a high degree of commercial activity, he did insist that the prime motive force for individual and social progress was ambition, "the specific principle of advancement uniformly directed to this end, and not satiated with any given measure of gratification." And ambition, in turn, he noted, operated no less "in the concerns of mere animal life; in the provision of subsistence, of accommodation, and ornament," as "in the progress of society, and in the choice of its institutions." [90] Further, and more important, Ferguson saw no conflict between those social arrangements that acted as guarantees of individual liberty and those that encouraged an increase in wealth. [91] He contended that the forces that lead to an expansion in population, which Ferguson equated with social wealth, required the successful pursuit of commerce coupled with a vigorous defense of individual rights. "The growth of industry," he wrote, "the endeavours of men to improve their arts, to extend their commerce, to secure their possessions, and to establish their rights, are the most effectual means to promote population." [92] Indeed, one intellectual historian has observed that one of the chief reasons for the popularity of Ferguson's *Essay* among Americans was its unambiguous defense of commercial society over more primitive cultures, despite other social costs that might possibly accompany civilization. [93]

All this is not to deny that Ferguson dealt extensively with the harmful effects of the increasing division of labor that marked advanced commercial societies. These effects he regarded as possessing the potential of producing a permanent subordination of rank, thus allowing for the rise of despotism. [94] "Many mechanical arts," he wrote,

> require no capacity; they succeed best under a total suppression of sentiment and reason; and ignorance is the mother of industry as well as of superstition. Reflection and fancy are subject to err; but a habit of moving the hand, or the foot, is independent of either. Manufactures, accordingly, prosper most, where the mind is least consulted, and where the workshop may, without any great effort of imagination, be considered as an engine, the parts of which are men. [95]

In elaborating the consequences of the division of labor, however, Ferguson did not conclude that it would inevitably prove to be a Trojan horse whose ultimate social effect would invariably be the destruction of a free and virtuous society. Although the division of labor might well place strains upon the social fabric and make possible a permanent subordination of the many by the few, it also facilitates the fullest expression of each individual's natural abilities and personal excellences and hence serves a particularly valuable moral and social purpose. "With the benefit of commerce . . . [and the division of labor which naturally accompanies it]," Ferguson noted, "every individual is enabled to avail himself, to the utmost, of the peculiar advantage of his place; to work on the peculiar materials with which nature has furnished him; to humour his genius or disposition, and betake himself to the task in which he is peculiarly qualified to proceed." [96]

Ferguson's response to the question of whether the dangers inherent in commercial societies could be averted was unambiguous. So long as the members of the community take an active role in civic affairs, so long as they prevent the division of labor from embracing the more crucial aspects of political and military life, [97] it is possible to secure the nation against despotism. In sum, while it is true that commercial societies bring with them the risks of despotism in the form of an over-specialization of function and a permanent system of subordination, a decline into tyranny need not follow. The stifling of public involvement in the affairs of state – either through the throttling of individual capacity consequent on an extensive division of labor or out of an all-consuming concern solely for one's private wealth is, in the end, what makes despotism possible. Encourage the populace to actively participate in the civic and military affairs of the nation and tyranny can be averted. Man's ability to uncover the laws that determine his condition provides him the opportunity to avoid what might otherwise be regarded as that corruption to which all commercial societies might possibly descend.

✳ ✳ ✳

These differences in their approach to political philosophy persisted in regard to the events in France two decades later. While Price was a fervent champion of the revolutionary cause, Ferguson was to express grave reservations respecting French attempts to "transform their Monarchy into a Democracy."[98] He could not tolerate the pretensions of French revolutionary ideology[99] and was dubious that any of the political tinkering undertaken by the various revolutionary bodies would prove of value in either establishing or maintaining a freer polity. At one point he even refers to the Revolutionary forces as "the Antichrist himself in the form of Democracy & Atheism."[100] Ferguson maintained that by abetting the revolutionaries in America the French court had set a dangerous example to its own people.[101] The cataclysm in France, he argued, posed a significant threat to the security of Great Britain and to the peace of the Continent. Indeed, Ferguson's particular concern was that Britain would be dragged into what had started as an internal French conflict but would likely become international.[102]

Price's views on the Revolution are, of course, well known, primarily because of Edmund Burke's *Reflections on the Revolution in France*, written in response to Price's comments. The sermon Price gave at the Old Jewry on 4 November 1789 before the Society for Commemorating the Revolution in Great Britain reflected his enormous enthusiasm for what was taking place in France. The nominal purpose of the address, which Price entitled *A Discourse on the Love of Our Country*, was to celebrate the hundredth anniversary of the Glorious Revolution. In doing so Price linked the events of 1688–89 with the American Revolution and the reforms in France in one of the most impassioned speeches delivered during the course of this tempestuous period "I have lived to see the rights of men better understood than ever," he said,

> and nations panting for liberty, which seemed to have lost the idea of it. I have lived to see thirty millions of people, indignant and resolute, spurning at slavery, and demanding liberty with an irresistible voice, their king led in triumph, and an arbitrary monarch surrendering himself to his subjects. After sharing in the benefits of one Revolution, I have been spared to be a witness to two other Revolutions, both glorious. And now, methinks, I see the ardor for liberty catching and spreading, a general amendment beginning in human affairs, the dominion of kings changed for the dominion of laws, and the dominion of priests giving way to the dominion of reason and conscience.
>
> Be encouraged, all ye friends of freedom and writers in its defence! The times are auspicious. Your labours have not been in vain. Behold kingdoms, admonished by you, starting from sleep, breaking their fetters, and claiming justice from their oppressors! Behold, the light you have struck out, after setting America free, reflected to France and there kindled into a blaze that lays despotism in ashes and warms and illuminates Europe![103]

   It is a reflection on the scope of the eighteenth-century Whig tradition that it could encompass two writers whose views were as dissimilar in certain particulars as were those of Price and Ferguson. Yet both were legatees of the Revolutionary Settlement of 1688 and both accepted its ideological premises. Both agreed that a free society was one that recognized the primacy of private property and the critical importance of the rule of law and both identified individual liberty with the rights of citizens to act as they choose, limited only by a modestly intrusive government. Finally, both had original insights into the nature of freedom and despotism that enlightened and informed. Whig doctrine clearly was broad enough to accommodate these two divergent views, neither of which fell victim to authoritarian leanings. In light of this, it is not difficult to see why, despite their differences, the American colonists were receptive, at one point or another in their arguments with Great Britain, to both these thinkers.

Ronald Hamowy
University of Alberta

Notes

1. The first of these traditions Hayek denominates as English while the second he associates most closely with French political theory, particularly that of the Physiocrats, the Encyclopedists, and Rousseau, despite the fact, as he points out, that it reflects the views of a number of English writers, among them Jeremy Bentham, the other Philosophical Radicals, William Godwin, and Richard Price. While the empiricist evolutionary approach to the development of political arrangements is compatible with a free and open society, Hayek contends, the French rationalist tradition invariably eventuates in the total state. Hayek first addressed what he perceived as this distinction in British and French liberal thought in *Individualism: True and False* [the 12th Finley Lecture delivered at University College, Dublin, 17 December 1945] (Dublin: Hodges, Figgis and Co., 1946), reprinted in *Individualism and Economic Order* (London: Routledge and Kegan Paul, 1949): 1–32. He resumed his discussion in "Freedom, Reason, and Tradition," *Ethics* 68 (1958): 229–45, which in turn was reprinted in slightly altered and its best known formulation in *The Constitution of Liberty* (Chicago: University of Chicago Press, 1960): 54–70.

2. Roland Thomas, *Richard Price: Philosopher and Apostle of Liberty* (Oxford: Oxford University Press, 1924): 74.

3. London's Roll of Fame, at the Guildhall Library, quoted in Thomas, *Richard Price*, 76.

4. "Preface," in Bernard Peach, ed., *Richard Price and the Ethical Foundations of the American Revolution* (Durham, N.C.: Duke University Press, 1979): 9.

5. Josiah Tucker, *A Series of Answers to certain Popular Objections, against Separating from the Rebellious Colonies, and discarding them Entirely* (Gloucester: Printed for R. Raikes, 1776); John Fletcher, *American Patriotism Farther Confronted with Reason, Scripture, and the Constitution* (Shrewsbury: Printed by J. Eddowes, 1776); John Wesley, *Some Observations on Liberty, occasioned by a late Tract* (Printed by R. Hawes, 1776).

6. The Act, passed in March 1766, declared that the colonies in America "have been, are, and of right ought to be, subordinate unto, and dependent upon the imperial crown and parliament of Great Britain; and that the King's majesty, by and with the advice and consent of the lords spiritual and temporal, and commons of Great Britain, in parliament assembled, had, hath, and of right ought to have, full power and authority to make laws and statutes of sufficient force and validity to bind the colonies and people of America, subjects of the crown of Great Britain, in all cases whatsoever," 6 George III, c. 12; *The Statutes at Large*, ed. Danby Pickering, (Cambridge: Printed for J. Bentham, 1767): 27:19–20. So heinous did Price find this Act that he wrote of it "I defy any one to express slavery in stronger language," "Observations on the Nature of Civil Liberty, the Principles of Government, and the Justice and Policy of the War with America", in Peach, *Ethical Foundations*, 82–3 [hereafter cited as *Observations*].

7. John Shebbeare, *An Essay on the Origin, Progress and Establishment of Natural Society; in which the Principles of Government, the Definitions of Physical, Moral, Civil, and Religious Liberty, Contained in Dr. Price's Observations, etc. are fairly Examined and fully Refuted* (London: Printed for J. Pew, 1776); Edmund Burke, *A Letter from Edmund Burke, Esq., one of the representatives in*

Parliament for the City of Bristol, to John Farr and John Harris, Esqrs., Sheriffs in that City, on the Affairs of America (Bristol: Printed by William Pine, 1777).

8. Neither Hume nor Smith were in complete agreement with this view. Hume was contemptuous of government policy and urged that the colonies should be allowed their independence, while Smith proposed that the colonies be extended representation in Parliament in proportion to the taxes levied on them. See Dalphy I. Fagerstrom, "Scottish Opinion and the American Revolution," *William and Mary Quarterly*, 3rd series, 11 (April 1954): 259–60.

9. Ferguson to Sir John MacPherson, Edinburgh, 1772 (No. 59), in Vincenzo Merolle, ed., *The Correspondence of Adam Ferguson* (2 vols.; London: William Pickering, 1995): 1: 95,

10. James MacPherson, *The Rights of Great Britain asserted against the Claims of America; being an Answer to the Declaration of the General Congress* (London: Printed for T. Caddell, 1775). Following publication of Price's *Observations on the Nature of Civil Liberty* in 1776 and beginning with the sixth edition of MacPherson's pamphlet, the essay was expanded and the following added to its title: *To which is now added a Refutation of Dr. Price's State of the National Debt.*

11. Ferguson to John Home, Edinburgh, 27 January 1776 (No. 83), in *Ferguson Correspondence*, 1: 134.

12. Herbert W. Schneider, *A History of American Philosophy* (2nd ed.; New York: Columbia University Press, 1963): 216. See also the detailed discussion of the favorable reception given eighteenth-century Scottish moral philosophy and epistemology by American intellectuals in Elizabeth Flowers and Murray G. Murphey, *A History of Philosophy in America* (2 vols.: New York: Capricorn Books, 1977): I: 203–361. William R. Brock deals with the extensive influence of Scottish thought in the colonies in *Scotus Americanus: A Survey of Sources for Links Between Scotland and America in the Eighteenth Century* (Edinburgh: Edinburgh University Press, 1982): 87–113.

13. Dennis F. Thompson, "The Education of a Founding Father: The Reading List for John Witherspoon's Course in Political Theory, Taken by James Madison," *Political Theory*, 4 (1976): 528. See also John Witherspoon, *Lectures on Moral Philosophy*, Varnum Lansing Collins, ed. (Princeton: Princeton University Press, 1912): 144.

14. Madison's debt to Scottish Enlightenment thinking is discussed at some length in Roy Branson, "James Madison and the Scottish Enlightenment," *Journal of the History of Ideas*, 11 (1979): 235–50.

15. David Lundberg and Henry F. May, "The Enlightened Reader in America," *American Quarterly*, 28 (1976): 262–93.

16. The basic library list that Jefferson prepared for a friend in 1771 contained works by Adam Smith, Thomas Reid, David Hume, and Henry Home, Lord Kames. Jefferson to Robert Skipwith, 3 August 1771, in Julian Boyd, ed., *The Papers of Thomas Jefferson*, 1 (Princeton: Princeton University Press, 1950): 78–80. Having studied for two years under William Small at the College of William and Mary it is inconceivable that Jefferson had not also read and digested Ferguson's works. One commentator has gone so far as to maintain that Jefferson was so thoroughly immersed in the thought of the Scottish Enlightenment that the Declaration of Independence cannot be properly understood except in terms of Scottish political and moral philosophy. See Garry Wills, *Inventing America: Jefferson's Declaration of Independence* (Garden City, N.Y.: Doubleday and Co., Inc., 1978). While there is no historical warrant whatever for this eccentric conclusion, there is much evidence that Jefferson was familiar with the major Scottish writers.

17. (2nd ed., corr.; London: A. Millar and T. Caddell, 1768). E. Millicent Sowerby, comp., *Catalogue of the Library of Thomas Jefferson* (5 vols.; Washington, D.C.: Library of Congress, 1952–59): 3: 20–21, item 2348.

18. Schneider, *American Philosophy*, 38.

19. Adam Ferguson, *An Essay on the History of Civil Society*, Fania Oz-Salzberger, ed. (Cambridge Texts in the History of Political Thought; Cambridge: Cambridge University Press, 1995): 12, 14 [hereafter cited as *Essay*].

20. Citing the condition of his health, Ferguson resigned his professorship in 1785, at the age of 62, to be succeeded in that position by his one-time student and friend, Dugald Stewart. In lieu of a pension, Ferguson had made arrangements with the University to continue to draw a salary as senior professor of mathematics. The position was, of course, a sinecure and all lectures in the field were, in fact, to be delivered by a junior professor. During his retirement Ferguson completed his major work in moral philosophy, a revision and expansion of his *Institutes*, entitled *Principles of Moral and Political Science*, which appeared in two volumes in 1792. Ferguson died on 22 February 1816, in his 93rd year, at St Andrews, Scotland, and is buried in the grounds of the cathedral there. By far the best biographical essay is by Jane B. Fagg, "Biographical Introduction," in Vincenzo Morelle, ed., *The Correspondence of Adam Ferguson*, 1: xx–cxvii. See also the biographical chapter on Ferguson in David Kettler, *The Social and Political Thought of Adam Ferguson* (Columbus: Ohio State University Press, 1965): 41–82.

21. While Ferguson, like his friend Lord Kames, had early sympathies with the colonists, he was convinced that their constitutional arguments were unjustified. However, Ferguson agreed with David Hume that the government's colonial policy was incompetent and doomed to failure.
22. While Macpherson was, at the time, a lower-ranking administrator of the East India Company, he was very well connected and eventually became Governor-General of India.
23. Ferguson to Sir John Macpherson, Edinburgh, 1772 (No. 59), in *Ferguson Correspondence*, 1: 96.
24. "If I had written the best that the occasion requires I should [not] be averse to be mentioned to Grafton as a writer." Letter to Sir John Macpherson, Edinburgh, 1772 (No. 59), in *Ferguson Correspondence*, 1: 96. The Duke of Grafton served as Prime Minister from late 1767 to 1770 and was appointed Privy Seal in the North government.
25. Jane Fagg, "Biographical Introduction," in *Ferguson Correspondence*, 1: xlix–l.
26. See Letter from Grey Cooper, London, 23 March 1776 (No. 85), in *Ferguson Correspondence*, 1: 137.
27. Jane Fagg, "Biographical Introduction," in *Ferguson Correspondence*, 1: l. The practice of rewarding authors sympathetic to the government and hiring publishers to place the Administration's point of view before the public was extremely common. See Solomon Lutnick, *The American Revolution and the British Press, 1775–1783* (Columbia, Mo.: University of Missouri Press, 1967): 12–34.
28. It should be pointed out that a professional such as a surgeon or high-level government clerk earned, on average, no more than £2 per week and that consequently, once bought, pamphlets of this nature were widely circulated from one reader to another and often read aloud in coffee houses. See Lutnick, *British Press*, 2.
29. *Additional Observations*, 140.
30. Ferguson to John Macpherson, 27 October 1777 (No. 100), in *Ferguson Correspondence*, 1: 156.
31. Ferguson to John Macpherson, 15 January 1778 (No. 105), in *Ferguson Correspondence*, 1: 162.
32. Ferguson to John Macpherson, 12 February 1778 (No. 108), in *Ferguson Correspondence*, 1: 166. "My Idea of a General Parliament for America may appear odd," Ferguson wrote. "What Unite them; should they not rather be keept Separate that we may govern by dividing. I have much to say on that Subject being much impressed with a notion that one great state is much more easily Governed than many Small ones."
33. The principal exceptions revolved around responsibility for the redemption of colonial paper money and assuming the financial burden undertaken by the colonies in the war.
34. It appears that Lord Shelburne had given serious thought to offering the post to Ferguson after Johnstone had returned to England in 1766. Jane Fagg, "Biographical Introduction," in *Ferguson Correspondence*, 1: xl.
35. Johnstone had entered Parliament following his tenure as governor of West Florida and, over the course of the next decade, had been an outspoken defender of the American cause. Ferguson's biographer recounts that Johnstone was encouraged by others to choose Ferguson as a companion in part because of Johnstone's hotheadedness, which, it was felt, would be moderated by Ferguson's more temperate disposition. Jane Fagg, "Biographical Introduction," in *Ferguson Correspondence*, 1: li.
36. The Commission's official letter to Congress was accompanied by personal notes from both Eden and Johnstone warmly commending Ferguson. Eden referred to the favorable reception to which Ferguson was entitled by virtue of his eminence in the literary world (Eden to Washington, 9 June 1778, in Benjamin Franklin Stevens, ed., *Stevens's Facsimiles of Manuscripts in European Archives Relating to America, 1773–1783* [24 vols.; London: Issued only to subscribers and printed by Malby and Sons, 1889–95], 5: 401, facsimile 498), while Johnstone's letter was even more generous. "I beg to recommend to your private civilities my friend Dr. Ferguson," he wrote. "He has been engaged from his early life, in inculcating to mankind the virtuous principles you practise," (Johnstone to Washington, 10 June 1778, in Jared Sparks, ed., *Correspondence of the American Revolution . . .* [4 vols.; Boston: Little, Brown, 1853], 2: 136).
37. There are good reasons to explain the colonists' refusal to treat with the Commission. The United States had just entered a treaty of alliance with France and it was clear that there were deepening divisions in Parliament regarding America. Washington was particularly adamant that the Commission's terms be rejected out of hand. Finally, with respect to the Commission's Secretary, one is tempted to speculate that Washington was familiar with Ferguson's rejoinder to Price's essay and, as a result, was especially ill-disposed towards the writer.
38. Extensive discussions of the Carlisle Commission appear in Weldon A. Brown, *Empire or Independence: a Study in the Failure of Reconciliation, 1774–1783* (University, La.: Louisiana State University Press, 1941): 244–92, and Carl Van Doren, *Secret History of the American Revolution* (Garden City, N.Y.: Garden City Publishing Co., 1941): 63–116.
39. Jane Fagg, "Biographical Introduction," in *Ferguson Correspondence*, 1: liii.

40. The Commission sought to remind the clergy that "the foreign power with which the Congress is endeavouring to connect them has ever been averse to toleration," Van Doren, *Secret History*, 112–13.

41. Brown, *Empire or Independence*, 284–5.

42. Thomas Paine, "The Crisis," No. 6 [20 October 1778], in Thomas Paine, *Collected Writings* (New York: Library of America, 1995): 186–90.

43. *Two Tracts on Civil Liberty, the War with America, and the Debts and Finances of the Kingdom* [With a General Introduction and Supplement] (London: T. Caddell, 1778).

44. "The consequences [of not acceding to America's demands] must be that the colonies will become the allies of France, that a general war will be kindled and, perhaps, this once happy country be made, in just retribution, the seat of that desolation and misery which it has produced in other countries," Richard Price, "The General Introduction and Supplement to the Two Tracts on Civil Liberty, the War with America, and the Finances of the Kingdom," in *Ethical Foundations*, 60.

45. D.O. Thomas, *The Honest Mind: The Thought and Work of Richard Price* (Oxford: At the Clarendon Press, 1977): 261–2.

46. *Constitution of Liberty*, 56.

47. Martha K. Zebrowski, "Richard Price: British Platonist of the Eighteenth Century," in *Journal of the History of Ideas*, 55 (1994): 29. See also Bernard Peach, "The Indefinability and Simplicity of Rightness in Richard Price's Review of Politics," *Philosophy and Phenomenological Research*, 14 (1954): 370–85.

48. The ethical foundations of Price's political views are discussed at some length in Peach, "Introduction," in *Ethical Foundations*, 18.

49. *Observations*, 70.

50. *Institutes of Moral Philosophy* [Edinburgh: A. Kincaid and W. Creech, 1769], p. 2.

51. *Principles of Moral and Political Science* (2 vols.; Edinburgh: Printed for A. Strahan and T. Cadell, 1972): 1: 5 [hereafter cited as *Principles*].

52. Peach, "Introduction," in *Ethical Foundations*, 19.

53. [Adam Ferguson], *Remarks on a Pamphlet Lately Published by Dr. Price* (London: Printed for T. Waddell, 1776, 7 [hereafter cited as *Remarks*]. "The liberty of every class and order is not proportional to the power they enjoy," Ferguson writes, "but to the security they have for the preservation of their rights," *Remarks*, 11.

54. *Remarks*, 5.

55. Carl B. Cone, *Torchbearer of Freedom: The Influence of Richard Price on Eighteenth Century Thought* (Lexington, Ky.: University of Kentucky Press, 1952): 73.

56. Price admits as much. In the Preface to the fifth edition of the *Observations*, Price acknowledges that "the principles on which I have argued form the foundation of every state as far as it is free; and are the same with those taught by Mr. Locke, and all the writers on civil liberty who have been hitherto most admired in this country," *Observations*, 65.

57. "Religious liberty signifies the power of exercising, without molestation, that mode of religion which we think best or of making the decisions of our consciences respecting religious truth the rule of our conduct, and not any of the decisions of our fellow-men," *Observations*, 68.

58. *Additional Observations*, 81.

59. *Observations*, 69.

60. *Essay*, 63–4.

61. *Remarks*, 16.

62. *Principles*, 2: 461.

63. *Remarks*, 41.

64. *Observations*, 80.

65. See Colin Bonwick, *English Radicals and the American Revolution* (Chapel Hill, N.C.: University of North Carolina Press, 1977): 93–102.

66. Adam Smith on the other hand, with whom Ferguson was on friendly terms, had embraced a federative view of empire as more consistent with free trade and the greatest generation of wealth. See Fagerstrom, "Scottish Opinion," 259.

67. *Remarks*, 18–19.

68. Ferguson goes so far as to make the following claim: "It is certainly true, that no nation ever planted Colonies with so liberal or so noble a hand as England has done," *Remarks*, 26.

69. *Essay*, 61.

70. "Appendix H," in *Ferguson Correspondence*, 2: 556.

71. P.J. Marshall, "Introduction," P.J. Marshall, ed., *The Oxford History of the British Empire*, 2: *The Eighteenth Century* (Oxford: Oxford University Press, 1998): 25–6.

72. *Observations*, 69. Every man is his own legislator in a free state, according to Price, in the sense that

every man, in a truly free state, participates in making the political decisions or in choosing those who make the political decisions that govern him. See *Additional Observations*, 140.

73. "Without all doubt, it is the choice of the people that makes civil governors. The people are the spring of all civil power, and they have a right to modify it as they please," *Additional Observations*, 148.

74. *Essay*, 4.

75. See David Hume, *A Treatise of Human Nature*, L.A. Selby-Bigge, ed. (2nd ed.; Oxford: Clarendon Press, 1978): 534–9.

76. *Essay*, 122–6. The notion that government itself, far from being the product of conscious design, took its form gradually and without deliberate intent has led one commentator to refer to Ferguson's rejection of the social contract as the boldest attack on the contractarian theory of political obligation that had been made up to that time (Hermann Huth, "Soziale und Individualistische Auffassung im 18. Jahrhundert, vornehmlich bei Adam Smith und Adam Ferguson," *Staats- und Sozialwissenschaftliche Forschungen* [Leipzig: Duncker and Humblot, 1907]: 46).

77. *Essay*, 121

78. "If the palace be unnatural," wrote Ferguson in an often-quoted passage, "the cottage is no less; and the highest refinements of political and moral apprehension, are not more artificial in their kind, than the first operation of sentiment and reason." (*Essay*, 8).

79. *Principles*, 1: 192.

80. *Observations*, 102–3.

81. *Observations*, 115.

82. "Observations on the Importance of the American Revolution, and the Means of Making it a Benefit to the World, To which is Added, a letter from Mr. Turgot, Late Comptroller of the Finances of France," in Peach, ed., *Ethical Foundations*, 210 [hereafter cited as *Importance of the Revolution*].

83. Price was a seminal contributor to the study of finance and insurance and was universally so regarded. His *Appeal to the Public on the Subject of the National Debt* (London, 1771) argued decisively against the increasing British public debt and called for its elimination. In the same year he published an essay, *Observations on Reversionary Payments*, that was of crucial importance in making possible a workable system of life insurance and pensions.

84. *Importance of the American Revolution*, 210.

85. Price to Ezra Stiles, Newington Green, 2 August 1785, in Bernard Peach and D.O. Thomas, eds., *The Correspondence of Richard Price* (3 vols.: Durham, N.C.: Duke University Press, 1991): 2: 297.

86. *Importance of the American Revolution*, 211.

87. *Principles*, 2: 371.

88. *Principles*, 1: 254, 253.

89. *Principles*, 1: 254.

90. *Principles*, 1: 235.

91. Ferguson writes in his *Essay* that "The laws made to secure the rights and liberties of the people, may serve as encouragements to population and commerce" (136).

92. *Essay*, 140.

93. "What generally emerges from Ferguson's *Essay* and from others like it, is a simple and clear demonstration from conjectural history of a proposition which Americans, in their feelings of pity and censure over the fate of the Indians, needed desperately to believe; that men in becoming civilized had gained much more than they had lost; and that civilization, the act of civilizing, for all of its destruction of primitive virtues, put something higher and greater in their place." (Roy Harvey Pearce, *The Savages of America: A Study of the Indian and the Idea of Civilization* [rev. ed.; Baltimore: The Johns Hopkins Press, 1965], p. 85). See also Jay G. Prokop, who writes: "The great achievement of the Scottish school of sociological historians was the recognition that a commercial organization of society had rendered obsolete much that had been believed about society before." Quoted in Robert W. Galvin, *America's Founding Secret: What the Scottish Enlightenment Taught Our Founding Fathers* (Lanham, Md.: Rowman and Littlefield, 2002): 30.

94. Ferguson's views respecting the dangers arising out of the division of labor are discussed at some length in Ronald Hamowy, "Adam Smith, Adam Ferguson, and the Division of Labour," *Economica*, 35 (1968): 249–59.

95. *Essay*, 182–3.

96. *Principles*, 2: 424.

97. Ferguson was a strong supporter of a civilian army and had written tracts pointing out the serious dangers that followed the creation of a professional military force and calling for the establishment of a civilian militia. See his *Reflections Previous to the Establishment of a Militia* (London: R. and J. Dodsley, 1756), published anonymously.

98. Ferguson to Sir John MacPherson, Edinburgh, 31 July 1790 (No. 269), in *Ferguson Correspondence*, 2: 340.

99. With reference to the French Convention, for example, Ferguson wrote ironically, "[they] are Surely very impudent in pretending to prescribe to the great Infallible Sovereign People of France whom they shall elect," Ferguson to Sir John MacPherson, Nydpath Castle, 17 September 1795 (No. 297), in *Ferguson Correspondence*, 2: 370.

100. Ferguson to Alexander Carlyle, Edinburgh, 23 November 1976 (No. 322), in *Ferguson Correspondence*, 2: 408.

101. Ferguson to Sir John MacPherson, Edinburgh, 19 January 1790 (No. 265), in *Ferguson Correspondence*, 2: 336–7.

102. Ferguson seems to have blamed the French military, drunk with notions of democracy, for the Revolution. "The French Revolution," he wrote in 1797, "it seems is still a Curiosity; many things certainly led to it and the French heads a stir after new things made bolder and wider steps than ever were made before by Mankind in any case whatever; but all this would have come to nothing if the French Army had Adhered to their noblesse officers & to the Crown: but they did not; & they made the Revolution. They made & will continue to make every change that is to happen in France to the end of time. They were struck with democracy as with a Spark of Electricity or a Stroke of Lightening & have continued changed ever Since. They will follow no General that swerves from Democracy & will cut the throats of all Representatives of the People of France if the Cry of Royalism is raised against them," Ferguson to Alexander Carlyle, Hallyards, 2 October 1797 (No. 332), in *Ferguson Correspondence*, 2: 423.

103. "A Discourse on the Love of Our Country," in D.O. Thomas, ed., *Political Writings*, Cambridge Texts in the History of Politcal Thought (Cambridge: Cambridge University Press, 1991): 195–6.

[5]

F. A. Hayek, on the Occasion of the Centenary of his Birth
Ronald Hamowy

At the time of his death, F.A. Hayek (1899–1992) was unquestionably the world's preeminent spokesman for classical liberalism and its most important thinker. He led an immensely productive life, over the course of which he made significant contributions to a variety of disciplines, among them economics, political and social theory, psychology, and the history of ideas. While his doctorate from the University of Vienna was in jurisprudence, his first interests were in economics and, to a lesser extent, in psychology. Hayek had done his work at the University under Friedrich Wieser and as a consequence had early adopted some of Wieser's socialist views. However, in 1922 Ludwig von Mises published his devastating critique of central planning (*Die Gemeinwirtschaft*), in which he demonstrated that in the absence of markets there exists no method of determining the values of goods and services and hence rational economic calculation becomes impossible. Indeed, the inevitable failure of socialism hinges on this central fact, that in the absence of a genuine price system, which requires truly free markets, planning boards are incapable of calculating real costs. Largely as a consequence of reading Mises, Hayek abandoned his early Fabian views and developed a close relationship with Mises, whose seminars Hayek began attending.

During a year-long visit to the United States, Hayek had become particularly interested in the relation between bank credit and the business cycle, and this interest eventuated in 1927 in Hayek's being appointed director of the newly created Institute for Business Cycle Research. Building on the theoretical framework earlier advanced by Mises in his *Theory of Money and Credit*, Hayek produced his first important work, *Monetary Theory and the Trade Cycle* (1929), in which he unraveled the relation between credit expansions and capital

Cato Journal, Vol. 19, No. 2 (Fall 1999). Copyright © Cato Institute. All rights reserved.
Ronald Hamowy is Professor Emeritus of Intellectual History at the University of Alberta.

malinvestment that lay at the root of business cycles. The work was very well received and as a result Hayek was invited by Lionel Robbins to deliver a series of lectures at the London School of Economics on the trade cycle. Those lectures, which soon appeared in book form under the title *Prices and Production*, were received with such enthusiasm by the assembled faculty of the LSE that, as Ronald Coase has reported, they could speak of nothing else for months. Indeed, in their initial excitement some economists had concluded that Hayek had laid bare the underlying groundwork on which all public policy would henceforth have to be built. The immediate result was that Hayek was offered a chair at the LSE, the Tooke Professorship of Economic Science, which he took up at the age of 32.

The Primacy of Spontaneous Order

It is doubtless from this period that Hayek's love affair with England began. Hayek had already read widely in the history of ideas, but it was while in Great Britain that his conclusions regarding the nature of social relationships and law were more fully formed. Thoroughly familiar with the history of early economic thought, Hayek found in the writings of such writers as Adam Smith and David Hume the key to a theory that provided the philosophical underpinning for a free society. Much like Smith's description of the invisible hand as an unseen and undirected coordinating mechanism for the production and distribution of wealth, the writers of the Scottish Enlightenment, and particularly Adam Ferguson, had, Hayek found, offered an account of the rise of social institutions as the product of spontaneously generated orders. The theory, simply put, is that the social arrangements under which we live are of such an order of complexity that they cannot be the product of deliberate calculation but are, rather, the unintended consequence of countless individual actions, none of which aims at the establishment of coherent social institutions and many of which are the product of instinct and habit. In sum, one does not need an orderer to have order. Thus, language, law, morals, social conventions, and the exchange of goods and services are all instances of spontaneous orders. Indeed, Hayek regarded the view that social arrangements must be controlled by some central authority lest disorder and chaos ensue as the opening door to totalitarianism, no matter whether the directing authority was reactionary or socialist.

Both conservatism and socialism, Hayek contended, share this distrust of uncontrolled social action, in the same way both lack an understanding of economic forces. So central was the idea of the complexity of social orders to Hayek's thinking that it provided him what was probably his greatest insight in the field of economics, that in a *dirigiste* society there is simply no way to bring to bear the dispersed bits of knowledge possessed by economic actors that makes economic coordination possible. In two brilliant essays, the first published in 1937 ("Economics and Knowledge") and the second in 1945 ("The Use of Knowledge in Society"), Hayek points out that this division of knowledge is in fact the central problem of economics and that only free markets can provide this necessary coordinating structure.

Hayek's distrust of comprehensive theories of government and society followed directly upon his notions of the extraordinary complexity of social arrangements and the dispersion of knowledge. The history of the idea of liberty in England, Hayek contended, was essentially empirical and unsystematic and tended to rest on interpreting traditions and institutions that took their form without conscious direction. Most British theorists were aware, Hayek observed, that freedom itself was an artifact that grew out of these institutions and was no more natural to man than were the other trappings of civilization. French theories of a free society, on the other hand, tended to be more speculative and rationalistic, based on the assumption that the human mind could comprehend the totality of social arrangements and that it was, at least in principle, possible to restructure these institutions consistent with the social laws that human reason could uncover. In identifying these two traditions in the theory of liberty, the one British, the other French, Hayek sought to account for why continental political doctrine, stemming as it did from the French tradition, so easily slipped into totalitarianism. If one believes that human reason can lay bear the laws governing social arrangements, then one may with impunity thoroughly redesign society to one's liking.

The British tradition that Hayek so much admired was best exemplified by the writers of the Scottish Enlightenment, Adam Smith, Adam Ferguson, and above all David Hume. Joining them were a number of their 18th century contemporaries including Josiah Tucker, Edmund Burke, and William Paley, and the jurisprudential theorists of the common law. To these Hayek opposed the intellectuals of the French Enlightenment, which included the Encyclopedists, the Physiocrats, Condorcet, and especially Rousseau. Poisoned by Cartesian rationalism and appealing to men's pride and ambition, these writers regarded all social arrangements as the product of an ordering intelligence that political wisdom could reshape. Of course, as Hayek himself concedes, not all writers in the British tradition were British, nor were all those corrupted by rationalistic hubris French. Hobbes, Bentham and the other Philosophical Radicals, and the British supporters of the French

Revolution, among them William Godwin, Thomas Paine, and Richard
Price, all rejected the insights of the Scottish Enlightenment into the
evolution of institutions under which men live. On the other hand, a
number of French liberals fit more easily in the British tradition:
Montesquieu, Benjamin Constant, and Alexis de Tocqueville.

Hayek's Liberalism

While I have some difficulty in accepting Hayek's model of the
history of liberalism, I do think it casts light on where Hayek placed
himself and why he regarded himself as a classical liberal. As such,
Hayek could not fail to admire Locke, whose empiricism appealed to
him. Certainly Hayek would have questioned the idea that government
is ultimately the creature of a social contract, but Hayek's skepticism
on the issue of natural law, like Hume's, was tempered by a rather
sophisticated understanding of the nature of justice. While Hume,
and Hayek after him, would have regarded the rules that comprise
our notion of justice as the product of convention, these rules are not
capricious but are, in fact, grounded in our nature as social animals
born into a universe of scarce resources. We all share certain values
by virtue of our living in a common environment, where the desires
of all men exceed the means to satisfy them. It is this condition
that gives rise to the fundamental rules of justice—what Hume had
designated "the fundamental laws of nature." This is as close to Locke's
conception of natural law as Hayek got, but it is close enough for him
to embrace Locke as a true Whig.

Hayek enlarged on his criticism of the rationalistic approach to
politics that characterized the French liberal tradition in a series of
essays attacking the uncritical application of the methodology of the
natural sciences to social questions. This scientistic analysis of society,
common to all social planning schemes, errs in assuming that all social
issues can be studied solely in terms of the observable behavior of
individuals comprising the social whole, without reference to their
subjective states of mind, and in asserting that we may make meaningful statements about social collectives independent of their constituent
components. In a series of articles that originally appeared in the
British journal *Economica* between 1942 and 1944 (later published
in book form as *The Counter-Revolution of Science: Studies in the
Abuse of Reason*), Hayek demonstrated that this fundamental method-
ological fallacy lies at the root of all social engineering. Tracing its
roots to the view put forward by many French Enlightenment thinkers
that all phenomena were in principle reducible to physics and that all
social ills were curable through the application of reason, scientism

found its fullest expression in the social physics of Henri de Saint-Simon and Auguste Comte and in Georg Hegel's scheme for a universal history of mankind. And from Comte and Hegel, this view descended to Karl Marx and his successors.

Hayek and Keynes

Hayek's concerns while at the London School of Economics were not, of course, confined to problems in social theory. Soon after arriving in London, Hayek found himself confronting Britain's (and possibly the world's) most celebrated economist, John Maynard Keynes. Keynes's *Treatise on Money* was published in 1930 and Lionel Robbins, at the time the editor of *Economica*, assigned the book to Hayek to review. Hayek's review, which was published in two parts, was sharply critical of Keynes's monetary theory, which, he pointed out, failed to appreciate the critical importance of monetary factors in altering the structure of production and in determining the trade cycle. Keynes replied to part one of Hayek's review, which appeared in August 1931, and, as editor of the *Economic Journal*, in turn selected Piero Sraffa of Cambridge to review Hayek's recently released *Prices and Production*, to which Hayek replied and Sraffa wrote a rejoinder. The debate between Keynes and Hayek soon spread throughout Great Britain and eventually involved every important economist then writing (including Sir Ralph Hawtry, Arthur Pigou, Sir Dennis Robertson, Arthur Marget, Alvin Hansen, and Herbert Tout).

It should not, by the way, be assumed that there developed a strong personal animosity between Hayek and Keynes because of their intellectual disagreements. Keynes apparently had an exceptionally engaging personality. He was quick, immensely witty, and an excellent raconteur, and, like most who met him, Hayek had early been charmed by his company, a charm that continued when the London School of Economics was moved to Cambridge early in the war as a consequence of the German bombing of the British capital.

Despite the fact that Keynes was later to concede the legitimacy of much of Hayek's criticism of his *Treatise*, the debate between the two economists was soon eclipsed by the publication of Keynes's *General Theory of Employment, Interest, and Money*. Released in 1936, at the height of the Depression, the academic world found in Keynes's recommendations regarding deficit spending and vigorous government activity a formula that had far more appeal than did Hayek's analysis of the causes of the business cycle and the need to allow the market to correct itself without more monetary intervention. The result was that Keynes's theory of underinvestment and undercon-

CATO JOURNAL

sumption during periods of slow or negative economic growth came to dominate economic theory for several decades.

The Road to Serfdom

The 1930s and 40s, coincident with Hayek's tenure as professor at the LSE, witnessed a massive increase in government intervention in the economy coupled with ever greater intrusions into what had hitherto been regarded as one's private life. The growth of government was, of course, substantially accelerated after the outbreak of war in 1939. At the same time the prevailing English and American political orthodoxy viewed fascism and particularly National Socialism as philosophically antithetical to welfare socialism, which was commonly thought to be capitalism's benign reaction to the depredations of an unbridled market economy. Hayek became so alarmed by this commonly held view that he felt compelled to write his first work aimed at a lay audience, *The Road to Serfdom*. The essay appeared in 1944 and quickly became a cause célèbre, castigated by intellectuals on both sides of the Atlantic. Hayek there argued that the collectivist attitudes that had become so popular in the western democracies were, by virtue of their distrust of market forces and their contempt for individual decisionmaking, intimately related to fascism and that both had similar statist, anti-individualist roots. Central planning, Hayek claimed, by destroying the spontaneous order of the market, had of necessity resulted in a wide array of unforeseen and undesired consequences, which, in turn, had led to even more extensive planning and to yet further unsatisfactory outcomes.

The public notice that *The Road to Serfdom* received in the United States, where the book also appeared in condensed form in the *Reader's Digest*, led to Hayek's being invited on a lecture tour of American cities in mid-1945. His taste for America having been whetted by this trip, he was prevailed upon to accept an appointment on the Committee on Social Thought at the University of Chicago, which he took up in 1950. Hayek's appointment was to the Committee on Social Thought rather than to the Economics Department, his natural home, because the economists at Chicago regarded *The Road to Serfdom* and Hayek's other publications during the 1940s as either in areas not central to the problems of economic science as they understood them or as aimed at too popular an audience to be considered serious academic works. Hayek remained at Chicago until 1962, when he accepted an appointment as professor of economics at the University of Freiburg.

F. A. HAYEK

The Constitution of Liberty

While Hayek published comparatively little in the field of pure economics during his tenure at Chicago, he did write a number of seminal works in a number of other disciplines, including psychology (*The Sensory Order*, 1952), the history of ideas (*The Counter-Revolution of Science*, 1952), economic history (the introductory essay to *Capitalism and the Historians*, 1954), and social philosophy (*The Constitution of Liberty*, 1960). *The Constitution of Liberty*, a theoretical treatise on the institutional foundations of a free society, was Hayek's most ambitious work. In its 570 pages, in which Hayek displayed truly breathtaking scholarship, he elaborated his theory of the interrelation between the rule of law and individual freedom and amplified his notion that the social arrangements under which men live are the product of spontaneously generated forces. By this, of course, Hayek did not in any way intend to rule out human intervention to ameliorate our condition or to improve our institutions. What he regarded as foolhardy was the idea that men could fashion complex social arrangements from the ground up and substitute these supposedly rationally designed institutions for those that had been build up over centuries, the product of numberless individual human interactions each of which sought some specific end distinct from the ordered arrangement to which it contributed.

Hayek as Mentor

It was immediately after the publication of *The Constitution of Liberty* that I met Hayek and had the pleasure of working under him. He was an extremely distinguished-looking man with impeccable manners and a gentle scholarly way about him. I confess to having found him somewhat formal, and although I grew to become quite fond of him and saw him a number of times after having received my doctorate, there always existed a wall, however tenuous, that separated professor from student. Indeed, I never ceased to call him professor even though I last met him when I was in my forties and had been a professor myself for a number of years.

Two things that struck me quite early about Hayek were his intellectual honesty and the modesty with which he wore his immense erudition. A close friend, Ralph Raico, had preceded me on the Committee on Social Thought by a year and was in residence working under Hayek when *The Constitution of Liberty* was first released. When I learned that I had been admitted to do graduate work there, Ralph presented me with a copy of Hayek's new book, with an inscription by the author: "As welcome to the Committee on Social Thought:

F.A. Hayek." My response to Hayek's kind gesture was to devote my first few months at Chicago to writing an article attacking a crucial aspect of Hayek's theoretical framework, his analysis of the relation between freedom, coercion, and the rule of law. Not only did Hayek have the opportunity to read this attack but a number of others did as well, since it appeared as a book review in a new student periodical Ralph and I had started. At the time it did not strike me as inappropriate for a new graduate student to try to point out failings in the philosophical reasoning of his professor, but not only did Hayek read and discuss my critique with me, he offered to respond in print to my comments. It was only after I became a professor in my own right that I really appreciated the modesty and love of true scholarship that Hayek displayed toward me, some jumped-up graduate student who decided he was going to take on the very man he had chosen to work under. I'm still breathless when I think of the chutzpah that I must have had.

Because of the inadequacy of the pension arrangements Hayek had with the University of Chicago, he decided to return to Europe in the fall of 1962, when he assumed a professorship at the University of Freiburg. I had mentioned earlier that Hayek had an ongoing love affair with Great Britain. One of his proudest achievements was his having become a British subject during his tenure at the LSE, and he was disappointed that he did not have the opportunity to return to Britain. During the years I studied at Oxford I was able to see Hayek in London, to which he occasionally came. We would meet for a drink or lunch and he would tell me stories of his years in England and why he regarded the British as the most civilized people on earth. The British more than any other nation, Hayek contended, understood that true liberty rested on an appreciation for the rule of law and on the institutions that evolved to protect the subject's freedom from arbitrary power. They had a keen (but not a blind) respect for the unwritten rules governing how we should deal with each other, which allowed them to function as a cohesive entity even in a crisis, without relying on the explicit commands of some arbitrary authority.

But beyond this, he was struck by the quiet courage and dignity that the British displayed during the Second World War and particularly during the bombing of London. One day over lunch at the Reform Club he recounted to me how, at that very same table some years earlier, he had been having lunch with a colleague when the screech of a buzz bomb was heard getting louder and louder, a sure sign that it would land, if not directly on the Club, then close by. When conversation no longer became possible over the mounting noise the dining room fell silent and remained so until the bomb landed. At that point, Hayek recalled, each person picked up his comments at the exact point where he had earlier stopped speaking. There were no cries of alarm, no confused rush for the doors, no panic, and, equally important, no one barking out orders to the waiters and guests. In the event, the club that stood immediately to the west of the Reform was totally destroyed.

For some reason, that event and Hayek's tremendous pride in having been part of it stayed with me as an indication of Hayek's own modest dignity. When Hayek became a British subject he ceased styling himself in the central European manner as Friedrich August von Hayek but became F.A. Hayek, or "Fritz," as he was known to his close friends. He loved the British people and, above all, her philosophers of liberty, from the Whigs of the 18th century to the great liberals who followed them, especially Macaulay, Gladstone, and Lord Acton. All his writings in political and social philosophy attest to his admiration for things British. It was therefore somewhat of a surprise that he should have been recognized by the Nobel Committee for his brilliant contributions to economics but never to have been knighted by the Queen. But, doubtless, this disappointment was more than made up for by Hayek's having been fortunate enough to witness the complete collapse of the Soviet Union and the introduction of market ideas into Eastern Europe and to realize, as large numbers of Eastern European academics and intellectuals have attested, that his work played a crucial role in the revolutions that swept through the Eastern Bloc. If the world is a better place now than it was 20 years ago, at least some of the credit must be laid at Hayek's door. Beyond that, we have all been enriched by Hayek's contributions to our understanding of what makes a free society free.

[6]

Book Reviews

F. A. Hayek, *Hayek on Hayek: An Autobiographical Dialogue.* Edited by Stephen Kresge and Leif Wenar. University of Chicago Press, Chicago, 1994. Pp. xi + 170. $27.50.

Hayek on Hayek comprises a series of autobiographical notes and interviews of the Anglo-Austrian economist and social theorist Friedrich Hayek, who received the Nobel Prize in economic science in 1974. This thin volume has been published as part of a projected 22-volume *Collected Works of F. A. Hayek* under the general editorship of Stephen Kresge, who, with Leif Wenar, edited this particular volume. The notes, interspersed with relevant sections taken from a half dozen interviews, are prefaced by a brief, somewhat muddled biographical introduction by Kresge that provides a sketchy and often confusing picture of Hayek's life that does little justice to his contributions to economics and social theory.

Indeed, even when dealing with the details of Hayek's life, the introductory essay often is sloppy and misleading. There seems no point in announcing in a casual aside that Hayek and Ludwig Wittgenstein were cousins except to leave the reader with the impression—false, as it turns out—that Hayek and Wittgenstein knew each other moderately well, if not intimately, when both young men lived in Vienna. However, as Hayek himself informs us in response to one interviewer's question (p. 60), he and Wittgenstein were only distantly related (Wittgenstein was a second cousin to Hayek's mother) and the two men appear to have met only once prior to encountering each other in England during the late 1930s. Hayek relates that his first memory of Wittgenstein was of bumping into him at a railway station and of their sharing a train journey back to Vienna while both were on furlough from the front during World War I. The two next met at Cambridge immediately prior to the outbreak of World War II, but their relationship seems never to have been a close one and did not extend to more than a few more encounters toward the close of the war.

When he discusses the background to Hayek's contributions to economic theory, Kresge is on equally uncertain ground. It is clearly unfair to single out Carl Menger as the preeminent spokesman for a subjective theory of value. As Kresge concedes, both Jevons and Walras had independently introduced the concept of marginal utility into economics. Jevons proposed the concept in his *Theory of Political Economy*, published in 1871 (the same year in which

Philosophy of the Social Sciences, Vol. 26 No. 3, September 1996 417-435
© 1996 Sage Publications, Inc.

417

Menger enunciated the theory in his *Grundsätze der Volkswirtschaftslehre*); Walras had arrived at similar conclusions at Lausanne, and his *Eléments d'économie politique pure* appeared in two parts in 1874 and 1877. Marginal utility theory logically implies that the value of any economic good, far from being an inherent property of the commodity or service, is subjective. This notion can hardly be regarded as a peculiarity of the Austrian school; certainly by the time Hayek was studying economics immediately after World War I, the subjective theory of value had pervaded almost all academic economics. Nor is it reasonable to imply that the concept of opportunity costs ("that value be rooted in a set of relations—alternatives or substitutions," as Kresge puts it) was, by the end of World War I, a particularly Austrian notion. The revolution in economics wrought by marginal analysis had, by the turn of the century, eclipsed classical economics and transformed the discipline from one whose emphasis was on economic aggregates to an examination of the actions of individuals. It is against this background that Hayek took his degree at the University of Vienna in 1921.

As Hayek recounts in his notes, of decisive importance in shaping his approach to economic questions was his association with Ludwig von Mises, who, between 1909 and 1934, was an economist at the Vienna Chamber of Commerce, a quasi-official body responsible for advising the Austrian government on economic issues. By 1921, when he and Hayek first became associated, Mises was already established as one of Europe's most distinguished economists and the most important living scholar of the Austrian school. With the publication of his *Theorie des Geldes und der Umlaufsmittel* in 1912 (translated in 1934 under the title *The Theory of Money and Credit*), Mises had extended Austrian marginal analysis to the question of money. In 1920, Mises authored a devastating critique of socialism in an article that appeared in the *Archiv für Sozialwissenschaft und Sozialpolitik*, which he expanded into his book *Die Gemeinwirtschaft* two years later (translated under the title *Socialism* in 1936). Mises here argued that any rational economic calculation was impossible in the absence of a genuine price system and that planning boards are incapable of calculating real costs without resource prices, which themselves require free markets.

Hayek writes that from 1921 to 1929, during which time he attended Mises' weekly *privatseminars*, "Mises was unquestionably the personal contact from whom I profited most, not only by way of intellectual stimulation but also for his direct assistance in my career" (pp. 68-69). During a one-year visit to the United States, Hayek had become particularly interested in the relation between bank credit and the business cycle, and this interest eventuated in Hayek being appointed the director of the newly created Austrian Institute for Business Cycle Research. It was to Mises that Hayek was indebted for establishing the institute in 1927, and Hayek's first important work in economics— *Geldtheorie und Konjunkturtheorie* (published in 1929 and translated in 1935 under the title *Monetary Theory and the Trade Cycle*)—was an extension of Mises' business cycle theory.

In 1931, Hayek was invited to deliver a series of lectures at the London School of Economics (LSE) on the trade cycle in which he elaborated the Austrian view that business cycles were a function of monetary changes in the economy that, in turn, brought about structural changes in production. The lectures, which later that year appeared in book form (*Prices and Production*), had an immense impact on English economics and led to Hayek being offered a professorship at the LSE. Probably the most interesting portion of these autobiographical notes and interviews, because it is the most personal, is devoted to Hayek's assessment of his colleagues in London. Thus we learn that socialist political theorist Harold Laski, who held the chairmanship of the Labour Party in 1945, was a pathological liar of such proportions that even his friends were forced to concede as much and that William Beveridge, the director of the LSE and author of the 1942 *Beveridge Report* (which became the blueprint for the modern welfare state), was an academic fraud. Although Beveridge was regarded as an economist, he in fact knew no economics and apparently was quite prepared to adopt whatever position would ensure him the greatest reward. He routinely misused the school's funds, spending monies earmarked for one project on another of his own choosing and raising funds on the basis of promises he had no intention of keeping. It is unfortunate that such personal reminiscences occupy only a small portion of this brief book and are confined to Hayek's years in England. American audiences would, I am certain, have been fascinated by similar assessments of his American colleagues.

Hayek's tenure as Tooke Professor of Economic Science and Statistics at the LSE, from 1932 to 1949, coincided with a massive increase in government intervention in the economy and with ever greater intrusions into what had hitherto been regarded as one's private life. This tendency was, of course, substantially accelerated after the outbreak of war in 1939. At the same time, the prevailing English and American political orthodoxy viewed fascism, and particularly national socialism, as philosophically antithetical to welfare socialism, a species of capitalist reaction to the benign and inevitable intervention occurring in the West. So alarmed was Hayek by this commonly held opinion that he felt compelled to write his first work aimed at a lay audience, *The Road to Serfdom*. The essay was published in 1944 and immediately became a cause célèbre, denounced by most intellectuals on both sides of the Atlantic. The argument that Hayek put forward was a simple one: that the collectivist attitudes so popular in the Western democracies were, by virtue of their distrust of market forces and their contempt for individual decision making, intimately related to fascism and that both had similar statist, anti-individualist philosophical roots. Government planning, by destroying the spontaneous order of the market, of necessity results in a host of unforeseen and undesired consequences, which, in turn, lead to more extensive planning and to a yet further unsatisfactory outcome. Although he was accused of ignoring the difference between the planning that accompanies welfare statism with the more extreme forms of collectivism and fascism, Hayek in fact did not argue that social democratic planning would inevitably eventuate in regimes as malevolent as Stalinist Russia or Hitler Germany. Indeed, Hayek is careful to point out that even the most extensive interventions into economic and social life, were they to take place in Britain and America, would almost certainly prove less noxious than those of the West's totalitarian enemies.

The notoriety that *The Road to Serfdom* received, especially in the United States where the book was condensed in *Reader's Digest*, resulted in Hayek's being invited on a lecture tour of American cities in mid-1945. One of the more interesting sections of *Hayek on Hayek* is a reprint of the transcript of a radio discussion between Hayek and two professors at the University of Chicago on the argument of *The Road to Serfdom*. Perhaps nothing better illustrates Hayek's thesis regarding the psychology of government planners than the contemptuous demeanor of Hayek's opponents in this interchange. Hayek was confronted by Maynard C. Krueger, a professor of economics and at the time the national chairman of the Socialist Party, and by Charles E. Merriam, an eminent professor of political science and an avid planner. Merriam particularly exemplifies the insolence, incivility, and self-importance that so often accompanies high-ranking bureaucrats, but both exude a contempt for personal freedom of choice and individual autonomy that surely should have induced the listener to have serious misgivings regarding government planning, or at least regarding government planners.

It is unfortunate that Hayek is reticent regarding his own move to Chicago in 1950 and back to Europe in 1962. Hayek's notes gloss over the details of his appointment to the University of Chicago, and Kresge's introductory essay contains only the briefest mention of the circumstances that led to Hayek's professorship with the Committee on Social Thought at the University of Chicago. Kresge quotes John Ulrich Nef, one of the founders (and at that time chairman) of the committee, to the effect that Hayek joined the Committee on Social Thought rather than the Economics Department, his natural home, because the economists had, four years earlier, regarded *The Road to Serfdom*, which Hayek published in 1944, as too popular a work to come from the pen of a reputable scholar (p. 24). What is left out of this narrative is the fact that the leading members of the Economics Department were unalterably opposed to Hayek's joining the department in large part because of his connection with the Austrian school, which they viewed as somewhat disreputable. Even when the William Volker Fund of Burlingame, California, which had been underwriting the costs of Mises' salary as a visiting professor of economics at New York University, offered to similarly subsidize Hayek's salary at the University of Chicago, this was not sufficient to induce the Economics Department to accept Hayek as a colleague. On the other hand, the Committee on Social Thought, an interdisciplinary department with few graduate students, was prepared to accept his appointment on these terms, and Hayek moved from London to Chicago in 1950. What needs emphasizing is that the University of Chicago, and particularly the Economics Department, can claim little, if any, credit for Hayek's tenure at the university, despite its eagerness to do so after Hayek was awarded the Nobel Prize in 1974. Indeed, inasmuch as the university had never actually paid Hayek a salary, it refused to provide him a pension, and this is what occasioned his moving to the University of Freiburg in the fall of 1962.

While at Chicago, Hayek conceived and wrote his most ambitious work, *The Constitution of Liberty*, a theoretical treatise on the institutional foundations of a free society. It is in this work that Hayek elaborates his theory of the interrelation between the rule of law and individual freedom and offers his most extended analysis of the notion that the social arrangements under which men live are the product of spontaneously generated forces. By this, Hayek did not intend to rule out human intervention to ameliorate our condition or to improve our institutions. What he regarded as foolhardy was the notion that men could fashion complex social arrangements de novo and substitute these rationally designed institutions for those that had been built up over centuries, the product of countless individual human interactions, each of which seeks some specific end distinct from the ordered arrangement to which it contributes. But there is nothing in Hayek to suggest that he embraced the pessimistic view that whatever institutions existed at the moment constituted the highest possible expression of the evolution of social arrangements and that all attempts to consciously reform these institutions are necessarily doomed to failure.

Hayek on Hayek, despite its skimpiness and weak introduction, is an entertaining book that students of Hayek's thought will find well worth reading. But having perused these autobiographical notes, one cannot help but wish that Hayek had written more extensively and more confidingly about his public and private life. Perhaps these omissions will be corrected by whomever takes on the task of offering the public a full-scale biography of this engrossing figure.

—*Ronald Hamowy*
University of Alberta, Edmonton

[7]

A Note on Hayek and Anti-Semitism

Ronald Hamowy

The winter 2000 issue of *HOPE* contains an article by Melvin W. Reder in which he seeks to show that several prominent twentieth-century economists were in reality anti-Semitic. The economists with whom Reder deals are John Maynard Keynes, Joseph Schumpeter, and F. A. Hayek. It is the charge leveled at Hayek that this note seeks to address.

The evidence pointing to Hayek's supposed anti-Semitism, Reder confesses, comes from only one source, an autobiographical account of Hayek's life and work given in a series of interviews that were published in *Hayek on Hayek* in 1994 as one of the volumes in his collected works. For those of us who knew Hayek, the charge that he was anti-Semitic can only seem perverse. Not only was he not anti-Semitic but in most regards he was in fact pro-Semitic. (I take anti-Semitism to mean the belief that Jews are in some way morally or socially inferior and/or that treating them as such either individually or collectively, as through the state, is legitimate.) Indeed, Reder admits as much when he quotes Hayek as saying:

> It is difficult to overestimate how much I owe to the fact that, almost from the beginning of my university career, I became connected with a group of contemporaries who belonged to the best type of the Jewish

Correspondence may be addressed to Ronald Hamowy, 708 Norfield Court, Westminster, Maryland 21158.

History of Political Economy 34:1 © 2002 by Duke University Press.

intelligentsia of Vienna and who proved to be far ahead of me in literary education and general precociousness. (845)

In what, then, does the evidence consist that leads Reder to conclude that Hayek was an anti-Semite? The totality of Reder's "evidence" lies in five quotations from *Hayek on Hayek* that touch on Jews in prewar Vienna. They are as follows:

1. Hayek recounts that Vienna tended to divide itself along religious lines in the 1920s and 1930s and as a result a three-part division took shape: on the one hand, Jews; on the other, Christians; and a third, middle group comprising, in the main, baptized Jews and Jews and Christians who were prepared to mingle with each other. It was to this group that Hayek belonged. Hayek goes on to note that those Jews who fell into the totally Jewish group did not fraternize with either Christians or members of the mixed group and that accounts for why it is out of the question that he could have met Freud, a member of the Jewish group (Kresge and Wenar 1994, 59).

This "perceived trichotomy" (Reder's term), in which two groups of Jews are distinguished, Reder finds suspect, although we are not told why there is something vaguely sinister in this account. What seems to particularly upset Reder is the fact that Hayek writes that Freud belonged to "the really Jewish group that was beyond my range of acquaintances." What Reder fails to include in his quotation are Hayek's words immediately prior to this:

> I became very much aware of this ["trichotomy"] quite recently, when I was asked whom of the great figures of Vienna I'd known at the time. For instance, Schrödinger, yes, of course; Wittgenstein, yes, of course; and so on. Then he came to Freud, and I couldn't possibly have known Freud. Why? Because he belonged to the really Jewish group, and that was beyond my range of acquaintances. (59)

2. Reder's second piece of evidence concerns Hayek's account of the precipitating factors behind the virulent anti-Semitism in Austria. Hayek notes that there were two groups of Jews in Vienna at the time he was growing up, an "old, established Jewish population . . ., partly of local origin, partly of Hungarian or Bohemian origin, who were fully accepted and recognized" and a group of more recent immigrants, "very primitive, poor Polish Jews [who had immigrated] before the war and partly in flight from the Russians during the war" (Reder 2000, 846). "Vienna,"

Hayek continues, "became filled with a type of Jew which hadn't been known before, with cap on and long beards, which we hadn't even seen before. And it was against them that anti-Semitism developed" (846).

Reder is prepared to eschew "the more scabrous adjectives" in Hayek's account, but, it is implied, readers who are not uncomfortable with descriptions of men "with cap on and long beards" should be aware that they are flirting with anti-Semitic feelings rather than simple depictions of Jews who only recently left the shtetl. What seems to most annoy Reder about this passage is the fact that Hayek does not give sufficient weight to the anti-Semitism of fin de siècle Vienna, the Vienna of Karl Lueger and the Christian Social Party. However, Reder is in fact in error regarding the history of Jewish migration into Vienna, and there is no excuse for his snide suggestion that Hayek's claim "reflects a quite distorted recollection of the attitude of Viennese society toward Jews prior to 1914" (846).

In point of fact, Hayek is correct. Strong anti-Jewish sentiments did indeed predate the large influx of Jews from Galicia and Bukovina, but it was the massive migration of Jews from these regions between 1890 and 1910 that changed the face of Viennese anti-Semitism. Prior to 1890, the bulk of Viennese Jews had come from Bohemia, Moravia, and Hungary. But in the twenty years following 1890 most Jews who converged on Vienna came from the economically backward regions of Galicia and swelled the Jewish population of the city from less than 100,000 to somewhat over 175,000 (Wistrich 1989; Rozenblit 1983). The more virulent anti-Semitism of which Hayek speaks was directed against recent immigrants from the East and was a far more common attitude among all classes of Viennese gentiles than was the class-bound anti-Semitism of the Christian Socialists.

3. When speaking of his friendship with Jews while at the university, Hayek recalls that he resented the fact that he was prohibited from offering any kind of characterization, either about Jews or Jewish culture and customs. "I was not allowed to speak about Jewish things," he relates, "[but] they did that all the time. Even the theme of 'Has he a Jewish accent?' was constantly discussed among them; if I would have said a word about it, it would have been bitterly resented."

Reder appears to feel that only an anti-Semite would object to being excluded from making such comments when in the company of his friends. People with a genuine sense of goodwill toward Jews would, presumably, be happy to unquestioningly accept these conditions without the least discomfort.

4. Hayek notes that his younger brother was quite swarthy and was often described by Hayek's Jewish friends as "looking Jewish." Out of curiosity regarding whether he had Jewish ancestors, Hayek tells us, he spent one summer compiling a genealogy of the family, which he managed to trace back for five generations. His conclusion was that his family had not intermarried with Jews.

In what has to be one of the most preposterous conclusions reached by the author, Reder takes Hayek's tracing of his family tree, especially when juxtaposed against the recollection that his brother had dark hair, as an example of a morbid concern regarding whether he had Jewish blood.

5. Hayek's mentor Ludwig von Mises, whose weekly seminars Hayek regularly attended during the 1920s, was almost certainly the economist whom Hayek felt closest to. Hayek notes that "Mises was unquestionably the personal contact from whom I profited most, not only by way of intellectual stimulation but also for his direct assistance in my career" (Kresge and Wenar 1994, 68–69). These two economists continued as close friends throughout their lives, and Hayek regularly conceded his debt to Mises for helping shape his views on economics. Mises was Jewish and, when Hayek met him, was regarded as one of the most distinguished economists in Europe and the most eminent living scholar of the Austrian school. Despite his reputation, however, Mises was unable to obtain a chair at the University of Vienna. Hayek relates that while Mises had always assumed that it was anti-Semitism that kept him from a post at the university, the real reason lay in Mises's promarket and antisocialist views. "But the Jews who were teaching," Hayek recounts, "were all socialists, and Mises was an anti-socialist, so he could not get the support of his own fellows. So the reason why he did not get a professorship was not really anti-Semitism, but [that] he wasn't liked by his Jewish colleagues" (Kresge and Wenar 1994, 59).

This paragraph Reder depicts as "tainted with ideological-ethnic bias" (848), because Hayek, while claiming that the Jewish socialists on the faculty would not support Mises, does not also indicate that gentile nonsocialists would also oppose Mises! It is truly breathtaking to find this offered as evidence of anti-Semitism.

This, then, is the sum total of Reder's "evidence" to impugn Hayek's reputation and to couple the name of this scholar, the author of more than twenty books and several hundred articles, with anti-Semitism: He described Viennese society as having been divided into three groups and noted that the more profoundly Jewish group tended not to mix with Christians; he attributed the most malignant period of anti-Semitism in Vienna to the years immediately before and during the Great War, when there was an influx of poorer Jews from the East; he resented being unable to speak freely about things Jewish with his Jewish friends while they permitted themselves that right; he undertook to trace his family tree, partly out of curiosity as to whether he had Jewish ancestors; and he concluded that Mises was denied a chair at the University of Vienna, not because he was Jewish, but because the professoriat was dominated by left-wing academics who were themselves Jewish but were opposed to Mises's promarket views.

It seems clear from this list that Reder is equating anti-Semitism with any characterization of Jews by a non-Jew that is not explicitly laudatory. Even statements of historical fact are not exempt. In sum, Reder's reading of Hayek's comments are, to put the most charitable light on it, idiosyncratic. Not only did I not interpret Hayek's references to Jews as suggesting anti-Semitism when I reviewed the book on which Reder relies (see Hamowy 1996), but, as far as I am aware, no other reader has arrived at conclusions remotely similar to those of Professor Reder.

Nor does the level of scholarship exhibited by Professor Reder's article meet professional standards. Reder did not even bother to consult any of Hayek's other writings before making these charges. While Hayek deals only sparingly with Jews in his other writings, he does speak of them in *The Road to Serfdom*, Hayek's wartime attack on collectivism in the West. Those who are familiar with Hayek's work are aware that he was particularly repelled by Marx's contempt for Jews and the implication in Marx's "On the Jewish Question" that anti-Semitism was justified because the Jews were engaged in exploitative "capitalist" pursuits like money-lending. The Nazi condemnation of Jews, Hayek realized, was of a piece with the movement's hatred of free markets and built on the contempt large numbers of Europeans had for those engaged in trade and industry:

> In Germany and Austria the Jew had come to be regarded as the representative of capitalism because a traditional dislike of large classes of the population for commercial pursuits had left these more readily accessible to a group that was practically excluded from the more

highly esteemed occupations. It is the old story of the alien race's being admitted only to the less respected trades and then being hated
still more for practicing them. The fact that German anti-Semitism
and anti-capitalism spring from the same root is of great importance
for the understanding of what has happened there, but this is rarely
grasped by foreign observers. (Hayek 1944, 139–40)

Finally, Reder, in quoting Hayek's observations about Jews as they appear in *Hayek on Hayek*, does not include what are probably Hayek's
most fulsome and generous comments. In speaking of his early friendship with his Jewish and partly Jewish comrades, Hayek notes:

And where I learnt perhaps most from them was in the fact that genuine devotion to things of the spirit need not mean being impractical
in the art of getting on in life, that a special gift in one field is no
excuse for not learning how to best utilize it, and that ignorance of
opportunities is as much a result of a particular kind of laziness or a
prejudiced disdain for a necessary task as any other lack of capacity
to make oneself useful. (Kresge and Wenar 1994, 58–59)

Not only is there not a hint of anti-Semitism in such remarks, but they
are a potent indication of Hayek's contempt for anti-Semitic sentiments.

Professor Reder's comments on Hayek are an insult both to Hayek and
to those many Jews, like myself, who worked closely with and under him
and should be dismissed as the somewhat jaundiced views of a writer
intent on finding malevolence where none exists.

References

Hamowy, Ronald. 1996. Hayek on Hayek. *Philosophy of the Social Sciences* 26
(September): 417–21.
Hayek, F. A. 1944. *The Road to Serfdom*. Chicago: University of Chicago Press.
Kresge, Stephen, and Leif Wenar, eds. 1994. *Hayek on Hayek: An Autobiographical
Dialogue*. Chicago: University of Chicago Press.
Reder, Melvin W. 2000. The Anti-Semitism of Some Eminent Economists. *HOPE*
32.4:833–56.
Rozenblit, Marsha L. 1983. *The Jews of Vienna: 1867–1914*. Albany: State Univer-
sity Press of New York.
Wistrich, Robert S. 1989. *The Jews of Vienna in the Age of Franz Joseph*. Oxford:
Oxford University Press.

FREEDOM AND THE RULE OF LAW IN F.A. HAYEK

by Ronald Hamowy (*)

One of the paramount difficulties which confronts the political or legal theorist involves the definition of such key terms as rights and freedom. Most contemporary authors who commonly use these terms do so without attempting a precise definition of them, relying principally on the « common sense » meaning these words convey. However, it is a task of crucial importance to anyone intent on an exposition of the theoretical nature of individual liberty and of the proper function of law to analyse the way these terms are employed. We shall, in this paper, be concerned with one of the most important and widely known of these expositions, that of Professor F. A. Hayek and with his interpretation of the rule of law.

Although the most extensive analytic treatment of the idea of the rule of law is that offered by Hayek, the idea is by no means new. Kenneth Davis has suggested that the notion of the rule of law can be equated with the concept of government under law which, in this form, can be found in Aristotle (1). Holdsworth indicates that the rule, in British legal theory, derives directly from the medieval notion that law — whether human or divine — rules the world (2). The doctrine lies at the core of English constitutional law throughout its development.

Its definitive statement in modern times is that offered by Dicey. In his *Law of the Constitution*, first published in 1885, Dicey saw the rule of law as consisting of the following three principles:

« We mean, in the first place, that no man is punishable or can be lawfully made to suffer in body or goods except for a distinct breach of law established in the ordinary legal manner before the ordinary courts of the land. In this sense the rule of law is contrasted with every system of government based on the exercise by persons in authority of wide, arbitrary, or discretionary powers of constraint » (3). « We mean in the second place ... not only that

---

(*) Department of History, University of Alberta, Edmonton, Canada.
(1) *Discretionary Justice: A Preliminary Inquiry*, Baton Rouge, La., Louisiana State University Press, 1969, p. 28.
(2) Sir WILLIAM HOLDSWORTH, *A History of English Law*, 7th ed., London, Methuen & Co., Ltd., 1956, X, 647.
(3) A. V. DICEY, *Introduction to the Study of the Law of the Constitution*, 10th ed., London, Macmillan and Company Ltd., 1959, p. 188.

with us no man is above the law, but (what is a different thing)
that here every man, whatever his rank or condition, is subject to
the ordinary law of the realm and amenable to the jurisdiction of
the ordinary tribunals » (4). « We may that the constitution is
pervaded by the rule of law on the ground that the general principles
of the constitution (as for example the right to personal liberty,
or the right of public meeting) are with us the results of judicial
decisions determining the rights of private persons in particular cases
brought before the courts; whereas under many foreign constitutions
the security (such as it is) given to the rights of individuals results,
or appears to result, from the general principles of the constitution » (5). These characteristics, especially the first two, form
the basis of all subsequent formulations of the rule of law by later
authors.

The same notion is offered by Lord Hewart in his attack on
the growing discretionary powers of government. For Hewart the
rule of law denotes the following: « No one can lawfully be restrained
or punished, or condemned in damages except for a violation of the
law established to the satisfaction of a judge or jury or magistrate
in proceedings regularly instituted in one of the ordinary Courts
of Justice. The rights of personal liberty and of freedom of speech,
the liberty of the press, and the right of public meeting, are all a
result of the application of this fundamental principle (6). Everyone,
whatever his position ... is governed by the ordinary law of the land
and personally liable for anything done by him contrary to that law,
and is subject to the jurisdiction of the ordinary Courts of Justice,
civil and criminal (7). No one who is charged with a violation of
the law can effectively plead, either in a civil or in a criminal Court
that his act was done in obedience to the command of a superior,
even the command of the King himself » (8).

The foremost proponent of this position in the United States is
John Dickinson, who holds that « nothing has been held more fundamental to the supremacy of law than the right of every citizen
to bring the action of government officials to trial in the ordinary
courts of the common law. That government officials, on the contrary,
should themselves assume to perform the functions of a law court
and determine the rights of individuals, as is the case under a system

---

(4) *Ibidem*, p. 193.
(5) *Ibidem*, pp. 195-96.
(6) The Rt. Hon. Lord HEWART of BURY, *The New Despotism*, London,
Ernest Benn Ltd., 1929, p. 26.
(7) *Ibidem*.
(8) *Ibidem*, p. 27.

of administrative justice, has been traditionally felt to be inconsistent with the supremacy of law... In short, every citizen is entitled, first, to have his rights adjudicated in a regular common-law court, and, secondly, to call into question in such a court the legality of any act done by an administrative official » (9).

Hayek's notion of the rule of law is fundamentally in agreement with the principles postulated by these authors. A society operating under the rule of law, according to Hayek, will be one in which its laws take the form of general, abstract rules, *i.e.*, « essentially long-term measures, referring to yet unknown cases, and containing no references to particular persons, places, or objects. Such laws must always be prospective, never retrospective in their effect ». They must be « known and certain », *i.e.*, they must be such that « the decisions of the courts can be predicted », and they must « apply equally to all » (10).

All of these writers have juxtaposed the rule of law, with arbitrary government. They all share the presumption that individual freedom is secure only under a government based on the rule of law and free of the bureaucratic encroachments of administrative agencies endowed with the power to make *ad hoc* decisions. It is the contention of this paper that the rule of law, in fact, does not guarantee a system of personal liberty of any greater dimensions than that afforded by a government delegated broad discretionary powers, that the free interplay of spontaneously generated social and economic forces can be just as much constrained under one system as under

---

(9) *Administrative Justice and the Supremacy of Law in the United States*, New York, Russell & Russell, Inc., 1959, pp. 33, 35. (First published in 1927).

(10) *The Constitution of Liberty*, Chicago, University of Chicago Press, 1960, pp. 208, 209. Professor Lon Fuller has suggested that a legal system must posses certain similar attributes to qualify as a true system of laws. Discussing the question in the negative, he writes: « ... the attempt to create and maintain a system of legal rules may miscarry in at least eight ways; ... The first and most obvious lies in a failure to achieve rules at all, so that every issue must be decided on an *ad hoc basis*. The other routes are: (2) a failure to publicize, or at least to make available to the affected party, the rules he is expected to observe; (3) the abuse of retroactive legislation, which not only cannot itself guide action, but undercuts the integrity of rules prospective in effect, since it puts them under the threat of retrospective change; (4) a failure to make rules understandable; (5) the enactment of contradictory rules or (6) rules that require conduct beyond the powers of the affected party; (7) introducing such frequent changes in the rules taht the subject cannot orient his action by them; and, finally, (8) a failure of congruence between the rules as announced and their actual administration.

« A total failure in any one of these eight directions does not simply result in a bad system of law; it results in something that is not properly called a legal system at all... » *The Morality of Law*, New Haven and London, Yale University Press, 1964, pp. 38-39.

206 _The Political Sociology of Freedom_

the other, and that a system of _formal_ restrictions (as opposed to _substantive_ restrictions) on government activity, in the end, has the force of no restrictions at all.

For the purpose of this essay, I have confined myself to an analysis of the idea of freedom and the rule of law as presented by F. A. Hayek. There are several reasons for this. First, Hayek's exposition is by far the most extensive and ambitious theoretical treatment of the subject. Secondly, of the important defenses of this position, his is the most recent. And thirdly and most importantly, Hayek leaves less room in his discussion of the rule of law for discretionary power in any system of government which qualifies as a government of law than that allowed by any of the other writers. To use Kenneth Davis' phrase, Hayek's is the most « extravagant version » of the rule of law (11). If, therefore, even Hayek's version should prove to permit incursions into the area of personal liberty substantially beyond those we would normally wish to allow, it follows that the less extreme statements of this position afford even fewer protections to individual freedom.

Since the rule of law, for Hayek, has reference to government activity only in so far as it limits the private sphere of individual activity (12), we shall first deal with his concept of freedom.

I.

Hayek begins the construction of his theoretical framework by defining freedom as the absence of coercion (13). Thus, in order to fully comprehend what he feels to be the basis of personal freedom in society we must turn to his definition of coercion. « Coercion », he writes, « occurs when one man's actions are made to serve another man's will, not for his own but for the other's purpose » (14). But, he continues, such coercion can occur only when the possibility of alternate action is open to the coerced. « Coercion implies ... that I still choose but that my mind is made someone else's tool, because the alternatives before me have been so manipulated that the conduct that the coercer wants me to choose becomes for me the least painful one » (15).

---

(11) For Davis' discusison of this version of the rule of law, see _Discretionary Justice_, pp. 27-51.

(12) ... the rule of law restricts government only in its coercive activities. » _Constitution of Liberty_, p. 206.

(13) In the following discussion of Hayek's concept of coercion, I have at times drawn on a previously published paper, « Hayek's Concept of Freedom: A Critique ». _New Individualist Review_ (Chicago), I, April, 1961, 28-31.

(14) _Constitution of Liberty_, p. 133.

(15) _Ibidem._

Let us examine this concept more closely. The absence of coercion (*i.e.*, freedom) would seem to be the following: freedom obtains when the possible alternative actions open to me are not such that, through the manipulation of such alternatives by someone else, the least painful choice for me is that which is the most beneficial to him. Or, more simply, freedom obtains when no one else manipulates my environment in such a way that my action (or actions) benefits him.

Now the first difficulty arising out of such a definition is that of determining just what particular actions are coercive. Professor Hayek attempts to distinguish coercive acts from « the conditions or terms on which our fellow men are willing to render us specific services or benefits » in the following way. « So long as the services of a particular person are not crucial to my existence or the preservation of what I most value, the conditions he exacts for rendering these services cannot properly be called ' coercion ' » (16). But it would seem that this lends little if any clarity to the distinction between coercive and non-coercive acts since we are left to define and make precise Hayek's qualifications for characterizing an action as a coercive one, namely being « crucial to existence » and preserving « what one most values ».

Let us take an example which Hayek himself uses. Suppose that the condition for my being invited to a particular party, which I had previously indicated I very much wanted to attend, were my wearing formal attire. Could it be said that my host, by demanding such an action on my part, was acting coercively towards me? It would appear, and so Hayek concludes, that the answer is clearly « no ». For, although it is true that my environment is being manipulated in such a way that my « least painful choice » (my wearing a dinner jacket and attending the party) is that which benefits the manipulator (the host), this situation does not, at least superficially, satisfy the terms of either of the qualifications necessary for falling into the category of coercive acts. Specifically, my attendance at this gathering could not be said to be either crucial to my existence or contributory to preserving what I most value. Yet it might be that I am a very socially conscious person and that my not attending this party would greatly endanger my social standing. Further, my dinner jacket is at the cleaners and will not be ready for a week. I do not have the time to order a new one as I am assured by my tailors that the fitting and altering involved would take close to a month, yet the party is tomorrow. Under these conditions, could it

---

(16) *Ibidem*, p. 136.

be said that my host's action in demanding my wearing formal attire
as the price of access to his home *is*, in fact, a coercive one, inasmuch
as it clearly threatens the preservation of one of the things I most
value, my social prestige? (17).

The above situation might be slightly altered to present what
might more clearly appear to be a coercive act in terms of Hayek's
definition. Suppose the price demanded by my host, in return for
inviting me to his home, were a commitment from me that I wash
all the silver and china used at the party. On the fact of it, this
would seem to be nothing more than an ordinary contract, voluntarily entered into by the parties to the agreement and with full knowledge on both sides of the terms of the agreement. But suppose
further that all the other conditions concerning my attachment to
social prestige still held. It then becomes the case, within the framework of Hayek's terms, that such a contract is of a coercive nature (18).

Professor Hayek spells out a case of « true coercion » of this
same type. « A monopolist could exercise true coercion ... if he were ...
the owner of a spring in an oasis. Let us say that other persons
settled there on the presumption that water would always be
available at a reasonable price and then found ... that they had no
choice but to do whatever the owner of the spring demanded of
them if they were to survive: here would be a clear case of coercion » (19). We assume that Hayek here means that a contract
entered into by the owner of the spring and the purchaser of water
which allowed for remuneration to the spring owner of any but a
« reasonable price » would be of a coercive nature. But here we are

---

(17) Hayek states: « To constitute coercion it is also necessary that
the action of the coercer should put the coerced in a position which he regards
as worse than that in which he would have been without that action ». « Freedom and Coercion: Some Comments on a Critique by Mr. Ronald Hamowy »,
Studies in Philosophy, Politics and Economics, Chicago, University of Chicago
Press, 1967, p. 349. The case just described seems to meet this condition as
well; for, while it is true that, in a sense, my would-be host has widened
my range of alternatives by the invitation, the *whole* situation (which must
include my inability to acquire formal attire and my consequent frustration)
is worse from my point of view than the situation which had obtained before
the invitation, certainly worse than had existed before my would-be host had
decided to have a party at that particular time.

(18) It might be argued that the preservation of one's social prestige
cannot properly be considered legitimate grounds to warrant those actions
which tend to endanger it as « coercive ». This, however, is not really relevant
to the problem. One can always construct a different set of hypothetical values which could be jeopardized by such action. For example, I might have
mentioned to my employer that I would be attending this party and it might
possibly cost me my job were I to fail to show up.

(19) *Constitution of Liberty*, p. 136.

faced with what appears to be an insurmountable problem—what constitutes a « reasonable » price (20)? By « reasonable » Hayek might mean « competitive ». But how is it possible to determine what the competitive price is in the absence of competition? Economics cannot predict the cardinal magnitude of any market price in the absence of a market. What, then, can we assume to be a « reasonable » price, or, more to the point, at what price does the contract alter its nature and become an instance of « coercion »? Is it at one cent a gallon, at one dollar a gallon, at ten dollars a gallon? What if the owner of the spring demands nothing more than the friendship of the settlers? Is such a « price » coercive? By what principle can we decide when the agreement is a simple contractual one and when it is not?

---

(20) The fact American law at times sanctions such vague language is admitted. Thus, as Professor Amsterdam notes, in *Nash v. United States*, 229 U.S. 373 (1913), the Supreme Court sustained « as a sufficiently definite criminal standard the " rule of reason " of the Sherman Act — a case which fathered such others as *Edgar A. Levy Leasing Co. v. Siegel* [25 U.S. 242 (1922)], upholding state rent control legislation which allowed as a defense to a landlord's action his tenant's showing that the rent charged was " unjust and unreasonable ", and *United States v. Ragen* [314 U.S. 513 (1942)], sustaining a conviction for federal income tax evasion predicated upon the defendant's having taken a deduction which violated the statutory mandate that only a " reasonable allowance for salaries " might be excluded from taxable income ». ANTHONY G. AMSTERDAM, « The Void-for-Vagueness Doctrine in the Supreme Court », *University of Pennsylvania Law Review*, CIX, November, 1960, 69-70.

There is, however, just as strong a counter-tradition in the law, *i.e.*, the doctrine of unconstitutional uncertainty, which requires that statutes be sufficiently definite to allow clear knowledge of the conduct prohibited. Thus, again quoting Professor Amsterdam, in *Cline v. Frink Dairy Co.*, 274 U.S. 445 (1927), the Court « held unconstitutional a statute that outlawed certain agreements and associations in restraint of trade, excepting those whose object was to market at a " reasonable profit " products which could not otherwise be so marketed. That case followed its more famous ancestor, *United States v. L. Cohen Grocery Co.* [255 U.S. 81 (1921)], which had voided for vagueness section 4 of the Lever Act, proscribing the making of " any unjust or unreasonable rate or charge in handling... any necessaries " ». *Ibid.*, p. 69.

In a still earlier case, a state law prohibiting price-fixing combinations aimed at selling commodities (excepting certain crops) at a price higher than their « real value » was held unconstitutional by the Court. In the unanimous decision of the Court to reverse conviction, Mr. Justice Holmes wrote that to determine « real value » was a « problem that no human ingenuity could solve ». « ... if business is to go on, men must unite to do it and must sell their wares. To compel them to guess on peril of indictment what the community would have given for them if the continually changing conditions were other than they are... ; to divine prophetically what the reaction of only partially determinate facts would be upon the imagination and desires of purchasers, is to exact gift that mankind does not possess ». *International Harvester Co., v. Kentucky*, 234 U.S. 216 at 223-24 (1914).

For excellent discussions of this problem, see Amsterdam's article, cited above, and REX A. COLLINGS, Jr., « Unconstitutional Uncertainty — An Appraisal », *Cornell Law Quarterly*, XL, Winter, 1955, 195-237.

But we must face yet a further difficulty. Is the owner acting coercively if he refuses to sell his water at *any* price? Suppose that he looks upon his spring as sacred and its water as holy. To offer the water to the settlers would contravene his deepest religious sentiments. Here is a situation which would not fall under Hayek's definition of coercion, since the owner of the spring forces *no* action on the settlers. Yet it would appear that, within Hayek's own framework, this is a far worse situation, since the only « choice » left open to the settlers now is dying of thirst.

Let us now turn to Professor Hayek's use of the term « coercion » in contexts where one can foresee the results of one's actions when certain conditions are realized. Just as the foregoing discussion points up too broad a definition for the term « coercion », here that area of actions which can properly be called « coercive » appears to be unreasonably narrowed. He writes: « Provided that I know beforehand that if I place myself in a particular position, I shall be coerced and provided that I can avoid putting myself in such a position, I need never be coerced [*i.e.*, I need never have my freedom curtailed] » (21). It follows from this that if Mr. X warns me that he is going to kill me if I buy anything from Mr. Y, and if the products available from Mr. Y are also available elsewhere (probably from Mr. X), such action on the part of Mr. X is non-coercive! Avoidability of the action is sufficient, according to this criterion, to set up a situation theoretically identical to one in which a threat does not occur at all. The threatened party is no *less* free than he was before the threat was made, if he can avoid the threatener's action (22). Thus, if I know in advance that I will be attacked by hoodlums if I enter a certain neighborhood, and if I can avoid that neighborhood, then I need never be coerced by the hoodlums.

This rather awkward relationship between avoidability and coercion, where the presence of the former entails the absence of the latter, stems from Hayek's attempt to create a necessary connection between general rules which prohibit specific actions (the rule of law) and freedom. Hayek goes on to say that « in so far as the rules providing for coercion are not aimed at me personally but are so framed as to apply equally to all people in similar circumstances, they are no different from any of the natural obstacles that affect my plans » (23). Hence, one could regard the hoodlum-infested neighborhood of the preceding example in the same way as

---

(21) *Constitution of Liberty*, p. 142.
(22) According to the logical structure of this argument, « threatening coercion » is not a coercive act.
(23) *Constitution of Liberty*, p. 142.

a plague-infested swamp, both avoidable obstacles, neither personally aimed at me.

J. W. N. Watkins has examined this position in some detail and argued that « Hayek has been over-impressed by the following logical consideration: a prohibition leaves an agent free to act in any of the indefinitely large number of ways compatible with not acting in the prohibited way, whereas a positive command leaves him unfree to act in any of the indefinitely large number of ways incompatible with acting in the commanded way. This seems to suggest that a prohibition is infinitely less coercive than a command. But we must not be dazzled by the largeness of the number of alternative courses left open by a prohibition. After all, the agent can select only one of them. To measure the degree of penalisation which a prohibition involves, what we have to weigh against the prohibited course is not the whole class of unprohibited alternatives but just the unprohibited alternative which he dislikes least. Now it may be that his best un-prohibited alternative will be little or no worse than the prohibited course, in which case he will not be penalised by the prohibition. But it may also be that he regards the best unprohibited alternative as *much* worse than the prohibited course. Suppose he is confronted by a ' general, abstract rule, equally applicable to all ' which forbids foreign travel; and suppose he has an ailing father abroad whom he wants to visit before he dies. On Hayek's argument, there is no coercion or loss of freedom here. This agent is not subject to anyone's will. He is just confronted by the fact that if he tries to go abroad he will be apprehended and punished. He might equally have been confronted by the fact that he has not enough money for the trip or that the trip would take so long that his father would be dead before he arrived. Instead of using the word ' coerced ' Hayek should, I think, have written: " Provided that I know before-hand if I place myself in a particular position, I shall not be *punished* and, provided that I can avoid putting myself in such a position, I need never be *punished* ". So amended, this statement is true, but no longer supports the contention that coercion is impossible under a rule of law (for the cost of avoiding punishment may be intolerable) or even the contention that there is less coercion under a rule of law (for under a *dirigiste* system one could likewise avoid punishment by obeying the specific commands directed at one personally) » (24).

This relationship between general rules and freedom is, indeed, the most important characteristic of Hayek's theory of law. Freedom,

(24) « Philosophy », *Agenda for a Free Society: Essays on Hayek's The Constitution of Liberty*, Arthur Seldon, ed. London, Published for the Institute of Economic Affairs by Hutchinson, 1961, pp. 39-40.

for him, is a logical consequence of a certain set of formal restrictions on legislative activity. He writes: « ... the conception of freedom under the law ... rests on the contention that when we obey laws, in the sense of general abstract rules laid down irrespective of their application to us, we are not subject to another man's will and are therefore free » (25). The implication is, of course, that these abstract rules, when applied impartially, without regard to person, are non-coercive, despite any substantive qualification. Further, the non-coercive nature of general rules seems to hold even when these rules take the form of specific directives rather than prohibitions. Though « taxation and the various compulsory services, especially the armed forces ... are not supposed to be avoidable, they are at least predictable and are enforced irrespective of how the individual would otherwise employ his energies: this deprives them largely of the evil nature of coercion » (26).

It is interesting to note that Hayek's theory of rights, although less explicitly dealt with than his idea of freedom, involves the notion that rights, rather than resting on some independent non-governmental social arrangement, proceed from governmental action. They are, in Hayek's words, « legal guarantees » that the legislature will not interfere in certain areas. Rights, like freedom, are a logical consequence of the rule of law. « Under a reign of freedom the free sphere of the individual [that area protected by rights] includes all action not explicitly restricted by a general law » (27). These rights do not logically antecede government but proceed from the rule of law and are formed by the legal arrangements which stem from it. Moreover, Hayek does not regard the area of legally guaranteed freedom as in any sense absolutely guaranteed. « We have up to this point represented these guaranties of individual freedom as if they were absolute rights which could never be infringed. In actual fact they cannot mean more than that the normal running of society is based on them and that any departure from them requires special justification [as does any departure from the rule of law] » (28).

II.

Inasmuch as rights may be infringed under certain circumstances, Hayek must differentiate between those governmental actions which are to be considered legitimate and those which are invasive or

---

(25) *Constitution of Liberty*, p. 153.
(26) *Ibidem*, p. 143.
(27) *Ibidem*, p. 216.
(28) *Ibidem*, p. 217.

coercive. In order to do so he has recourse to the concept of the rule of law.

« Law », Hayek asserts, « in its ideal form might be described as a 'once-and-for-all' command that is directed to unknown people and that is abstracted from all particular circumstances of time and place and refers only to such conditions as may occur anywhere and at any time » (29). We see, then, that the rule of law constitutes a set of abstract rules governing society which in no way discriminates among citizens and, hence, are equally applicable to all. It is from this legal framework, Hayek contends, that the whole body of rights ultimately emanates, emerging from and defined in terms of the legal rules by which society operates; these « rights » are guarantees against action falling outside the rule of law.

Ideally, according to Hayek's understanding of the rule of law, legislatures would be prohibited from making laws that explicitly apply only to specific persons or groups: « As a true law should not name particulars, so it should especially not single out any specific persons or group of persons » (30). This strict interpretation Hayek is forced to modify, however, since it is immediately apparent that certain sets of rules apply to specific sets of people, *e.g.*, at common law rape can be committed only against a woman (31). Hayek suggests two criteria which, if met, would place such laws regulating the behavior of specific groups outside the range of arbitrary government and make them consistent with the rule of law. These criteria are, first, that no proper names be employed in the law and, second, that the distinctions are permissible « so long as the distinction is favored by the majority both inside and outside the group » (32). We shall deal with each of these criteria in turn.

It would seem that the first criterion, that no proper names be mentioned in a law, would protect against particular persons or groups being either harassed by the government by laws which discriminate against them or being granted special privileges denied the rest of the population. But, on closer examination, such a guarantee is specious for it is always possible to contrive a set of descriptive terms which can apply exclusively to a person or group without recourse to proper names. As an example, suppose that the legislature wishes to pass a statute allowing the deportation of Al Capone and, further, suppose that it is prohibited from passing legislation aimed

(29) *Ibidem*, pp. 149-50.
(30) *Ibidem*, pp. 153-54.
(31) 75 *Corpus Juris Secundum* 461, Section 1.   There are, of course, a host of laws which have application only to juveniles, others, to the aged, etc.
(32) *Constitution of Liberty*, p. 154.

at deporting a citizen by name but does not wish anyone else deported. It is possible to contrive a set of descriptive terms which can apply exclusively to Capone without recourse to proper names. Thus, « all persons born in a country presently a member of the Common Market, arrested more than x times, suspected of engaging in illegal conduct, earning more than $20,000,000 in one year, etc. [i.e., all persons possessing characteristics a, b, c, ... n], shall be held liable for deportation ». Legislatures today are constantly faced with the problem of defining groups for the purpose of special legislation and often describe them according to specific and related traits. Descriptions are set up in such a way that the parameters of the group and the characteristics possessed by a certain set of persons are neither over- nor under- inclusive, *i.e.*, a one-member class is created. In such a way legislation aimed at specific groups avoids the apparently unconstitutional device of singling them out by name (33). Further, groups, unlike specific individuals, are possessed of a set of *defining* characteristics which, when listed in the law, would serve the same function as the use of proper names.

The second criterion, that legislation referring to specific groups is permissible when it is recognized as justified by a majority of those both inside and outside the group, appears to be much stronger protection. The term « group », however, can be interpreted in either of two ways. Either « group » can refer to the specific group which is the subject of legislation, or it can refer to a wider group of « those concerned with the legislation », whose membership is left undetermined. In the first case, if the proposed legislation aims at discriminating against a particular group, it is difficult to imagine a majority of that group (those « inside » the group) concurring in such legislation and I cannot believe that this is what Hayek has in mind (34). In the second sense, and it must be to the wider group

---

(33) There are numerous examples which could be offered of states circumventing constitutional provisions prohibiting « special legislation » of this type. For example, the New York State Rapid Transit Act (April 28 Laws 1941), Chapter 800 (Chapter 48 (a) of the Consolidated Laws), has reference exclusively to New York City without once mentioning the city by name. The statute simply defines « city » for its purposes as « a city containing a population of more than one million inhabitants according to the last Federal census ». Section 2a (7). This device is by no means confined to New York and such statutes can be found in most states. The Georgia statutes are an especially fertile ground for finding laws which can have reference only to its capital city, although Atlanta is never referred to by name.

(34) If the purpose of specific legislation is to grant privileges to a certain minority, rather than to discriminate against them, then, of course, the majority of those « inside the group » would most likely concur in such legislation. Hayek contends that a statute aimed at a specific group which is favored by the majority both inside and outside the group can be presumed to serve the ends of both. (*Constitution of Liberty*, p. 154). This strikes me

that Hayek is referring, this restraint on governmental activity suffers from the weakness that the « group » to which the legislation applies is not unitary but consists in fact of a series of broader, more inclusive groups and, more often than not, of several such series of ever more inclusive groups. Let us, for example, pass on the propriety of a proposal to outlaw the Communist Party. Now, who is to be considered inside the group? All those who are members of the Communist Party? They would clearly never consent to such legislation and I do not think it is what Hayek intends when he writes that the consent of the majority inside the group is necessary for the passage of discriminatory legislation. Who then? I suspect that what Hayek is getting at by this criterion is that the consent of those who *might* be affected by the legislation is necessary, *i.e.*, the group consists of those who *might* become members of the Communist Party. But who is included « within » the group then? Those active in extreme-left politics? Those active in left-wing politics of whatever sort? Those active in politics, regardless of their political views? Several such series are possible. Another might be: those sympathetic to Communism; those who are interested in Communism; those who know anything about Communism, etc. The categories of those who fall within and those who are outside the group are totally dependent on which « group » is chosen and, generally, approval or disapproval of the proposed law would be a function of the particular dividing line employed. If this is true and gerrymandering of this sort is possible, the suggested criterion for permissible legislation boils down to an uncontrolled majoritarianism.

It might be argued that when Hayek here refers to rules relating to « specific groups » he is concerned solely with legislation referring to classes of people who, of necessity, possess certain sets of properties such as nationality, sex, race, age, blood-type, and so on. In such

---

as an unwarranted assumption if « being favored by the majority outside the group » of a statute granting special privileges to a minority is simply the acquiescence of the majority to the statute. Modern law is replete with legislation granting special economic privileges to a certain group (tariffs, subsidies, restriction of entry into professions and businesses, local monopolies, special privileges of other sorts, etc.) which are clearly detrimental to the majority of the population. The dynamics of political life offer evidence of why such statutes can be enacted without much opposition. The few who stand to gain by the legislation, stand to gain much and will lobby accordingly; those who stand to lose, the bulk of the population, each individually, stand to lose only a little and are politically unorganized for the purpose of preventing the legislation. In addition, proponents of the legislation often gain the acquiescence of many people by invoking « the national interest » or « our defense posture ». The result, almost invariably, is that the legislation is passed and accepted by those « outside the group ».

a case the protections offered against discriminatory legislation would be much stronger. The problems inherent in defining groups would no longer hold since the legislation would *necessarily* indicate the group to be considered and the dividing line between those in and those outside the group would be an obvious one, But the argument is still open to serious objection on another ground. Coercive legislation remains a possibility in cases where legislation is contemplated at all on the basis of group membership alone. Thus, it is possible that proscription of interracial marriages would have the sanction of majorities in both groups. In connection with Hayek's argument here, we would do well to remember that Hayek defines « rights » in terms of the legal guarantees of the rule of law. If governmental action is consistent with the rule of law, as this example appears to be, it becomes meaningless to speak of the denial of one's « rights ». Yet, in spite of this, it clearly appears that such a law denies the « right » to marry whom one chooses to members of either group who favor miscegenation. I can find no way, within the terms of Hayek's theory, to reconcile this conflict.

Having examined the criteria which Hayek sets up as necessary to allow legislation directed at specific persons or groups, let us now discuss the original strict interpretation of the rule of law. Ideally, Hayek holds, laws must consist of general rules equally applicable to all members of society. What he is here aiming at is a system of law based on a set of rules which allows one to predict with a good measure of certainty when one is within and when outside the law—in short, a system in which one is protected from apparently arbitrary decisions of the government and where conflict with the law is avoidable. Hayek's argument here centers about the protection afforded by these three safeguards: first, that the law does not distinguish among citizens in its application (the « equality » of the law); second, that it consist of general rules without regard to particular time or place (its « generality »); and lastly, that its incidence be predictable (its « certainty »).

Hayek does not specify what is meant by the term « equally applicable » when he refers to the effects of legislation on individuals. Let us, for the moment, assume that what he means is that actions prohibited to some must be prohibited to all—in other words, that laws should be the same for all members of society. Thus, if homosexual behavior were placed outside the range of allowable actions by the law, it would be outside the permissible sphere for all, and so on. But careful examination indicates that this limitation on the form legislation must take in order to be consonant with the rule of law hardly represents a serious curtailment on the content of legislation. It still remains possible to legislate against specific groups or persons inasmuch as some laws clearly have a harsher impact on certain people than they do on others. For example, if it were thought necessary for some reason to restrict trade to a particular foreign country, the law, in a sense, would « apply equally » to all; no one would be permitted to engage in such trade. But the *effect* of the law would be to benefit some—in this case, merchants who deal with countries exporting and importing the same or similar products as are affected by the legislation — at the expense of others — those engaged in the now prohibited trade. And there is no end to such examples. All of the following laws meet the criterion of being « equally applicable »; it is a punishable offense to support subversive political groups (defined in the law as all groups other than the one presently in power); it is a punishable offense to undermine faith in the United States government (thereby curtailing all political criticism); it is a punishable offense to read any literature not approved by the Censor, to smoke, to take certain drugs, to drink alcoholic beverages, to engage in « immoral » sexual activities, etc. Such laws obviously represent gross infringements on individual freedom of action. That laws be equally applicable in no way curtails the power of the government to enforce uniformity in those areas where it desires it. Further, by prohibiting *certain* things from being done by anybody, the government is in a position to strike at any particular person or group by legislating against the behavior which is peculiar to that person or group. That the laws be the same for all is hardly a safeguard against gross harassment of any minority by the state.

But Hayek does not even contend that the law *must* be the same for all, inasmuch as he recognizes the legitimacy of allowing specified exceptions to the law provided only that they be stipulated in the text of the law. Thus, « the law will prohibit killing another person or killing except under certain conditions so defined that they may occur at any time or place, but not killing of particular individuals » (35). Now this is perfectly reasonable; killing is not always murder and it is murder which the law wishes to prohibit. Exceptions to general proscriptions of stipulated physical actions are allowable since the law is interested not so much in the physical act (generally) as in attempts to subvert the structure of ordered relationships by contravening the intent of the laws. But this problem is not dealt with by Hayek and we have no guidelines to indicate

---

(35) *Ibidem*, p. 152. It would be consistent with this criterion, I think, to empower agents of the government (the police, the hangman, etc.) to kill in situations where others were prohibited from acting in this way.

in what way legal terms (such as theft, murder, rape, etc.) are to be defined. What exceptions are to be made and, what, if any, are the general principles for deciding whether the content of the exception is legitimate or otherwise? Are licensing laws — which are merely prohibitory laws which stipulate the requirements for exemption — to be regarded as consonant with the rule of law? If so, may the government license entry into *any* profession or business? If licensing is once allowed and if we lack a juridical theory concerning the limits of such action, we are faced with the possibility of a society of status based on principles totally consistent with the rule of law (36).

There is yet a further difficulty with Hayek's « equal applicability » thesis (37). Not all laws which Hayek feels are consistent with this principle are in any meaningful sense « equally applicable ». Thus, we are told that conscription is consistent with the rule of law theory, even when it explicitly applies only to a particular segment of the population, in the United States specifically to males between the ages of eighteen and thirty-five who meet certain stipulated physical and psychological requirements. We are now reduced

---

(36) The criterion dealt with earlier, that legislation aimed at specific groups, to be legitimate must have the concurrence of the majority of both those within and those outside the group, is not too helpful a protection here. It might be that the majority favor the general prohibition (say, on anyone being permitted to practice medicine) but not any one particular set of exemption requirements (although there might be unanimity on the question of the propriety of some exemption). In any case, this argument still suffers from a majoritarian bias which would permit enormous latitude to permissible legislative actions.

(37) The similarities between the problems raised by Hayek's concept of « equality of the law » and the constitutional concept of « equal protection of the laws » are very suggestive. For a discussion of the latter, see Joseph Tussman and Jacobus ten Broek, « The Equal Protection of the Laws », *California Law Review*, XXXVII, September, 1949, 341-81.

The following example gives some idea of how the « equal protection » clause of the Fourteenth Amendment has, at times, received a rather awkward interpretation by the Supreme Court.

A Michigan statute requires licensing of bartenders in all cities with a population of over 50,000, but no female may be so licensed unless she be « the wife or daughter of the male owner » of a licensed liquor establishment. [Public Acts of Michigan, Act 133, Section 19(a)]. In *Goesaert v. Cleary*, 335 U.S. 464 (1948), the Supreme Court was confronted with the question of whether the classification between wives and daughters of male owners and wives and daughters of non-owners made by the Michigan statute violated the equal protection guarantee of the Fourteenth Amendment. Mr. Justice Frankfurter, writing for the majority, noted that « while Michigan may deny to all women opportunities for bartending, Michigan cannot play favorites among women without rhyme or reason ». *Ibidem*, at 466. *However*, « since the line they have drawn is not without a basis in reason », he continued, « we cannot give ear to the suggestion that the real impulse behind the legislation was an unchivalrous desire of male bartenders to try to monopolize the calling ». *Ibidem*, at 467.

to defining « equal applicability » of the law in terms of « equal applicability to all those the law applies to ». As Bruno Leoni points out in connection with this: « We can form as many categories of people as we want in order to apply the same laws to them. Within each category people will alle be " equal " before the particular law that applies to them, regardless of the fact that other people, grouped in other categories, will be treated differently by other laws » (38). This in no sense can be considered an effective safeguard against the content of legislation since we are assured nothing more than that the law will be consistent in its application towards those it legislates against. How much protection does such a requirement afford from governmental involvement in the ordinary affairs of citizens?

Let us now turn to the second requirement which a legal system must fulfill in order that it be consistent with the rule of law. Laws must be general in nature, they must be such that « they do not refer to particulars but apply whenever certain abstractly defined conditions are satisfied » (39). Proponents of the rule of law have been disturbed at the growing power of administrative tribunals in Britain and in the United States, exercising powers which before had been confined to the courts and often making decisions which follow from no general rules. The rule of law has, thus, been contrasted with a system of « administrative law » under which certain autonomous administrative agencies created by statute are granted discretionary power to make *ad hoc* decisions in certain areas (40). The rule of law, they claim, does not sanction such

---

(38) *Freedom and the Law*, Princeton, N.J., D. Van Nostrand Co., Inc., 1961, pp. 68-69.

(39) F. A. HAYEK, *The Political Ideal of the Rule of Law*, Cairo, National Bank of Egypt, p. 35.

(40) Dicey saw a system of administrative law as foreign to England and as antithetical to the rule of law. See his chapter on the *droit administratif* in *The Law of the Constitution*, pp. 328-405, and E.C.S. Wade's « Introduction », *ibidem*, pp. cxiii-cli. Lord Hewart remarks that « between the " Rule of Law " and what is called " administrative law " (happily there is no English name for it) there is the sharpest possible contrast. One is substantially the opposite of the other ». *The New Despotism*, p. 37. Perhaps the most detailed discussion of the rise of administrative agencies in the United States and their effect upon the doctrine of the supremacy of the law is that offered by Dickinson. « The multiplication in recent years of bodies like public-service commissions and industrial-accident boards, accompanied by the vesting of ampler powers in health officers, building inspectors, and the like, has raised anew for our law, after three centuries, the problem of executive justice. That government officials should assume the traditional function of courts of law, and be permitted to determine the rights of individuals, is a development so out of line with the supposed path of our legal growth as to challenge renewed attention to certain underlying principles of our jurisprudence ». *Administrative Justice and the Supremacy of the Law*, p. 3. See, also, the

governmental activity, and Hayek, following this tradition, holds
that discretionary administrative activity which goes beyond deciding
questions of internal administration of government is proscribed by
the idea of the supremacy of the law. « When administration interferes with the private sphere of the citizen », he writes, « the
problem of discretion becomes relevant to us; and the principle of
the rule of law, in effect, means that the administrative authorities
should have no discretionary powers in this respect » (41). The requirement that all laws must be general would thus limit the courts
and any other judicial or quasi-judicial organs of the state from
rendering *ad hoc* decisions.

But what, in fact, would be prohibited by this criterion of the
rule of law? In examining the efficacy of this principle of law we are
confronted with the same difficulty which was met in our discussion
of proper names in the law. For, here too, inasmuch as a sufficiently
specific general characterization fitting only one condition or a
particular set of conditions can be provided, it remains possible to
meet this requirement in law and yet allow legislation directed
towards specific situations. A clear understanding of what « generality » of the law entails is further confused by the fact that some
law — as we have seen — may be applicable to only certain groups,
other laws applicable to others, and so on. As Leoni has indicated,
« it is not easy to establish what renders one law *general* in comparison with another. There are many 'genera' under which
'general' laws may be contrived... » (42).

III.

We have yet to consider that requirement which Hayek considers
most important to the operation of the rule of law, that the law be
certain. « There is probably no single factor which has contributed
more to the prosperity of the West than the relative certainty of
of the law which has prevailed here » (43). By « certainty of the
law » Hayek clearly means that its incidence be predictable. I have
no argument with Hayek that a clear knowledge of what conduct
is either demanded or proscribed by law and a fair degree of certainty
concerning its enforcement advances the supremacy of law in society.
What I will argue is that such predictability neither exists nor can
exist in some vital areas of our legal system, that the very nature

---

Report of the Committee on Administrative Tribunals and Enquiries, London,
Her Majesty's Stationery Office, 1957.
  (41) *Constitution of Liberty*, p. 213.
  (42) *Freedom and the Law*, p. 70.
  (43) *Constitution of Liberty*, p. 208.

of the system cannot help but allow far-reaching discretionary powers to the executive and its servants and to the judiciary (44), and that this area of discretionary power touches upon the average person to a much greater extent than that area governed by rigid rules.

There are an enormous number of laws, Federal, state, and local, touching on every conceivable area of human action, to which we are all subject. It is beyond the means of the executive authorities in all cases to enforce the bulk of them. For this reason, the most immediate agent of law enforcement, the policeman, is possessed of a great deal of discretionary power centering around when to enforce a particular law. In most cases, there appears to be no clear pattern as to when a certain law will be disregarded and when it will not be. We are all familiar with the case of traffic policemen warning a violator rather than writing a ticket or of the police officer who breaks up a loud argument or fight on the street and tells the participants to go home rather than arresting them for a breach of the peace. These examples could be multiplied a thousand-fold.

The President's Commission on Law Enforcement and Criminal Justice, in their report, noted the extensive discretionary powers accorded police. « The police are not accustomed to thinking of themselves as employees of an agency that much more often enforces laws administratively than by invoking the formal criminal process through arrest. Yet a decision by a policeman to order a sidewalk gathering to ' break it up ', or to take a delinquent youth home rather than formally charge him, is an administrative decision ... [The police] do not arrest all, or even most, offenders they know of. Among the factors accounting for this exercise of discretion are the volume of and the public desire for nonenforcement of many statutes and ordinances, the reluctance of many victims to complain and, most important, an entirely proper conviction by policemen that the invocation of criminal sanctions is too drastic a response to many offenses » (45).

---

(44) In *The Road to Serfdom*, Hayek writes that the rule of law « means that government in all its action is bound by rules fixed and announced beforehand-rules which make it possible to foresee with fair certainty how te authority will use its coercive powers in given circumstances and to plan one's individual affairs on the basis of this knowledge ». (Chicago, University of Chicago Press, 1944, p. 72). Kenneth Davis rightly contends that this statement is either an absurdity or an inadvertence, since the legislature, obviously, cannot be bound by rules fixed and announced beforehand. (*Discretionary Justice*, p. 32). What Hayek here means, I think, is that the legislature, if it is to act consistent with the rule of law, is limited to passing into law only fixed rules which then must be made known, and that the other branches of government are constrained to act only under such rules.

(45) *The Challenge of Crime in a Free Society*, Washington, D.C., Gov-

The discretionary power of the policeman, including the decision to arrest, extends even into areas where no crime is involved. For example, as Mr. Justice Douglas notes, « there is no crime known as ' suspicion '. Nor is there any federal crime known as ' holding for investigation '. Yet it is common in the District of Columbia to make arrests for the latter purpose. There were 7,367 so arrested in 1958, *all of whom were later released* » (46).

Even in instances where the statutes define certain crimes, these definitions can be so vague as to preclude prediction of whether an offense has been committed. For example, the District of Columbia statutes define a vagrant as, among other things, « any person wandering abroad and lodging ... in the open air and not giving a good account of himself », and « any person who wanders about the streets at late or unusual hours of the night without any visible or lawful business and not giving a good account of himself » (47). The California vagrancy statute reads in part, « every person (except a California Indian) without visible means of living who has the physical ability to work and who does not seek employment » is a vagrant (48). Although several similar statutes have been held unconstitutional by the courts (49), a number of equally vague laws concerning vagrancy are still on the books in a number of states.

---

ernment Printing Office, 1967, pp. 104, 106. It is interesting to note that the Commission report tends to stress the more beneficent aspects of police discretion rather than the possible dangers. Kenneth Davis has gone even further, remarking that « perhaps it is not too much to say that the essence of criminal justice lies in the exercise of discretionary power... » *Discretionary Justice*, p. 18. Davis devotes a good portion of his monograph to discussing the benefits which he feels accrue to society from endowing its judicial and administrative bodies with some measure of discretion. He points out that injustices often result from the application of rigid rules which are being enforced by someone lacking the power to modify them to make their application sensible to the particular case at hand. « When [discretionary power] is too narrow, justice may suffer from insufficient individualizing ». *Ibidem*, p. 52.

(46) WILLIAM O. DOUGLAS, « Vagrancy and Arrest on Suspicion », *Yale Law Journal*, LXX, November, 1960, p. 12. « The extent of arrests for no specific crime may be estimated when it showed that in 1960, local police departments reported 136,325 arrests on suspicion to the FBI ». SIDNEY H. ASCH, *Police Authority and the Rights of the Individual*, New York, Arco Publishing Co., Inc., 1967, p. 48.

(47) D. C. Code Ann., Section 22-3302 (Suppl. VIII 1960), quoted in Douglas, « Vagrancy and Arrest on Suspicion », p. 6, n. 26.

(48) Ca. Pen. Code, Section 647, quoted in ARTHUR SHERRY, « Vagrants, Rogues and Vagabonds—Old Concepts in Need of Revision », *California Law Review*, XLVII, October, 1960, 562, n. 38.

(49) Both the New York and Massachusetts statutes on vagrancy have been struck dows as unconstitutional on grounds of vagueness. See *Fenster v. Leary*, 20 N. Y. 2d 309, 229 N. E. 2d 426 (1967), and *Alegata v. Commonwealth*, 253 Mass. 287, 231 N. E. 2d 201 (Mass. 1967).

It is, further, a matter of dispute whether in many cases (generally those concerning a lower order of offenses) the decisions of the courts are any less discretionary than those of the policeman. How can one be sure at what point waiting for someone on a street corner becomes the crime of loitering? At what point does general liveliness at a party become a disturbance of the peace? At what point does acting an unusual way or taking unpopular views become an offense against public morals? In many such instances the difference between having committed a crime and having stayed within the law rests upon whether a policeman happens to feel like pressing charges. The « crime » of failing to disperse upon a declaration that a particular gathering is illegal apparently is committed only if a policeman decides to take you into custody. This problem is compounded by the fact that the lower courts, in dealing with minor offenses, are known to hold a strong presumption in favor of upholding policeman's decision unless there is overwhelming evidence contrary to the claims of the arresting officer concerning the situation at the time of the arrest (50).

Judicial discretion is, of course, not confined to minor infringemetns of the law. Judge-made law based upon reinterpretations of statute or the Constitution represents an important part of the legislative process and such changes in interpretation are almost impossible to predict. Lon Fuller has noted that a « criminal statute may be so drawn that, though its meaning is reasonably plain in nine cases out of ten, in the tenth case, where some special situation of fact arises, it may be so unclear as to give the particular defendant no real warning that what he was doing was criminal. This is especially likely to be the case where economic regulations are involved. The courts have generally assumed that in this kind of case they have no choice but to resolve the doubt, thus creating retrospective criminal law » (51).

I offer the following example as an instance where predictability of the ultimat decision by the courts is minimal. In 1964, the Supreme Court of California held, in *People v. Woody* (52), that the California statute prohibiting the possession of peyote was unconstitutional when applied to members of the Native American Church on the ground that it was an infringement of the First Amendment guarantee regarding the free exercise of religion. This decision was

---

(50)   « ... the tendency of the lower courts [is] to identify their mission with that of maintaining the morale of the police force ». Lon Fuller, *The Morality of Law*, p. 82.

(51)   *Ibidem*, p. 58.

(52)   61 Cal. 2d 716, 394 P. 2d 813, 40 Cal. Rptr. 69 (1964).

a surprising one. However, no encroachment on the First Amendment guarantee was found by the United States Fifth Circuit Court of Appeals when it affirmed the conviction of Dr. Timothy Leary for possession of marihuana in 1967. There the court held that there was a distinction between « the use of peyote in the limited *bona fide* religious ceremonies of the relatively small, unknown Native American Church », and « the private and personal use of marihuana by any person who claims he is using it as a religious practice » (53). As one legal authority has noted, the distinction drawn by the Fifth Circuit appears to contravene the Supreme Court's holding in *United States v. Seeger* that « belonging to an organized church or belief in a supreme being is not necessarily a prerequisite to the application of a guarantee of freedom of religion » (54). It is asking too much to have expected Dr. Leary, or anyone else for that matter, to have predicted, in light of the Woody and Seeger decisions, that possession of marihuana for personal, « religious » purposes would be held a crime (55).

I should like to deal with one more example of judicial discretion and the difficulty of predicting the law, which I take from a case involving obscenity law. Admittedly this is a particularly confused area of the law today, inasmuch as interpretations of the First Amendment guarantee of freedom of the press are undergoing rapid change. However, the example is still instructive since there are always some areas of the law undergoing radical reinterpretation by the courts at any given time and issues involved are usually of such far-reaching consequence that they affect the lives of most of us. In the case in point, the question concerns what we have the right to read.

When G. P. Putnam's Sons decided in 1963 to publish *Fanny Hill* (56) (under the title « John Cleland's Memoirs of a Woman of Pleasure »), there was no way of predicting whether the courts would consider the book obscene or entitled to the protection of the First Amendment. The publishers were first brought to trial in the New York Supreme Court, Special and Trial Term, New York

---

(53) *Leary v. United States*, 383 F. 2d 851 (5th Cir. 1967), at 861, n. 11.

(54) MARK S. DICHTER, « Marijuana and the Law : The Constitutional Challenges to Marijuana Laws in Light of the Social Aspects of Marijuana Use », *Villanova Law Review*, XIII (Summer, 1968), 860. See *United States v. Seeger*, 380 U.S. 163 (1965).

(55) Dr. Leary was sentenced to a thirty-year prison term and fined $ 40,000 for possession of less than one-half ounce of marihuana. MARK S. DICHTER, « Marijuana and the Law », p. 860.

(56) I am grateful to Mr. Allen Cadgene of the Yale Law School for having researched the facts of the Fanny Hill cases and for other helpful suggestions concerning this paper.

County (57), where a preliminary injunction against the distribution and sale of the book was issued in late July, 1963. In August, the book was held not obscene and its sale then became legal in New York. This decision was reversed in a *per curiam* opinion of the Supreme Court of New York, Appellate Division (58), by a vote of three to two, in February, 1964, at which time it again became illegal to sell the book in New York. The case was again appealed, to the Court of Appeals of New York (59). There *Fanny Hill* was held to be entitled to the protection of the First Amendment by a four to three vote. This decision was reached in mid-July, 1964. Thus, in New York State, it was illegal to sell *Fanny Hill* from July 26, 1963 (when the temporary injunction was issued) until August 23, 1963 (when the book was held not obscene by the trial judge), legal to sell it from August 23, 1963, to February 27, 1964 (when the lower court decision was reversed by the Appellate Division), illegal to sell it from February 27, 1964, to July 10, 1964 (at which time the book was held not obscene by the Court of Appeals), and legal to sell it from July 10, 1964, on. The case was heard by thirteen judges in New York, seven of whom found the book entitled to First Amendment protection, six of whom found it obscene.

In Massachusetts, *Fanny Hill* was held obscene by the Superior Court, Suffolk County, and this decision was affirmed in a four to three decision by the Supreme Court of Massachusetts (60) in April, 1965.

Finally, in an appeal of the Massachusetts decision to the United States Supreme Court (61), the Court held the book not obscene in a six to three decision. Besides the thirteen judges in New York, eight Massachusetts judges had ruled on the book, five finding it obscene, three finding that it was not. In addition, the book had been held obscene by a lower court in New Jersey (62). If we include the Justices of the Supreme Court, thirty-one judges ruled on the work. Fifteen thought the book obscene, sixteen thought that it was not. All were more or less trying to make their decision consistent with the standards for judging obscenity set down by the majority of the High Court in 1957 in the *Roth* decision (63) (except-

---

(57) *Larkin v. G.P. Putnam's Sons, et. al.*, 48 Misc. 2d 28, 242 N.Y.S. 2d 746 (1963).

(58) 20 A.D. 2d 702, 247 N.Y.S. 2d 275 (1964).

(59) 40 N.Y. 2d 399, 252 N.Y.S. 2d 71, 200 N.E. 2d 760 (1964).

(60) *Attorney General v. A Book Named ‹John Cleland's Memoirs of a Woman of Pleasure ›*, 349 Mass. 69, 206 N.E. 2d 403 (1965).

(61) 383 U.S. 413 (1966).

(62) *G.P. Putnam's Sons v. Calissi*, 86 N.J. Super. 82, 205 A. 2d 913 (1964).

(63) *Roth v. United States*, 354 U.S. 476 (1957).

ing Mr. Justice Black and Mr. Justice Douglas, who argued against all obscenity censorship in their dissenting opinion in *Roth*).

It is no surprise that Mr. Justice Harlan, in his dissent in the *Fanny Hill* case, was prompted to write that « no stable approach to the obscenity problem has yet been devised by this court » (64). Between June, 1957, when the Supreme Court handed down its decision in *Roth v. United States,* and March, 1966, the Supreme Court made ten major obscenity decisions. These ten decisions, as Raymond Sebastian has pointed out, had given rise to no fewer than forty-five different opinions by the Justices of the Court (65).

On the same day as the Fanny Hill decision, the Court ruled in the case of *Ginzburg v. United States* (66). The Ginzburg decision introduced yet another uncertainty into the question of obscenity statutes. Besides previously designated « standards » by which a book must be judged in determining whether it is obscene, a new standard, « pandering », is added. Pandering in itself, the Court held, does not constitute an offense against the obscenity statute, but evidence that the seller placed emphasis upon the prurient appeal of the material for sale, when the material is already of a highly erotic nature may be decisive. Mr. Justice Black wrote in his dissenting opinion in this case that « not even the most learned judge, much less a layman, is capable of knowing in advance ... whether certain material comes within the area of ' obscenity ' as that term is confused by the Court today » (67).

The law of obscenity is just one of the many areas presently undergoing reinterpretation by the courts and where predictability of the outcome of any case is limited. Law and procedures relating to arrest, search and seizure and the right to counsel, laws touching on the question of privacy of the individual, laws which have possible implications with respect to racial discrimination, libel laws and their relation to freedom of the press, are all areas in which the law is being radically altered by the courts and in which newly established legal precedents are being formed .

Another way in which the predictability of the law is limited involves all those cases falling within the imprecise border areas

---

(64) 383 U.S. 413, at 455 (1966).
(65) « Obscenity and the Supreme Court: Nine Years of Confusion », *Stanford Law Review*, XIX, November, 1966, 167.
(66) 383 U. S. 463 (1966).
(67) At 480-81. The question of obscenity law is further confounded by the Supreme Court decision in *Stanley v. Georgia*, 394 U.S. 557 (1969), which concerns the relationship between the individual's right to privacy and the possession of obscene matter. For a discussion of this case and its effect on the tangle of obscenity law today, see AL KATZ, « Privacy and Pornography: Stanley v. Georgia », *The Supreme Court Review* (1969), pp. 203-17.

of a law's applicability. Much litigation arises through genuine dispute over whether a particular law is, in fact, applicable to a given situation. Is a doctor who is unaware of the latest advances in his field guilty of negligence when his patient dies as the result of the doctor's ignorance of a life-saving drug? Is a man who misses a road sign and, as a result, drives up some private lane guilty of trespass? It might be argued that almost all cases, at least to some extent, concern themselves with questions of law as well as of fact. The judge's task would be a fairly easy one if it were confined to determining the admissibility of certain evidence or to deciding on the truth or falsity of evidence presented to the court. But he is further faced with ascertaining law in each case. If decisions concerning questions of law could be predicted with a good measure of certainty, there would be little disagreement among trained lawyers over such questions. The very existence of appellate courts belies this. Professor Llewellyn remarks, with reference to his treatise on appeals, that « the *rules of law, alone*, do not, because they cannot, decide any appealed case *which has been worth an appeal and a response*... I hope ... that the present material may make permanently untenable any notion that creativeness — choice or creation of effective policy by appellate judges — is limited to the crucial case, the unusual case, the borderline case, the case that calls for lasting conscious worry. My material aims to put beyond challenge that such creativeness is instead everyday stuff, almost every-case stuff, and need not be conscious at all » (68). To the extent that

---

(68) KARL N. LLEWELLYN, *The Common Law Tradition: Deciding Appeals* (Little, Brown and Company, 1960), pp. 189, 190.   Professor Llewellyn has argued that the sort of certainty which follows from strict obedience to a set of rules was a hallmark of a particular period of American appellate judicial history, a period for which he has little sympathy. It was a period, he writes, « in which the appellate judges *sought* to do their deciding without reference to much except the rules, *sought* to eliminate the impact of sense, as an intrusion, and *sought* to write their opinions as if wisdom (in contrast to logic) were hardly a decent doctrine of a responsible appellate court.   I call this way of work the Formal Style; ... 'The Law', as seen and understood in the Formal period, tended in lawyers' minds more and more to coincide until it substantially coalesced with 'the law' as discussed by lawyers in court: the *mere rules* of law.   And in action, the whole drive of the Formal Style was toward making sure, so far as might be, that it should be just those phrased rules which did do the deciding ». *Ibidem*, pp. 5-6, 186.

This « Formal Style » has been supplanted, Llewellyn claims, by a more creative, just style of adjudication which provides a different sort of certainty, a « psychological » certainty *after* the event that the decision arrived at was correct.   « The *certainty* in question is that certainty *after the event* which makes ordinary men and lawyers *recognize as soon as they see the result* that however hard it has been to reach, it is the right result... In such a world there is no lack of office for the court, nor for the great creator on the bench ; no lack of room, either for litigants and lawyers. And the consequent

judges are creative, of course, the amount of « certainty » or predictability of any particular decision is reduced.

It is, I think, clear that our legal system permits, at times of
necessity even encourages, extensive discretionary powers to the executive and the judiciary, even in the criminal law, an area where
it might at first be supposed to be minimal. Kenneth Davis has
noted in this regard: « All the rules that call for punishment can
be nullified by any one of five sets of discretionary power—the
discretion of the police not to arrest, the discretion of the prosecutor
not to prosecute or to trade a lesser charge for a plea of guilty,
the discretion of the judge in favor of suspended sentence or pro-
bation, the discretion of the parole officer to release, the discretion
of the executive to pardon » (69).

We have yet to consider one argument bearing upon the law's
certainty which is raised by Professor Leoni. Assume a body of
written laws, precisely worded and unambiguous, certain of enforcement and allowing a minimum of judicial discretion concerning
either its application or the penalties imposed for its transgression.
In such a case, « we are always ' certain ' as far as the literal
content of each rule is concerned at any given moment, but we are
never certain that tomorrow we shall still have the rules we have
today » (70). This, of course, becomes increasingly applicable as the
amount of legislation in a society increases (71).

IV.

One of Hayek's main purposes in setting up the various criteria
of the rule of law is to build a theoretical framework within which
individual freedom is maximized. However, this framework seems to
allow for the concentration in and use of power by the state which
can result in a system the nature of which aims at the overthrow
of personal liberty. The limitations on the formal aspects of legislation as they are interpreted by Hayek, and which together form his
concept of the rule of law, appear to allow so much power to govern-

---

' certainty ' of outcome is the truest certainty legal work can have, a certainty
reached not by deduction but by dynamics, moving in step with human need
yet along and out of the lines laid out by history of the Law and of the
Culture ; the certainty, then, not of logical conclusion from a static *universal*,
but of that *reasonable regularity* which is law's proper interplay with life ».
Ibidem, pp. 185-86.

    (69) *Discretionary Justice,* p. 18.
    (70) *Freedom and the Law,* p. 76.
    (71) We are here dealing with the idea of the « certainty » of the law
as a criterion of the *form* law must take. It can, of course, be considered as
a *substantive* restriction on legislation (« long-run certainty »), but this seems
to be going beyond what Hayek is saying.

ment that freedom as we commonly understand it rests on a foundation no more secure than government good will.

Hayek rejects any special set of substantive limitations on
government action, relying exclusively on the formal restrictions
imposed by the rule of law: « There is a great variety possible in
the particular content of these rules [defining the area of government activity] and the classical formulae about 'private property'
and the ' freedom of contract' do not tell us much about what the
content of these rules ought to be. The important point, however,
is merely that they should be stated in terms of general rules, that
the sphere in which the individual can follow his own will and the
conditions and the manner in which he can be coerced shall be
clearly known » (72).

The rule of law requires no more than that legislation be characterized by equality, generality, and certainty. These characteristics, as defined by Hayek, either cannot or do not act as any real
check on the power of government. It is true that there are certain
limitations imposed by the rule of law on the form the law can
take. Administrative orders directly commanding specific actions
might be reduced and citizens would have the right to demand that
what they consider extra-legal administrative actions be reviewed
by an independent court system (73). But these restrictions are of

---

(72) *The Political Ideal of the Rule of Law*, p. 44.

(73) The rule of law, as Hayek presents it, would not preclude far-
reaching government regulation of the economy. It would simply require that
such regulation take the form of more or less fixed rules rather than direction
via administrative bodies armed with extensive discretionary powers. Even
here it is not certain whether the rule of law as postulated would prohibit
the legislature from delegating its authority to administrative agencies provided that meaningful standards governing administrative policy-making are incorporated into the statute and provided that judicial review of administrative
decisions is allowed. « It is evident, Hayek writes, « that not all acts of
government can be bound by fixed rules and that at every stage of the governmental hierarchy considerable discretion must be granted to the subordinate
agencies ». But this discretionary power « must be controlled by the possibility
of a review of the substance of the decision by an independent court ». « What
is required under the rule of law », he continues, « is that a court should have
the power to decide whether the law provided for a particular action that an
authority has taken ». *Constitution of Liberty*, pp. 213, 214.

That the rule of law is not inconsistent with government regulation of
the economy is suggested by Donald B. Molteno. « ... the fundamentals of the
rule of law are capable of adaptation to the new social and economic conditions... They have largely been embodied in legislation in England and in
the U.S.A., thereby reconciling the inevitable—and largely beneficial—extension
of the powers of the Executive, for the purposes of economic collectivism and
of the Welfare State, with the fundamentals of the rule of law ». *The Rules
Behind the Rule of Law*, Pietermaritzburg, University of Natal Press (Published for the Students Representative Council of the University of Natal), 1965,
p. 10.

a small order of magnitude when compared with the area of allowable governmental involvement in the ordinary affairs of the individual.

In light of defining such concepts as « freedom » and « rights » in terms of the rule of law, those who feel that certain legislation is restrictive of freedom are left in somewhat of a theoretical bind. For, although it might be shown that a particular restriction on individual behavior would prove detrimental to society, so long as the restriction meets the criteria Hayek sets down for the rule of law, such a restriction could not be held to be an invasion of individual freedom. Once consistency with the rule of law is taken as the sole basis for determining legitimate state action, we can no longer bring to bear a discussion of the state's interference with personal liberty (74).

On the basis of the arguments presented in this paper, then, there appear to be two main difficulties posed by Hayek's theory of the rule of law.

First, Hayek's concepts of « freedom » and of « rights » are logically tied to the rule of law rather than being definitionally independent. As a result they tend, in these restricted senses, to lose much of their value as political concepts and to unreasonably limit the range of political discourse.

Second, the rule of law, whose presence is perhaps a *necessary* condition for a free society, is offered as a *sufficient* condition.

Since Hayek's notion of the rule of law, the keystone of his conceptual political system, is open to criticism on several counts, most particularly in that it permits certain seemingly peaceful, non-violent actions of individuals to be classified as coercive and, further, that it excludes from the category of coercive activity numerous actions which we should ordinarily call coercive, we conclude that Hayek's account of the nature of coercion, rights and freedom requires philosophical refinement before it can fully serve as a valid account of the nature of political behavior.

RONALD HAMOWY

---

(74) Hayek himself acknowledges this restriction on political discussion: « ... so long as [government measures] are compatible with the rule of law, tney cannot be rejected out of hand as government intervention but must be examined in each instance from the viewpoint of expediency ». *Constitution of Liberty*, p. 221.

[9]

The *Journal of Libertarian Studies*, Vol. VI, No. 2 (Spring 1982)

The Hayekian Model of Government in an Open Society*

by Ronald Hamowy

Department of History, University of Alberta

F. A. Hayek, whose most important work in the area of political and legal theory, *The Constitution of Liberty,* was published in 1960,[1] has, since that time, followed up his original analysis of the structure of a free society in a three-volume work, appearing under the general title *Law, Legislation, and Liberty.*[2] I shall here concern myself with the third of these volumes (published in 1979) and, specifically, with a brief discussion of his model of an ideal constitution. I should like to make one point clear at the outset. By concentrating on this area of Hayek's thought, as I have done in the past, I do not mean to denigrate his insights respecting the shortcomings of socialist economic and political doctrine or his contributions to an analysis of the modern democratic state. Indeed, I have deliberately chosen those areas of Hayek's work where he has attempted to suggest alternatives to the current orthodoxy. I realize that I might be doing the totality of his work an injustice by criticizing that which is most difficult to accomplish and consequently easiest to find fault with. But I think it of pressing importance to point out what I believe to be fatal errors in Hayek's argument, lest we end up accepting a system no better than the one we now have under the mistaken notion that we have thereby enlarged the area of individual autonomy and personal freedom.

The major feature, and doubtless the most novel, of Hayek's constitution is his proposal for a separation of function between the two houses of what appears to be a bicameral legislature. Hayek observes:

> When...at the end of the seventeenth century the exclusive right of the Commons over "money bills" was definitely conceded by the House of Lords, the latter, as the highest court in the country, still retained ultimate control of the development of the rules of common law. What would have been more natural than that, in conceding to the Commons sole control of the current conduct of government, the second chamber should have in return claimed the exclusive right to alter by statute the enforceable rules of just conduct?[3]

---

*The original version of this paper was delivered at the "Interdisciplinary Seminar on the Contributions of F. A. Hayek" held in New York City in May 1982 and sponsored by the Institute for Humane Studies, Menlo Park.

Now, I find nothing particularly "natural" in this division. The Commons never regarded itself as solely a taxing and administrative agency of government, a kind of large executive committee with the added power of raising revenue, but as the legislature of the nation. This meant, until the nineteenth century, that for the most part it confined itself to levying taxes, raising armies and navies, and deciding questions of war and peace. To a lesser degreee, it enacted such statutes governing the lives of British subjects as were at the time thought necessary and desirable. Most such rules, however, were laid down, not by the legislature, but by the courts and, in an earlier period, by the executive, through orders-in-council. The extensive intervention in all aspects of private and public life that now describes the legislative function was unknown to the British Parliament until after the Napoleonic wars. At that point, it was natural that the Commons, having control over the government's purse and having effectively absorbed the executive power, should demand that it be the body that determined which rules were enacted.

The division that Hayek suggests is so artificial as to be unworkable. If the lower house were to confine itself to questions of revenue and expenditure, while the upper house possessed sole authority to determine the rules of conduct, ultimate control would eventually fall to that body empowered to collect and disperse funds. Every law requires expenditures for its enforcement and every money bill is passed towards some end. If the lower house were to tax and allocate huge sums towards some project, are we to suppose that such a measure would not have extensive implications respecting the behavior of citizens? Indeed, the power to tax and to spend involves the power to alter behavior, in the same way a fine punishes and a grant rewards. The effect of such a division of powers would be (and, indeed, was) to place in the hands of the lower house all substantive power to govern; for, while it could pick and choose which rules of conduct enacted by the upper house it wished to enforce, it could further enforce its own rules via the taxing power. The situation that would prevail would—in its essentials—differ very little from parliamentary government as it now exists.

Far more significant in terms of a theory of freedom is not the creation of an upper chamber itself but the basic principles which are to govern the specific rules of conduct it may enact. These rules, Hayek writes,

> should be intended to apply to an indefinite number of unknown future instances, to serve the formation and preservation of an abstract order whose concrete contents were unforeseeable, but not the achievement of particular concrete purposes, and finally to exclude all provisions intended or known to affect principally particular identifiable individuals and groups.[4]

The first criterion, "intended to apply to an indefinite number of unknown future instances," appears to be a restatement of Hayek's rule of generality. The second, that rules should only "serve the formation and preservation of an abstract order whose concrete contents were unforeseeable, but not the achievement of particular concrete purposes," strikes me as almost impossible to fulfill. *All* statute law is enacted to achieve certain concrete purposes, whether it be as broad as prohibiting theft or as narrow as proscribing entry into a specific defense installation without authorization. What would it mean to enact a law that did not aim at achieving a concrete purpose? If Hayek here means that all rules of conduct should also aim at achieving some abstract purpose, such as "justice," or "fairness," or such like, then all laws, no matter how invasive, can be regarded as falling into such categories as well. "Social equality," "order," "public peace," "national well-being," "social harmony," are all rubrics under which specific rules might fall. Frankly, I am unsure of what Hayek here means and I cannot imagine the courts of any nation struggling with the notion of whether or not a resolution of the legislature possessed this property.

The third criterion is stunning in its implications. That all legitimate rules "exclude all provisions intended or known to affect principally particular identifiable individrals or groups" is — without question — the strongest protection against government intrusion. Indeed, it is so strong that it appears to defeat the purpose of Hayek's upper house altogether; for, if no laws may avail before the courts should they violate this criterion, then the legislature is logically prevented from ever enacting a prohibition in reaction to certain conduct previously allowed. Since the provisions of all such laws would at least be *intended* to affect identifiable individuals or groups, namely, those engaged in the specific activity constituting the subject of the prohibition, then the courts, under Hayek's criteria of judicial review, would be bound to nullify all such acts. But, then, why have an upper chamber (a "Legislative Assembly," as Hayek calls it) at all? If its compass is limited to setting down the basic rules of conduct and never to enlarge this body of rules in response to specific events, then the legislature need never meet.

When Hayek observes that this criterion "would by itself achieve all and more than the traditional Bills of Rights were meant to secure,"[5] he appears to be aware of the far-reaching nature of this restriction on legislation. However, these limitations on the form law may take also seem to contravene Hayek's intentions regarding an ongoing legislative body. He writes of the freedoms guaranteed in the American Bill of Rights that, for example, "freedom of speech does not of course mean that we are free to slander, libel, deceive, incite to crime or cause a panic by false alarm, etc."[6] Now these limitations, as Hayek is aware, are the product of judicial decisions and not of a legislative assembly. But Hayek views one of the functions of the upper chamber as passing into law the "not yet articulated decisions" implicit in the courts' decisions. If so, he has gutted the very restriction on legislative authority that might have proven most effective, by reducing his criterion (that no law may be enacted that, either by intent or knowledge, principally affects identifiable individuals) to some vague generality, and, in the process, he has made the upper chamber a creature of the courts. In any case, what would be the point of such laws? Legislatures are already bound by judicial decisions; they would hardly pass into law statutes that the courts would void. Why have a legislature that confines itself to nothing more than enacting general rules which have been previously set down by the courts and, by that very fact, are already binding?

But no sooner has Hayek set down these restrictions on the nature of the rules that his upper chamber may enact than he removes them by observing:

> The Constitution should. . . guard against the eventuality of the Legis-
> lative Assembly becoming wholly inactive by providing that, while it
> should have exclusive powers to lay down general rules of just conduct,
> this power might devolve temporarily to the Governmental Assembly
> [the lower house] if the former did not respond within a reasonable
> period to a notice given by government that some rules should be laid
> down on a particular question.[7]

Thus, having first specified criteria that would have provided workable limits on what can be legislated, we have returned full circle to a legislature empowered to enact laws on virtually any particular issue.

The lower house, what Hayek calls the Governmental Assembly, would, we are told, resemble existing parliamentary bodies, in that the executive and the day-to-day legislative power would be combined in the same hands. With respect to its orders, it would be bound by the general rules of conduct set down by the upper house. In other words, it would be bound by the Constitution, by establishing rules of just conduct, and by the courts' various interpretative rulings. How exactly this differs in principle from the situation now prevailing in the legislatures of parliamentary democracies is unclear. Hayek states that the lower house would be "complete master in organizing the apparatus of government and deciding about the use of material and personal resources entrusted to the government."[8] But, if it is to have any legislative function at all, it is the lower house itself that is empowered to determine which and how many resources are to be entrusted to government. Indeed, this is Hayek's whole point in classifying the lower house as a legislature and not simply a huge executive committee. But if it is a legislature, then how can it be bound by the *same* rules of conduct that apply to all citizens? Individuals cannot extort wealth from others under authority of government. In what sense, then, is the lower chamber obligated to conform to the rules of conduct enacted by the upper house? Hayek does not say that there are special rules it must obey, but that it must obey the *same* rules as apply to all citizens. He is here left in a quandary. Either the lower house is nothing more than an executive authority, and Hayek's model provides no body authorized to tax and to determine how the wealth it controls is to be spent, or it is in fact a legislature, with the power to raise and expend funds and to pass laws respecting the conduct of government. But, by the nature of the fact that legislatures pass laws, they cannot be bound by the rules that limit other members of society. Private citizens cannot employ force to execute their dictates, while governments are defined by their power to do exactly that.

There is yet a further problem. Many laws fall within the jurisdictions of both Hayek's chambers. How are we to determine when a law constitutes a "general rule of just conduct" and when it pertains to "the conduct of government"? What of a law regulating access to the streets? Or a statute providing that all actions of the executive be kept secret? What chamber determines who is to be enfranchised? And, finally, why have two chambers at all, if, between one or the other, there are no limits on what laws may be enacted?

The constitution itself neither solves these jurisdictional problems nor, more importantly, does it contain any substantive limitations on the powers of the legislature, regardless of which of its two houses might have jurisdiction. The constitution, we are told,

> ought to consist wholly of organizational rules, and need touch on substantive law in the sense of universal rules of just conduct only by stating the general attributes such laws must possess in order to entitle government to use coercion for their enforcement.[9]

Thus, despite his elaborate and complex schema of government, in the end Hayek returns to his original restrictions on the formal qualities of rules of conduct that he first laid down in his *Constitution of Liberty* as the only protection against arbitrary government.

I would suggest that this approach has been discredited and that it has been shown that no purely formal criteria of the sort Hayek has offered, that is, that all laws be general, predictable, and certain, can effectively curtail the extent of governmental intrusion, all the structural changes notwithstanding.[10] You cannot make a silk purse out of a sow's ear and you cannot limit the power of government by tinkering with its structure. Only by placing unequivocal, substantive limitations on what laws may be enacted would it be possible to control the areas in which the legislature may intervene, and, even then, one would still require a vigilant and suspicious judiciary to ride herd on the legislature. The decisions concerning which areas must be off limits to the legislature can be made only on the basis of a theory of rights, which logically precedes a theory of government. This is a conception that Hayek, for some reason, fails to come to grips with and it is nowhere more evident than in his discussion of the emergency powers for which his model constitution provides. Hayek is so wedded to the notion that rights are a product of good government — and not anterior to it — that when good government is endangered, he is quite prepared to sacrifice the lesser value, the citizen's rights. Hayek observes:

> When an external enemy threatens, when rebellion or lawless violence
> has broken out, or a natural catastrophe requires quick action by what-
> ever means can be secured, powers of compulsory organization, which
> normally nobody possesses, must be granted to somebody. Like an
> animal in flight from mortal danger society may in such situations have
> to suspend temporarily even vital functions on which in the long run its
> existence depends if it is to escape destruction.[11]

Now, what is being preserved here? Surely not the rights of citizens, but
the government, as it is constituted, and from whom one's rights flow. Else,
why go through the trouble of preserving it at such cost? But even allowing
this, why is it necessary to provide for powers which no society calling itself
free would tolerate? It is particularly surprising that Hayek, whose contributions to social theory are predicated on the notion that ordered social
arrangements do not require an orderer, should fall victim to the idea that
in times of domestic crisis it becomes necessary to bestow authoritarian
powers on a leader. If what appear to be the simplest social patterns are
beyond the capacity of government to manipulate without seriously damag-
ing the spontaneously generated order created by the free interactions of
individuals, then why would this not hold true as these patterns become
increasingly complex? Why is a government endowed with extraordinary
powers of compulsion better able to cope with a natural catastrophe than
the unfettered forces of the market and the charity of free men? And why
should the political mechanism be granted a warrant to exercise coercion
unrestrained by its usual checks in cases of lawless violence? Any government already possesses ample authority to deal with those who commit
violent acts. Extra powers would serve no purpose unless they were used to
also coerce the innocent, such as occurred when all Americans of Japanese
origin were interned during World War II.

Hayek's whole model of government, emergency powers and all, is conceived in the mistaken notion that the political mechanism in society can
itself be made subject to its own orders. However, the fact is that one cannot bind a legislature by a higher legislature and thus compel the lower
house to obey rules applicable to everyone else. Legislatures, to the extent
they legislate, are not like private citizens, since their instruments of compli-
ance are not suasion and exchange but main force. And even if Hayek is
right and the circle can be squared, what difference would it really make?
After all, what binds the higher legislature? Certainly not the constitution,
which places no substantive limitations on which law may be enacted.

In his *Counter-Revolution of Science,* Hayek quotes Saint-Simon as
having said: "I cannot conceive of association without government by someone."[12] Yet Hayek's penetrating insights into the anti-libertarian foundations of positivist social theory seem difficult to reconcile with his own
suggestions on the constitutional structure of a free society. For at least two
hundred years, social philosophers have known that association does not
need government, that, indeed, government is destructive of association.

And no modern thinker has written more incisively on this issue than has Hayek.

The central problem that confronts modern libertarian political theory is not the development of formal criteria respecting the rules government may enact and the political structure that ensures that these criteria will be met. It is, rather, the problem of how to place limits on the *number* and *kinds* of intrusions in which government may engage and how to ensure that it will confine itself to these limits. That laws meeting Hayek's criteria might make government less arbitrary does not really matter in the end if the government will be no less invasive and if men will be no freer.

NOTES

1. F. A. Hayek, *The Constitution of Liberty* (Chicago: University of Chicago Press, 1960).
2. Hayek, *Law, Legislation, and Liberty,* vol. 1, *Rules and Order* (Chicago: University of Chicago Press, 1973); vol. 2, *The Mirage of Social Justice* (Chicago: University of Chicago Press, 1976); vol. 3, *The Political Order of a Free People* (Chicago: University of Chicago Press, 1979).
3. Hayek, *The Political Order of a Free People,* p. 106.
4. *Ibid.,* p. 109.
5. *Ibid.,* p. 110.
6. *Ibid.*
7. *Ibid.,* p. 116.
8. *Ibid.,* p. 119.
9. *Ibid.,* p. 122.
10. Among the many criticisms respecting Hayek's contention that the rule of law is a sufficient condition for a free society, see especially: Ronald Hamowy, "Freedom and the Rule of Law in F. A. Hayek," *Il Politico* 36 (1971):349-77, and a revised version of this article, "Law and the Liberal Society: F. A. Hayek's Constitution of Liberty," *Journal of Libertarian Studies* 2 (Winter 1978):287-97; Joseph Raz, "The Rule of Law and Its Virtue," *Law Quarterly Review* 93 (April 1977):185-211, reprinted in R. L. Cunningham, ed., *Liberty and the Rule of Law* (College Station, Tex.: Texas A & M University Press, 1979), pp. 3-21; John N. Gray, "F. A. Hayek on Liberty and Tradition," *Journal of Libertarian Studies* 4 (Spring 1980):119-37; and Murray N. Rothbard, *The Ethics of Liberty* (Atlantic Highlands, N.J.: Humanities Press, 1982), pp. 219-28.
11. Hayek, *The Political Order of a Free People,* p. 124.
12. Hayek, *The Counter-Revolution of Science: Studies in the Abuse of Reason* (New York: The Free Press of Glencoe, 1955), p. 127.

[10]

F. A. HAYEK AND THE COMMON LAW
Ronald Hamowy

One of the most significant insights into the history of Anglo-American law offered by F. A. Hayek concerns the superiority of common over statute law in framing a free society.

Hayek's Legal Theory

English common law, like much medieval law, Hayek maintained, reflected the underlying notion that law was not so much created as uncovered and that its principles were identical to the fundamental canons of justice upon which all free societies rest.[1] It was this view of law that predominated in England until the 15th and 16th centu-

---

Cato Journal, Vol. 23. No. 2 (Fall 2003). Copyright © Cato Institute. All rights reserved.

Ronald Hamowy is Professor Emeritus of Intellectual History at the University of Alberta. An earlier version of this essay was delivered as the F. A. Hayek Memorial Lecture at the Mises Institute, Auburn, Alabama, in March 2002.

[1] Hayek's is by no means the only argument offered in defense of the common law. In 1973, Richard Posner, one of the nation's most prolific legal scholars, maintained that the legal rules that emerged from the common law courts, by virtue of relying on precedent, are more efficient—where efficiency is understood as wealth-maximizing—than are the enactments of a legislative body and that they in turn promote social efficiency. Since that time there have been numerous attempts to corroborate this claim, among the most notable those by William Landes and Posner (1987) and by George Priest (1978). Robert Cooter and Lewis Kornhauser (1980: 139) have observed that arguments justifying the common law as more efficient have taken three forms: first, that common law judges in their decisions actively seek efficiency; second, that it is highly likely that inefficient legal rules will be litigated more often than will efficient rules; and, third, that litigants who are likely to benefit from an efficient rule will invest more in litigating their cases than will those who favor inefficient rules. The literature on the relation between the common law and efficiency is capably summarized in Gillian Hadfield (1992). As interesting and valuable as this literature is, however, it is irrelevant to the subject of this study.

It should be emphasized that these arguments supporting the common law on grounds of efficiency are in no way reiterations of Hayek's earlier argument. Hayek maintained that, at least before the 17th century, the common law, for a variety of reasons set forth in this study, was crucial in contributing to England's comparative freedom and served as a barrier against the arbitrary power of the monarch. Hayek's arguments in favor of the common law have very little, if anything, to do with the efficiency of the common law and nothing whatever to do with questions of public choice nor whether the decisions of the common law courts were Pareto optimal. His principal concern was to offer a theory of what political

241

ries, when for the first time the European nation states sought to use legislation to effect specific policies.[2] As Hayek maintains (1973: 83):

> Until the discovery of Aristotle's *Politics* in the thirteenth century and the reception of Justinian's code in the fifteenth . . . Western Europe passed through . . . [an] epoch of nearly a thousand years when law was . . . regarded as something given independently of human will, something to be discovered, not made, and when the conception that law could be deliberately made or altered seemed almost sacrilegious.[3]

The reason why England, unlike the continental countries, did not develop a highly centralized absolute monarchy in the 16th and 17th centuries, he argues, was its distinctive system of legal rules and procedures. "What prevented such development," writes Hayek (1973: 84–85), "was the deeply entrenched tradition of a common law that was not conceived as the product of anyone's will but rather as a barrier to all power, including that of the king—a tradition which Sir Edward Coke was to defend against King James I and his Chancellor, Sir Francis Bacon, and which Sir Matthew Hale brilliantly restated at the end of the seventeenth century in opposition to Thomas Hobbes."

Indeed, according to Hayek, all early conceptions of law took this form, that law was unalterably given and that while legislation might attempt to purify the law of its accumulated corruptions it could not go beyond this to make completely new law. Thus, the great early lawgivers, those semimythic figures of which early civilizations

---

and legal institutions are consistent with a free and open society, and it is within this context that he singled out the common law—that is, a body of law based primarily on custom and undergoing change through slow evolution—as an essential element of early English liberty. His discussion does not concern itself with questions of efficiency nor is this justification as it touches on the structure of law relevant to his thesis. Indeed, not to distinguish between these two clearly distinct reasons for supporting the common law constitutes the pons asinorum of scholarship bearing on Hayek's work.

If the arguments offered by Posner and others supporting the comparative efficiency of common law judgments are justified, however, this might well account for why the common law courts proved as successful as they proved in the end to be.

[2]Hayek's discussions of the common law are scattered throughout his writings on political philosophy but are dealt with at some length in "The Origins of the Rule of Law" (Hayek 1960:162–75) and "The Changing Concept of Law" (Hayek 1973:72–93).

[3]Elsewhere Hayek (1960:163) writes: "This medieval view, which is profoundly important as background for modern developments, though completely accepted perhaps only during the early Middle Ages, was that 'the state cannot itself create or make law, and of course as little abolish or violate law, because this would mean to abolish justice itself, it would be absurd, a sin, a rebellion against God who alone creates law.' For centuries it was recognized doctrine that kings or any other human authority could only declare or find the existing law, or modify abuses that had crept in, and not create law. Only gradually, during the later Middle Ages, did the conception of deliberate creation of new law—legislation as we know it—come to be accepted."

boasted, among them Ur-Nammu, Hammurabi, Solon, Lykurgus, and the authors of the Roman Twelve Tables, did not set down new law but rather codified what the law was and had always been (Hayek 1973: 81). The law, as originally understood, stood above and separate from the will of the civil magistrate and bound both ruler and ruled. This notion of law as residing in the unwritten rules that governed social interaction in the community was particularly true of England, where, Hayek contends, the ordinances of the Norman and Angevin monarchs played a more muted role in shaping social regulation and where the law administered by the king's courts had its origins in the judicial articulation of preexisting rules and practices that were common to the community.

As cases were brought before the common law courts, judges sought precedents for their decisions in the principles that had been laid down in earlier cases. This doctrine of *stare decisis* bound judges to apply similar principles in analogous cases. However, this development of the common law, Hayek noted, did not entail that it remained static and unchanging. The law did indeed change, through its application to new circumstances and through variations in interpretation that emerged in specific legal decisions. Common law thus evolved over time as judge-made law, the product of countless judicial decisions each having a specific end in view but the whole body of which reflected no deliberate intention or plan. Like language, common law formed a spontaneously generated arrangement, the product of human action but not of human design (Hayek 1973: 81).

The reason why England was the object of such great admiration by Europeans in the 18th century, according to Hayek (1973: 85), was because the law administered in its courts was the common law, which existed, he argues, "independently of anyone's will and at the same time binding upon and developed by the independent courts; a law with which parliament only rarely interfered and, when it did, mainly only to clear up doubtful points within a given body of law." While this division of powers was erroneously attributed by Montesquieu to the separation of the executive from the legislature, it would be more correct to claim, Hayek concludes, it was "not because the 'legislature' alone made law, but because it did *not*; because the law was determined by courts independent of the power which organized and directed government, the power namely of what was misleadingly called the 'legislature.'"

Hayek's characterization of the common law as an institutional bulwark against the depredations of the Stuart monarchs is not dissimilar to that offered by J. G. A. Pocock in his *The Ancient Constitution and the Feudal Law*, where he argues that the legal rules under which Englishmen operated had their origins in ancient custom, not statute, and took their form through a process of evolution over many centuries. Pocock (1987: 46) maintains that it is this aspect of English political history that provided the parliamentarians the legal principles with which they armed themselves in their struggles with the Crown:

> What occurred was that belief in the antiquity of the common law encouraged belief in the existence of the ancient constitution, reference to which was constantly made, precedents, maxims and principles from which were constantly alleged, and which was constantly asserted to be in some way immune from the king's prerogative action; and discussion in these terms formed one of the century's chief modes of political argument. Parliamentary debates and pamphlet controversies involving the law or the constitution were almost invariably carried on either wholly or partially in terms of an appeal to the past made in this way.

All the leading 17th-century British lawyers sympathetic to the parliamentary cause embraced the view that the common law stood as the great protector of prescriptive rights and of parliamentary government. As the fundamental law of England whose roots lay in ancient custom and whose social value was attested to by its having survived over time, the common law, it was claimed, constituted a body of rules that took precedence even over the commands of the sovereign. Perhaps the best 17th-century summary of the common law—which comports with the way Hayek was later to interpret it—was put forward in 1612 by Sir John Davies. Davies was then attorney general for Ireland and had introduced British common law to Ireland after the Tudor Conquest. He maintained that

> the *Common Law of England* is nothing else but the *Common Custome* of the Realm: and a Custome which hath obtained the force of a Law is always said to be *jus non scriptum*; for it cannot be made or created either by Charter, or by Parliament, which are Acts reduced to writing, and are alwaies matter of Record; but being onely matter of fact, and consisting in use and practice, it can be recorded and registered no-where but in the memory of the people.
>
> For a Custome taketh beginning and groweth to perfection in this matter: When a reasonable act once done is found to be good and beneficiall to the people, and agreeable to their nature and disposition, then do they use it and practise it again and again, and so by often interation and multiplication of the act it becometh a *Custome*; and being continued without interruption time out of mind, it obtaineth the force of a *Law*.
>
> And this *Customary Law* is the most perfect and most excellent, and without comparison the best, to make and preserve a Commonwealth. For the *written Laws* which are made either by the

> Edicts of Princes, or by Councils of Estates, are imposed upon the
> Subject before any Triall or Probation made, whether the same be
> fit and agreeable to the nature and disposition of the people, or
> whether they will breed any inconvenience or no. But a *Custome*
> doth never become a Law to bind the people, untill it hath been
> tried and approved time out of mind, during all which time there
> did thereby arise no inconvenience: for if it had been found incon-
> venient at any time, it had been used no longer, but had been
> interrupted, and consequently it had lost the virtue and force of a
> Law.[4]

It is interesting that Davies' account of the development of the
common law relies on a species of evolutionary theory close to that
later put forward by Edmund Burke and given systematic expression
by Hayek. Davies appears to be suggesting that legal rules are of an
order of complexity such that only an evolutionary test through trial
and error could determine their ultimate social value. "The edicts of
princes" and the "councils of estates," when they attempt to contrive
fundamental legal rules whose justification is rationally demonstrated,
will fail because the process of coordination with existing rules will
fail. The strength of the common law, indeed of all law based on
precedent, is that its rules are compatible with ancient custom and
therefore irreconcilable with a sovereign who seeks to issue arbitrary
commands. As Hayek (1973: 94) notes, "The ideal of individual liberty
seems to have flourished chiefly among people where, at least for long
periods, judge-made law predominated."

What I should like to suggest in this essay is that while this characterization has some merit it fails as an accurate description of the
genesis and development of the common law. More important, it does
not address the common law's weaknesses and inadequacies, which
were so extensive that it was only by supplementing it with other
systems of substantive and procedural rules, particularly the law of
equity, that it was able to survive its early history. At the outset I
should make clear that in dealing with the early history of English law
we are dealing with a subject of truly immense complexity. The historical description that follows therefore is of necessity somewhat
oversimplified.[5]

A word of explanation might be useful. Although the term "com-

---

[4]From the Preface Dedicatory to *Irish Reports* (London 1674), quoted in Pocock (1987:
32–33).

[5]This study is indebted for many of the details respecting the development of English legal
procedure to Sir William Holdsworth's masterful and exhaustive account of the history of
English law (see Holdsworth 1982).

mon law" is regarded, in the minds of many, as synonymous with English law, especially the form that English law took until the 18th century, this is not the common law Hayek has in mind when he writes of its greatest virtue.[6] By the 18th century, elements of equity had been incorporated into the common law and, in addition, during the second half of the century, Lord Chief Justice William Manfield had made the law merchant, which governed a substantial portion of all commercial transactions, a part of the common law.[7] The common law that Hayek holds in such esteem is the common law as understood by the medieval lawyers and legal theorists, when its legal rules reflected custom and precedent and where statute and deliberate design played no, or at best a minimal, role. What Hayek wishes to emphasize is the *spontaneous* nature of the common law, that is, that aspect of law that was the creature of an unformulated web of rules governing the way Englishmen were expected to deal with each other.

Commentators who have addressed Hayek's legal theory appear to have all underscored this conclusion, that the common law is a particularly appropriate example of a spontaneously generated institution that developed as a consequence of innumerable human actions, each having as their object a specific and different end but was not consciously and deliberately designed to achieve any specific purposes. To the extent that there existed certain legal principles, those principles were not the creation of any mind or group of minds but rather were embedded in the disparate and unarticulated rules under which Englishmen operated in dealing with each other.[8] What this study seeks to show, however, is that the common law as it in fact arose was not the idealized system of justice that Hayek portrayed it to be.

The Royal Courts

Common law was the law administered by the royal courts and, as such, was enforced throughout the whole of England. But before the 14th century the royal courts were by no means the only courts to

---

[6]It is customary even today to refer to those countries whose legal systems had their origin in English law as "common law" nations despite the fact that statute law might well have superceded common law. Such is the case, for example, with certain jurisdictions in the United States.

[7]The Judicature Act of 1873 formally amalgamated law and equity in England.

[8]The literature on Hayek's social and political philosophy is substantial and daily growing. Although a great deal of attention has been given to Hayek's discussion of the structure of law necessary for a free society, very little has been written on his treatment of the common law. For particularly insightful discussions of this aspect of Hayek's thought, see Ogus (1989: 393–409); Kley (1994: 135–47), and particularly Barry (1979: 76–102).

which Englishmen could have access. With the exception of cases in which a freehold was at issue, plaintiffs were free to have their cases heard in a variety of different courts, each enforcing a distinct set of rules. Among them were local county courts, which dated back to the period before the Conquest and which administered the customary rules of the region, the borough courts, which administered commercial law and the rules that prevailed in towns, and the manorial and other seignorial courts, which enforced feudal law. In addition, the ecclesiastical courts administered canon law, which included jurisdiction over issues of marriage and divorce, wills and testaments, and contracts sealed by a pledge of faith. Even in the face of these choices, however, the king's courts and the common law gained steadily in popularity, especially during the 12th and 13th centuries when those courts actively expanded their authority. By the mid-13th century, the great English jurist Henry Bracton noted that the king was the proper judge for all temporal causes (Plucknett 1956: 80–81).

This shift away from those courts competing with the courts of common law was due in large measure to the fact that the royal courts offered far more efficient protection. Not only did the kings' courts have professional judges a good deal earlier than the local courts but the method of determining guilt was different. In the local courts, judgment—amazing as it might seem—preceded proof. A group of freeholders of the region were called to sit as judges, called suitors, before the plaintiff and defendant and determined which of the litigants should present proof of their claim. Proof was not what we currently understand as proof but rather an appeal to the supernatural, through ordeal, battle, or what was called wager of law, that is, swearing to the truth of one's claim and rounding up a sufficient number of "oath-helpers" who would testify that one's oath was clean and unperjured. Although ordeal, battle, and wager of law were all, at one time, used in the royal courts, by 1215 they were replaced by trial by jury,[9] which, at about the same time, was also extended from private cases to questions of criminal guilt.[10] Indeed, plaintiffs were

[9]Trial by ordeal was abolished by order of the Lateran Council of 1215. Trial by battle and wager of law were not formally abolished until 1819 and 1833, respectively. Battle had become archaic even during the late Middle Ages and there is no evidence that any battle was fought after 1485. However, it was not legally abolished until a gauntlet was thrown into a startled court of King's Bench in 1818 (*Ashford v. Thornton* [1818] B & Ald 405).

[10]The original jury took the form of a group of neighbors who were impaneled to tell the truth about the matter before the court. They were thus more like witnesses than judges of fact. Trial by battle was clearly an unreliable method of determining guilt, which was of especial concern to the king when the charge involved the dispossession of the rightful

compelled to take their cases to the king's courts to avoid trial by battle or wager of law inasmuch as only the king could grant the privilege of jury trial. Finally, the increased activity of the royal courts was greatly accelerated by virtue of the fact that the king claimed a virtual monopoly over criminal justice since it proved a valuable source of revenue through the forfeitures and fines collected. Private actions for dispossession [disseisen] often brought with them a criminal complaint against the defendant against whom judgment was given, who was required not only to pay damages to the plaintiff but also a fine to the king.

As one legal historian has pointed out, the old courts were not deprived of their competence to hear cases. Rather, the alternative of bringing suit in the royal courts, unhampered by the antiquated and sluggish processes with which the older courts were burdened, clearly was a superior option to most prospective litigants (Caenegem 1973: 33).[11] There can be little doubt that the king's courts indeed reflected the genuine preferences of litigants since, unlike the older courts, the king's courts charged for their services by requiring the plaintiff to purchase a writ, which would provide him access to the court. Each writ governed a separate and distinct procedure and was devised for a specific type of grievance. The plaintiff's complaint thus had to fit into one of the existing forms of action. The specific writ was addressed to the sheriff, who was directed to demand of the named defendant that he remedy the wrongful act complained of or, should he not, to appear in a royal court to answer why he had not done so.

By the end of the 13th century, three great royal courts had emerged, all functioning in much the same way and all administering the same rules. These were (1) the Court of King's Bench, whose authority originated in the royal right to preserve the peace and which, as a result, had unlimited criminal jurisdiction, that is, authority to try all cases involving appeals of felony and breaches of the peace. The court originally accompanied a perambulating king in his circuit throughout the kingdom and the king himself would, from time to time, participate in the operation of the court.[12] The other supreme courts of common law were (2) the Common Bench or

---

occupier of a piece of land. As a result in 1179 Henry II enacted the Grand Assize, which permitted the decision in such cases to be determined by jury trial.

[11]The older courts, whose origin and authority were independent of the king, gradually lost their independent status and were absorbed into the system of royal justice. In the end, they were either abolished or were displaced by other institutions.

[12]Given the more intimate relationship with the king and his council, the King's Bench originally had appellate jurisdiction over appeals of error from the Court of Common Pleas.

Court of Common Pleas, which sat as a permanent court in West-minster and which had exclusive jurisdiction over suits in which the king had no interest, and (3) the Court of Exchequer, whose juris-diction largely concerned issues touching the royal finances. Although each of these courts originally tended to specialize in a specific area of the law, by the reign of Edward III they all judged cases by common law and the Courts of King's Bench and Common Pleas exercised what amounted to concurrent jurisdiction over civil actions. And all, by virtue of being common law courts, relied on one form of writ or another before a case could be initiated.

Writs were issued through the Chancery, the royal secretariat. As the disputes before the king's courts raised new and recurring issues, the Chancery would frame new forms of writ, ordering the sheriffs to call juries to deal with the specific complaint. For example, to secure enforcement of an agreement, the plaintiff would obtain a *writ of covenant*; to collect a certain sum of money earlier lent the defendant, the plaintiff would bring an action of *debt*; to recover personal prop-erty or chattels illegally taken, the plaintiff would apply for a *writ of replevin*. By the end of Henry II's reign in 1189, there were approxi-mately 39 writs and these increased to more than 470 in the reign of Edward II (1271–1307). During the 12th and 13th centuries, the Chancery appears to have been prepared to create appropriate writs to address new instances where any private right had been violated. However, by the end of the 13th century, this process slowed con-siderably and by the 14th century had stopped altogether. By that time the writ system in use in the common law courts had hardened to the point where no new forms were devised, partly because the common law judges opposed the issuance of writs that had no prec-edent.

Although 470 writs might suggest that the common law was able to address an almost unlimited spectrum of private wrongs, this was not in fact the case. Many of the original writs fell into groups or families, with similar formulas grounded on a single principle that varied only slightly from writ to writ. Thus, writs of entry, invented during the reigns of Richard I, John, and Henry III (1189–1272), all concerned themselves with recovering the possession of land wrongfully held through a flaw in title. However, there were a large number of pos-sible causes of such flaws, including wrongful transfers by a host of different officials. Each of these instances required a distinct writ.

By the end of the 14th century the King's Bench has ceased to go on circuit and settled permanently in Westminster.

Consequently, by the reign of Edward I (1272–1307), there were 18 different writs of entry. Although the earliest writs referred in the main to landed property, personal actions made their appearance toward the end of the 12th century in the form of actions for debt and detinue. An action for debt ordered that a specific sum of money be returned to the plaintiff, while an action for detinue ordered the defendant to surrender certain chattels (or their value). Thus, should one of the parties to the transaction refuse to fulfill his obligation, the seller could sue for debt or the buyer could bring an action for detinue.

Possibly the most important of all the personal actions developed during this period was that for trespass, "the fertile mother of actions,"[13] which was not to become a writ until very late in the reign of Henry III. As a civil action, trespass, whether against land, against the person, or against goods, was based on the principle that force had been misused against the plaintiff. It appears that before 1252 one was expected to act on one's own behalf in defense of one's person, goods, or land (Ames 1913: 50, 56). Should someone wronged pursue and catch the thief, he was allowed, and expected, to execute him on the spot. However, this private use of force often proved awkward and ineffective. The introduction of writs of trespass permitted the intervention of the king's officials in such instances and they quickly became extremely popular. Not only did these writs bring to bear the majesty of royal authority but they also served to expand the criminal law and criminal procedure inasmuch as most trespasses constituted breaches of the king's peace.[14]

Limitations of the Common Law

Despite the fact that the common law had, by the end of the 13th century, extended its reach to address what appears to have been a large number of offenses, the law's ability to provide remedies for the complaints brought before the common law courts was in fact quite limited. Despite the proliferation of writs, there was insufficient expansion of the courts' competence to redress injuries, not because of

[13] In the words of the great British legal scholar F. W. Maitland (1971: 39).

[14] "The action of trespass," writes Maitland (1971: 40), "is founded on a breach of the king's peace: with force and arms the defendant has assaulted and beaten the plaintiff; broken the plaintiff's close, or carried off the plaintiff's goods; he is sued for damages. The plaintiff seeks not violence but compensation, but the unsuccessful defendant will also be punished and pretty severely."

the actions of the Chancery but because of strong objections from the common lawyers themselves. They were fearful that with the authority to invent new remedies came an authority to create new rights and duties, thus placing too much power in the hands of the Chancery. Indeed, the early common lawyers appear to have suffered from such a strong prejudice in favor of precedent that by the end of the 13th century they were prepared to abandon support for any novel legal solution, even in the interests of justice. There existed an early maxim, quoted in Plunkett (1956: 680), to which most of the common lawyers adhered, that it was better to tolerate a "mischief" (by which they meant a failure of substantive justice in a particular case) than an "inconvenience" (by which was meant a breach of legal principle). As early as 1285, the second Statute of Westminster noted that "men have been obliged to depart from the Chancery without getting writs, because there are none which will exactly fit their cases, although cases fall within admitted principles."[15] Certainly by the middle of the 14th century this rule had seized hold of the common law, whose procedures became firmly fixed, and by the end of the reign of Edward III in 1377 all innovation had effectively ceased and the common law courts had become totally inflexible. As Frederic Maitland (1971: 42) notes, by this point in the development of English law, "the king's courts had come to be regarded as omnicompetent courts; [but] they had to do all the important civil justice of the realm and to do it with the limited supply of forms of action which had been gradually accumulated in the days when feudal justice and ecclesiastical justice were serious competitors with royal justice."

The ingrained conservatism of the common lawyers and their power to translate their concerns into curbs on the king and his chancellor to create new forms of action acted to seriously limit the ability of the common law courts to resolve the disputes that came before them. Regardless of the circumstances of the case, its remedies were limited to a judgment for money or to ordering the return of specific real or personal property or its value. Fortunately, the Chancery was under no such constraint respecting its own authority to respond to the petitions it received and to dispense substantive justice. The king always held residual discretionary power to do justice among his subjects where, for some reason, it could not be obtained in his courts. As a result, his Chancellor, the highest ranking official in the king's secretariat, and the Chancery clerks gradually began to exercise independent jurisdiction as judges in legal disputes

---

[15]Statute of Westminster II. 13 Edw. I c. 24.

heard in the Chancery courts. However, unlike the common law courts—whose central focus was the application of existing legal principle–courts of equity concerned themselves with what ought to be the results of their decisions, that is, with whether the remedies handed down served the interests of justice. In the words of one legal historian, "The distinction between *what is* and *what ought to be* may serve as a rough guide to the difference between common law and equity in the centuries after the 14th. Equity supplements the common law; its rules do not contradict the common law; rather, they aim at securing substantial justice when the strict rule of common law might work hardship" (Hogue 1985: 175). There is no way that the common law could have served as an exclusive body of legal rules governing a society as complex as was England in the 14th century. Over the course of the preceding 150 years commercial activity had become increasingly important to the economic life of the nation, and the common law courts were simply not equipped to deal with cases arising out of mercantile transactions. The numerous artificial restrictions with which the common law was tied down, many of its own making, made it impossible to adequately treat a large number of legal relations, particularly those having to do with trade. As a result, the equity courts assumed the jurisdiction that the common law courts had abdicated to remedy these inadequacies. The failings of the common law were acute and far-reaching. Since its courts were circumscribed in their judgments to awards of money or to directing that specific real or personal property be returned, the common law lacked the ability to right a huge range of wrongs, including—most importantly—the enforcement of fiduciary trusts. The Chancery courts, however, could cancel a document, compel the delivery of deeds or of specific personal property, grant specific performance of a contract, liberate a freeman wrongly held as a serf, and so on. They could issue declaratory judgments and injunctions. Indeed, the whole range of possible remedies was available to it. In sum, the courts of Chancery were in a position to grant relief in any of the countless instances in which a petitioner could not be awarded a remedy in the ordinary course of justice, even when entitled to a remedy.

There are any number of examples of the limitations under which the common law courts were forced to operate because of the writ system. For example, if a debtor failed to cancel his sealed bond on paying his debt, common law was obligated to regard the bond as incontrovertible evidence of the debt and to award payment to the plaintiff, thus forcing the debtor to pay a second time. Only if the debtor should have obtained from the creditor a release under seal would the common law courts adjudge his debt to have been paid.

The Chancery courts were under no such limitation. Should the complaining debtor advise the court of equity that he had either been sued and judgment given against him or that he was about to be sued upon a bond that he had paid, the chancellor exercised his authority to issue a subpoena to the creditor, requiring him to answer under oath as to the payment. If the creditor admitted the payment, or if, under examination, it were found that payment had been made, the chancellor would cancel the bond. Should the creditor have already been awarded a common law judgment, the chancellor would issue a writ of injunction forbidding the creditor to proceed further under the judgment.

Similarly, if a man entered into an oral contract for which the law required written evidence, even though the facts were undisputed, the complainant was without remedy. Because of the technical requirements associated with the common law, the law was filled with such aberrations. The limitations of common law were particularly acute with respect to commerce, but the common law was also occasionally inadequate with regard to land tenure. Should a man grant land to someone else in trust on condition that the trustee carry out the original owner's wishes, the original holder of the land had no recourse if the grantee, who was recognized in law as absolute owner of the property, refused to act as he had agreed.

Nor was the common law able to deal with situations in which goods were sold that had not yet been manufactured. The law held that upon the sale of goods, property in the goods immediately transferred to the purchaser and, totally independent of delivery, the seller could at once sue in an action of debt for the stipulated price, and the buyer could sue in an action of detinue for the goods. That being the case, the sale of nonexistent goods was regarded by the courts as a nullity and no remedy existed for breaches of such agreements.

Nowhere were the limitations of the common law more dramatic than in the area of trusts. Despite any prior agreement between the original owner and the person to whom ownership was transferred, all transfers of titles to property were regarded by the common law courts as unconditional. The result was that the courts were helpless to enforce the original owner's intentions. Once title had transferred, ownership was regarded as absolute and this was true even when fraud was involved in the transfer. The Chancery courts were under no such constraint. They could and did order that, despite the fact that A owned, say, a piece of land, it must be held for the exclusive benefit of B, if those were the terms under which the transfer was made. In addition, A was enjoined from suing in a court of law (that is, a common law court) to establish his legal rights, or from exercising them had they been established by an earlier suit.[16] The effect of such decisions was to create a distinction between legal and beneficial ownership, or *ownership in law* and *ownership in equity*. These decisions were far-reaching and opened up the law to the possibility of permanent endowments for charitable ventures and to the whole range of commercial activities that relied on being able to transfer title to real property or chattels to someone else to be used for specific purposes.

Growing Inflexibility of Common Law Courts

The refusal of the common lawyers either to permit flexibility in the legal rules or to permit the Chancery from issuing writs for new causes of action inevitably led common law courts to lose ground to the Chancery courts. In this way the common law's addiction to precedent was in large part responsible for protecting it from the changes that all social institutions require if they are to remain vibrant and relevant. So rigid and complex did the procedural requirements of the common law become that litigants, in many instances with the connivance of the courts, took to relying on fictions to expedite access and to reduce the costs involved in bringing suit. These fictions, known by all parties to be false and used to extend the substantive remedies available to the courts, became so common that by the 17th century only highly trained experts in the law were aware of how best to proceed in bringing an action.

One example of the numerous fictions to which the common law courts had recourse will suffice. Because of the complexities and the cost to plaintiffs of acquiring the necessary writs, there was a steady decline over the course of the 15th century in the number of cases taken to these courts. This was especially true of the Court of King's Bench, which had settled permanently at Westminster and which could not ordinarily entertain writs of debt or other suits between private individuals—over which the Court of Common Pleas held exclusive jurisdiction. In order to increase the number of litigants appearing before it, the King's Bench took to encouraging employment of a more streamlined procedure, the use of bills rather than writs.

---

[16]Hanbury's *Modern Equity* (1969: 7) lists several reasons why land might be conveyed to another person for the benefit of the conveyor. If the conveyor were going on a crusade, feudal services would still have to be performed and received. A community of Franciscan friars, who because of their rule of poverty could not hold property, would need to find someone to hold land for the group's benefit. In cases where a landowner was attempting to escape his creditors or where he feared a conviction for felony, he might wish to transfer his lands "to his use," that is, to be used for his benefit after the transfer.

A bill was a petition addressed directly to a court to commence an action, thus bypassing the expense and inconvenience of lodging a complaint at the Chancery and of purchasing a writ, which would then be sent to the court in which the proceedings were to take place. This made it a far superior device for initiating action against someone than was a writ. In addition, bills were substantially less expensive than were writs. However, a bill's reach was severely circumscribed. One could bring an action via bill procedure only in two instances: (1) where the defendant was at the time either an officer of the court or a prisoner of the court, that is, only if the prospective defendant were at that moment the defendant in another case, or (2) if the prospective defendant were accused of having committed the offense in the county in which the court was sitting.

By the 16th century these two exceptions provided a loophole sufficiently large that a substantial number of legal actions via bill were undertaken in the Court of King's Bench, including actions for debt and covenant, which, being private, were ordinarily the prerogative of the Court of Common Pleas. If the fiction were maintained that the defendant committed a wrong in Middlesex (the county in which Westminster was situated and in which the King's Bench sat) and that the wrong was a trespass in which the King had an interest, this would constitute sufficient cause to arrest the defendant. And once arrested, a bill would suffice to institute legal proceedings on the particular wrong that the plaintiff wished to have addressed by the court.[17]

The inflexible formalism of the common law courts was not alone the cause of their declining popularity. Curiously, juries, which constituted one of the great strengths of the common law courts in the early history of English law, later proved a critical weakness.[18] As earlier noted, juries, at least as they originally functioned and unlike those with which we are familiar, were not charged with determining the facts of a case on the basis of the evidence placed before them. Rather, before the 16th century, jurors were selected from the district in which the wrong was alleged to have been committed and were asked to bear witness regarding the truth or falsity of the plaintiff's charge. The use of juries was confined to the king's courts in-

[17]Should the defendant not be found in Middlesex, as was most often the case, the plaintiff would then inform the court that the defendant "lurks and runs about" in a particular county, at which point the court would issue a writ of arrest (*latitat*) to the sheriff of that county.

[18]An excellent overview of the history of the English jury is provided by Sir Patrick Devlin (1956).

asmuch as the king alone could compel the taking of an oath. The jurors in a proceeding were taken to have knowledge of all the relevant facts of the case and were required under oath to answer which of the disputants was in the right. Initially juries consisted of 12 men and if they did not agree, then others were added until 12 concurred in a verdict. It was not until the mid-14th century that juries were required to render a unanimous verdict.

Henry II had been responsible for turning the jury into an essential instrument of English law, first, in 1166, when jury trials were extended to all criminal cases by the Assize of Clarendon, and second, with enactment of the Grand Assize in 1179, which provided that in disputes involving title to land, litigants had a choice between a wager of battle or trial before a jury. Both these uses of the early jury as testifier of fact made some sense. With regard to questions of real property, the disputants' neighbors would almost certainly have been aware of recent changes in possession. And those living in the district could be expected to have knowledge of the crimes committed in the district and who was likely to be responsible.[19] Indeed, the use of this type of jury in criminal cases adumbrates the modern grand jury. But it soon became apparent that the knowledge that juries possessed was inadequate to most of the cases before them. The growth in trade and the expansion of urban life both worked to seriously limit what one knew about one's neighbors.

The problems confronting the common law jury were compounded by the rules respecting the giving of evidence. With few exceptions, particularly before the 15th century, jurors were the only witnesses and were free to get their information out of court in any way they chose (Zane 1998: 158, 254). However, they were thoroughly shielded from any testimony that might be presented in court. Indeed, early juries were called in only when the defendant requested a definitive decision on the issue in dispute. Anyone who voluntarily testified to the jury when he had no interest in the case or where he was not a relative of one of the parties was guilty of the crime of maintenance. Indeed, in criminal cases before the reign of Elizabeth, even when court rules were relaxed sufficiently to permit juries to hear testimony, only the Crown could adduce witnesses. Even when the defendant was finally permitted to call witnesses in his defense, they had to remain unsworn, sworn inquisition being a prerogative of the Crown. These limitations on the abilities of juries in common law

---

[19]Juries in criminal cases were not required to speak of their own knowledge but could report what was reputed to be the case in their districts.

courts to arrive at just verdicts contributed substantially to the increasing popularity of the courts of Chancery, which were free from such constraints. Chancery courts, armed with the subpoena power, routinely summoned witnesses, whose testimony was written down.

In the 15th century the Chancery courts had assumed jurisdiction over cases that fell outside the common law, including those concerning foreign merchants and those based on maritime or ecclesiastical law. At about the same time the authority of these courts was extended to include appeals from litigants who had lost in a common law court through fraud (for example, the use of perjured evidence) or as the result of an excusable inadvertence or by the petitioner's failure to produce evidence that would have proved the verdict and judgment wrong, provided the failure was not the fault of the losing party. In such cases the Chancery court would enjoin enforcement of the common law judgment, thus compelling the winning party to agree to a new trial.

The common law courts were further burdened by the fact that pleadings and judgments were made in Norman French, which persisted until the 16th century. Even as late as 1631, the records of the Salisbury assizes noted that the Chief Justice of the Court of Common Pleas condemned a prisoner, who *"ject un Brickbat a le dit Justice que narrowly mist,"* for which *"son dexter manue amputee,"* and the man himself *"immediatment hange in presence de Court"* (quoted in Harding 1966: 205). Attempts had been made by Parliament to change this but these were disregarded by the common lawyers, who insisted that they could not express the necessary legal niceties without recourse to Norman French and who treasured the priest-like status mastery of this esoteric language accorded them. That most plaintiffs and defendants could not follow the proceedings proved a serious blow to the common law courts and contributed to a shift of litigation into the courts of Chancery, where the proceedings were in English and where, after 1435, the pleadings were in the same language.

The Origin of Common Law Revisited

Not only is Hayek's account defective in that it does not reflect the severe limitations of the early common law, but his conclusions regarding the origin of its rules are questionable. Hayek's claim that the common law, because it reflected customary rules, was superior to the statutes and ordinances that issued from the king and his council, cannot stand up to historical scrutiny. The common law as it developed over time comprised not only a body of principles derived from precedent but also the ordinances and royal regulations that issued from the king and the *curia reges*. Even by the middle of the 13th century no clear distinction between legislation and judicial actions was possible and every rule, no matter its origin, was regarded as binding only by virtue of "the consent of the barons and the king in his feudal capacity" (Ullmann 1961: 167). It is true that the term "common law," which became current during the reign of Edward I (1272–1307), was borrowed from the Canon Law jurists to describe that part of the law that was unenacted, or nonstatutory (Maitland 1969: 2), but in fact the legal and procedural rules of civil and criminal procedure comprised statute as much as custom. Indeed, one of the most important advances in common law that played a crucial role in structuring the criminal law in the royal courts was the Assize of Clarendon, which was enacted as a statute by Henry II in 1166.[20] And one of the earliest surviving legal treatises, dating from around 1188 and attributed to Henry II's justiciar (the king's viceroy in England), Ranulf Glanvill, noted that "although the laws of England are not written, it does not seem absurd to call them laws—those, that is, which are known to have been promulgated about problems settled in council on the advice of the magnates and with the supporting authority of the prince" (Hall 1965: 2).

Indeed, the procedures by which the common law courts operated were ultimately dependent on the king and his council. The staffing, location, and jurisdiction of the courts themselves, as well as the rules governing their operation, all reflected administrative decisions originating in the king's council and particularly in his secretariat. Clause 17 of the Magna Carta explicitly provided that the Court of Common Pleas sit permanently at Westminster. These procedural rules, which gave shape and direction to the legal rules that the king's courts applied when determining the outcome of the cases before them, while in some instances reflecting traditional elements, were instituted through what amounted to legislation.[21]

---

[20]Enacted by Henry II, the Assize of Clarendon was issued to the sheriffs of every county in England, calling on them to assemble a specified group from each country: 12 men from each 100, plus the priest, the reeve, and 4 men from every village. This "presenting jury" was in turn, asked to name, under oath, all persons in the area suspected for murder or theft since Henry's coronation 10 years earlier. The list of names, known as presentments, were then taken before the royal justices, who ordered the arrest of the suspects and proceeded to put them through trial by ordeal.

[21]With respect to the question of how legislation was enacted in medieval England, one historian writes: "The parliamentary form of modern legislation is rarely encountered before the end of the thirteenth century, and the consent of the House of Commons was probably not regarded as indispensable until after 1400. The present bill procedure was not settled until early Tudor times. It is therefore anachronistic to regard medieval legislation

HAYEK AND THE COMMON LAW

In understanding the framework of the common law throughout most of its history, it is essential that we are fully aware of the singular importance played by the forms of action and the writs associated with them. Maitland (1971: 1) went so far as to note that "the system of Forms of Action or the Writ System is the most important characteristic of English medieval law, and it was not abolished until its piecemeal destruction in the nineteenth century." These writs ultimately determined the remedies available to plaintiffs in the king's courts. And being creatures of the Chancery, an integral arm of the *curia regis*, writs partake in large part of statutory determinations. By varying the existing writs or, indeed, by inventing new ones when he was permitted to do so, the chancellor played a crucial role in shaping the development of English law.

While Hayek is correct in noting that the central concern of the common law is property, the property of which the early common law speaks is real property. Moreover, it was only changes in the common law brought about by decisions of equity, by the law merchant, and by statute that English law began to address the complex interrelationships of commerce and to make provision for the instrumentalities of finance that we associate with modern capitalism (Atiyah 1979).[22] The common law of which Hayek is such a proponent operated in what was primarily an agrarian society where people dealt with those whom they knew and where custom was sufficient to structure their legal relationships. Historically, however, the laws that developed in England that proved necessary for the operation of an advanced commercial society seem to have been far too complex to have relied solely on rules that were never made explicit and that did not grow by deliberate design. Its principles had first to have been contrived and consciously applied by judges who had learned the law and then applied it.

---

as an authoritative text in quite the modern sense. The text was written law, certainly, but it was not a text which had been pored over word for word in both houses, with debates upon verbal amendments. In the case of the early statrutes, the drafting was done by the clerks and judges after assent had been given. A statute represented the terms of a decision upon a complaint or petition; a decision of the highest authority in the land, but not different in kind from decisions by inferior branches of the *Curia Regis*" (Baker 1979: 178).

[22]Atiyah traces the 18th-century transition of English law from one whose primary concern is the law of property to one where the law of contract plays the most crucial role. As he points out, "Between 1688 and 1770 the common law, with the aid of the Court of Chancery, created the legal principles necessary to support...[a] credit system [compatible with a flourishing market economy], though not without travail, and not wholly successfully" (Atiyah 1979: 135).

Common Law as a Barrier to State Power

Given the limitations of the common law and of the courts whose function it was to enforce its rules and given the fact that the common law itself was as much a product of conscious design as it was of unarticulated custom, how could Hayek have concluded that the English common law had served as an effective barrier to the incursions of state power? There are, I think, two principal reasons for this. First, all the great 17th-century common law jurists, most notably Sir Matthew Hale and Sir Edward Coke, were associated with the parliamentarians' struggle against arbitrary government and the oppressive policies of the Tudor and Stuart monarchs. Coke was the earlier of the two great jurists and, in large measure because of his *Institutes of the Laws of England*, was to leave a deeper impression.[23]

Coke was appointed Chief Justice of the Court of Common Pleas in 1606 by James I and, in 1613, was transferred to the position of Chief Justice of the Court of King's Bench in the hope that he would be more sympathetic to the prerogatives claimed by the king. Throughout his tenure on the bench, he was an uncompromising defender of the common law and viewed with great suspicion not only the Chancery courts, whose jurisdiction he made every effort to limit,[24] but with the ecclesiastical courts as well. While Coke employed the common law, of which he had a brilliant mastery, as a tool against the encroachments of the Stuart kings, his knowledge of the early legal and political history of England is now conceded to have been quite poor and it was largely through a series of misinterpretations of early common law that Coke was successful in voiding a number of royal edicts. Coke's zeal in defending the common law courts against the prerogative courts and the Parliamentary cause against the king was in large measure responsible for the reputation the common law earned as a defense against arbitrary government.

The second reason why Hayek appears so taken with the common law as an institutional deterrent to a tyrannical and capricious state is that he ascribes to the common law the properties normally associated with natural law, whose great proponent in England is John

---

[23]Hayek's conception of the common law derives primarily from that of Sir Edward Coke, whom Hayek regarded as "the great fountain of Whig principles."

[24]Coke's attempts to limit the authority of the Chancery courts to enjoin proceedings in the common law courts brought him into conflict with Francis Bacon. Coke had attempted to gain the post of attorney general, which was eventually awarded to Bacon in 1613, and both Bacon and Coke engaged in a bitter competition for the hand of a young and wealthy widow, in which Coke, despite his age, prevailed. Coke's life and career is dealt with at some length in Bowen (1957).

Locke. As Locke maintained, natural law dictates that men, by virtue of their nature and the nature of the universe in which they all exist, are subject to a system of objective rules, good for all times and all places, governing how they are to behave toward each other, and that man's reasoning ability provides him the instrument whereby he can uncover these rules. From natural law derive a spectrum of natural rights that all men possess by virtue of their humanity that protect them from the encroachments of an oppressive government. When governments violate these rights they pervert their natural purposes and men may attempt to replace them with others more fitting.

Hayek's description and analysis of the English common law locates the law's origins in the unwritten rules and conventions to which English society adhered, which were then taken up by the king's courts and which, through the vehicle of precedent, became the law of the land. To the extent that Englishmen had rights over and against the king, these rights followed from the unwritten rules that comprised the law and were historical and prescriptive in origin. Although there appears to be a sharp divergence between discovering our legal rules in right reason on the one hand or in the traditional rules of the group on the other, the distinction, as Hayek understands it, is less than one might at first suppose. What is significant in this regard is that Hayek (1973: 98) concedes that the unwritten rules that form the basis of the common law must meet certain strict criteria, that "only some order of rules of individual conduct will produce an overall order while others would make such an order impossible." There are some rules that conduce to a peaceful, free, and ordered society and others that do not and it is only the former that will, in the end, be selected. The only difference between natural law theory and Hayek's conclusions respecting these rules is how they are discovered. For Hayek they can only be uncovered by a process of evolution, while a Lockean would maintain that reason alone is sufficient to decipher them.[25]

Indeed, there is a striking similarity between Hayek's treatment of the common law and Hume's discussion of the nature of justice. As Knud Haakonssen (1981: 12–21) has observed of Hume's ethical

---

[25]The conflation of the common law with natural law was not unusual among the 17th-century common lawyers. The claim that historical precedent existed for almost every limitation on the power of the sovereign to make law was extended in *Dr. Bonham's Case* (8 Co, Rep. 197 [1610] by Coke, who wrote: "In many cases, the common law will control acts of parliament, and sometimes adjudge them to be utterly void: for when an act of parliament is against common right and reason, or repugnant, or impossible to be performed, the common law will control it, and adjudge such act to be void" (quoted in Kurland and Lerner 1987, V: 303).

theory, while it is true that the rules that comprise justice are the product of convention, these rules are not capricious but reflect our common nature as social beings born into a universe of scarce resources (see also Dun 1994: 269–86). We thus all share certain values simply by virtue of the fact that we share a common environment in which our wants exceed the means to satisfy them In like manner it is possible to reconcile the common law, which has its origin in the unarticulated rules that have slowly evolved over time and which are the product of convention, with natural law, which comprises a series of objective moral rules determinable by reason. The rules that form the matrix of the common law, like Hume's rules of justice, also reflect the common environment in which we find ourselves and thus give rise to certain values that we all more or less embrace. Hence, although Hayek (1988: 10) maintained that there are no universally valid principles of justice, his theory of law is spared being relativistic by taking on certain crucial characteristics of natural law.

Conclusion

Hayek, however, wishes to go further. Not only does he want to explain the dynamic by which the legal rules of a free society develop but he also wishes to provide an historical instance of this dynamic in the form of the English common law. But the facts of the matter simply do not warrant this conclusion. The early common law cannot be said to be either the product of evolution, any more than any other medieval English institution, nor a workable system of justice.

It was only with the rise of the law of equity that English law was able to deal with the legal needs of a growing commercial society. Hayek's distrust of social institutions that are clearly the product of deliberate design is so deep and his reliance on the historical misinterpretations of the common law made by those jurists who opposed the arbitrary power of the Stuarts so great that he misconceived the strengths and weaknesses of early English law and made of the common law one of the strongest bulwarks against tyrannical government with which the Parliamentarians were armed. The truth is that, even admitting all its strengths, it was much less.

References

Ames, J. B. (1913) *Lectures on Legal History: and Miscellaneous Legal Essays.* Cambridge, Mass.: Harvard University Press.

Atiyah, P. S. (1979) *Rise and Fall of Freedom of Contract.* Oxford: Clarendon Press.

Baker, J. H. (1979) *An Introduction to English Legal History.* London: Butterworths.

Barry, N. (1979) *Hayek's Social and Economic Philosophy.* London: Macmillan.

Bowen, C. D. (1957) *The Lion and the Throne: The Life and Times of Sir Edward Coke, 1552–1634.* Boston: Little, Brown.

Caenegem, R. C. van (1973) *The Birth of the English Common Law.* 2d ed. Cambridge: Cambridge University Press.

Cooter, R., and Kornhauser, L (1980) "Can Litigation Improve the Law Without the Help of Judges?" *Journal of Legal Studies* 9 (January): 139–63.

Devlin, P. (1956) *Trial by Jury.* The Hamlyn Lectures. Revised ed. London: Stevens & Sons.

Dun, F. van (1994) "Hayek and Natural Law: The Humean Connection," In J. Birner and R. van Zijp (eds.) *Hayek, Co-ordination and Evolution: His Legacy in Philosophy, Politics, Economics and the History of Ideas.* London: Routledge.

Haakonnsen, K. (1981) *The Science of a Legislator: The Natural Jurisprudence of David Hume and Adam Smith.* New York: Cambridge University Press.

Hadfield, G. K. (1992) "Bias in the Evolution of Legal Rules." *Georgetown University Law Journal* 80: 583–616

Hall, G. D. G, ed. (1965) *The Treatise on the Laws and Customs of the Realm of England, Commonly Called Glanvill.* London: Nelson.

Hanbury, H. G. (1969) *Modern Equity.* Edited by R. H. Maudsley. 9th ed. London: Stevens & Sons.

Harding, A. (1966) *A Social History of English Law.* Baltimore: Penguin Books.

Hayek, F. A. (1960) The *Constitution of Liberty.* Chicago: University of Chicago Press.

———— (1988) *The Fatal Conceit: The Errors of Socialism.* Chicago: University of Chicago Press.

———— (1973) *Law, Legislation, and Liberty.* Vol. 1: *Rules and Order.* Chicago: University of Chicago Press.

Hogue, A. R. (1985) *Origins of the Common Law.* Indianapolis: Liberty Press.

Holdsworth, W. (1982) *History of English Law.* London: Methuen.

Kley, R. (1994) *Hayek's Social and Political Thought.* Oxford: Clarendon Press.

Kurland, P. B., and Lerner, R., eds. (1987) *The Founders' Constitution.* Chicago: University of Chicago Press.

Landes, W. M., and Posner, R. A. (1987) *The Economic Structure of Tort Law.* Cambridge, Mass.: Harvard University Press.

Maitland, F. W. (1969) *Equity: A Course of Lectures.* Cambridge: Cambridge University Press.

———— (1971) *The Forms of Action at Common Law.* Edited by A. H. Cadre and W. J. Whitaker. Cambridge: Cambridge University Press.

Ogus, A. I. (1989) "Law and Spontaneous Order: Hayek's Contribution to Legal Theory." *Journal of Law and Society* 16 (Winter): 393–409. Reprinted in P. J. Boettke, ed. (1999) *The Legacy of Friedrich von Hayek.* Vol. 1: *Politics*, 416–32. Chelteham: Elgar Reference Collection.

Plucknett, T. F. T. (1956) *A Concise History of the Common Law* 5th ed. Boston: Little, Brown and Company.

Pocock, J. G. A. (1987) *The Ancient Constitution and the Feudal Law: A Study of English Historical Thought in the Seventeenth Century.* Cambridge: Cambridge University Press.

Posner, R. A. (1973) *Economic Analysis.* Boston: Little, Brown and Company.

Priest, G. L. (1978) "Breach and Remedy for the Tender of Nonconforming Goods under the Uniform Commercial Code: An Economic Approach." *Harvard Law Review* 91 (Winter): 960–1001.

Ullmann, W. (1961) *Principles of Government and Politics in the Middle Ages.* London: Methuen.

Zane, J. M. (1998) *The Story of Law* 2d ed. Indianapolis: Liberty Fund. (This work was originally published in 1928.)

Name index